Michael Lisin and Jim Joseph

Microsoft® SQL Server 2005

Reporting Services

Microsoft® SQL Server™ 2005

Microsoft® SQL Server 2005 Reporting Services

International Standard Book Number: 0-672-32799-6

Library of Congress Catalog Card Number: 2005937212

Printed in the United States of America

First Printing: March 2006

08 07 06 4 3 2 1

Trademarks

All terms mentioned in this book that are known to be trademarks or service marks have been appropriately capitalized. Sams Publishing cannot attest to the accuracy of this information. Use of a term in this book should not be regarded as affecting the validity of any trademark or service mark.

Warning and Disclaimer

Every effort has been made to make this book as complete and as accurate as possible, but no warranty or fitness is implied. The information provided is on an "as is" basis. The author(s) and the publisher shall have neither liability nor responsibility to any person or entity with respect to any loss or damages arising from the information contained in this book.

Bulk Sales

Sams Publishing offers excellent discounts on this book when ordered in quantity for bulk purchases or special sales. For more information, please contact

U.S. Corporate and Government Sales
1-800-382-3419
corpsales@pearsontechgroup.com

For sales outside of the U.S., please contact

International Sales
international@pearsoned.com

Publisher
Paul Boger

Acquisitions Editor
Neil Rowe

Development Editor
Mark Renfrow

Managing Editor
Charlotte Clapp

Project Editor
George Nedeff

Copy Editor
Karen Annett

Indexer
Ken Johnson

Proofreader
Kathy Bidwell

Technical Editor
J. Boyd Nolan

Publishing Coordinator
Cindy Teeters

Interior Designer
Gary Adair

Cover Designer
Gary Adair

Page Layout
Nonie Ratcliff

Contents at a Glance

Table of Contents

About the Authors

Michael Lisin has been in the software industry for more than 14 years with 7 of those years working with Microsoft. He is currently working as a senior strategy consultant with Microsoft Consulting Services. Michael has been working with SQL Server for six years and with SQL Server Reporting Services starting from the pre-Beta version in 2002. Michael has taught Reporting Services classes and presented SQL Server–related topics during various events. Michael will complete his MBA degree at Texas A&M this year.

Jim Joseph is a manager at Continental Airlines Inc. He currently functions as a SQL Server DBA within the Financial Systems Group with Continental Technology. He earned his MBA at the University of St Thomas in 2003, and undergraduate degree in mathematics from there in 1999. In his spare time, he enjoys spending time with his infant son, Christopher, and wife Deseere.

Dedication

Michael Lisin: Dedicated to my family: my wife Anna, my daughter Helen, my mother, and the memory of my grandfather. Thank you for always being extremely supportive in my life endeavors.

Jim Joseph: Dedicated to my wife Deseere and my son Christopher.

Acknowledgments

The authors would like to thank the publishing team working with us on this book. Special thanks to: Neil, Mark, George, Karen, and Alex. Thank you for your valuable feedback, answers, and hard work on this book. Without you all, this book would not be complete.

Thank you to Brian Welcker, Richard Waymire, Robert Bruckner, Thierry D'Hers, David Crawford, Bogdan Crivat, Donovan Smith, and Eli Ilionsky for helping with questions that arose while writing this book. Thank you to Matt Whitten and Stephen Rauch for getting Michael started with Reporting Services. Thank you to Kevin Swales for pointers about exception reports.

We Want to Hear from You!

As the reader of this book, *you* are our most important critic and commentator. We value your opinion and want to know what we're doing right, what we could do better, what areas you'd like to see us publish in, and any other words of wisdom you're willing to pass our way.

As an associate publisher for Sams Publishing, I welcome your comments. You can email or write me directly to let me know what you did or didn't like about this book—as well as what we can do to make our books better.

Please note that I cannot help you with technical problems related to the topic of this book. We do have a User Services group, however, where I will forward specific technical questions related to the book.

When you write, please be sure to include this book's title and author as well as your name, email address, and phone number. I will carefully review your comments and share them with the author and editors who worked on the book.

Email: feedback@samspublishing.com

Mail: Paul Boger
Publisher
Sams Publishing
800 East 96th Street
Indianapolis, IN 46240 USA

For more information about this book or another Sams Publishing title, visit our website at www.samspublishing.com. Type the ISBN (excluding hyphens) or the title of a book in the Search field to find the page you're looking for.

Introduction

SQL Server Reporting Services is a server-based, extensible and scalable platform that delivers and presents information based on data that a business collects during its operation. Information, in turn, helps business managers to evaluate the current state of the enterprise and make decisions on how to increase revenues, reduce costs, and increase customer and employee satisfaction.

The Reporting Services scope extends from traditional paper reports to interactive content and various forms of delivery: email, file shares, and so on. SSRS is capable of generating reports in various formats, such as Hypertext Markup Language (HTML), Extensible Markup Language (XML), and Excel formats, thus allowing users to manipulate their data in whatever format is required.

Before diving into this book, let's take a moment to understand the layout as well as some of the conventions used in the book. First, we cover how this book is organized and what you can expect in each section. Second, we cover the style and formatting conventions used in this book. It is particularly noteworthy to note the style changes in reference to code lines, including SQL Server and .NET code.

How This Book Is Organized

This book begins with an introductory overview of SQL Server 2005 Reporting Services and covers a broad range of topics in the areas of report authoring, Reporting Services deployment and administration, and custom code development for Reporting Services.

The chapters in Part I, "Introduction to Reporting Services," provide a high-level overview of Reporting Services and highlight key features of the Reporting Services, deployment scenarios, typical users of Reporting Services, and Reporting Services architecture. This part allows for leisurely reading and does not require you to have access to a computer.

The chapters in Part II, "Report Authoring from Basic to Advanced," take you through report development tools and processes. This part describes report building blocks and walks through building a report from simple to complex.

The chapters in Part III, "Reporting Services Administration and Operations," discuss advanced topics of Reporting Services administration, such as setting proper security, managing Reporting Services as individual servers and in a web farm, and gathering report execution information.

The chapters in Part IV, "Developing for Reporting Services," are for those of you who might want to extend Reporting Services and incorporate reports in their applications. This part covers key programmable aspects of Reporting Services.

Conventions Used in This Book

SQL Server 2005 Reporting Services is frequently abbreviated as **SSRS**.

Business Intelligence Development Studio is frequently abbreviated as **BIDS**.

New features available in SQL Server 2005 Reporting Services as compared to SQL Server 2000 Reporting Services (SSRS2K) are labeled with *"NEW in 2005"*.

Names of products, tools, individual windows (docking or not), titles, and abbreviations are capitalized. For example, SQL Server 2005, SQL Server Reporting Services, Visual Studio 2005, Report Designer, Report Builder, Report Manager, Windows, and so on.

Monospace is used to highlight:

- Sections of code that are included in the flow of the text—"Add a text box to a report and place the following code in the Background Color property: =Code.Highlight(value)."
- Filenames—"Visual Studio creates a project with a single class Class1. Let's rename file Class1.cs in Solution Explorer to MainClass.cs."
- Pathnames—"The compiled assembly must be located in directories where it is accessible by Report Designer (the default directory is C:\Program Files\Microsoft Visual Studio 8\Common7\IDE\PrivateAssemblies) and SSRS (default is C:\Program Files\Microsoft SQL Server\MSSQL.3\Reporting Services\ReportServer\bin)."
- Error numbers, codes, and messages: "[rsInvalidReportParameterDependency] The report parameter 'SalesOrderId' has a DefaultValue or a ValidValue that depends on the report parameter "MaxOrderId". Forward dependencies are not valid."
- Names of permissions, constants, properties, collections, and variables: Execute, Fields, ReportParameter, Parent.

To indicate adjustable information, we use

- "{}", mostly where the variable information can be confused with XML, for example <Value>{EXPRESSION}</Value>. In this example, an {EXPRESSION} is any valid expression, such as =Fields!ProductImage.Value.
- "<>", where the variable information cannot be confused with XML, for example =Fields!<Field Name>.Value.

PART I

Introduction to Reporting Services

IN THIS PART

CHAPTER 1

Introduction to SQL Server Reporting Services (SSRS)

IN THIS CHAPTER

- What Is SSRS?
- SSRS for End Users
- Overview of Features
- Enterprise Report Examples
- SSRS in the Report Development Life Cycle
- Editions of Reporting Services
- How Is SSRS Licensed?

NOTE

This book abbreviates SQL Server 2005 Reporting Services as SSRS and SQL Server 2000 Reporting Services as SSRS2K.

New features available in SSRS and not in SSRS2K are labeled with "NEW in 2005".

In today's ultracompetitive business environment, having good information is essential. Companies are awash in information, and with the advent of technologies such as RFID, more and more information is coming. Technology has made the job of gathering information trivial, but making sense of it all still remains elusive. This makes good reporting and business intelligence tools essential.

This first chapter is strictly nontechnical. This chapter focuses on the following:

- Capabilities of SSRS
- How it fits into the Microsoft Business Intelligence platform
- Report development life cycle as it relates to SSRS
- Editions of SSRS
- Licensing SSRS

What Is SSRS?

SSRS is Microsoft's answer to business reporting. It provides a unified, server-based, extensible, and scalable platform from which to deliver and present information. Its scope extends from traditional paper reports, to web-based delivery and interactive content. SSRS can also be configured to deliver reports to peoples' inboxes, file shares, and so on. SSRS is capable of generating reports in various formats, such as the web-oriented Hypertext Markup Language (HTML) and desktop application (Microsoft Excel and CSV) formats, thus allowing users to manipulate their data in whatever format is required.

SSRS is just one of the components in the Microsoft Business Intelligence (BI) platform. Combined, those components provide an excellent platform for enterprise data analysis. The Microsoft BI platform includes the following:

- **SQL Server**—The traditional database engine, which also stores SSRS' catalog data.
- **SQL Server Analysis Services (SSAS)**—A component for online analytical processing (OLAP) and data mining. OLAP performs data aggregation and allows users to traverse from aggregations to details looking though the dimensions (such as geography or time) of data. Data mining helps users to discover patterns in data.
- **SQL Server Integration Services (SSIS)**—A component for extracting, transforming, and loading (ETL) data.
- **SQL Server Notification Services (SSNS)**—A component for deploying and sending notifications of changing data.

SSRS for End Users

SSRS is unique in the Microsoft Business Intelligence suite, as it covers a variety of information users. Microsoft divides users into three groups: information consumers, information explorers, and analysts.

Table 1.1 briefly summarizes the percentages of users in each group, the level of technical experience, and the expectations from an enterprise reporting tool. All of these factors will vary from company to company, but generally the breakdown holds true.

TABLE 1.1 Breakdown of Information Workers

Type of User	Percentage	Technical Expertise	Expectation
Analysts	5%–10%	High	Analysts can develop reports, work with ad hoc reports, and perform sophisticated calculations (such as linear regressions and trend analysis). Analysts often publish reports to explorers and consumers.

TABLE 1.1 Continued

Type of User	Percentage	Technical Expertise	Expectation
Information explorers	15%–30%	Medium	Information explorers want to interact with reports to some degree, such as applying filters or performing drill down through.
Information consumers	55%–85%	Low	Information consumers use static, predefined, and preformatted reports.

To address the varying needs of these types of users, SSRS provides three main tools from the user perspective:

- **Report Viewer**—The primary mechanism for viewing reports over the Web. Report Manager is the name of the website that SSRS sets up. It provides a very clean and neatly organized user interface for end users. Developers can also embed a Report Viewer control into both ASP.NET and Windows Forms applications.
- **Report Builder**—The tool that provides users with a front end for ad hoc reporting against a SQL Server or Analysis Services database. Unlike most ad hoc reporting tools, users of Report Builder do not need to know Structured Query Language (SQL), or anything about joins or grouping to create reports.
- **Report Designer**—The tool that takes on the job of building advanced reports. Although Report Builder does a good job as an ad hoc reporting tool, Report Designer was made to tackle really advanced reports.

Figure 1.1 summarizes the type of reporting users, and mentions some of the tools SSRS brings to the table for them.

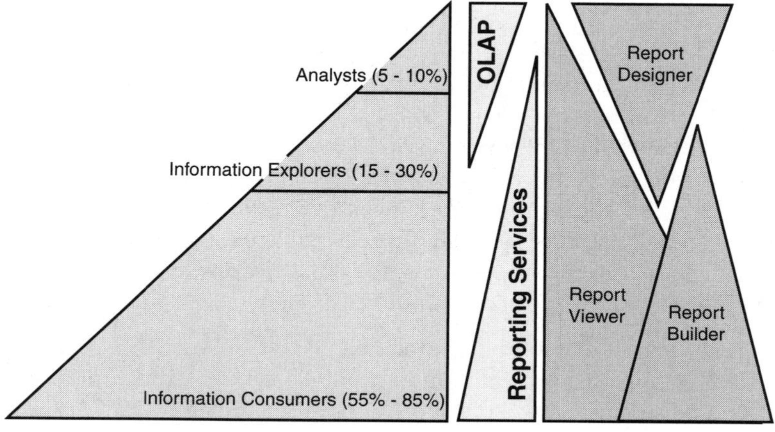

FIGURE 1.1 Reporting Services users and tools.

Overview of Features

SSRS has a number of features to address complex business reporting needs. Over the course of this book, these features are explored more closely. For now, here is a brief overview:

- SSRS can be used across the enterprise by various users simultaneously.
- SSRS leverages .NET data providers and can query a variety of data sources. Examples of the .NET providers are SQL Server, Oracle, Analysis Services, Microsoft Access, and many more. If needed, SSRS can also be extended through the custom data-processing extensions.
- SSRS includes delivery mechanisms to distribute reports to individual users on demand or on a scheduled basis.
- SSRS reports can be rendered to a number of formats, including Excel or HTML. The reports themselves can also be used as data sources for other applications when rendered to XML.
- SSRS provides mechanisms for ad hoc reporting.
- SSRS is highly available. Many enterprises are multinational companies and perform work in multiple shifts; to be a true enterprise reporting solution, SSRS had to include high-availability features.

As you can see, SSRS provides a comprehensive set of features out of the box. Another nice feature of SSRS is its extensibility. Because there is no way that the developers of SSRS could have anticipated every need of an enterprise reporting solution, they made SSRS extensible. This allows developers to use SSRS in any number of ways from embedded reports to customized reporting solutions.

Enterprise Report Examples

Each user is likely to have favorite reports to make timely and effective business decisions and although it is not possible to cover a whole gamut of reports in this book, some common ideas can help you think through practical applications of SSRS.

Score card reports are frequently used in today's businesses and provide information for each manager on how well his group is doing as compared to the goals set for the group. Usually, a score card implements a "traffic light" type of highlight or a "gage" indicator. Values on the score card are highlighted in green when the group is meeting its goals, in yellow when the group is doing so-so, and in red when the group's performance requires immediate attention. Score card reports can now take advantage of the new feature of Analysis Services 2005: Key Performance Indicators (KPI).

When users are looking to combine a comprehensive set of business health and "speed" gages (score card) and related information in a small space, a dashboard is used to accomplish this goal. A dashboard provides a short, typically one-page, summary view of a business (much like a car's dashboard summarizes a car's status) and allows drill down through the items on the top page to retrieve detailed information. SharePoint is an excellent platform to host dashboards and greatly simplifies arranging reports in the meaningful fashion on a page.

Today, when everybody is so short on time, it might be easy to miss an information point that could prove fatal for a business. Exception reporting is what comes to the rescue of a time-constrained user. Unlike regularly scheduled reports or summaries provided by score cards, exception reports are created and delivered to a user when an unusual event occurs. An exception report removes the "noise" created in periodic reports, focusing instead on mission-critical anomalies. An example of such an anomaly could be a sudden drop in daily sales for a particular region.

Other typical reports include various views of sales (geographic, demographic, product, promotion breakdowns), inventory, customer satisfaction, production, services, and financial information.

SSRS in the Report Development Life Cycle

To understand all of the ways SSRS can be used and deployed, you can simply walk through the report development life cycle, and see what features are useful in each stage.

A typical reporting application goes through three stages (see Figure 1.2): authoring, managing, and delivery. SSRS provides all the necessary tools to work with a reporting application in all three stages.

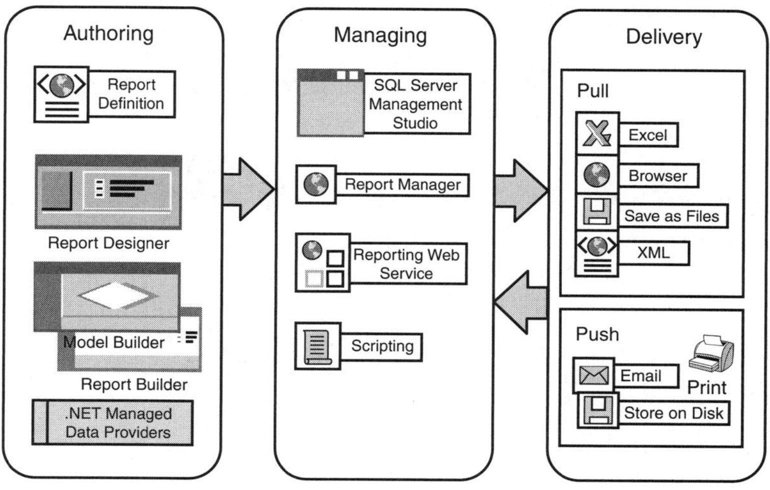

FIGURE 1.2 Reporting life cycle.

Authoring Stage of the Reporting Life Cycle

During this stage, the report author defines the report layout and sources of data. For authoring, SSRS maintains all of the features of SSRS2K and adds some new features.

Report Designer is a tool that was previously available for SSRS2K. For SSRS2K, developers had to install Visual Studio 2003 Integrated Development Environment (IDE) for the Report Designer to function. Although integration with Visual Studio is still available in SSRS, today developers have a choice to use Report Designer within Visual Studio IDE or to use Report Designer within Business Intelligence Development Studio (BIDS). The Business Intelligence Development Studio shell has gone through changes from Beta 2 of SSRS. Starting from the Community Technology Preview release of SSRS, Visual Studio Express Edition, a free version of Visual Studio 2005 is included with SQL Server 2005 as a shell for the Report Designer. The Report Designer interface is shown in Figure 1.3.

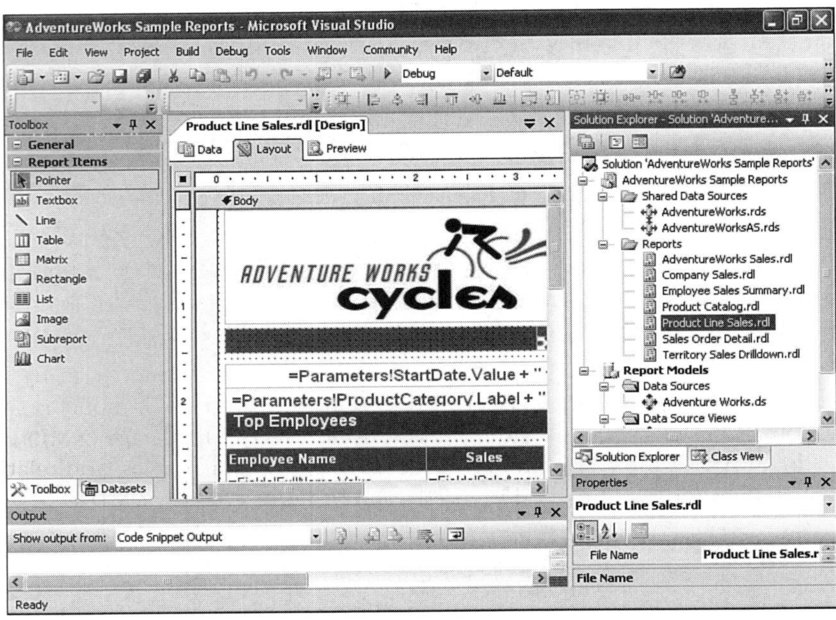

FIGURE 1.3 Report Designer.

Report Designer is a full-featured report authoring tool that targets developers and provides extensive design capabilities and can handle a variety of data sources. Report Designer can work with all reports generated for SSRS, including reports generated by Report Builder. Report Designer incorporates the following productivity features:

- Import Access reports, which allows designers to import Microsoft Access reports and creates a report definition in turn. In complex cases, it might not be able to successfully or completely import an Access report. The general rule of thumb is that SSRS will be able to convert approximately 80% of the existing Access reports.

- *NEW in 2005* IntelliSense for expression editing, which provides assistance with the syntax of a function used in expressions, names of class members, and indicates syntax errors in expressions by underlining them with squiggly red lines. You will see more details of this feature in Chapter 8, "Expressions."

- *NEW in 2005* Multidimensional Expressions (MDX) and Data Mining Expressions (DMX) query designer, which provides a drag-and-drop interface for writing MDX and DMX queries. This feature is covered in more details in Chapter 15, "Working with Multidimensional Data Sources."
- Relational query designer, which provides a drag-and-drop interface for writing SQL queries.
- Report Wizard, which provides step-by-step instructions to create a report.
- Preview mode, which allows a report author to preview the report design and layout before he publishes the report. This is a very powerful feature of a report designer that does not require Reporting Services to be installed on a computer on which the preview is generated.
- Publishing and deployment functionality, which allows a report designer to publish a report to a target server. For example, the developer might choose to publish to a development or to a test reporting server.

The end user's ability to design reports is a new feature in SSRS. There are two tools that make this possible: Report Builder and Model Builder. The combination of both tools allows an end user to develop, modify, and share her reports from SQL Server databases—both relational and OLAP—without the need to know either SQL or MDX.

Before an end user can develop a report, a developer must create a model, using the Model Builder tool. Figure 1.4 depicts the Model Builder's interface. A model is similar to a report, in that a model is a file written in Extensible Markup Language (XML) with an extension of .SMDL. A model defines layout, data sources, data entities, and relationships in terms that are understood by end users and not in terms of SQL or MDX.

When a model is published, an end user can choose a report's layout and drag and drop model items on a report. This is how an end user can create ad hoc reports, based on the published model. Figure 1.5 shows the Report Builder interface.

Report Builder targets end users and provides access to data sources predefined in a mode.

NOTE

Report Builder cannot modify reports generated by Report Designer.

Report Builder is a click once .NET smart client application that is launched from Report Manager's toolbar.

Report Designer and Report Builder generate reports in Report Definition Language (RDL). RDL is an XML-based language, a code presentation of a report that defines data, presentation elements of a report, calls to the outside .NET assemblies, custom VB.NET functions, and expressions. RDL has powerful design elements (controls) such as the familiar Table, Chart, Subreport, and Matrix. SSRS has the capability to parameterize, sort, filter, drill down through, and aggregate data. RDL can be saved as a file on a file system or as data in the Reporting Services database. RDL is an open language that allows third-party vendors to develop custom authoring tools.

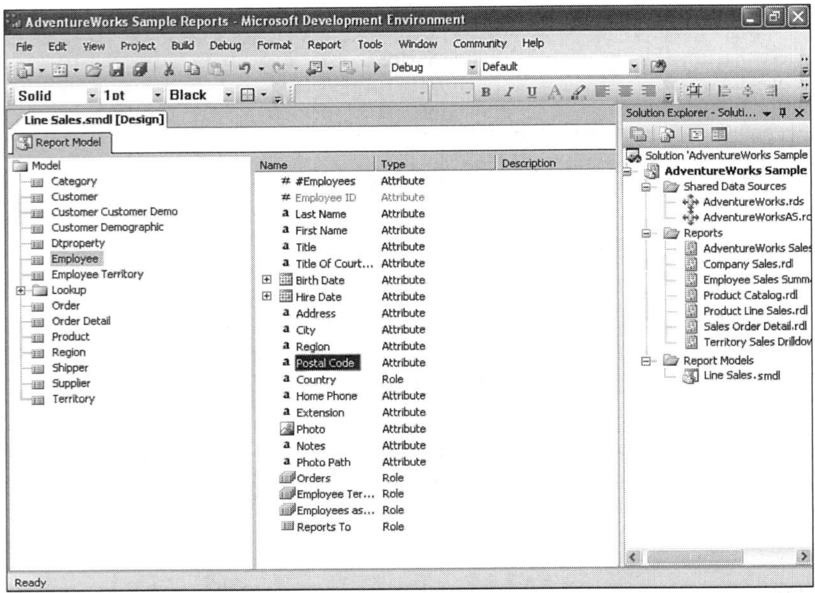

FIGURE 1.4 Model Builder.

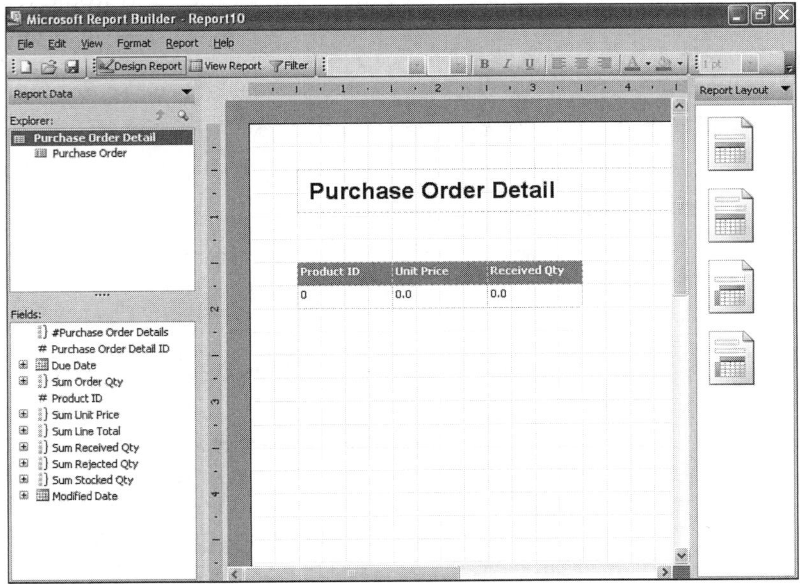

FIGURE 1.5 Report Builder.

Managing Stage of the Reporting Life Cycle

During this stage, the report author publishes the report to a central location where it can be managed by a report administrator in terms of security and delivery. This central location is a SSRS database. After the report is published, the administrator can use Report Manager, custom written scripts, third-party tools, or SQL Server Management Studio to manage published reports. The report administrator can

- Assign the report's security or the right a user might have to a report.
- Establish execution control, such as selecting a time of an execution or caching options.
- Access and organize subscriptions from a single location.
- Control report execution properties, which controls how and when reports are processed. For example, the administrator can set processing options to prevent a large report from running on demand.
- Set timeout values to prevent a single report from overloading system resources.
- Automate report delivery through a standard subscription. Users can use subscriptions to set report presentation preferences. Users who prefer to view a report in Excel, for example, can specify that format in a subscription.
- Automate report distribution through data-driven subscriptions. A data-driven subscription generates a recipient list and delivery instructions at runtime from an external data source. A data-driven subscription uses a query and column-mapping information to customize report output for a large number of users.
- Set delivery methods for a report, such as file share, printer (this would require a custom extension in the current release, which is discussed in Chapter 26, "Writing Custom Reporting Services Extensions"), or email.

Figure 1.6 depicts the Report Manager's interface.

The default URL for Report Manager is http://<server>/reports (as shown in Figure 1.6). This is a default virtual directory in which Report Manager is installed. A report administrator can later change this URL by editing configuration files or using the Reporting Services Configuration Manager, as shown in Figure 1.7.

Using SQL Server Management Studio, shown here in Figure 1.8, an administrator can perform most of the operations that she would otherwise perform through Report Manager. SQL Server Management Studio can access the SSRS catalog directly and does not require the SSRS Windows Service to be running to change the report's properties. However, an administrator will not be able to view the report if the SSRS Windows Service is not running.

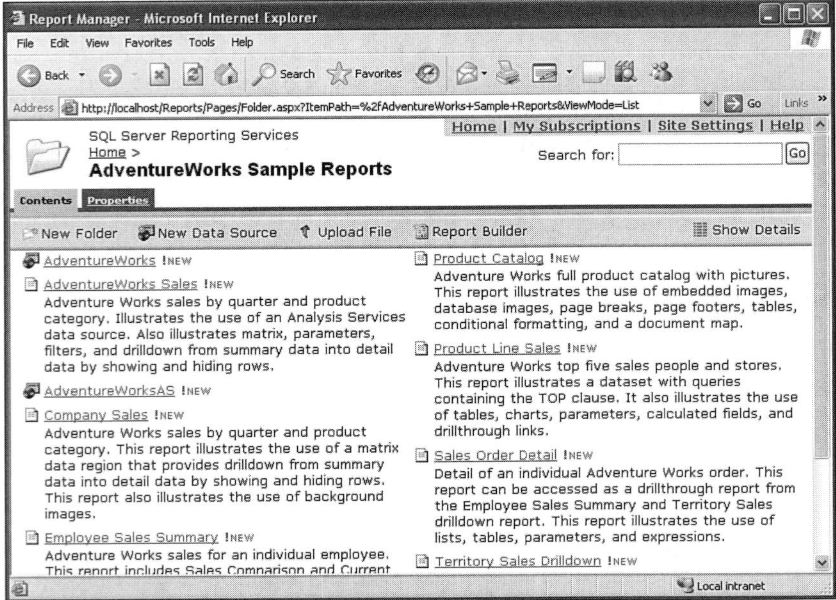

FIGURE 1.6 Report Manager.

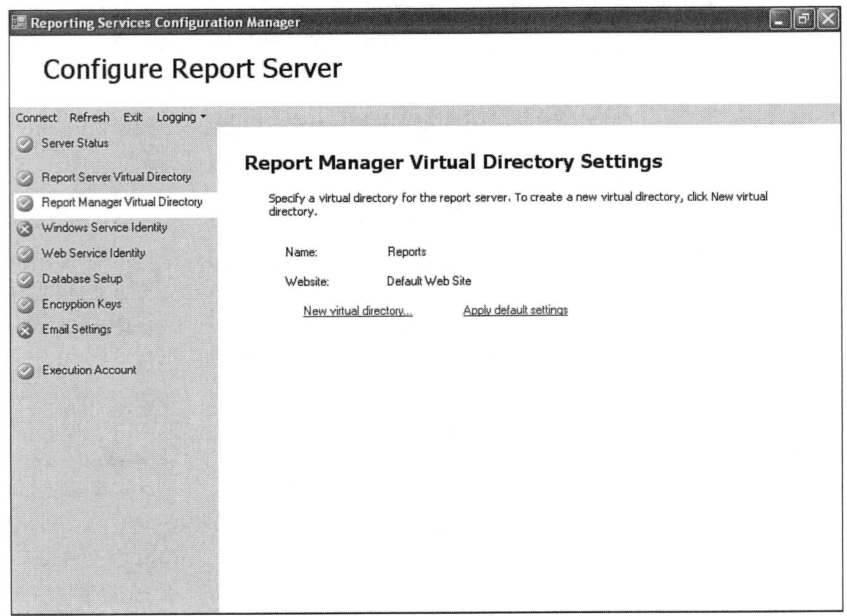

FIGURE 1.7 Reporting Services Configuration Manager.

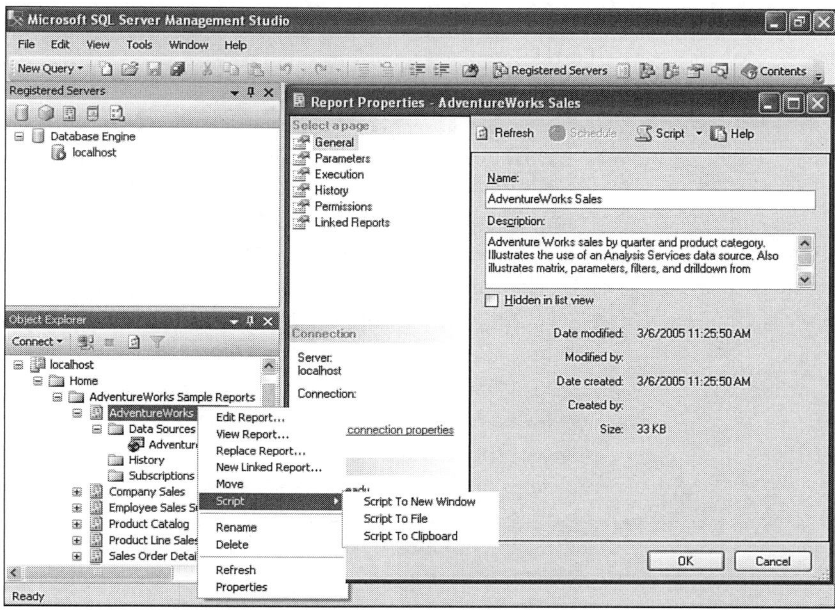

FIGURE 1.8 Managing within SQL Server Management Studio.

Table 1.2 presents a summary of the management features of SSRS.

TABLE 1.2 SSRS Management Features

Feature	Details
Browser-based management: Report Manager	Manages and maintains reports and the reporting environment.
Windows-based management: SQL Server Management Studio **NEW in 2005**	Manages and maintains reports and the reporting environment; included in SQL Server Management Studio. Provides slightly better performance than the browser-based tool in addition to the convenience of a single point of access (SQL Server Management Studio) for management of all SQL Server–related components.
Command-line utilities	Configure, activate, manage keys, and perform scripted operations.
Scripting support	Helps automate server administration tasks. For example, an administrator can script deployment and security settings for the group of reports, instead of doing the same one by one using Report Manager.
Folder hierarchy	Organizes reports by certain criteria, such as reports for specific groups of users (for example, a folder for the sales department).

TABLE 1.2 Continued

Feature	Details
Role-based security	Controls access to folders, reports, and resources. Security settings get inherited through the folder structure, similar to Windows folders security inheritance. Security can be inherited through the hierarchy or redefined at any level of hierarchy: folder or report. Role-based security works with Windows authentication. Security is installed during SSRS installation.
Job management	Monitors and cancels pending or in-process reports.
Shared data sources	Share data source connections between multiple reports and are managed independently from any of the reports.
Shared schedules	Share schedules between multiple reports and are managed independently from any of the reports.
History	Allows storing snapshots of a report at any particular moment of time. You can add report snapshots on an ad hoc basis or as a recurring scheduled operation. History can be used to view past versions of a report and see how information on a report has changed.
Linked reports	Create a link to an existing report that provides a different set of properties, parameter values, or security settings to the original report. To the user, each linked report appears to be a standalone report.
XML-based server configuration	Edits configuration files to customize email delivery, security tracing, and more.
Database, server, and report logging capability	Contains information about the reports that execute on a server or on multiple servers in a single web farm. You can use the report execution log to find out how often a report is requested, what formats are used the most, and what percentage of processing time is spent on each processing phase.

The true test of an enterprise system is shown by its ability to scale from a single user to up to thousands across an enterprise. The second test of an enterprise system is to maintain uptime and reliability. SSRS passes both tests.

SSRS manages these tasks by using underlying Windows technologies. The simplest deployment of SSRS simply places all of the components on a single machine. That single machine can then be updated with bigger and better hardware. The single machine deployment model provides a relatively cheap and cost-effective way to get up and running with SSRS.

SSRS can also be deployed across a network load balanced (NLB) cluster, giving it scalability and availability. The database catalog that SSRS uses can also be deployed across a clustered database server apart from the web servers. This allows for virtually limitless growth in terms of number of users (scalability) and, at the same time, maximum availability.

Delivery Stage of the Reporting Life Cycle

During this stage, the report is distributed to the report's users and is available in multiple output formats. The SSRS retrieval mechanism allows users to quickly change an output format.

SSRS supports various delivery methods: email, interactively online (usually through a browser, portal, or custom application), printer (requires custom extension), or file system. If the delivery method of interest is not available by default from SSRS, you can relatively easily develop custom delivery extensions. SSRS Books-On-Line provides a complete set of samples for various custom delivery extensions. You can learn more about custom extensions in Chapter 26.

Reports are structured as items in a folder structure and allow for easy browsing and execution. You can see an example of viewing a report online in Figure 1.9. Please note that the report is shown inside of Report Manager. Report Manager provides an additional functionality, such as assigning security or subscribing to a report. You can also view the report directly in the browser without Report Manager.

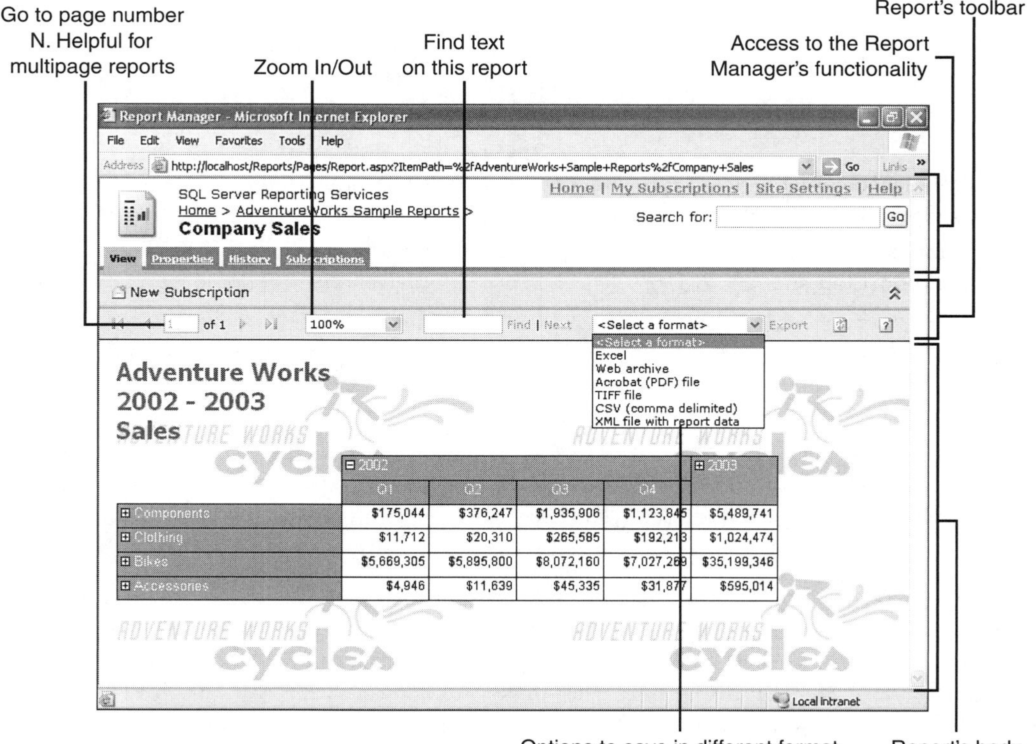

FIGURE 1.9 Online viewing.

Alternatively, a user can subscribe to a report that subsequently will be delivered via email, as shown in Figure 1.10. Email delivery is a push-model of report delivery. Push-model is especially useful for the cases in which report generation takes a long time, the report needs to be delivered to an outside user, or there is an emergency situation that generates an exception report.

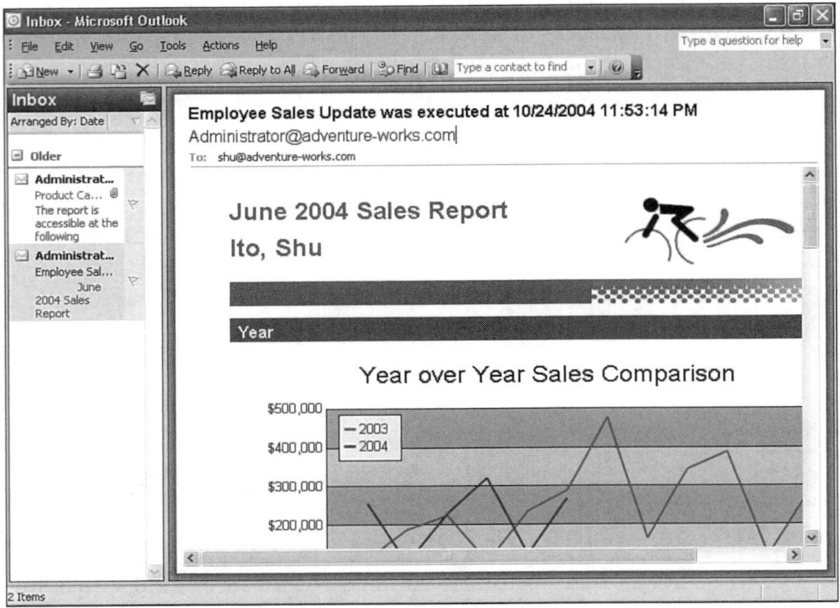

FIGURE 1.10 Email delivery.

Online view and scheduled delivery are great, but for a single solution to be truly ubiquitous, it has to offer more. SSRS does this, again, by making itself extensible rather than being all-encompassing.

A perfect example of this is via embedded reporting. With Visual Studio 2005, Microsoft has developed an integrated Report Viewer control. This control allows developers to embed SSRS reports into their Windows and web applications. Figure 1.11 shows the Report Viewer control.

If developers need to do more than simply view reports, they can access the SSRS web services directly. This set of SOAP-based calls (SOAP Application Programming Interface or SOAP API) provides access to just about every function on the report server. In fact, Report Manager does nothing more than make the same web service calls. For example, with the API, developers can modify permissions and create custom from ends.

Lastly, SSRS security is extensible. This allows access to SSRS reports from any custom portal such as SharePoint. SSRS includes Report Viewer and Report Browser SharePoint controls—the same set of controls that became available in SSRS2K SP2.

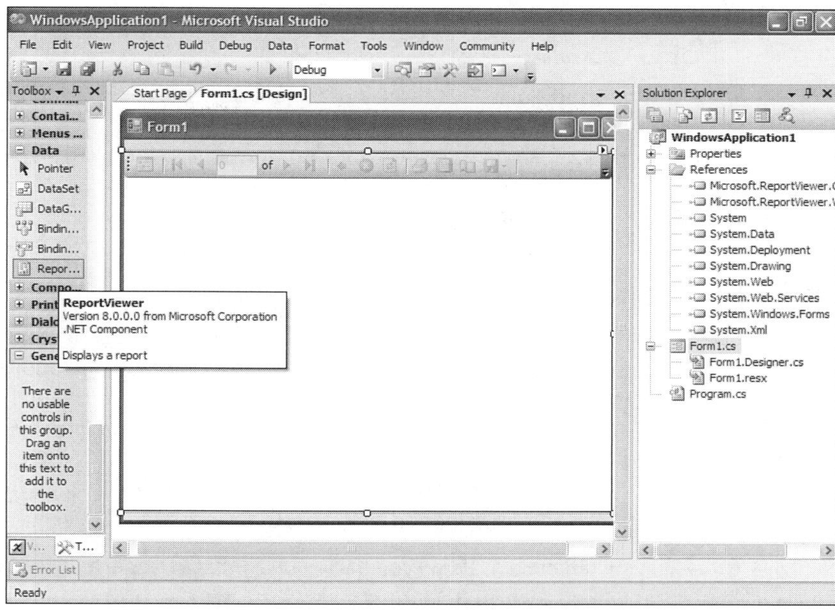

FIGURE 1.11 Report Viewer control.

Editions of Reporting Services

SSRS comes in four editions that mirror the editions of SQL Server and Visual Studio. These editions range from free starter editions to full-scale Enterprise editions.

Chapter 4, "Reporting Services Deployment Scenarios," has more information on the different editions and supported features. Table 1.3 offers a high-level overview of the different editions of SSRS.

TABLE 1.3 Overview of SSRS Editions

Edition	Quick Overview
Express	Express edition offers a lightweight edition of SSRS for developers who want to learn how to use SSRS.
Workgroup	Workgroup edition is for use in small departmental organizations or branch offices. Should needs increase, Workgroup edition can be upgraded to Standard or Enterprise editions.
Standard	Standard edition is for use in small- to medium-sized organizations, or in a single server environment. Standard edition supports all of the features of SSRS, except highly specialized data-driven subscriptions, and infinite drill down through Report Builder.
Enterprise	Enterprise edition is for use in large organizations with complex database and reporting needs. Enterprise edition is fully functional, and supports scale out functionality across a web farm.

TABLE 1.3 Continued

Edition	Quick Overview
Developer	Developer edition is essentially the same as Enterprise edition, but has different licensing requirements to make it easy for people to develop enterprise applications. Developer edition is licensed per developer in development (nonproduction) environments.

How Is SSRS Licensed?

The short answer is that every machine running SSRS has to be licensed as if it were running SQL Server. This means that any machine running SQL Server is automatically licensed for not just SQL Server, but for the entire Microsoft Business Intelligence platform. This includes SSRS, SSAS, SSNS, and SSIS. This makes it really easy to get one's feet wet with SSRS. Simply install SQL Server on one machine, and then install SSRS. On the flip side, if the choice was made to use Enterprise edition in a web farm scale–out scenario, every machine in the web farm has to be licensed to run SQL Server.

Microsoft offers three ways to license SQL Server. Table 1.4 summarizes the licensing options for SQL Server. For more information and specific costing options, you should contact your Microsoft sales representative or reseller.

TABLE 1.4 Licensing Options for SQL Server

License Options	Description
Per processor	Licenses are paid for each processor on the machine running SQL Server. This license is optimal for web facing or Business to Business machines running SQL Server. It is also helpful for very large user populations.
Server licence plus device Client Access Licenses (CALs)	Licenses are paid for the machine running SQL Server, and for every device connecting to SQL Server. An ideal situation for this is kiosks for which there are multiple users per device.
Server licence plus user CALs	Licenses are paid for the machine running SQL Server and per user accessing the machine. This is useful for enterprises in which every user can access the SQL Server machine for multiple devices.

TIP

When determining the most appropriate licensing model, please make sure to calculate the total license cost for each option and combination of licensing options. Select a licensing model combination that is the most financially sound for your business.

Summary

This chapter provided a high-level overview of SSRS features. It started with an overview of tools for the end user. From there, it showed how different SSRS features can be leveraged in the report development life cycle. Finally, it concluded with an overview of the different editions of SSRS, and how it is licensed.

The following chapters build on the content covered here, and delve into the capabilities of SSRS reports and into the architecture of SSRS. Chapter 5 concludes Part I, by discussing different installation scenarios and how to install SSRS.

Reporting Services Capabilities: Presentation, Navigation, and Programmability

CHAPTER 2

IN THIS CHAPTER

Building on basics covered in the previous chapter, this chapter provides a deeper overview of features in SSRS, from rendering reports to programmability. Along the way, any new features that were not available in the previous version are pointed out. Specific topics include the following:

- Report layout and rendering
- Report items
- Report navigation
- Ad hoc reporting
- Data access and programmability

Report Layouts

SSRS has three report layout options for developers to choose from during the design phase: tabular (top-down, row-by-row, column aligned output), matrix (top to bottom and left to right, column- and row-aligned output), and free-form. Developers can combine various layouts on a single report. More detailed discussion about report layouts is available in Chapter 11, "Working with Report Items."

The report presented in Figure 2.1, taken as a whole, has a combination of layouts: free-form and tabular.

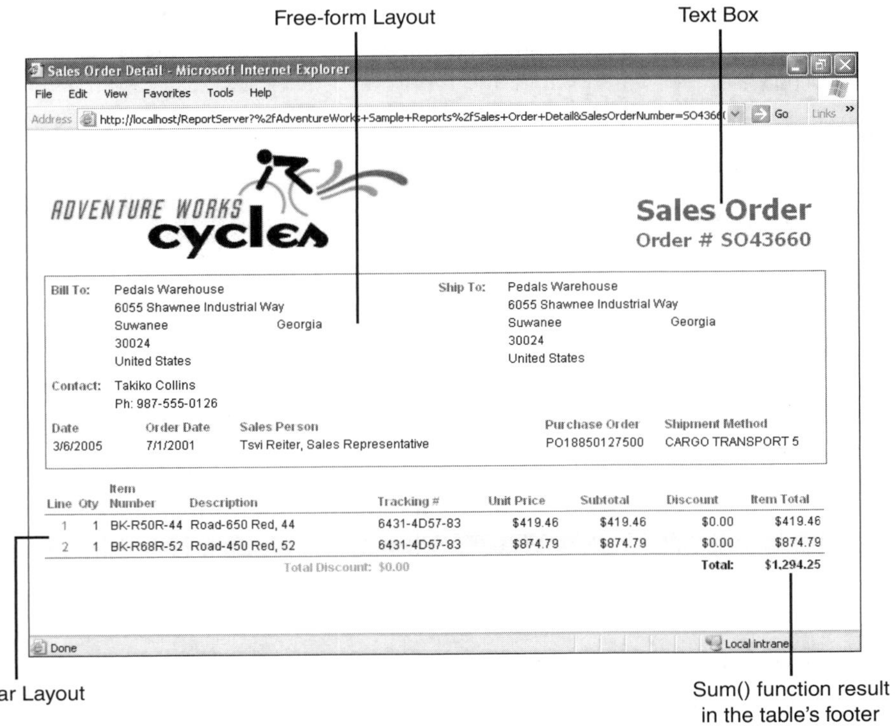

FIGURE 2.1 Tabular and free-form layout.

Tabular Report Layout

The tabular report layout is designed to display column-based data. This type of report is very similar to the way data is presented in a Microsoft Excel worksheet.

In the tabular report, developers can group and summarize data using aggregate functions. Aggregate functions include `Sum`, `Avg`, `Min`, `Max`, and `Count`. Tabular report layout propagates from top to bottom, row-by-row and allows grouping rows. Using a Table data region is the most common way to generate the tabular report layout. Unlike a table, a list does not provide item alignment; however, this type of layout could also be created using a list. Figure 2.1 includes a tabular layout.

A large portion of reports are developed in a tabular layout.

Free-Form Report Layout

As the name implies, free-form layout can contain repetitive or nonrepetitive data; items can be free-form, grouped, nested within each other (providing multiple levels of grouping), and/or located side by side. Much like a Microsoft Office document, a report contains three main areas: the body (the main informational content of a report), a page header (the information that repeats at the top of each page of a report), and a page footer (the information that repeats at the bottom of each page of a report).

A header and a footer can contain a limited subset of report items: images, text boxes, and lines. A report's body can contain any report item. Each report area serves as a free-form container in that it allows you to place report items in any position and, unlike tabular (or matrix) layout, does not restrict this position.

In addition, rectangle and list report items can be used as free-form containers for other report items. A free-form layout is shown in Figure 2.1.

Matrix Report Layout

Matrix layout (see Figure 2.2) is similar to a cross-tab or pivot table in Excel. Unlike table layout, which has a static number of columns and a dynamic number of rows, matrix layout has a dynamic number of rows and a dynamic number of columns. In other words, matrix layout propagates from top to bottom and from left to right. In turn, matrix layout allows grouping and summarizing by rows and columns. Developers can use aggregate functions for each group of rows and/or columns.

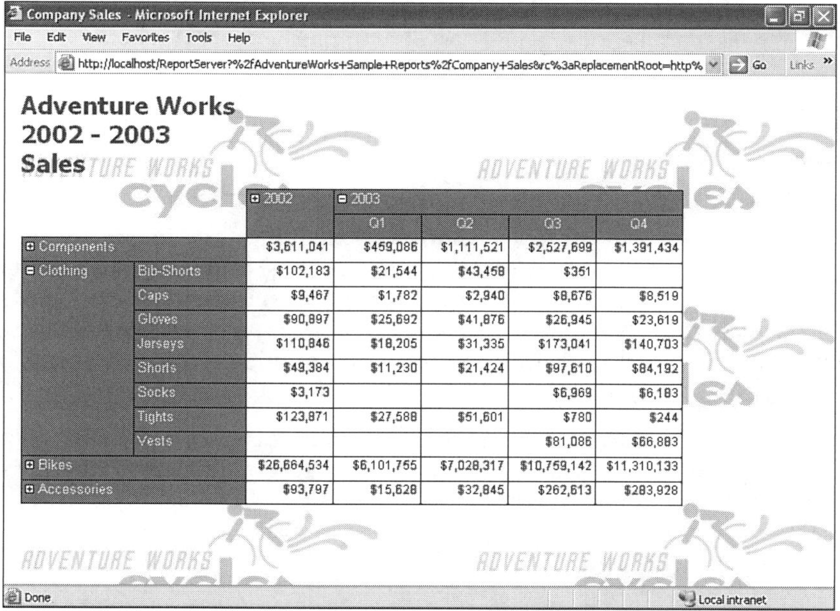

		2002	2003			
			Q1	Q2	Q3	Q4
Components		$3,611,041	$459,086	$1,111,521	$2,527,699	$1,391,434
Clothing	Bib-Shorts	$102,183	$21,544	$43,458	$351	
	Caps	$9,467	$1,782	$2,940	$8,676	$8,519
	Gloves	$90,897	$25,692	$41,876	$26,945	$23,619
	Jerseys	$110,846	$18,205	$31,335	$173,041	$140,703
	Shorts	$49,384	$11,230	$21,424	$97,610	$84,192
	Socks	$3,173			$6,969	$6,183
	Tights	$123,871	$27,588	$51,601	$780	$244
	Vests				$81,086	$66,883
Bikes		$26,664,534	$6,101,755	$7,028,317	$10,759,142	$11,310,133
Accessories		$93,797	$15,628	$32,845	$262,613	$283,928

FIGURE 2.2 Matrix report layout.

Matrix layout is accomplished using a Matrix data region and cannot be created by any other container.

Report Presentation (Rendering) Formats

SSRS offers a choice of presentation formats for the report. The following formats are available: Extensible Markup Language (XML), web-oriented Hypertext Markup Language (HTML, HTML with Office Web Components, and Web archive MHT), page-oriented such as Tagged Image File Format (TIFF) or Portable Document Format (PDF), and desktop application (Excel and CSV) formats.

Switching between presentation formats is very fast and does not requery data sources. This is accomplished by separation of data processing from final rendering, enabling multiple users to choose different rendering options for the same report.

Report Items, Visual Effects, and Charting

Presentation elements in SSRS are called report items. Report items are very similar to visual controls available in Visual Studio languages, such as Visual Basic and C#. Report items are classified as data regions, containers, and independent report items. Data regions support grouping and sorting of data and provide repetitive display of rows (or groups of rows) from a data set associated with a data region. Independent report items display a single value or a single image.

Containers contain other report elements, including data regions. A container is fixed when the position of a report item is fixed. Most, but not all, of the containers are also data regions. Thus, data regions can be nested within other data regions.

NOTE

Report Builder does not support nested data regions.

Developers can create visual effects by using rectangles, lines, and images (embedded or referenced) in a report. SSRS has extensive capabilities to specify properties of items on a report, including border, color, background color, and so on. For example, a report can include bold totals and red negative numbers. A report can include score card graphics, like a traffic light, with red indicating problematic areas and green highlighting areas where everything is well.

In addition to static graphical images, reports can include charts. Just like any other data region, a chart has to be associated with one of the report's data sets to be able to display data. See Figure 2.3 for sample charts.

A chart has comprehensive functionality and is very similar by capabilities to an Excel chart with a variety of chart types, 3-D effects, and more. Unlike an Excel chart, an SSRS chart does not build a trend line internally; however, this limit can be overcome by calculating values for a trend line in the data set and then providing it to a chart.

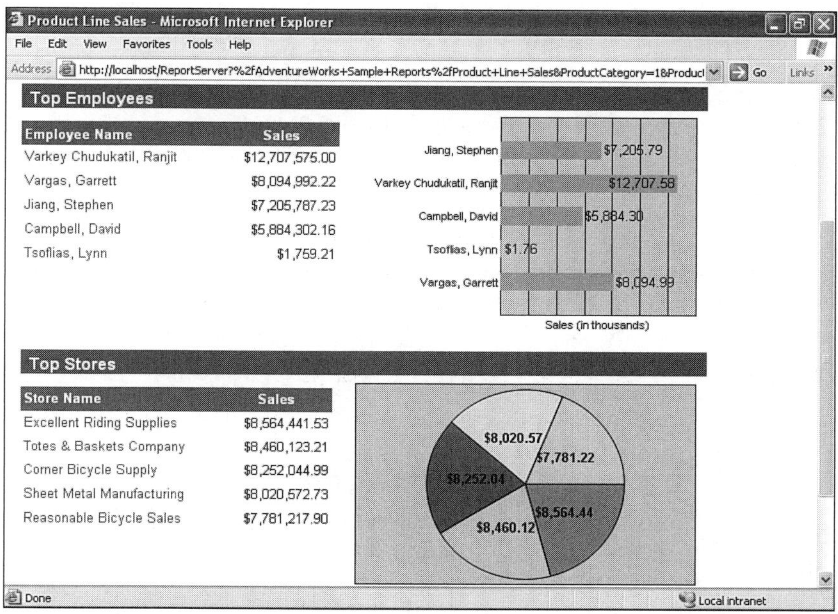

FIGURE 2.3 Report using bar and pie charts.

NOTE

The chart control used in this release of Reporting Services is licensed from Dundas Software (www.dundas.com). In addition, a more comprehensive version of the chart can be purchased from Dundas Software.

List, Table, Matrix, and Chart report items are data regions. The Line, Text Box, Image, Rectangle, and Subreport report are independent items. Table 2.1 provides a summary of SSRS design elements.

TABLE 2.1 Report Items

Design Element	Description	Data Region	Container
Table	Presents data with static columns and expands row by row. Allows developers to group and sort rows of data. Can have multiple groups. Table is faster than Matrix and List, which makes Table the fastest of all data regions. Table is a very powerful control and can be used for most reports.	Yes	Fixed

TABLE 2.1 Continued

Design Element	Description	Data Region	Container
Matrix	Capable of having a dynamic number of rows and columns and expands row by row and column by column. Can act like a table (fixed columns, dynamic rows) or like a transposed table (fixed rows and dynamic columns). Allows developers to group and sort rows and columns of data. Can have multiple groups. Matrix can also be used when you want to transpose your data, that is, when you want to turn records into columns of your data. Also known as cross-tab or pivot.	Yes	Fixed
List[1]	Presents data in a free-form fashion for complex repeating areas. List repeats items based on the associated data set. Allows developers to group and sort rows of data. A single list can have only a single group, but lists can be nested within each other to provide multiple grouping.	Yes	Free-form
Chart	Provides a graphic presentation of data. Supports bar, pie, line, and many more chart types. Functionality is comparable to an Excel chart.	Yes	Fixed
Text Box	Displays all text data in the report. A table or matrix cell is a text box by default. Individual text boxes can be placed anywhere on a report and can include labels, data set fields, or calculated data.	No	No
Image	Displays an image. An image can be loaded from a URL, embedded in a report, or stored in a database. SSRS supports `.bmp`, `.jpeg`, `.jpe`, `.gif`, and `.png` image formats.	No	No
Line	Graphical element with no data associated with it. Can be placed anywhere on a report. Has styles commonly associated with lines: weight, color, and so on.	No	No
Rectangle	Provides a graphical element or a container for other report items. Can be placed anywhere on a report.	No	Free-form
Subreport	Provides a container for the body of another report on the report server. Better performance can be achieved by using data regions, instead of subreports.	No	Free-form

[1]This item is not supported in Report Builder. All other items in this table are supported by both Report Designer and Report Builder.

Report Navigation

Developers can add interactive features to navigate to related reports (jump to report or URL) or within a single report (find, go to page, jump to bookmark, and document map). Developers can add links to related reports, reports that have more details (drill down through or simply drill through), or, in general, to any web page. Bookmarks and document maps provide navigation within a large report.

For multipage reports, SSRS provides functionality to move through pages of the report, go to a specified page, and go to the beginning or the end of the report. In addition, users can search through a report for a string that they specify in search criteria.

If a report is too big or too small for a page, the zoom capability comes in handy. Users can zoom-in and zoom-out on the report's page when using web-oriented formats (HTML, HTMLOWA). Other formats such as PDF handle zoom through corresponding applications, such as Adobe Acrobat Reader.

After a user accesses the Reporting Services site, she can navigate a folder hierarchy to find reports and other items. In addition, reports can be added to a Favorites list in a web browser, presented via a web portal. Users can store and manage reports and other items in a personal workspace.

In addition, users can use an interactive sorting feature—the end users can sort rows in the table interactively by clicking on the column heading. Report developers can enable or disable this functionality.

Ad Hoc Reports *NEW in 2005*

This is a new capability that was added for SSRS and was not available prior to this release. Microsoft provides the Windows application Report Builder *NEW in 2005* tool to support this functionality. Report Builder uses models generated by the Model Builder *NEW in 2005* tool.

Model Builder is a tool used by database developers to abstract the complexities of the database schema, and provide information analysts with a view of "business objects" to which analysts can relate. The model also allows developers to relate the business objects (or entities) to other objects within the database. Because the model contains information on the underlying database schema, as well as how to abstract it, it becomes integral to ad hoc reporting. After a model is complete, it is published to the report server, just as any report.

The Report Builder uses models to provide the end user views of business objects and how they relate to each other. Because the model has information on the relationship between entities, and the underlying database schema, it allows for a feature called "infinite drill down." This feature allows information analysts to browse through company data with little or no knowledge of SQL.

Reporting Services Data Access Features

SSRS data-processing extensions use ADO.NET-managed providers and support a variety of data sources. SSRS includes the following providers: SQL Server (7.0-2005), SQL Server Analysis Services (2000-2005), Oracle, ODBC, and OLEDB. Other providers are usually available from corresponding database vendors. In general, SSRS can populate reports with relational and multidimensional data from SQL Server, Analysis Services, and other .NET Framework data providers. Developers can also create custom data-processing extensions if there is no provider available for the specific data source.

SSRS allows using multiple data sources and multiple data sets within a single report. This allows developers, for example, to combine data from the SQL Server transactional database, SQL Server Analysis Services data warehouse, and Oracle database on the same report.

Developers can add parameters to refine a query or filter a data set. Dynamic parameters get values at runtime based on user selections (the selection of one parameter can build the value list for a second parameter).

Several new features were added to SSRS:

- *NEW in 2005* **Multidimensional Expressions (MDX) query parameters**—A tool that allows you to pass parameters to multidimensional queries.
- *NEW in 2005* **MDX query designer**—An intuitive tool to develop multidimensional queries with a simple drag and drop.
- *NEW in 2005* **Data Mining Extension (DMX) query designer**—An intuitive tool to develop data-mining queries with a simple drag and drop.
- *NEW in 2005* **Multivalued parameters**—A tool that allows you to select multiple parameters. For example, a user might like to be presented with sales data for 2002 and 2003, but not for 2001 and 2004. In technical terms, this is IN(list) selection criteria.

Programmability

This feature provides endless possibilities for developers to extend SSRS. For example, developers can script administrative functionality, execute a report asynchronously[1] (using `BeginRender` and `EndRender` functions) within their code, and more. Table 2.2 provides a summary of programmable features in SSRS.

NOTE

[1] **Asynchronous execution can be also accomplished within a custom extension. Additional asynchronous options are to schedule a snapshot or to subscribe to a report.**

TABLE 2.2 Reporting Services Programmability and Extensibility Features

Programmable Functionality	Notes	Language
Custom embedded code	A code is embedded as a part of the report definition file and compiled together with the container report. Many errors are caught by the compiler when a reporting solution is built. Although embedded code allows a developer to use full object-oriented functionality of VB.NET, embedded code is mostly used for simple logic. Developing complex embedded code is possible, but not usually done due to limited debugging facilities and limited functionality of the embedded code editor. The embedded code editor is a simple text box that does not have advanced features, such as code completion, which is available in Visual Studio.	VB.NET
Custom assembly	A .NET assembly, which can be written in any .NET language and can be called from a report. Visual Studio .NET is the most popular tool for .NET development and provides full debugging capacities for .NET assemblies. Custom assemblies can be used for complex logic and, for example, in cases when access to a file I/O or database is needed.	Any .NET language: VB.NET, C#, and so on
Reporting Services web service/SOAP API	The programmatic interfaces that provide an entry point to the complete functionality of SSRS. Reporting Services web service can be called from .NET or SOAP-enabled applications and provides access to full Reporting Services functionality, including rendering, report management, report and folder browsing, and report deployment. Mainly used to incorporate report processing or management in custom web or Windows applications.	Can be used from any .NET or SOAP-enabled application
SSRS scripts (rs.exe utility)	The utility that provides access to Reporting Services web service by executing VB.NET scripts. Scripting allows a developer to use full object-oriented functionality of VB.NET and is mainly used to automate SSRS' management.	VB.NET

TABLE 2.2 Continued

Programmable Functionality	Notes	Language
URL Access	The tool that provides access to various features of Reporting Services through a parameterized URL string. Designed to retrieve rendered output, URL Access can be used with GET and POST methods and can be integrated in a web portal "as is" or as a source for a frame. URL Access can also be incorporated in a Windows or a web application using WebBrowser control.	HTML/URL
Report Definition Language (RDL)	The language that is an open and extensible XML-based language that describes a report. Developers can write tools to customize RDL files, for example tools similar to the Report Designer. In addition, developers can add support for elements or features that are not present in the existing RDL schema, and then build custom tools and report-rendering extensions to handle new functionality.	RDL (XML)
Reporting Services extensions	The appropriate hooks to enable developers to extend SSRS' functionality and write custom extensions. For example, delivery (cell phones, pagers, other applications), data processing, rendering, report processing, and security (security extensions are not available in Express edition) can be extended with new extensions.	Any .NET language: VB.NET, C#, and so on
WMI interfaces (manage SSRS configuration)	The interface used to manage Report Server Windows service configuration.	Can be used from any .NET application
Report Viewer control *NEW in 2005*	The Web and Windows controls that make it easier to integrate reporting functionality into applications. Report Viewer can view server and local reports. Local reports rendered by the Report Viewer control do not require access to SSRS. In Reporting Services 2000 (as well as 2005), developers can use the WebBrowser control to embed reports in an application. WebBrowser is a simple HTML viewer and does not have advanced capabilities of Report Viewer, such as an ability to render reports.	Can be used from any .NET language application

TABLE 2.2 Continued

Programmable Functionality	Notes	Language
`RSPrintClient` NEW in 2005	The control that presents the Print dialog box for a user to initiate a print job, preview a report, specify pages to print, and change the margins. Developers can use this control in the code to enable report printing functionality.	Can be used from any .NET language application
SharePoint Web Parts (Viewer and Explorer)	Similar to report controls, the control that assists integration with SharePoint Portal applications. Web Parts had shipped with Reporting Services 2000 SP2. SSRS 2005 is the first version that includes it in the initial install.	SharePoint serves as a container
Expressions	A combination of variables, constants, functions, and operators that evaluate to a single data value. Simple expressions can be a constant, variable, column, or scalar function. Complex expressions are one or more simple expressions connected by operators. Most properties of the report take expressions. Expressions use VB.NET syntax and are technically very similar to Excel formulas. Expressions use Visual Basic runtime functions, most identical to functions used in Excel, such as `IIF`.	VB.NET
Custom report items NEW in 2005	The server controls that extend report processing. Custom report items can be data bound and use familiar SSRS VB.NET, functionality, such as expressions, grouping, sorting, and filtering. Custom report items can have its custom user interface and properties. Developers can add custom report items to a Report Designer toolbox. SSRS provides an infrastructure to support custom report items.	Any .NET language: C#, and so on

More detailed discussion about each of the programmability features is available in Chapters 22 through 28.

Summary

This chapter provided an overview of features in SSRS in the areas of data retrieval, presentation, navigation, and programmability. SSRS added several new features to the future mix that was available in the previous version, to name a few:

- End-user capability to develop ad hoc reports
- Intuitive, drag-and-drop editors for Multidimensional Expressions (MDX) and Data Mining Extensions (DMX)
- New controls to integrate reports (ReportViewer) and report printing (`RSPrintClient`) in Windows or web applications
- Ability to add custom (not defined in RDL) report items

The next chapter discusses a high-level architecture of SSRS.

Reporting Services Architecture

CHAPTER 3

IN THIS CHAPTER

- Report Server Web and Windows Service
- Programmatic Interfaces
- Report Processor
- Command-Line Utilities
- Reporting Services Extensions
- Report Server Databases
- Scheduling and Delivery Processor
- Report Builder *NEW in 2005*
- Report Model Designer *NEW in 2005*
- Report Designer
- Report Manager
- SQL Server Management Studio *NEW in 2005*
- Reporting Services Configuration Tool *NEW in 2005*
- RSPrintClient Control *NEW in 2005*
- WMI Provider
- Performance Monitoring Objects

SSRS is a comprehensive and extensible reporting platform, which includes an integrated set of processing components, programmatic interfaces, and tools. Processing components are the basis for the multilayered architecture of SSRS and interact with each other to retrieve data, process layout, render, and deliver a report to a target destination. SSRS supports two categories of components:

- **Processors**—Ensure integrity of SSRS and supply an infrastructure that enables developers to add a new functionality (extensions). Processors itself are not extendable in this release of SSRS.
- **Extensions**—Assemblies that are invoked by processors and perform specific processing functionality, such as data retrieval. Developers can write custom extensions.

Reporting Services architecture diagram is depicted in Figure 3.1; components are described in more details later in this chapter. Arrows on the diagram show a data flow between components "within" and "outside" of SSRS (external tools, applications, services, and utilities).

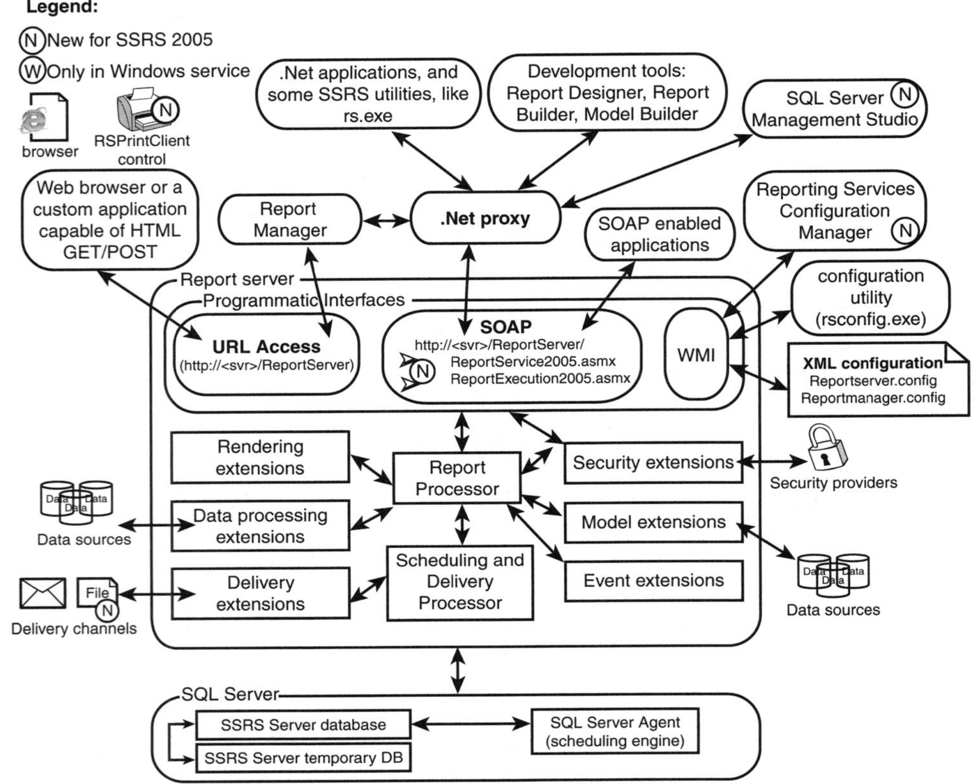

FIGURE 3.1 Reporting Services architecture.

Report Server Web and Windows Service

The Report Server is implemented as a symbiosis between a web service and Windows service. Services work together to host, process, and deliver reports.

NOTE

In SSRS 2005, Report Server supports multiple instances on a single computer.

When SSRS Windows service starts, it initially loads basic supporting assemblies (such as a SQL data provider and interface library), but it does not load extensions. In this release, SSRS Windows service handles encryption and decryption and serves as a host for the Scheduling and Delivery Processor. The Scheduling and Delivery Processor uses a `PollingInterval` configuration setting to monitor SSRS catalog's `Event` table for "events" (such as timed subscription). Events instruct SSRS to "wake up" and start processing.

Similar to any .NET web service, SSRS web service is invoked ("wakened up") via Internet Information Server (IIS) and executes in the ASP.NET worker process (`aspnet_wp.exe`). "Wake up" events are facilitated by programmatic interfaces.

Programmatic Interfaces

The Reporting Services programmatic interfaces accept SOAP (via SSRS web service) and HTTP requests (via URL Access). For more information about SSRS web service, please see Chapter 25, "How to Use Reporting Services Web Service." For more information about SSRS URL Access, please see Chapter 24, "How to Use URL Access."

SSRS 2005 web service provides three endpoints:

- http://localhost/ReportServer/ReportService.asmx is provided for backward compatibility with SSRS 2000.
- http://<server>/ReportServer/ReportService2005.asmx is the new management endpoint in SSRS 2005.
- http://<server>/ReportServer/ReportExecution2005.asmx is the new execution endpoint.

The name of an endpoint describes the purpose. For example, the execution endpoint is designed to provide report execution (processing) interfaces and, with that, an access to functions, such as `Render`. Function `Render` returns a rendered report as a stream with a specified format, such as HTML.

Programmatic interfaces facilitate retrieval of information from the SSRS catalog and information exchange between SSRS components.

When a report is requested, either interactively or by the Scheduling and Delivery Processor, programmatic interfaces initialize the Report Processor component and start processing a report.

Report Processor

The Report Processor ties components of a report server together and takes care of caching within SSRS. Caching refers to an ability of the SSRS to keep a copy of a processed report and return that copy when a user opens the report. Caching can shorten the time required to retrieve a report, especially if the report is large or is accessed frequently. All report caches are stored in the SSRS catalog (specifically ReportServerTempDB database) and survive both SQL Server and Report Server restarts.

Report Processor performs the following operations:

- **Execution**—Retrieves a report definition and combines it with data retrieved by the data-processing extension. This operation generates an intermediate format.
- **Rendering**—Renders the intermediate format to a requested output format using rendering extensions.

- **Processing of models**—This is similar to Execution operation for reports that are generated by Report Builder and contain a semantic model (or simply a model, which serves as a data source for a report) and a semantic query. Semantic query refers to a query performed against a model that, in turn, just like a SQL query, generates a report's data set.

This is how Report Processor responds to users' requests:

- **New interactive report request**—Intermediate format is generated and passed to the rendering extension; user receives rendered report.
- **Request to generate cache or snapshot**—Intermediate format is generated and stored in the database.
- **Request for cached report or snapshot**—Intermediate format is retrieved from cache (or snapshot) and passed to the rendering extension; user receives rendered report.

Command-Line Utilities

Three administration assistance utilities are installed automatically during the Reporting Services install:

- `rs.exe`—Host scripting operations. Developers can, for example, create VB.NET script to deploy a set of reports. You can find more details about this utility in Chapter 25.
- `rsconfig.exe`—Use to modify encrypted connection information to the Report Server database.
- `rskeymgmt.exe`—Back up/restore symmetric keys for encrypted data used by a report server or delete encrypted data if the key is lost. For more details, please see Chapter 21, "Deploying and Configuring SSRS."

NOTE

SSRS 2005 discontinued the `rsactivate.exe` utility, which was used in the previous release to activate new SSRS instances in a web farm. In SSRS 2005, activation is performed using the Reporting Services Configuration Tool.

Reporting Services Extensions

An extension is a .NET Assembly that is invoked by the Report Processor to perform certain processing functions. There are several types of extensions: Data Processing, Delivery, Rendering, Security (authentication and authorization), SemanticQuery, ModelGeneration, and EventProcessing.

For an extension to be used by a report server, it has to be installed (assuming default SSRS configuration) to the `C:\Program Files\Microsoft SQL Server\MSSQL.3\Reporting Services\ReportServer\bin` directory and configured in `C:\Program Files\Microsoft SQL Server\MSSQL.3\Reporting Services\ReportServer\rsreportserver.config`.

The last part of an extension filename usually implies the extension's functionality. For example, the HTML rendering extension's filename is `Microsoft.ReportingServices.HtmlRendering.dll`.

Custom extensions allow developers to add complementing functionality that is not available in SSRS "out-of-the-box." For example, a company can implement an extension that delivers reports to a phone or a fax. You can learn more about extensions in Chapter 26, "Writing Custom Reporting Services Extensions."

NOTE

This release of SSRS does not allow custom SemanticQuery, ModelGeneration, or EventProcessing extensions.

Data-Processing Extensions

Data-processing extensions retrieve data from the report data source. Some of the tasks performed by data-processing extensions include open connection to a data source, analyze query and return field names, pass parameters, and retrieve and iterate data set. Table 3.1 outlines the data-processing extensions included and configured with SSRS.

TABLE 3.1 Data-Processing Extensions Configured with SSRS

Extension	Description/Notes
SQL Server	Connects to and retrieves data from the SQL Server database engine versions 7.0 through 2005.
OLE DB	Connects to and retrieves data from OLE DB-compliant data sources.
Microsoft SQL Server Analysis	Connects to and retrieves data from the SQL Server Analysis Services Services 2000 and 2005. For Analysis Services 2005, this extension supports both Multidimensional Expressions (MDX) and Data Mining Expressions (DMX). For Analysis Services 2000, this extension supports nonparameterized MDX only.
Oracle	Connects to and retrieves data from an Oracle database; requires Oracle client 8i Release 3 (8.1.7) to be installed on a computer on which Reporting Server is installed.
ODBC	Connects to and retrieves data from ODBC-compliant data sources.
XML	Retrieves XML data from any XML web source (such as a web server) that can be accessed through a URL.

All extensions, which are installed with SSRS (except XML), leverage corresponding .NET data providers. `Microsoft.ReportingServices.DataExtensions` library provides wrapper classes that supply SSRS data-processing extension interfaces to .NET data providers.

Developers can create additional custom data-processing extensions.

Delivery Extensions

Delivery extensions deliver reports to specific devices or formats. Extensions included with RS include email and file share delivery. The delivery method and, therefore, corresponding extension are selected when a user (or an administrator) creates a subscription.

A sample of printer delivery extension is included with SQL Server samples and discussed in Chapter 26. Table 3.2 outlines the delivery extensions included and configured with SSRS.

TABLE 3.2 Delivery Extensions Included with SSRS

Extension	Purpose
Email delivery	Delivers a rendered report to an email inbox. Allows setting delivery options that control an output format and whether the report is delivered as a link or as an attachment.
File share delivery	Delivers a rendered report to a shared folder. Allows setting delivery options that control a destination folder path, an output format, and whether the report overrides an older version or is added as a new version.

Developers can create additional custom delivery extensions.

Rendering Extensions

Report Server Rendering extensions transform a report's layout and data into a device-specific format. Extensions included with RS include HTML (3.2 and 4.0), Microsoft Excel, Text/CSV, XML, Image (BMP, EMF, GIF, JPEG, PNG, TIFF, WMF), and PDF rendering.

NOTE

Unlike SSRS 2000, which rendered Excel files as an MHTML file carrying special Excel metatags, SSRS 2005 renders reports to Excel's native binary format.

Because the final rendering phase is only loosely coupled with data processing, it enables users to choose different rendering options for the same report without the need to requery data sources.

Developers can create additional custom rendering extensions.

Security Extensions

This book frequently uses the term "security extension" as if it refers to a single unit. In actuality, there are two interrelated extensions:

- Authentication extension, which handles a process that establishes user's identity
- Authorization extension, which handles a process that checks if an identity has access to a particular SSRS resource

SSRS includes a security extension based on Windows authentication. After a user's identity is established, an authorization process determines whether a Windows user (or a Windows group that contains a user) is configured to access a particular resource on a reporting server.

Developers can create additional custom security extensions. An instance of SSRS can use only one security extension. In other words, either the Windows or a custom extension can be used, but not both at the same time.

Report Server Databases

The SSRS catalog encompasses two databases: Report Server database (the default name is `ReportServer`) and Report Server temporary database (the default name is `ReportServerTempDB`). Report Server database is a SQL Server database that stores part of SSRS configuration, report definitions, report metadata, report history, cache policy, snapshots, resources, security settings, encrypted data, scheduling and delivery data, and extension information.

NOTE

Although users can certainly directly access databases in the SSRS catalog and directly modify objects that SSRS uses, this is not a recommended (or supported) practice. Underlying data and structures within the SSRS catalog are not guaranteed to be compatible between different releases of SSRS, service packs, or patches.

Please treat the `ReportServer` database as one of the production databases. Although many developers store report detentions (RDL) in a separate repository, and, thus, RDL is often recoverable, a loss of snapshot data can carry a negative business impact. For example, users might make some business decisions using snapshot's capabilities to report "frozen-in-time" data.

Another database that SSRS uses is the Report Server temporary database. This database is responsible for storing intermediate processing products, such as cached reports, and session and execution data.

NOTE

To store temporary snapshots in the file system, instead of the database, administrators should complete the following steps. First modify `RSReportServer.config` **and set** `WebServiceUseFileShareStorage` **and** `WindowsServiceUseFileShareStorage` **to True.**

Then set `FileShareStorageLocation` **to a fully qualified path. The default path is** `C:\Program Files\Microsoft SQL Server\MSSQL.3\Reporting Services\RSTempFiles`.

Unlike SQL Server's `tempdb`, data in `ReportServerTempDB` survives SQL Server and Report Server restarts. Report Server periodically cleans expired and orphan data in `ReportServerTempDB`.

All data in `ReportServerTempDB` can be deleted at any time with minimal or no impact. The minimal impact that a user might experience, for example, is a temporary performance reduction due to lost cache data and a loss of an execution state. The execution state is stored in the table `SessionData`. Loss of the execution state results in an error: "Execution 'j4j3vfblcanzv3qzcqhvml55' cannot be found (rsExecutionNotFound)." To resolve the loss of the execution state, a user would need to reopen a report.

TIP

SSRS does not recover deleted `ReportServerTempDB` **or tables within this database. To quickly recover from erroneous deletions of objects in this database, keep a script or a backup of an empty** `ReportServerTempDB` **handy.**

In a scale-out deployment, the SSRS catalog is shared across all of the report servers in the deployment.

Scheduling and Delivery Processor

The Scheduling and Delivery Processor is hosted in SSRS Windows service and monitors for events. When the Scheduling and Delivery Processor receives an event, the Scheduling and Delivery Processor collaborates with the Report Processor to render a report. After a report is rendered, the Scheduling and Delivery Processor uses delivery extensions to deliver a report.

The Scheduling and Delivery Processor leverages the SQL Server Agent as a scheduling engine. The schedule is based on the local time of the Report Server that owns the schedule. When an administrator creates a new schedule, the SSRS creates a SQL Server Agent job to run on the requested schedule. Then SSRS adds a row in the `Schedule` table of the `ReportServer` database. The row's `ScheduleId` field is the job's identifier. Administrators can schedule subscriptions, report history, and snapshot execution.

When the scheduled time comes, the SQL Server Agent generates an event by executing the scheduled job. The job inserts a row in the `Event` table of the `ReportServer` database. This row serves as an event for the Scheduling and Delivery Processor.

The Scheduling and Delivery Processor checks the `Event` table every `PollingInterval` seconds and initiates appropriate actions as a response to an event.

NOTE

The `PollingInterval` is specified in the `rsreportserver.config` configuration file and is set to 10 seconds by default.

The scheduling and delivery process "breaks" when either (or both) the SSRS Windows service is not running (the Scheduling and Delivery Processor is not processing events) or the SQL Server Agent is not running (the agent is not generating events).

NOTE

When the SSRS Windows service is not running and the SQL Server Agent is running, the job history for SQL Server Agent would indicate that the scheduled request ("insert event") ran successfully. The job will be successful despite the fact that the scheduled operation could complete because the Scheduling and Delivery Processor is not running to process the event.

Report Builder *NEW in 2005*

One of the most requested features in the previous version of SSRS was an ability to develop end-user reports. Microsoft delivered this functionality in SSRS 2005.

Report Builder is a ClickOnce, ad hoc, end-user report authoring and publishing tool, which provides drag-and-drop, easy-to-use report design functionality.

NOTE

You can find more information about ClickOnce applications by searching http://www.microsoft.com and reading http://msdn.microsoft.com/msdnmag/issues/04/05/clickonce/default.aspx.

As a typical ClickOnce application, Report Builder is deployed from a browser and executes on a client's computer. Report Builder does not require administrative permissions during installation and runs in a secure sandbox provided by .NET code access security.

To deploy Report Builder, click on the Report Builder button on the Report Manager's toolbar. Alternatively, you can use http://<server>/ReportServer/ReportBuilder/ReportBuilder.application URL to launch Report Builder. Report Builder is deployed to `C:\Documents and Settings\<UserName>\Local Settings\Apps\2.0\<obfuscated directory>`.

Before you can use Report Builder,

- You must have appropriate permissions, and be a member of the Report Consumer role or a custom role that includes the Consume Reports task.
- At least one report model has to be published.
- An Internet browser must allow you to download files.

Reports developed by Report Builder can be interpreted by Report Designer.

Report Model Designer *NEW in 2005*

The Report Model Designer generates report models for use by Report Builder. A model abstracts complexities of an underlying data; for example, a model allows mapping names of tables and columns to business terms that an end user can easily understand.

The Report Model Designer is hosted in Business Intelligence Development Studio (BIDS for short) or Visual Studio and is intended for use by developers. Actually, BIDS is a Visual Studio shell with only Business Intelligence projects and no language projects. One of the Business Intelligence projects is the Report Model Project, which launches the Report Model Designer and allows developers to create models.

In this release, models and, therefore, ad hoc reports can only work with SQL Server data sources: SQL Server database engine and SQL Server Analysis Services. However, developers can work around this limitation and access other data sources by using link servers or Analysis Services Unified Data Model. Both provide a thin layer of abstraction and allow access to any OLE DB- or ODBC-compliant data source including Oracle.

Report Designer

Report Designer is a developer-oriented, comprehensive report authoring, previewing, and publishing tool hosted in Business Intelligence Development Studio or Visual Studio.

To organize the report development process, Report Designer provides three tab views of a report: Data, Layout, and Preview.

The Data tab helps developers to define data sources and design data set queries. Report Designer provides three drag-and-drop graphical query designers to assist with SQL queries, Analysis Services Multidimensional Expressions (MDX query designer is a new feature of SSRS 2005), and Analysis Services Data Mining Expressions (DMX query designer is a new feature of SSRS 2005) .

The Layout tab helps developers to design graphical presentations of a report and associate graphical presentation with data. Report Designer provides a drag-and-drop layout designer and toolbox with reporting controls. Layout design is very similar to a user interface design that Visual Studio provides for Windows and web applications: You can drag and drop reporting controls to a report, arrange them as needed, set properties, and associate with data sets that were designed through the Data tab.

The Preview tab provides a preview for a report so developers can test and adjust the report as needed.

Report Designer provides the Report Wizard that takes developers through the guided steps to create a report. As such, the wizard provides a limited number of layouts to choose from, but a report developer can modify the layout as needed by using the Layout tab after the wizard's steps are completed.

Finally, Report Designer allows developers to build and deploy reports to SSRS.

NOTE

Reports developed by Report Designer cannot be interpreted or edited by Report Builder.

Report Manager

Report Manager is a web-based report access and management tool providing access to a single instance of a Report Server. Some of the operations that users can perform using the Report Manager include view, search and subscribe to reports, manage security (report access and roles), create folders and move reports around folders, manage data sources, set report parameters, and more. Actions that a user can perform using Report Manager depend on the user's security permissions. The default URL that invokes Report Manager is http://<server>/reports. The default directory that contains the Report Manager's binaries, pages, and so on is `C:\Program Files\Microsoft SQL Server\MSSQL.3\Reporting Services\ReportManager`.

Although Report Manager provides for a limited customization, it is neither designed nor supplied with sufficient documentation to support customization. This leaves companies with several customization options, which can be combined:

- Accept limited customization capabilities of Report Manager, such as modification of style sheets it uses (by default located at `C:\Program Files\Microsoft SQL Server\MSSQL.3\Reporting Services\ReportManager\Styles`) and adjusting the name the Report Manager displays through the site settings (http://<server>/Reports/Pages/Settings.aspx).
- Understand how Report Manager functions internally through the use of classes in the `ReportingServicesWebUserInterface` assembly and leverage its undocumented functionality.
- Write custom management pages to replace one or more management pages in Report Manager (by default located at `C:\Program Files\Microsoft SQL Server\MSSQL.3\Reporting Services\ReportManager\Pages`).
- Write a custom façade that would display a company's information and eventually take a user to the Report Manager pages.
- Write a custom report management application to replace Report Manager.

SQL Server Management Studio *NEW in 2005*

SQL Server Management Studio provides a Windows form-based, integrated environment that can manage various SQL Server components. From the SSRS perspective, the Management Studio has similar functionality to Report Manager when used to manage a single instance of SSRS.

The advantages of using the SQL Server Management Studio include consolidated content view for SSRS web farm (scale-out) deployment, slightly better performance, an ability to script and replay administrative tasks, and a finer granularity for role-based security settings.

TIP

Use the SQL Server Management Studio for a consolidated view of a SSRS web farm.

Reporting Services Configuration Tool *NEW in 2005*

The Reporting Services Configuration Tool is a Windows form application that can be used to start and stop the Report Server Windows Service and reconfigure report servers. For example, administrators can change the Report Server's database and SQL Server names, change SSRS' Windows service identity, and change the virtual directories used to access the Report Server and Report Manager. Administrators can start the Reporting Services Configuration Tool from SQL Server 2005, Configuration Tools, Reporting Services Configuration menu or from the SQL Server Configuration Manager using the Configure button in the SQL Server Reporting Services Properties dialog box.

RSPrintClient Control *NEW in 2005*

The `RSPrintClient` ActiveX control provides client-side printing for reports viewed in Report Manager. The control presents the Print dialog box for a user to initiate a print job, preview a report, specify pages to print, and change the margins. Developers can access this control programmatically in the code to enable report-printing functionality in their applications.

WMI Provider

SSRS includes a WMI provider that maps SSRS' XML configuration files to a set of classes to simplify configuration management of the Report Server and Report Manager, and to minimize configuration errors. WMI provider also supplies a class that provides basic properties and status information for a SSRS instance, and thus assists with discovery of SSRS instances on a network.

Both the Reporting Services Configuration Tool and the `rsconfig.exe` utility use the SSRS WMI provider.

Performance Monitoring Objects

SSRS Windows and Web Service include performance objects that supply performance counters that provide information about report processing and resource consumption. The objects are called RS Windows Service and RS Web Service, respectively.

NOTE

In SSRS 2000, the web service performance object was called Reporting Services and the Windows service performance object was called Delivery Processor.

To have a more complete picture and to gather more information, an administrator can also monitor SQL Server, ASP.NET, Processor, Memory, and Physical or Logical Disk counters.

Summary

This chapter discussed the SQL Server Reporting Services (SSRS) architecture. Table 3.3 presents the SSRS components summary.

TABLE 3.3 Reporting Services Components Summary

Component	Brief Description
Programmatic interfaces	Provides access to SSRS functionality through SOAP and HTTP requests.
Report Processor	Facilitates a set of report generation operations from data retrieval to rendering. Report Processor invokes other components, such as data extensions to assist with report generation.
Data-processing extensions	Retrieves report's data from a data source. Developers can develop additional custom data-processing extensions.
Command-line utilities	Three utilities, designed to assist with scripting of administrative tasks, installed automatically during the Reporting Services install.
Rendering extensions	Transform the report's intermediate format (a combination of report's layout and data) into a device-specific format, such as HTML. Developers can create new rendering extensions.
Report Server database	Stores report definitions, report metadata, report history, cached reports, snapshots, resources, security settings, encrypted data, scheduling and delivery data, and more.
Report Server temporary database	Stores intermediate processing products, cache, and data.
Scheduling and Delivery Processor	Monitors for events (such as timed subscription), collaborates with Report Processor to render a report, and delivery extensions to deliver scheduled reports to a location specified in the subscription.

TABLE 3.3 Continued

Component	Brief Description
Delivery extensions	Deliver reports to specific devices, such as email or a file system. Developers can create new delivery extensions.
Report Manager	Provides web-based report access and management capabilities. Default URL that invokes Report Manager is http://<server>/reports.
Report Model Designer	Generates report models for use in Report Builder.
Report Builder	Provides drag-and-drop, easy-to-use report design functionality. Report Builder is an ad hoc end-user report authoring and publishing tool executed on a client computer.
Report Designer	Allows developers to develop complex reports. Report Designer is a comprehensive report authoring and publishing tool, hosted in Business Intelligence Development Studio or Visual Studio.
Security extensions	Enable authentication and authorization of users and groups. Developers can (excluding SQL Server Express edition) create new security extensions.
SQL Server Management Studio	Provides administrators with Windows form-based, integrated environment to manage SQL Server components including SSRS. From the report management perspective, Management Studio has similar functionality to Report Manager, but provides additional capabilities, such as consolidated web-farm management.
Reporting Services Configuration Tool	Provide administrators with functionality to start and stop Report Server Windows service and reconfigure report servers. This is a Windows forms application.
WMI provider	Provides a set of WMI interfaces to manage settings of a Report Server and assists with SSRS instance discovery on a network.
Performance monitoring objects	Provide a view of SSRS Windows and web service performance.

In the next chapter, authors discuss various SSRS deployment scenarios and features of SSRS editions.

Reporting Services Deployment Scenarios

CHAPTER 4

IN THIS CHAPTER

- High-Availability Deployment Considerations
- Internet Deployment Considerations
- Minimum Hardware Requirements
- Software Requirements
- Key Features of SSRS by SQL Server 2005 Editions
- Licensing

This chapter provides an overview of Reporting Services deployment scenarios (including Internet deployment), discusses SSRS' hardware and software requirements, licensing, and security around Reporting Services deployments. More technical details of security are covered in Chapter 18, "Securing Report Server Items."

An example of SSRS deployment is depicted in Figure 4.1. When an administrator installs SSRS, she has a choice to install one or more client- and server-side components outlined in Table 4.1.

NOTE

Although the test (staging) environment might not be as "powerful" as production, it is best to have a total match for the most effective and realistic scalability testing.

In the Enterprise Production Environment, support for web farms and scale-up capabilities of Enterprise Edition comes in very handy for high-volume reporting. Web farm deployment is very flexible and allows administrators to add capacity to a Report Server web farm as demand grows. In addition, if one of the servers in the web farm fails, the remaining servers will pick up the load. Thus, a web farm provides high availability for a report processing layer, but not the SSRS catalog.

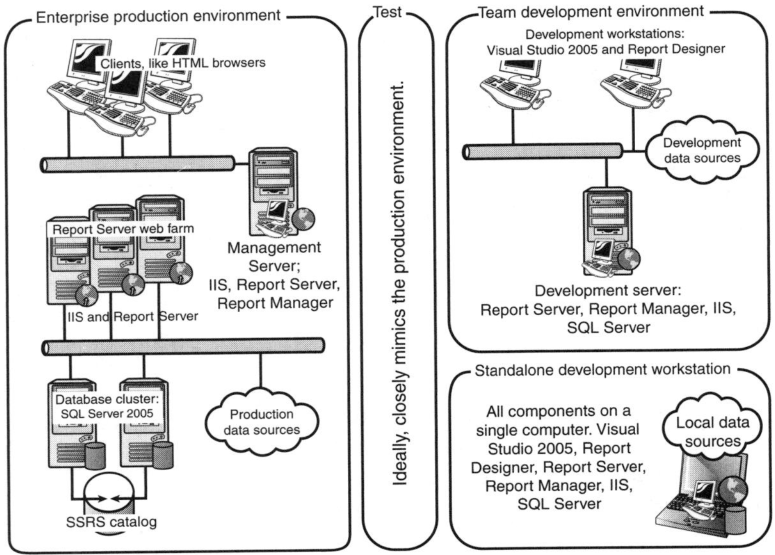

FIGURE 4.1 Deployment scenarios.

To achieve complete high availability for a reporting solution, a company can install a Reporting Services catalog on a SQL Server 2005 cluster.

For an environment that does not have high performance or availability requirements, you can simplify deployment and use a single Report Server instance with a catalog placed in a nonclustered instance of SQL Server 2005.

You can further simplify deployment in a development environment, install all the Reporting Services components on a single server, and install development tools on a set of workstations.

If a developer or a user needs to be completely mobile, he can install all the necessary components and a subset of data sources on a laptop, as depicted in the Development Environment box in Figure 4.1.

TABLE 4.1 Reporting Services Deployable Elements

Component	Approximate Size (MB) 32-bit Platform	Typical Install Location Prerequisites	Notes
Report Designer	105	Developer's Workstation, Visual Studio 2005, .NET Framework	Visual Studio 2005 add-on that enables visual development and publishing of reports

TABLE 4.1 Continued

Component	Approximate Size (MB) 32-bit Platform	Typical Install Location Prerequisites	Notes
Business Intelligence Development Studio (BIDS)	20	Developer's Workstation, .NET Framework	Visual Studio 2005 shell that includes only Business Intelligence projects
SSRS administrative utilities	1	Server/Client, .NET Framework	Configuration and scripting utilities
Books-On-Line	100	Server/Client	Help file with many useful development-related materials and code snippets
Report Server	60	IIS Server, .NET Framework	Integrated set of Windows and web software component that processes and delivers reports
Report Manager	9	IIS Server, Report Server, .NET Framework	Web-based report management and viewing tool
Report Server catalog	Initially empty database, final size depends on the number of reports deployed, caching, and snapshot settings	SQL Server 2005 standalone or cluster	Combination of two databases that store report definitions, settings, caching data, and so on

NOTE

There is no separate Books-On-Line for SSRS. Books-On-Line covers all the SQL Server 2005 components: Reporting Services, SQL Server engine, T-SQL, and so on.

SSRS is a fairly memory- and CPU-intensive application. It is hard to be precise with the exact hardware configuration that an administrator might need for her installation. Table 4.2 presents approximate CPU needs that depend on the number of concurrent users.

TABLE 4.2 Estimates of Reporting Server CPUs Needs

Concurrent Users	Approximate Number of CPUs
<150	1
<700	2
700 > <2000	4–8
2000> <4000	8–16
4000>	16+

Table 4.2 provides estimates for a 3-GHz 32-bit Intel Xeon CPU server and is based on SSRS performance for rendering a report of an average layout complexity, which retrieves approximately 5,000 rows of data from a data source, and provides users with HTML output and reasonable completion times of no more than 25–30 seconds. The data source used in this analysis is well tuned and available without significant latency.

Please keep in mind that your results will likely be different from the result in the table. A test is the best way to determine precise configuration needs that are the best suitable for your deployment scenario.

Configuration tips that you might want to consider when deploying SSRS (or specifically a Report Server) are as follows:

1. A 32-bit instance of a Report Server can use memory up to 3GB (requires the /3GB switch in boot.ini). Because of this, efficient hardware use would be at 4GB per instance (3GB for a Report Server and 1GB for OS). To effectively utilize servers with larger amounts of memory, consider installing multiple instances of SSRS per server.

2. For performance, start with scaling up (fastest CPU available, 4GB of RAM, and capable IO subsystem), then move to scale out, and add capacity as necessary (add Report Servers to a web farm). Host the Report Server catalog in a SQL Server instance on a separate box from your data sources (transactional, data warehouse, or line-of-business database) or at least make sure that a SQL Server instance can handle additional workload.

3. For scale-up scenarios, SSRS 2005 supports a 64-bit platform for both x64 (Opteron, Athlon64, and Xeon EMT64T CPUs) and IA64 (Itanium CPU). A 64-bit platform overcomes the 4GB memory limitation of the 32-bit platform and should be considered for reporting applications with high memory demand. A reporting application that renders a fair amount of or large Microsoft Excel or PDF reports is an example of a high memory demand application.

4. For reliability, use redundant components: at least two SSRS web servers and a database cluster for the Reporting Services catalog database, redundant disk arrays, and network pathways. Although high availability requires at least two servers, three is a better number. With three servers, you can do maintenance on one of the servers and still have a high-availability configuration running in your environment.

5. For cost evaluation and decision about buying more servers with a smaller number of CPUs versus fewer servers with a larger number of CPUs in each, consider the price of the hardware, the additional costs associated with extra servers, and the cost of a reporting solution failure. As the number of servers grow, so does the server management overhead and other costs, such as cost of additional space, cooling, and energy costs.

High-Availability Deployment Considerations

To create a highly available Reporting Services installation, an administrator can deploy Reporting Services on a web farm and use clustering for the Reporting Services catalog database. Enterprise Edition of Reporting Services is the only edition that supports web farm deployment in the production environment. Developer Edition and Evaluation Edition can be deployed on a web farm, but only in a testing environment. No other editions support the web farm feature.

Although the Enterprise Edition of SSRS supports a web farm, it does not include a functionality to create and manage a web farm. This is why a company would have to use separate software (or hardware) to create and manage a web farm. An example of web farm management software is the Network Load Balancing (NLB) feature of Windows Server. The steps to install Reporting Services on a web farm (scale-out configuration) are covered in Chapter 21, "Deploying and Configuring SSRS."

To protect the catalog database, companies can deploy a SQL Server 2005 cluster. Because of Windows authentication between the Report Server and the catalog database, both Report Server and the SQL Server 2005 cluster have to be in either the same or in the trusted domains. Both nodes of the SQL Server 2005 cluster must have an exact match and all hardware and software installed on a cluster must be supported; please see http://www.microsoft.com/windows/catalog/server/default.aspx?subID=22&xslt=category&pgn=904c28be-5a41-4db0-9c12-032dcb893c8b.

Alternative high-availability options can be used to protect from a database server failure: hardware-based data replication or the new peer-to-peer replication in SQL Server 2005.

NOTE

The new database mirroring functionality of the SQL Server 2005 would have been another high-availability option and although the database mirroring is included in this release of the SQL Server 2005—the mirroring is not currently supported in production environments; see http://support.microsoft.com/kb/907741.

Internet Deployment Considerations

Reporting Services is not specifically designed for Internet-facing scenarios. This is, partially, because the default authentication mechanism of Reporting Services is Windows integrated security. For security reasons, SQL Server setup does not provide options to deploy SSRS with anonymous access to reports.

NOTE

Chapter 18 provides additional details on securing Reporting Services installations.

Several deployment options are available to a SSRS administrator to make reports accessible over the Internet:

- Keep only public data in the SSRS catalog and enable Report Server for anonymous access.
- Deploy SSRS with Windows authentication and leverage Kerberos delegation to authenticate users.
- Use programmatic options (such as custom security extensions) to authenticate and authorize users.

NOTE

When an administrator deploys Reporting Services on the Internet, his web server security might not allow installation to proceed. The work-around is to block the target server from Internet access, relax security, install SSRS, and tighten security again.

Internet Deployment Option 1: Enable Report Server for Anonymous Access

This scenario is designed to distribute public information. In this scenario, none of the reports are secured and all of the users would get the same information. When accessing Reporting Services deployed in this fashion, Internet users **will not** be prompted for login credentials. Best practice for this scenario is to place the SSRS catalog database on the same server with an instance of the Report Server. Because the Report Server has web components, this option means that the SQL Server 2005 instance that hosts catalog data will also be running on the web server and there are no queries that cross boundaries of the web server.

To reduce data exposure in this scenario, the catalog must only contain a limited subset of public data. To further reduce data exposure, reports can be configured to be rendered from an execution snapshot; in this latter case, the SSRS catalog would only contain the snapshot data.

NOTE

To configure a report's rendering from a report execution snapshot, an administrator can use the Report Manager, navigate to a report that needs to be configured, then navigate to the Properties tab, Execution screen and select the Render This Report from a Report Execution Snapshot option.

Because this scenario does not protect data from unauthorized access, it might only be used when a company intends to publish public data, such as a product catalog. Secure Sockets Layer (SSL) configuration is not required for this scenario.

To provide public data (or snapshots with public data) to the SSRS catalog in this configuration, an administrator can use replication or SQL Server Integration Services to "copy" public data (or snapshots) from an internal data source to the SSRS catalog placed on a web server.

Internet Deployment Option 2: Deploy Report Server with Windows Authentication

This scenario leverages a default authentication mechanism of SSRS and uses a corresponding security extension.

In this scenario:

1. A company would have a domain associated with web-facing servers and use Kerberos delegation to validate a user by interacting with a corporate domain inside the firewall.
2. Customers can configure Reporting Services virtual directories with either Windows Integrated or Basic authentication.
3. When accessing Reporting Services deployed in this fashion, Internet users **will be** prompted for credentials. After a user is validated, she will have the level of access to a report corresponding to her credentials.

If this option is chosen, an administrator must configure SSL for proper security, especially for basic authentication.

Internet Deployment Option 3: Use the Programmatic Approach

Some of the situations in which a programmatic approach can be used:

- Users do not have Windows accounts.
- User IDs and passwords are stored in a third-party security provider, which, in turn, is used for user authentication.
- Single sign-on technology (such as Microsoft Passport) is used in place of Windows authentication.

To programmatically handle security, a company can develop a custom Security Extension, handle security within a .NET application, or use the new Report Viewer control.

NOTE

Please keep in mind that security breaches can have far-reaching financial consequences for a business; thus, use custom security solutions with caution, especially when a reporting solution is exposed on the Internet.

This book discusses some aspects of security extensions in Chapter 26, "Writing Custom Reporting Services Extensions." An example of a security extension is provided with SQL Server 2005.

On a high level, to handle security within an application, a developer could

- Authenticate a user in the code by either collaborating authentication processing with a third-party security provider or perhaps simply comparing the user's identifier and password to the values stored in a database.
- After the user is successfully authenticated, the code would either query a third-party security provider or a database for the user's security access options.
- Lastly, the code needs to control access to a report, based on the user's security access options.

You have several options to control a user's access to a report. Depending on the need of the reporting application, a code can impersonate a Windows user, who mapped to the SSRS Content Manager role (an administrative access). In turn, the code itself would control which reports can be accessed by a user.

Alternatively, depending on the actions that the code must take, the code may impersonate different Windows users who have finer granularity of permissions. In this case, there could be a Windows user who has access to just a single report.

After a user is impersonated, the code can, for example, use the function `Render` to access the report's data stream or use the Report Viewer control.

The Report Viewer control can process remote server as well as local reports. When the Report Viewer control processes local reports, it does it internally and does not need access to a Report Server.

Most data sources (like SQL Server) that a Report Viewer control uses require user identification and a password to access data. In this case, an application can collect, for example, a user's SQL Server credentials and pass those credentials to a data source, thereby restricting the user's access to data.

Enabling a Report Manager for Internet Access

A couple of options allow users to access the Report Manager over the Internet:

A. Install a Report Manager on the same computer as the Report Server.

B. Install a Report Manager on a different computer than the Report Server.

The following are the steps to enable report management over the Internet (unless marked otherwise, steps are applicable to both options A and B):

1. Install SSRS on the Internet-facing web server using the Install But Do Not Configure installation option.
2. Option B only. The instance installed in step 1 hosts only the Report Manager. Use the SQL Server Surface Area Configuration tool to disable the Reporting Services service.
3. Option B only. Repeat step 1 to install another instance of SSRS on a different computer, normally behind the firewall. This instance hosts the Reporting Services service.
4. Option A only. Secure the connection between the web server and SQL Server computer that will host the SSRS catalog. This can be achieved using IPSec.
5. Run the Reporting Services Configuration Tool, connect to the server that hosts the Reporting Services service, specify service accounts, configure virtual directories, and create the SSRS catalog (if SQL Server is in a different domain and Kerberos is not enabled, use SQL Server credentials to connect to the database server).
6. Option B only. On the computer that hosts Report Manager, modify `RsWebApplication.config` so the `<UI>` tag looks like:

```
<UI>
   <ReportServerVirtualDirectory></ReportServerVirtualDirectory>
   <ReportServerUrl>https://{SERVER}/ReportServer</ReportServerExternalURL>
   <ReportServerExternalURL>https://{SERVER}/ReportServer</
   ➥ReportServerExternalURL>
   <ReportBuilderTrustLevel>FullTrust</ReportBuilderTrustLevel>
</UI>
```

   Where `<ReportServerUrl>` indicates to the Report Manager that it should access remote server, `<ReportServerExternalURL>` allows Internet users to use the Report Builder, and {SERVER} is a fully qualified domain name (like www.microsoft.com) of the computer that runs the Reporting Services service.

NOTE

Just like with any SSRS deployment, to make sure that Reporting Services Internet deployment is successful, users should be able to access SSRS by typing: `http(s)://` **{SERVER}**`/ReportServer`.

Minimum Hardware Requirements

Table 4.3 outlines hardware requirements for SQL Server 2005 installations.

The following is the terminology used in relation to the 64-bit platform:

- IA64 refers to Itanium-compatible hardware architecture. This architecture can run IA64 software and 32-bit software using the Windows-On-Windows (WOW64) software emulator. The Itanium CPU cannot natively run 32-bit x86-compatible instructions and uses instruction emulation as a part of WOW64 processing.
- x64 refers to Extended Memory Technology support compatible architecture and includes systems, based on Opteron, Athlon 64, Intel Xeon EM64T, and Intel Pentium EM64T. x64 architecture can run classic 32-bit x86 compatible instructions natively on the CPU. One of the advantages of this architecture is an ability to support both 32- and 64-bit code. To ease an adoption of the 64-bit platform and optimize a hardware purchase, some companies might first deploy a 32-bit operating system and software on x64 hardware and then upgrade to 64-bit software on the same hardware.

TABLE 4.3 Minimum Hardware Requirements

Hardware	Minimum Requirements 32-Bit	Minimum Requirements 64-Bit
CPU	Intel or compatible Pentium III or higher Minimum: 600MHz Recommended: 1GHz or higher	IA64 recommended: 1GHz X64 minimum: 1GHz
Memory (RAM)	512MB minimum, 1GB or more recommended, 4GB maximum per a Report Server instance Report Server will utilize a maximum of 3GB (with /3GB switch in boot.ini).	512MB minimum, 1GB or more recommended
Hard disk space	A combination of hard drive requirements for the installed component: Report Server, Report Manager, and so on. A set of SSRS-related components is shown in Table 4.1. Full SQL Server Install is approximately 1.5 GB.	Approximately 2–3 times of the size of 32-bit components
Monitor (Visual tools will function at a lower resolution, such as 640x480)	VGA or higher resolution 1024x768 or higher resolution recommended for SQL Server graphical tools.	VGA or higher resolution 1024x768 or higher resolution recommended for SQL Server graphical tools

TABLE 4.3 Continued

Hardware	Minimum Requirements 32-Bit	Minimum Requirements 64-Bit
Pointing device	Microsoft Mouse or compatible pointing device.	Microsoft Mouse or compatible pointing device
CD-ROM drive	Required for CD installation.	Required for CD installation

NOTE

System Configuration Check blocks setup from running if the CPU type (Pentium III or higher) requirement is not met. Setup issues a warning, but allows you to proceed, if the CPU speed or minimum memory requirement is not met.

Software Requirements

Authors recommend installing Reporting Services on Windows 2003 SP1 (Service Pack 1). Although Windows 2000 is a fully supported platform, Windows 2003 SP1 reflects the latest technological advances, including enhanced coverage in the areas of security and high availability.

All editions of Reporting Services support installation on Virtual Server or Virtual PC, provided that the supported operating system is installed.

Tables 4.4, 4.5, and 4.6 list operating system requirements and additional software requirements for installation of Reporting Services on 32- and 64-bit platforms correspondingly.

TABLE 4.4 Operating Systems That Can Run 32-Bit Versions of Report Server

Software	Enterprise Edition	Developer Edition, Evaluation Edition	Standard Edition, Workgroup Edition, Express Edition
Windows 2000 SP4 Professional Edition	No	Yes	Yes
Windows 2000 Servers SP4 all editions (Server, Advanced, Data Center)	Yes	Yes	Yes
Windows XP SP2 Home Edition	No	Yes	No for Standard and Workgroup, Yes for Express
Windows XP SP2 Professional Edition	No	Yes	Yes
Windows XP SP2 Media Edition	No	Yes	Yes

TABLE 4.4 Continued

Software	Enterprise Edition	Developer Edition, Evaluation Edition	Standard Edition, Workgroup Edition, Express Edition
Windows XP SP2 Tablet Edition	No	Yes	Yes
Windows 2003 SP1 Servers all editions (Server, Enterprise, Data Center, Small Business Server 2003 Standard and Premium Editions)	Yes	Yes	Yes
Windows 2003 Web Edition	No	No	No for Standard and Workgroup, Yes for Express
Windows 2003 Server SP1 64-Bit X64 Standard, Enterprise, and Data Center Editions	WOW64	WOW64	WOW64

NOTE

Systems that are not explicitly listed in Table 4.4 are not supported by Reporting Services; for example, Reporting Services 32-bit is not supported on Windows 2003 64-bit Itanium.

For situations with heavy memory or IO requirements, such as heavy graphics and PDF rendering, customers can benefit from deploying SSRS on a 64-bit platform. Table 4.5 outlines SSRS support on a 64-bit platform.

TABLE 4.5 Operating System Requirements 64-Bit

SQL Server Version Operating System	x64 SQL Server 2005 Developer Edition	x64 SQL Server 2005 Enterprise Edition	x64 SQL Server 2005 Standard Edition	IA64 SQL Server 2005 Developer, Standard, Enterprise Editions
Windows XP X64 Professional 2003	Yes	**No**	Yes	**No**
Windows 2003 SP1 64-Bit Itanium Data Center and Enterprise Editions	**No**	**No**	**No**	Yes
Windows 2003 SP1 64-Bit X64 All Editions (Standard, Enterprise, Data Center)	Yes	Yes	Yes	**No**

NOTE

64-bit versions of SQL Server Workgroup and Express editions are not available in this release.

Development tools such as Business Intelligence Development Studio are neither installed nor supported on the IA64 platform. For IA64 deployments, use development tools installed on a separate 32-bit or x64 workstation.

Table 4.6 outlines additional software requirements for both 32- and 64-bit platforms and optional software that can be installed to benefit Reporting Services.

TABLE 4.6 Additional Software Requirements 32- and 64-Bit

Software	All Editions
Web Server	Internet Information Services 5.0 or later.
SQL Server	SQL Server 2005 that will store the Reporting Services catalog database and Reporting Services temporary database.
.NET Framework	.NET Framework 2.0 will be installed during the Reporting Services install process, if it has not been previously installed. There are two mutually exclusive install options for 64-bit platforms: ▪ Reporting Services 64-bit and ASP.NET 64-bit ▪ Reporting Services 32-bit and ASP.NET 32-bit, both running on WOW64
SMTP Server	Optional software. If you want to use report email capabilities of Reporting Services, you need to install SMTP Server. Access to SMTP Server can be configured after SSRS installation using the Reporting Services Configuration Tool.

Key Features of SSRS by SQL Server 2005 Editions

At least some components of SSRS are available in almost all editions of SQL Server 2005: Workgroup, Standard, Enterprise, Developer, and Evaluation.

NOTE

The Reporting Services install is now bundled with SQL Server Install. This is unlike Reporting Services 2000, which has an independent setup.

At the time of writing, SQL Server Express Edition did not have a version of SSRS. SQL Server Express Edition may eventually include an Express Edition of SSRS.

Whether a customer is a large enterprise or a small company, the key features of Reporting Services that are always available include the following:

- **Manageability**—Reporting Services is easy to deploy and manage. In addition to having a convenient web-based management interface, both deployment and management of Reporting Services can be scripted.
- **Security**—Reporting Services keeps corporate data secure. Reports and information are not accessible, unless sufficient privilege is granted to a user.
- **Programmability**—Reporting Services allows developing of a custom functionality that can be embedded in a report, called from a report, or scripted.
- **Reporting controls and wizard**—Windows and web-based Report Viewer controls are supplied with Visual Studio 2005. Report controls simplify adding reporting functionality to Windows and web-based applications.

Additional features available in the Standard Edition of Reporting Services include the following:

- **Extensibility**—Reporting Services allows adding new server functionality. Report Definition Language (RDL) is an XML-based language and is designed to be extensible. SSRS also allows extending data processing, rendering, and delivery extensions.

Additional features available in Enterprise Edition of Reporting Services include the following:

- **Scalability**—Reporting Services Enterprise Edition supports large workloads and high-volume reporting. Support for web farms in Enterprise Edition allows easy scale out, providing an ability to add extra capacity as needed. In addition, Enterprise Edition scales up, supporting more than two CPUs.
- **Availability**—Web farm support of Reporting Services Enterprise Edition paired with the Reporting Services catalog installed on a SQL Server 2005 cluster enables high-availability reporting solutions.
- **Data-driven subscriptions**—Reporting Services Enterprise Edition allows customers to dynamically change the recipient list, report parameters, and processing options. In contrast, Standard Subscription, available in Standard Edition of Reporting Services, is for a single predefined user and single predefined parameter set.

To help determine the most appropriate version, you can refer to Table 4.7 to review key features of SSRS editions

TABLE 4.7 Key Features by Reporting Services Editions

Feature	Workgroup	Standard	Enterprise
Data Source(s)	Local server and relational only	Support all data sources (OLAP and Relational)	
Rendering	Excel, PDF, Image (RGDI, Print), DHTML	Support all output formats	

TABLE 4.7 Continued

<table>
<tr><th>Feature</th><th>Workgroup</th><th>Standard</th><th>Enterprise</th></tr>
<tr><td>Management</td><td colspan="3">Support SQL Server Management Studio and Report Manager</td></tr>
<tr><td>Caching</td><td></td><td colspan="2">Supported</td></tr>
<tr><td>History</td><td></td><td colspan="2">Supported</td></tr>
<tr><td>Delivery</td><td></td><td colspan="2">Supported</td></tr>
<tr><td>Scheduling</td><td></td><td colspan="2">Supported</td></tr>
<tr><td>Extensibility</td><td></td><td colspan="2">Can add/remove renderers, data sources, and delivery</td></tr>
<tr><td>Custom Authentication</td><td></td><td colspan="2">Supported</td></tr>
<tr><td>SharePoint Integration</td><td></td><td colspan="2">Supported</td></tr>
<tr><td>Scale-out Report Servers</td><td></td><td></td><td>Supported</td></tr>
<tr><td>Subscription</td><td></td><td colspan="2">Supported</td></tr>
<tr><td>Data-Driven Subscription</td><td></td><td></td><td>Supported</td></tr>
<tr><td>Role-Based Security</td><td>Fixed Roles</td><td colspan="2">Can add roles</td></tr>
<tr><td>Report Builder</td><td colspan="3">Supported</td></tr>
<tr><td>Report Builder Data Sources</td><td>Local server and relational only</td><td colspan="2">Supported</td></tr>
<tr><td>Model Level Security</td><td></td><td colspan="2">Yes</td></tr>
<tr><td>Infinite Clickthrough</td><td></td><td></td><td>Yes</td></tr>
</table>

Source: http://www.microsoft.com/sql/technologies/reporting/rsfeatures.mspx

NOTE

Developer and Evaluation editions have the same capabilities as the Enterprise Edition of SSRS. However, the Developer Edition is only licensed and supported in the development environment and Evaluation Edition expires after 180 days.

Licensing

Complete details of SSRS licensing can be found on the Microsoft licensing website at http://www.microsoft.com/licensing/default.mspx and in the following document http://download.microsoft.com/download/e/3/7/e37e542f-f90c-4d5f-864c-3f428d5add5e/SQL2005_Licensing.doc.

In a "nutshell," a Server license (for Workgroup, Standard, or Enterprise editions) is required for every operating system environment on which that edition of SQL Server software or any of its components (for example, Reporting Services) is running.

This means that a company does not have to buy a separate license if SSRS is installed with SQL Server 2005 together on a single computer. For scale-out (web farm) deployments, each web server that runs Report Server would have to have a SQL Server license.

Summary

In this chapter, you have learned about various SSRS deployment choices. Deployment choices for SSRS components range from a developer's workstation, in which all SSRS components are installed on a single computer, to an enterprise, high-availability and high-performance, multiserver, web-farm deployment.

This chapter also covered several options of deploying SSRS for Internet access: enable Report Server for anonymous access and publish only public data, deploy SSRS on the Internet using default Windows authentication and programmatic authentication, and access options.

Lastly, this chapter covered hardware and software requirements, licensing, and key features of SSRS editions.

The next chapter delves into the SSRS installation process.

Installing Reporting Services

CHAPTER 5

By now, you should be able to approximate hardware requirements, have an idea about software prerequisites, and be ready to proceed with installation.

Unlike the SSRS 2000 install, the new Reporting Services is integrated with SQL Server 2005 and is significantly streamlined.

NOTE

Before running setup, please note the following:

1. **You need access to an account with administrative privileges to run SQL Server 2005 setup.**
2. **Set up several Windows accounts to run SQL Server services, such as Report Server and SQL Server.**
3. **Secure a computer on which you are planning to install SQL Server components: use a firewall, service accounts with least privileges, and so on.**
4. **Avoid hosting a Report Server on a computer that has an underscore in its name. Computers with underscores in the name break state management capabilities of the Report Server.**

On computers on which AutoPlay functionality is enabled, SQL Server 2005 setup starts automatically when the install disk is inserted into, depending on the install media, the CD or DVD drive.

If setup does not start automatically, you can either run `<setup directory>\servers\splash.hta` or `<setup directory>\servers\setup.exe`.

`splash.hta` provides options to install additional components, such as SQL Server Upgrade Advisor and more. Because this book is focusing on SSRS, it concentrates on the actions necessary to install SSRS.

To launch SQL Server 2005 install, select the Server Components, Tools, Books Online, and Samples link on the splash screen or run `<setup directory>\servers\setup.exe` directly.

The following are the SSRS-related setup steps:

1. On the End User License Agreement screen, read the license. If you agree with the license terms, check the I Accept the Licensing Terms and Conditions check box. Click Next.
2. Next, SQL Server setup checks if necessary prerequisites are installed. Depending on what has been installed already, SQL Server setup might install: .NET Framework 2.0, SQL Server Native Client, and SQL Server support files. Click Next after setup had competed this process.
3. Then, setup runs two stages of configuration checks. Click Next at the completion of the first stage. System Configuration Check checks for minimum hardware requirements, whether IIS is installed, and so on. The configuration check also reports if there are any problems that may require attention prior to installing SQL Server 2005. One of the possible warnings, for example, informs that IIS is not installed on the computer that is selected as the target for installation. After the second stage runs, fix errors, if any, rerun setup, and on the successful completion of this step, click Next.

NOTE

As you have seen in Chapter 4, "Reporting Services Deployment Scenarios," System Configuration Check blocks setup from running if the CPU type (Pentium III or higher) requirement is not met. Setup issues a warning, but will allow you to proceed, if the CPU speed or minimum memory requirement is not met.

4. Enter registration information in the Registration Information dialog box, and click Next.
5. In this step, setup allows you to select SQL Server related services to install without the need to specify details. Basic setup options are frequently sufficient for a simple install. Advanced install options are also available. The Components to Install dialog box that selects SSRS server-side components is shown in Figure 5.1. For a server-side component installation, check Reporting Services. For a client-side component installation, check Workstation Components, Books Online and Development Tools.

   Summary of the options available in the Components to Install dialog box is outlined in Table 5.1.

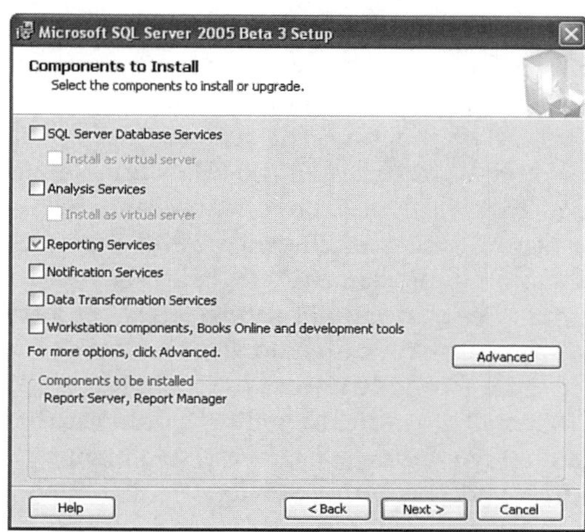

FIGURE 5.1 Selecting SQL Server components to install.

TABLE 5.1 SQL Server 2005 Installable Groups of Components

Component Group	Explanation
SQL Server Database Services	Core database services to store and manage data: database engine, replication, full-text search, and shared tools, such as BCP (bulk copy utility).
Analysis Services	Services that support online analytical processing (OLAP), data mining, and Integration Services (rewrite of DTS).
Reporting Services	Report processing services: Report Servers, extensions, catalog database, Report Manager, and Report Builder.
Notification Services	A platform for developing and deploying applications that generate and send notifications. Notification Services can send notification, for example, when data in a table has changed.
Integration Services	A set of tools and programmable objects for extracting, transforming, and loading data (ETL).
Workstation Components, Books Online and Development Tools	Connectivity components (including libraries for OLEDB and ODBC communications), management tools (including SQL Server Management Studio, Configuration Manager, Profiler, Replication Monitor, and Books Online). This option does not install samples. For sample installation, click the Advanced button.

NOTE

Report Manager provides access to the Report Builder and, thus, the Report Manager must be installed if the end-user ad hoc report design functionality is desired.

6. This step allows selecting finer granularity of software components for the installation. For example, you can Sample Databases and Sample Code and Applications. This book uses databases and some samples installed by those options. Click the Advanced button to initiate this step. The Feature Selection dialog box opens (see Figure 5.2). It is recommended to install the following: Reporting Services (Report Manager and Shared Tools), Client Components (connectivity components, Management Tools, and Business Intelligence Development Studio), and Documentation, and samples and sample databases (SQL Server Books Online, Sample Databases, and Sample Code and Applications). To select a feature, click on the icon depicting a disk in front of the feature you want to install and select Will Install on Local Hard Drive to install a single feature or Entire Feature Will Be Installed on Local Hard Drive to install a feature, including its subfeatures. For more details about features and deployment options, please see Chapters 3 and 4, "Reporting Services Architecture," and "Reporting Services Deployment Scenarios," respectively.

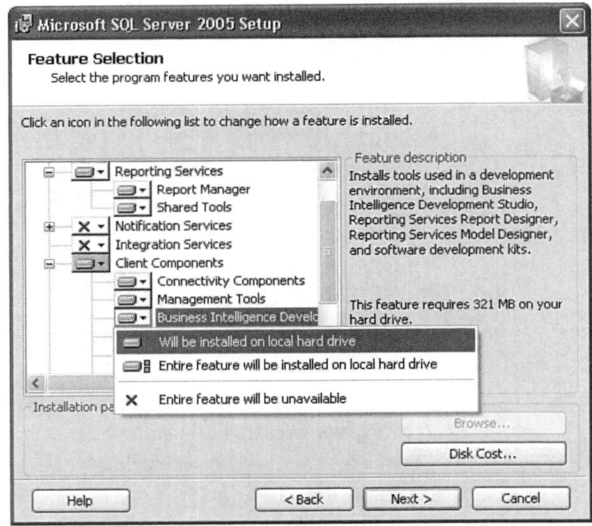

FIGURE 5.2 Selecting advanced SQL Server components to install.

7. Click Next and set up an instance name (Default or Named instance).
8. Click Next and enter the Service Account information.
9. Click Next to get to the Report Server Installation Options dialog box, which requests to either install the default configuration (this option is available only when the database engine and SSRS are installed as a single process) or install without configuration at all, as shown in Figure 5.3. In either case, an administrator can modify configuration information after the install using the Reporting Services Configuration Tool.

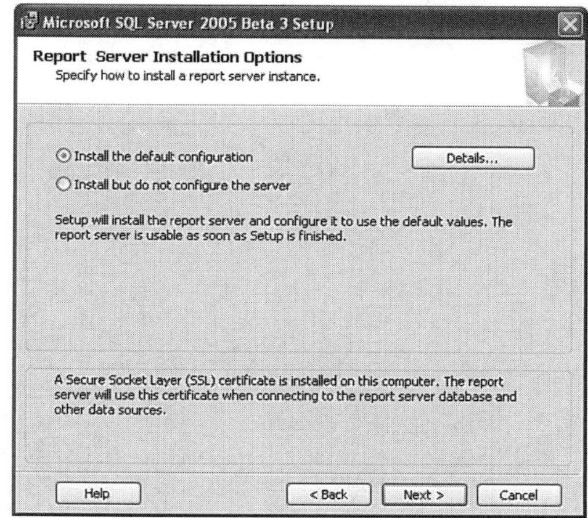

FIGURE 5.3 Report Server Installation Options dialog box.

If you have chosen a default configuration, setup installs SSRS with defaults:

- `ReportServer` and `ReportServerTemDB` databases on the instance of the SQL Server database services installed during the same setup as SSRS.
- Report Server Virtual Directory: http(s)://<server>/ReportServer
- Report Manager Virtual Directory: http(s)://<Server>/Reports

The defaults can be viewed by clicking the Details button in the Report Server Installation Options dialog box.

Setup configures SSL if the certificate is installed prior to Reporting Services installation. Administrators can always install an SSL certificate post SSRS installation but would consequently need to adjust SSRS configuration (specifically whether or not https:// is used in URLs).

After SSRS is installed, we are ready to move to more advanced topics.

Summary

This chapter discussed the SSRS installation steps. To install Reporting Services, run SQL Server 2005 setup, check Reporting Services on the Components to Install dialog box for server component installation and Workstation Components, Books Online and Development Tools for client component installation. Click both if you want to have a complete environment on a single computer.

If the same setup installs both SSRS and a database instance, you can install the default configuration, which automatically creates virtual directories and an SSRS catalog database. Another option is to install without configuration at all. In either case, an administrator can modify configuration information after the install using the Reporting Services Configuration Tool.

PART II

Report Authoring from Basic to Advanced

IN THIS PART

Report Designer

CHAPTER 6

IN THIS CHAPTER

- Two Main Report Designers from Microsoft
- Visual Studio Haves Versus Have Nots
- Solution, Project, File Hierarchy
- Generating Reports with Visual Studio

Report Designer is the main tool Microsoft provides for developers and tech-savvy information analysts to design and develop reports. This chapter begins by discussing Report Designer and how it gets installed either through Visual Studio or SQL Server Business Development Studio. Then, you use Report Designer to author your first report.

Two Main Report Designers from Microsoft

Microsoft offers two main report designers. The first one is Microsoft SQL Server Report Designer, or simply Report Designer, integrated with Visual Studio. Starting in SQL Server 2005, if you do not have Visual Studio installed, SQL Server setup installs the Visual Studio shell and labels it SQL Server Business Intelligence Developer Studio.

The second report designer is a standalone application called Report Builder. Report Builder is also new for SSRS in 2005. As covered in Chapter 3, "Reporting Services Architecture," Report Builder provides end users the ability to create their own reports knowing little to no SQL.

The largest difference between the two designers is the target audience, and how they access the designer itself. Visual Studio/SQL Server Business Intelligence Developer Studio is targeted at the developer community in general. To enable end-user reporting, the Report Builder is launched within a browser window from the SSRS Report Manager application. Although it is launched over the web, it is a Windows forms application. To use Report Builder, the end user must have access to a report model. The model contains metadata about the report data source, and it must be created using Visual Studio or Business Intelligence Developer Studio.

Visual Studio Haves Versus Have Nots

At this point, you might be wondering what the difference is between Visual Studio and Business Intelligence Developer Studio. In truth, there is not much difference.

In the first version of SSRS, the only report development tool available was Visual Studio. Many report development shops wanted the ability to use SSRS without having to purchase Visual Studio. In response to this, Microsoft bundled SQL Server Business Intelligence Developer Studio with SSRS 2005. Effectively, SQL Server Business Developer Intelligence Studio is simply a shell of Visual Studio with the ability to develop reports. In fact, throughout the rest of the book, we will use the terms interchangeably.

During the installation, the setup program detects if you have Visual Studio. If you do, the program simply installs the files needed to create reports. If you do not have Visual Studio, setup installs SQL Server Business Intelligence Developer Studio.

Solution, Project, File Hierarchy

As with anything else developed with Visual Studio, it helps to understand some of the basics of how Visual Studio handles files.

If you are developing reports, the developer's basic unit of work will be the Report Definition Language (RDL) files and associated data sources. Developers can also include the shared data sources, which have an `.rds` extension. Likewise, if you are working with report models, the default file extension is `.smdl` (SMDL abbreviates the term Semantic Data Modeling Language).

The files will be contained in a type of project called a "Report Server Project." If you are creating a SMDL file for use in the client-side Report Builder, the project type is called `Report Model Project`. A model project will likely also have Data Source View (DSV) and Data Sources (DS). All SSRS-related files (RDL, SMDL, DSV, and DS) are plaintext XML files.

Each of these files gets included into a project. A project has folders to organize the different components. A solution contains many projects. Combined, solutions and projects create a management hierarchy. A solution has multiple projects; a project has multiple files. The solution is nothing more than a container for related projects that might or might not be of the same type.

Generating Reports with Visual Studio

The easy way to get an overview of Visual Studio is to use it to develop a simple report. The following steps are the steps necessary to start Visual Studio and create a report project.

1. Click Start, point to All Programs, point to Microsoft SQL Server 2005, and then click SQL Server Business Intelligence Developer Studio.

2. Click the File menu, click New, and then click Project. The New Project dialog box opens.

3. In the Project Types section on the left, click Business Intelligence Projects.

4. In the Templates section on the right, click Report Server Project, as shown in Figure 6.1.

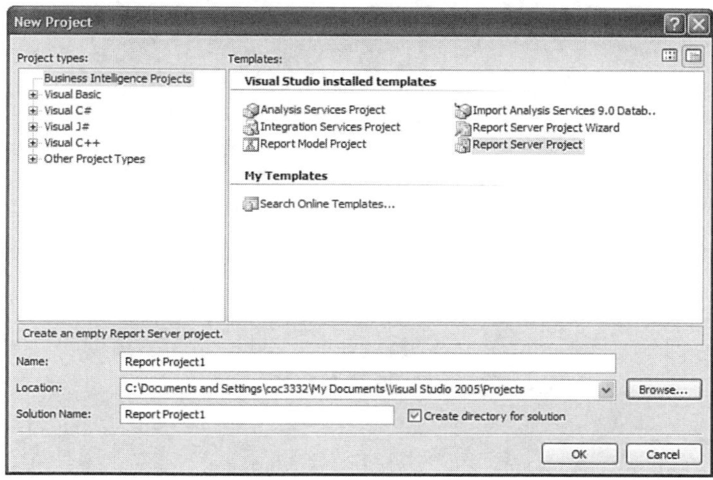

FIGURE 6.1 Creating a new report server project.

The Templates section should contain a number of options. You might notice that the Name (project name) and the Solution Name keep changing with each option. (These fields are located at the bottom of the dialog box.) You should also make note of the Location, as this is where the project and solution files are stored. For now, simply type AdventureWorksReports in the Name text box because you will be dealing with the AdventureWorks sample database. Your New Project dialog box should look similar to Figure 6.1.

5. Click OK to accept your changes and close the New Project dialog box.

At this point, you should have an empty shell of a project ready to accept new reports and data sources. The project should be contained in a solution called AdventureWorksReports. This will serve as the basis for moving forward. Your screen should look similar to Figure 6.2.

Choosing a data source(s) for the report is probably the most crucial step in the report developing process, albeit one of the easiest. The difficulty involves judging the quality of the data presented to the analyst. As the saying goes: "Garbage in—garbage out."

Having said that, it is a fairly straightforward task to connect Reporting Services to a data source. Using .NET technologies, it is possible to connect to SQL Server, Oracle, and

Analysis Services natively. Other possible data sources include using XML either from web services or flat files, and a ODBC- or OLEDB-compliant data source. You can also create reports using data from an SSIS package.

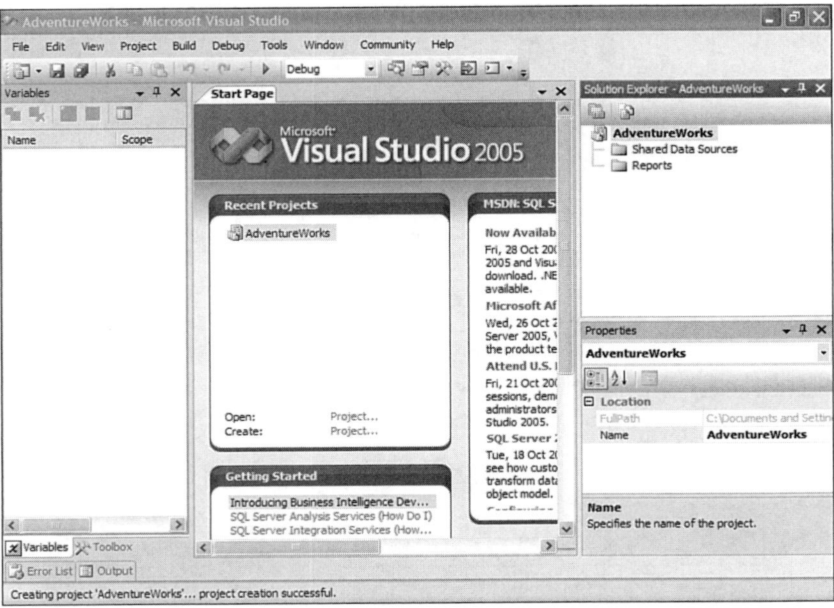

FIGURE 6.2 Empty project and solution.

Developers can also use ODBC and OLEDB to connect to a database that does not have native .NET data providers.

This opens Reporting Services up to any number of third-party databases. As if this were not enough, it is possible to write your own adapter using the interfaces provided by Microsoft. This way, report developers could report against any internal or proprietary data source.

Remember that a report data set can contain an embedded data source or it can be pointed to a shared data source. The following steps create a shared data source as the building block for your reports.

1. To open Solution Explorer, click the View menu, and then click Solution Explorer. Right-click Shared Data Sources, and then select Add New Data Source.

2. Name is used to enter the unique name of the data source. Enter AdventureWorks in the text box.

3. Type is a list of all native data sources. At this point, if you want to connect to other types of data sources, such as Oracle or Microsoft SQL Server Analysis Services, you could choose them here. For simplicity's sake, leave this as Microsoft SQL Server for now.

4. The next major step in setting up a data source is to set the connection string. To get the options, click the Edit button.

At this point, the Connection Properties dialog box should be open. From here, developers can set the properties of the connection and it will develop the connection string. The resulting connection string is nothing more than a .NET style connection string for the data source.

5. Enter localhost (or the name or Report Server you have installed) in the Server Name drop-down list.
6. Because you are working with SQL Server, Use Windows Authentication is already selected by default in the Log On to the Server section.
7. Select AdventureWorks from the list box under Select or Enter a Database Name. The Connection Properties dialog box should look similar to Figure 6.3.

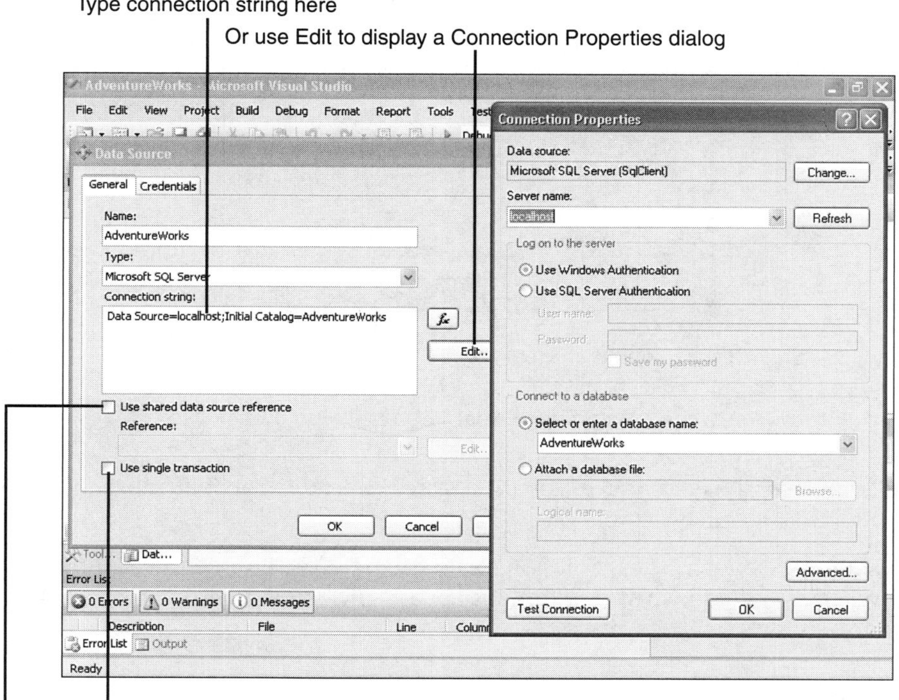
Type connection string here
Or use Edit to display a Connection Properties dialog
Select to indicate that Datasets that use this data source are executed in a single transaction
If there is already a shared Datasource readers can select it here

FIGURE 6.3 Connection Properties dialog box.

8. Test the connection by clicking the Test Connection button. If everything checks out, a pop-up should appear that says Test Connection Succeeded. Click OK on the pop-up box, and then click OK in the Connection Properties dialog box.

9. The Connection String box should have a line in it that says `Data Source=localhost;Initial Catalog=AdventureWorks`.

10. Click the Credentials tab. You should see a window similar to Figure 6.4. Because you are using SQL Server with Windows authentication, the default settings should suffice.

    If you were using SQL Server authentication, or another data source type that required a specialized user ID and password, you could enter it here or have Reporting Services prompt you for it. In special cases such as XML files or web services where no authentication is required, developers could use the No credentials option.

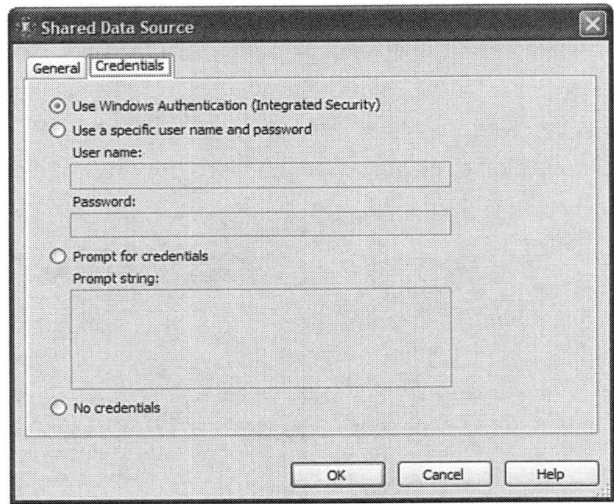

FIGURE 6.4 Shared data source credentials.

11. Click OK for the Shared Data Source dialog box to close.

Now that you have the data source, you can create the report. The following steps create an empty report on which to build on.

1. In Solution Explorer (View, Solution Explorer), right-click on Reports, and then hover over Add and when new options appear, click New Item. See Figure 6.5 as a reference.

NOTE

If you selected Add New Report, the Report Wizard appears. Click Cancel to exit the wizard.

2. The Add New Item dialog box opens. From this dialog box, select Report from the Templates menu.

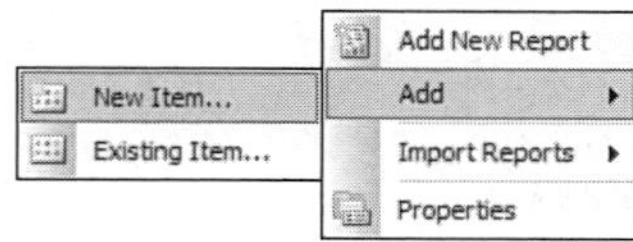

FIGURE 6.5 Adding a new item.

3. Enter the Name of the report Sales by Territory by Salesperson in the Name text box. The screen should look similar to Figure 6.6. When you are finished, click Add.

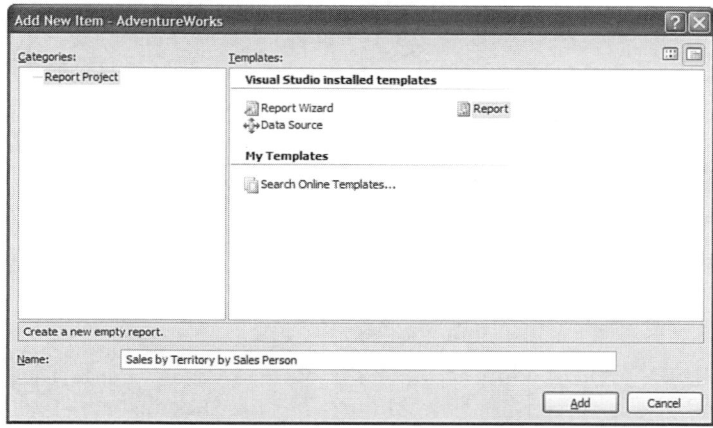

FIGURE 6.6 Add New Item dialog box.

At this point, you should have a new solution, project, and an empty report file. Figure 6.7 show the empty report created inside the project. From here, all that is needed to make a simple report is to collect data from the data source, choose a layout, and preview the report. Note that Report Designer conveniently lays out this process with the tabs across the Report—Data, Layout, and Preview.

SSRS reports collect data into an object called a data set. The results of the query, the SQL statement used for the query, and a pointer to the data source are all stored in the data set. In fact with a little work, you can make Reporting Services read from a `System.Data.DataSet` object over a web service. The SQL Server Business Intelligence Developer Studio contains a Graphical Query Builder to help write queries. It also allows for free-form queries to be specified by the developer. As we continue, we will see both views.

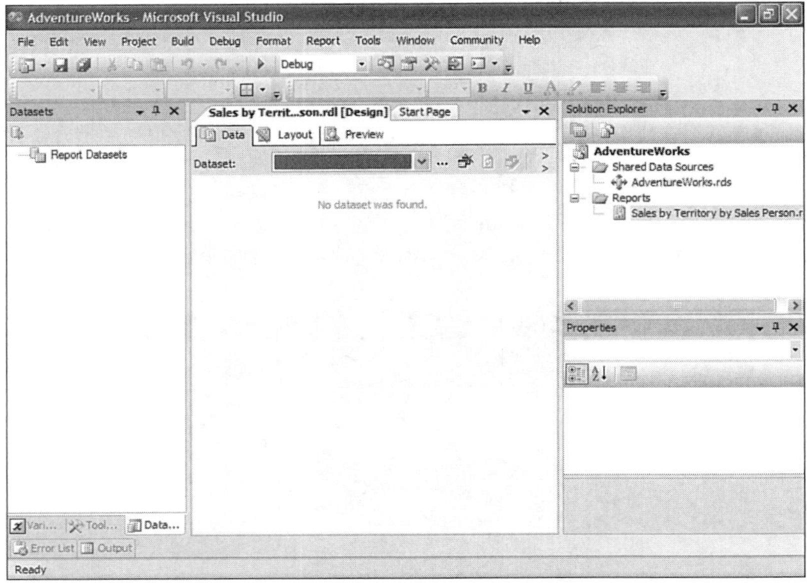

FIGURE 6.7 An empty report.

To continue the life cycle of your report, let's continue by adding a data set to collect and store your data. The data set you create will use the shared data source to execute a SQL statement and return a resultset. The following steps list how to proceed:

1. From the Data tab, select New Dataset. See Figure 6.8. The Dataset dialog box opens.

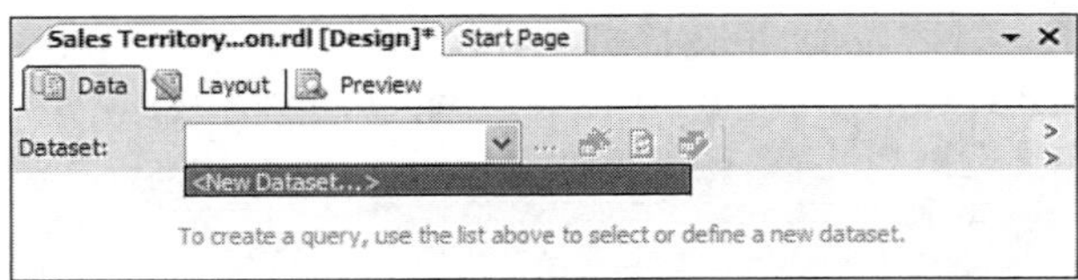

FIGURE 6.8 New Dataset option.

2. The first thing to do is to name the data set. Enter the AdventureWorksDataSet in the Name text box. This uniquely identifies the data set throughout the course of a report. At this point, there are also other text boxes, such as the Query, Command type, and Timeout. The Query text box contains the text of the actual query. Command type has the ADO.NET command type, and Timeout specifies the command timeout value. No value in the command Timeout text box lets the query run indefinitely. Some of the other tabs contain the more advanced options in the data set. The Fields tab contains the list of fields returned by the data set, and is also the place where report developers can enter calculated fields. The Data Options tab contains connection options for the underlying database connection. The Parameters tab contains a list of parameters to be passed onto the query. The most

common use of the Parameters tab is to store stored procedure parameters. Lastly, the Filters tab is used to filter the data from the resultset.

3. The dialog box should now look similar to Figure 6.9. At this point, click the OK button to close the dialog box.

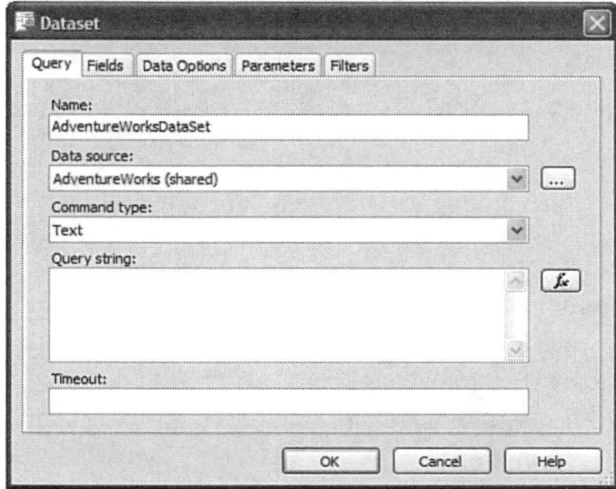

FIGURE 6.9 Dataset dialog box.

Now, you are ready to enter your query. Two main views are available for creating queries. The first one is the Generic Query Designer. This provides an open-ended text view for inputting the query. Basically, it assumes you know what you are doing as a developer. Figure 6.10 shows the Generic Query Designer.

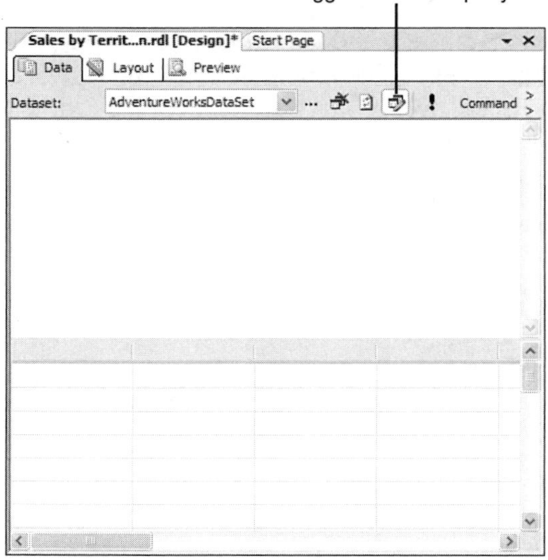

FIGURE 6.10 Generic Query Designer.

After clicking the OK button in step 3, you should be at the Generic Query Designer. If not, click on the button and you will get there.

4. Enter the following query into the Generic Query Designer:

```
SELECT
    c.[FirstName]+ ' '+ c.[LastName]as SalesPersonName
    ,[CountryRegionName] = cr.[Name]
    ,[TerritoryName] = st.[Name]
    ,[TerritoryGroup] = st.[Group]
    ,s.[SalesQuota]
    ,s.[SalesYTD]
    ,s.[SalesLastYear]
FROM [Sales].[SalesPerson] s
    INNER JOIN [HumanResources].[Employee] e
    ON e.[EmployeeID] = s.[SalesPersonID]
    LEFT OUTER JOIN [Sales].[SalesTerritory] st
    ON st.[TerritoryID] = s.[TerritoryID]
    INNER JOIN [Person].[Contact] c
    ON c.[ContactID] = e.[ContactID]
    INNER JOIN [HumanResources].[EmployeeAddress] ea
    ON e.[EmployeeID] = ea.[EmployeeID]
    INNER JOIN [Person].[Address] a
    ON ea.[AddressID] = a.[AddressID]
    INNER JOIN [Person].[StateProvince] sp
    ON sp.[StateProvinceID] = a.[StateProvinceID]
    INNER JOIN [Person].[CountryRegion] cr
    ON cr.[CountryRegionCode] = sp.[CountryRegionCode];
```

The second view is the Graphical Query Designer. It shows the same data, but it is a graphical view. Developers can toggle between the two tools using the toolbar button shown in Figure 6.10. Experienced Visual Studio developers will recognize this as the Visual Query Builder. Figure 6.11 shows the graphical view.

As with any tool to make life easier, you usually have to give up some control. Some queries are too complex to be displayed graphically. For example, derived tables would not be displayed in the first release of SSRS. SSRS 2005 now has that capability, but you might run into other syntaxes that it does not know how to display graphically.

Layout Screen

After selecting your data, the next step is to lay out or present the data. Layout assistance is provided by the Toolbox, Dataset view, and Layout dockable windows.

After you are finished selecting data in the Data view, select the Layout tab in the Report Design window. This brings up a grid similar to Figure 6.12.

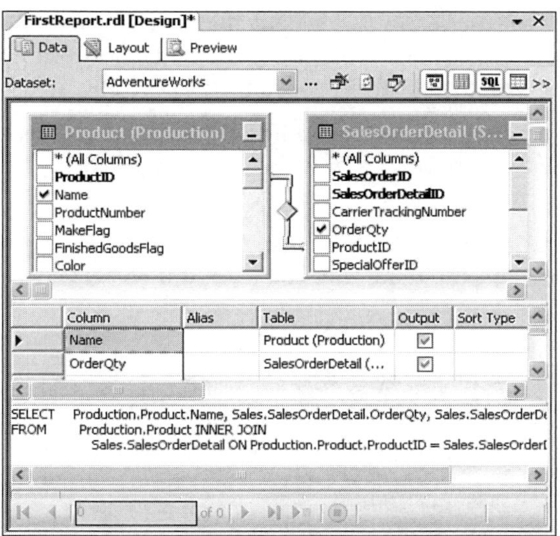

FIGURE 6.11 Visual Query Builder.

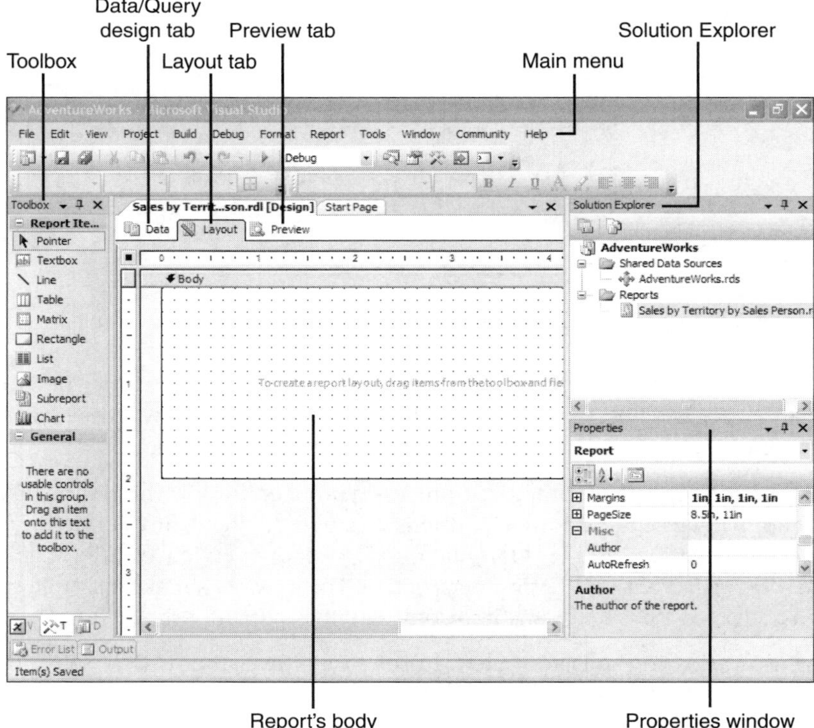

FIGURE 6.12 Report Layout view.

The toolbox (shown in Figure 6.12) is accessible by selecting the View, Toolbox menu. This has all the report item controls you might use while authoring reports. The simplest way to use them is to drag the control you want onto the layout.

Data can be inserted from the Datasets window (View, Datasets menu). In the first release of SSRS, this was called Fields. The Datasets view (see Figure 6.13) contains a treelist of available fields to use from the data sets.

Use of the fields is similar to the report items; drag the field onto a report item or onto the layout itself. If you add the field onto the layout, it creates a text box to contain the field.

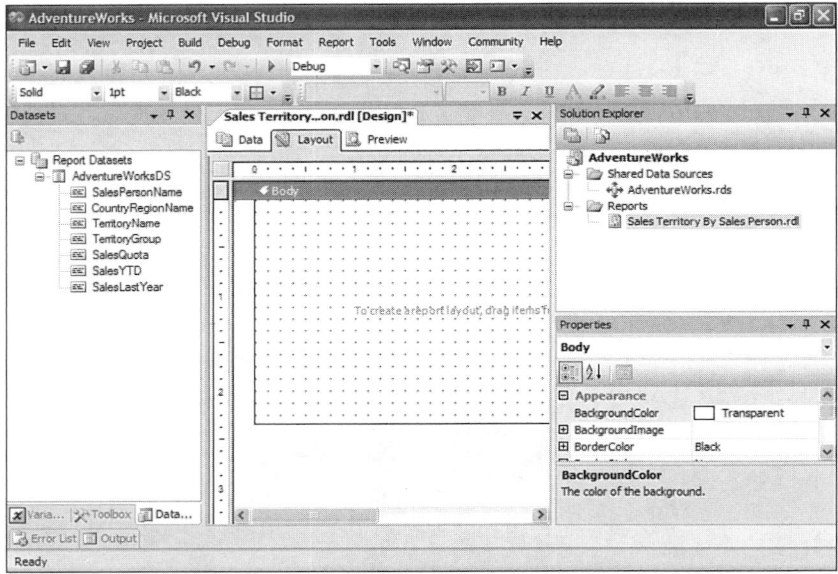

FIGURE 6.13 Treelist with data set fields.

Any item on the report can be modified through the Properties window. The Properties window can be accessed by pressing the F4 key, or by selecting View, Properties Window from the menu. Figure 6.14 shows the Properties window for a text box.

At this point in the report development process, you need to take the results of your query and apply a layout and format to them. Chapter 2, "Reporting Services Capabilities: Presentation, Navigation, and Programmability," gave an overview of the capabilities of SSRS from a report layout and design perspective. For now, let's make a simple tabular report and add a few bells and whistles. Complete the following steps:

1. Drag a text box to the Layout view. In the Properties window (F4), select the text box (most likely the text box you just added is already selected). Continue to change the following property values to those specified for the control named "`ReportTitle`."

Name: ReportTitle

Value: My First Report

Location: Top=0, Left=0

Size: Height=.33in, Width 3.5

Color: #1c3a70

Font: FontStyle=Normal, FontFamily=Tahoma, FontSize=18pt, FontWeight=Normal

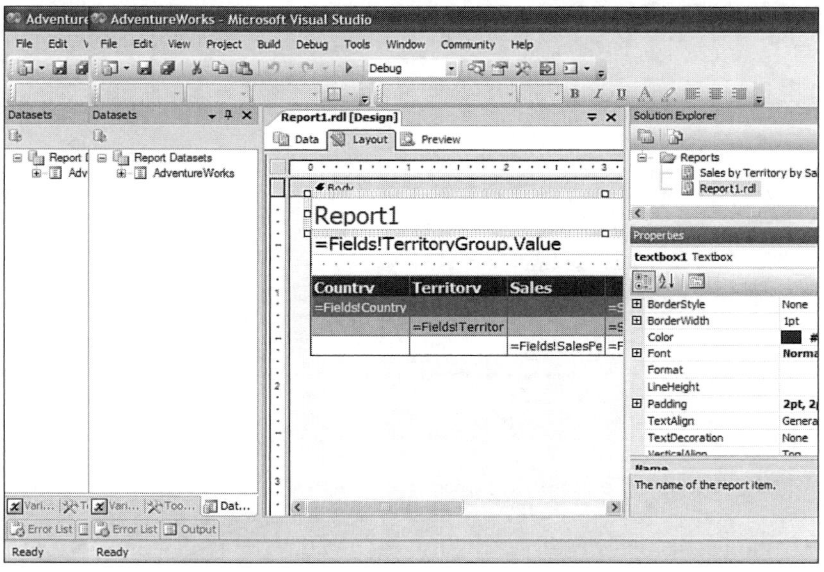

FIGURE 6.14 Properties window.

2. Drag a list onto the layout view. Set the following properties:

   Location: Top=0, Left= .33in

   Size: Height=1.35in, Width 6in

   DatasetName: AdventureWorksDS (can be selected from the drop-down list)

3. Click the "..." button in the Properties window for the list. The Grouping and Sorting Properties dialog box should open. Change the properties on the dialog box to match those in Figure 6.15.

4. Drag a second text box to the layout and place it inside the list. Change the following properties

Name: TerritoryGroup

Value: =Fields!TerritoryGroup.Value (this can be dragged onto the control from the datasets toolbox, or selected from the drop-down list)

```
Location: Top=0, Left=0

Size: Height=.27in, Width 6

Font: FontStyle=Normal, FontFamily=Tahoma, FontSize=14pt, FontWeight=Normal
```

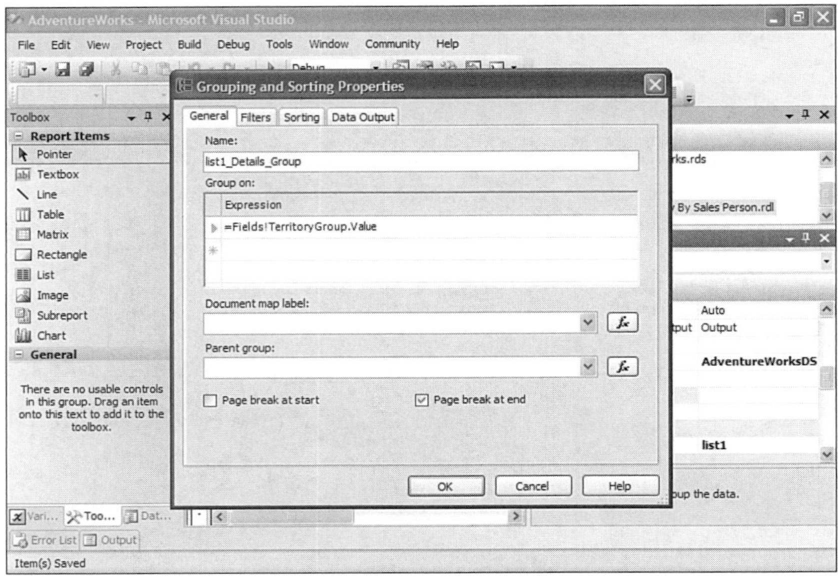

FIGURE 6.15 Grouping and sorting properties for the list.

5. Drag a table and place it inside the list. By default, the table comes with three columns, which are all a little more than 2 inches. Click on the bar above each column; if selected successfully, the entire column should be selected. After a column is selected, use the Properties window and change the width property to 1in. Continue to do this for all three columns. After you are finished, select the rightmost column, right-click on the column, and select Insert Column to the Right. Refer to Figure 6.16. Repeat three times. The table should now have six columns equally spaced at 1-inch wide.

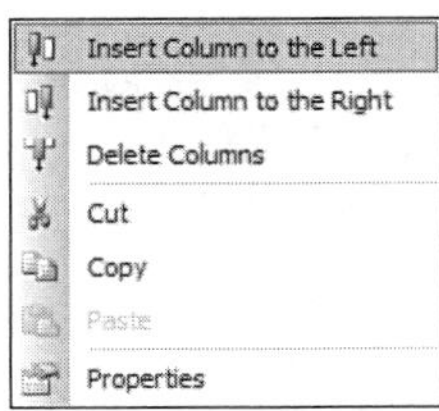

FIGURE 6.16 Selecting columns for a table.

6. Right-click on the button next to the table footer row. From the pop-up menu, deselect Table Footer. See Figure 6.17.

FIGURE 6.17 Table Row menu.

7. Click on the button next to the report header row. After the row is selected, use the Properties window to set the following properties:

```
BackgroundColor: #1c3a70

Color: White

Font: FontStyle=Bold, FontFamily=Tahoma, FontSize=11pt, FontWeight=Normal
```

8. Click the button at the upper-left corner of the table. By doing this, the entire table should now be selected. If so, right-click on the upper-left corner of the table and select Properties from the pop-up menu. The Table Properties dialog box opens.

9. Under Dataset Name, select AdventureWorksDS from the drop-down menu. Check Repeat Header Rows on Each Page from the Header/footer section.

10. Click the Groups tab. Then click the Add button. The Grouping and Sorting Properties dialog box opens. Under the Group On: section, there is a list box where you tell the table to group on one or more than one value. To illustrate, you will group on Country Region, and then Territory Name. From the drop-down menu in the list box, select the expression `=Fields!CountryRegionName.Value`. Under the Name text box, enter the value `table1_CountryRegion_Group`. Uncheck Include Group Footer. Figure 6.18 illustrates. Click OK when you are finished.

11. Proceed to make a second group by repeating the process described in step 10. This time, name the group `table1_TerritoryName_Group` and have it group on the expression `=Fields!TerritoryName.Value`. Click OK to exit the Grouping and Sorting Properties dialog box, and click OK again to exit the Table Properties dialog box. See Figure 6.19 for a view of the table.

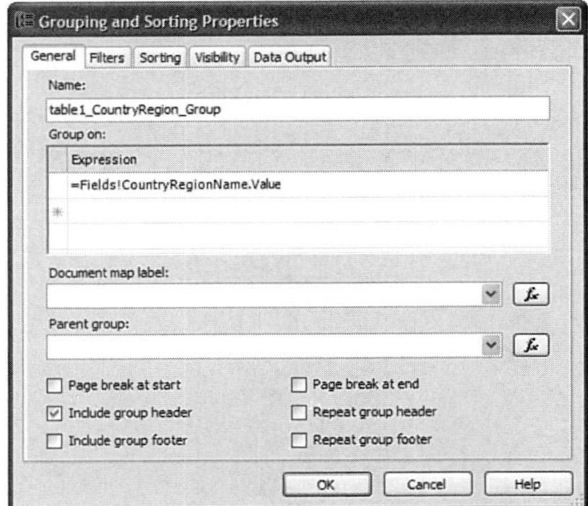

FIGURE 6.18 Grouping and Sorting Properties.

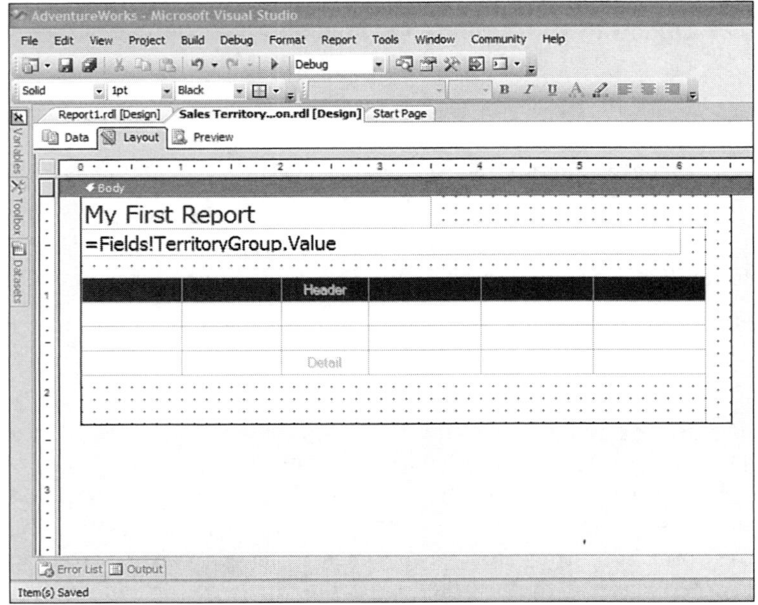

FIGURE 6.19 Completed table layout.

12. Now that the table groups have been created, let's add the data to the table. Start by dragging the field `CountryRegionName` from the Dataset field collection over to the uppermost row (labeled 1) on the left column. Be sure not to place it in the table header. Drag the `TerritoryName` fields to the lower-right side of the

CountryRegionName field. Continue to drag the fields SalesPersonName, SalesQuota, Sales YTD, and SalesLastYear to the detail row.

13. Add SalesQuota, Sales YTD, and SalesLastYear into both of the header rows. Notice how the expression changes from the detail row. In the detail, the value is displayed by salesperson, whereas for each of the headers the value is the sum of the amount for the grouping used. Hence Group 1 is the sum of the amount for Country, and Group 2 is the sum of the amount for Terrritory.

14. Select all of the text boxes used to display dollars. Using the Properties window, change the format property of all the text boxes to c2. This formats all of the dollars as currency. Adjust the table headings as appropriate. Figure 6.20 shows the completed report in Layout mode.

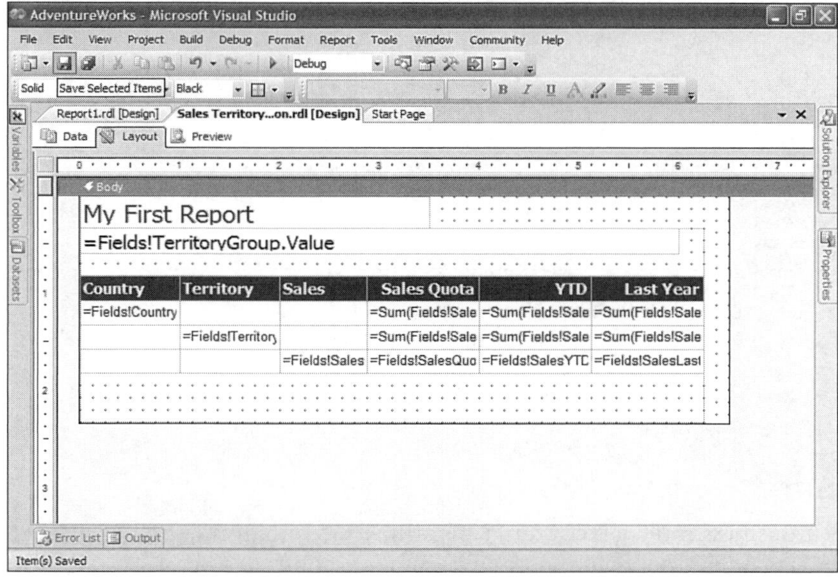

FIGURE 6.20 Completed report in Layout mode.

This concludes the starter report. To preview this report, click on the Preview tab in Report Designer. The Preview tab renders the report within the SQL Server Business Intelligence Studio. The tab also has the capability to preview parameters and print preview. Figure 6.21 shows the completed report in Preview mode.

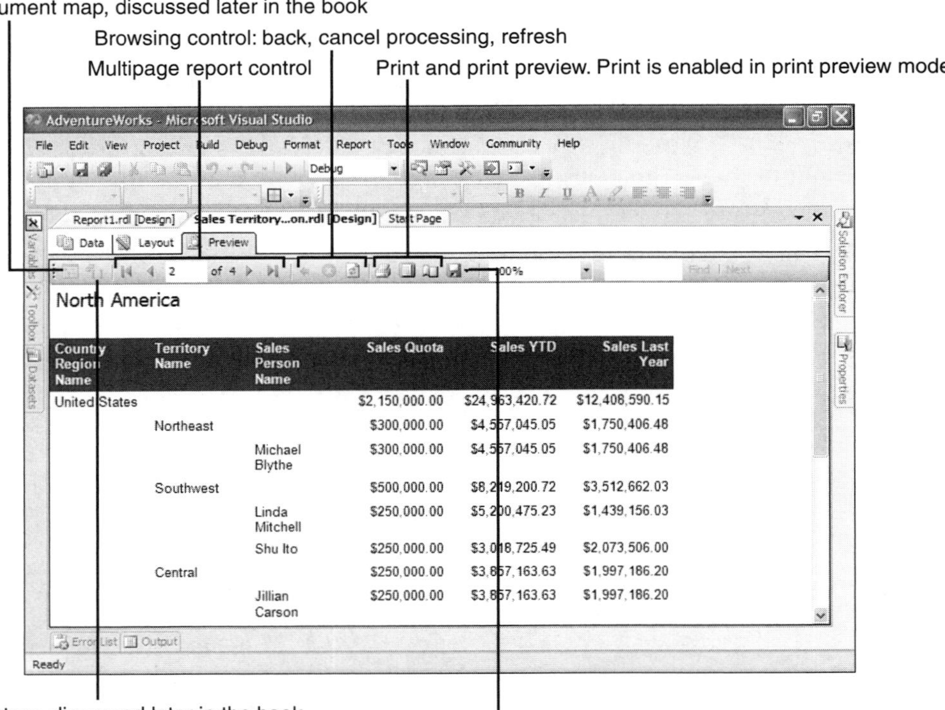

FIGURE 6.21 Completed report in Preview mode.

Summary

SQL Server Business Intelligence Studio is nothing more than the shell of Visual Studio. Both products house the main report development tool from Microsoft—SQL Server Report Designer. Over the next several chapters, you will see how to use Report Designer to develop powerful and visually appealing reports for all kinds of end users.

Report Definition Language

CHAPTER 7

IN THIS CHAPTER

The preceding chapter provided an introduction to Report Designer and Report Builder. This chapter takes a look at the output from these tools.

SSRS is unique in that it uses XML to generate reports. This chapter provides an insight into why Microsoft uses XML as their report generation language, and then delves into the structure of the resulting document.

Language: A Way to Communicate

At first glance, the name Report Definition Language (RDL) might appear to be a misnomer. As you've already seen, it is nothing more than an XML document, just like any other XML document. Why would they call this a language? After all, there is no compiler necessary and the syntax is nothing like C++, C#, or any other programming language. To answer this, you need to think of things at a bit higher level than most programming paradigms allow.

Remember, one of the goals of SSRS is to remain an open-ended environment.

Likewise, as you have already seen, SSRS is composed of many different components. Figure 3.1 (found in Chapter 3, "Reporting Services Architecture") provides a graphical overview of the different components of SSRS.

There is the database server, the Windows service, the Report Server Web Service, and so on.

Most importantly, at least from an end-user perspective, are the report designers and the rendering engine. As you have seen, Microsoft already offers two designers—Report Designer and Report Builder.

Both designers use the same rendering engine, and even within this engine there are multiple formats. For all of this to work together seamlessly, all these components need to communicate with the same underlying principles. This is where the common language comes in to play—it is simply a common way to communicate instructions between the various entities.

Use of XML

Most enterprise reporting solutions use proprietary binary formats. This locks developers into using that vendor's tools to generate and deploy reports. Obviously, this runs counter to SSRS's design goal of generating open standards. The other thing to note about SSRS is the idea to keep report designers and generators separate. This poses the fundamental challenge of what open format allows such disparate things to communicate. Thankfully, the answer already existed—XML.

XML is already in use throughout the Web and even in many non-Web systems as a communication mechanism. It easily allows anyone with a text editor to create an XML file. XML is similar to HTML in that it is a form of markup language. There are a few major differences.

With XML, a document has to be well formed, meaning every beginning markup tag (called a node) has to have a corresponding ending tag. Second, HTML only has a few keywords that can be used to mark up text. XML doesn't have any such limitation because the end user is the one responsible for the creation of tags. The tags are used to describe the data encompassed by them. This is in stark contrast to HTML, which describes how to handle presentation of data. This makes XML an ideal communication medium or language.

The one drawback about such a flexible medium is, ironically enough, its flexibility. Immediately, you might wonder the following: If any node can be in any place, and any node can have any attribute, how can this be effective? There have to be some rules. To solve this problem, you need to create an XML schema. An XML schema allows the creation of a contract to adhere to between different systems by defining when and where in the document a set of XML nodes should appear, and which nodes should have attributes describing them.

The RDL specification is the XML schema that describes the layout of the XML used to create reports. The XML itself basically becomes the programming language of the report.

Declarative Programming

Just as a programming language lets a programmer tell a computer how and what to produce to the end user, the RDL tells the report server what data to use and how to lay it out. Now, there is a little trick here: Most programming languages communicate a *what* and a *how* to do something. There is no way to tell ASP.NET to produce a web page just by giving it a template. However, that is what the RDL does. The RDL communicates what the output is to look like and where the source data is to come from. This leaves the application free to decide how to generate the defined look and feel, regardless of the programming language or underlying architecture. This model is called the declarative model.

A producer application is an application that is used to generate RDL files. Business Intelligence Development Studio and Report Builder fall into this category. For most users, it is helpful to have a graphical user interface (GUI), although you can develop a report purely in your favorite text editor.

A consumer application is simply one that takes the RDL from the producer and creates the desired output. In its simplest form, it queries for the data and displays the results in the specified format. This is where a lot of the custom elements come in. Using the custom elements, it is possible to send instructions for one output format, which could then be ignored by all others.

Report Elements

To create a report, you need to know a few things:

- Where and what is your source data?
- What is the report layout?
- Are there any other properties, such as external images or parameters?

To cover this much information, the RDL schema has many elements. The RDL specification (schema) itself is an open schema, and Microsoft fully expects third parties to add onto it to extend it. In the scope of this book, it would be very time consuming and arduous to cover every element, so this book covers just a few main elements. For more information, the RDL specification is available for download on the Microsoft website at the following location:

http://www.microsoft.com/sql/technologies/reporting/rdlspec.mspx

You can also view the XML of any report, by opening the report in SQL Server Business Intelligence Studio and selecting the View, Code menu while in Design view. Alternatively, you can view a report's XML by right-clicking the report in Solution Explorer and selecting View Code from a drop-down menu.

Report Element

The Report element is the highest-level element in the RDL XML hierarchy. The Report element contains all the information needed to process the report. There can be only one Report element in every report. In fact, every other element is a child node of the Report element. Examples of these child elements include PageHeader, Body, PageFooter, DataSources, DataSets, and Parameters.

The following code listing shows an example of the Report element:

```
<?xml version="1.0" encoding="utf-8"?>
<Report xmlns="http://schemas.microsoft.com/sqlserver/reporting/2005/01/
➥reportdefinition" xmlns:rd="http://schemas.microsoft.com/SQLServer/reporting/
➥reportdesigner">
  <DataSources></DataSources>
  <BottomMargin>1in</BottomMargin>
  <RightMargin>1in</RightMargin>
  <InteractiveWidth>8.5in</InteractiveWidth>
    <Body>
    <ReportItems>
      <Table Name="table1"></Table>
    </ReportItems>
    <Height>2in</Height>
  </Body>
  <LeftMargin>1in</LeftMargin>
  <DataSets></DataSets>
  <Width>6.5in</Width>
  <InteractiveHeight>11in</InteractiveHeight>
  <Language>en-US</Language>
  <TopMargin>1in</TopMargin>
</Report>
```

Report Parameters

This element lists the parameters for a report (see Table 7.1). This is an ordered list of ReportParameters elements.

NOTE

Because all XML is character based, technically, any data type (Type) that is specified in Table 7.1 and further is a String. To be more specific about a range of possible string values, this book generally uses acceptable descriptions. For example, Boolean indicates that the string value could be `true` or `false`.

TABLE 7.1 Report Parameters

Element Name	Required or Optional	Type	Description
Name	Required	String	Unique name of the parameter (the value of this element is used when other expressions need to refer back to this parameter). Note: Parameter names must be unique within the ReportParameters parent element.

TABLE 7.1 Continued

Element Name	Required or Optional	Type	Description
DataType	Required	Enum	Programmatic data type of the parameter. Because it is a required value, there is no default. Boolean | DateTime | Integer | Float | String
Nullable	Optional	Boolean	Whether the value of the parameter can be null. Defaults to False if excluded.
DefaultValue	Optional	Element	Value used for the parameter when not supplied by the end user. If the Prompt element is omitted, the value is null. DefaultValue becomes required when there is no Prompt element and when either Nullable is False or a ValidValues element exists that does not contain Null (an omitted value).
AllowBlank	Optional	Boolean	Whether an empty string is an acceptable value for the parameter. The default value is False, and the element is ignored if the DataType is not String.
Hidden	Optional	Boolean	The element that determines whether a user should be prompted to enter a parameter. If this element is false, the user interface prompts a user to enter the parameter.
Prompt	Optional	String	The element that designates the text that the user interface should display when prompting the user for parameter values. If the element is omitted, the user is not prompted for a parameter's value and additionally the parameter *cannot* be modified any other way. For example, it can't be modified through URL Access. Report Designer does not allow this element to be blank. Manual RDL editing and setting this element to blank or removing this element have a similar effect to the Hidden element being set to true.

DataSets

The DataSets element is a collection of individual DataSet elements (see Table 7.2). As a whole, the collection contains information about how to get the data used in the reports.

Each individual DataSet element has to have a unique name element. The DataSet element itself contains elements for basic properties, such as AccentSensitivity, CaseSensitivity, Collation, and so on.

The actual database query is contained in the Query element. Each data set can only have one query. When using the Query element, you can see some of the influences of the .NET Framework, particularly ADO.NET. The child elements are CommandText, CommandType, DataSourceName, QueryParameters, and Timeout.

The Fields collection contains Field elements. In an Online Transaction Processing (OLTP) system, the Fields collection usually maps to the columns returned by your database query. There is also the ability to add calculated fields. The field name is the name referenced in the layout sections of the report. The Field element must have either a DataField child element or a Value child element, but not both. As you might have guessed, the DataField simply maps to a query column. A Value element should contain an expression used to calculate a field. In the designer, this shows up as a calculated value. An example of the Fields collection follows:

```
<Fields>
  <Field Name="ProductID">
    <rd:TypeName>System.Int32</rd:TypeName>
    <DataField>ProductID</DataField>
  </Field>
  <Field Name="Name">
    <rd:TypeName>System.String</rd:TypeName>
    <DataField>Name</DataField>
  </Field>
</Fields>
```

In a lot of cases, a database query or stored procedure returns more information than most readers would like or need. In this case, you can apply a filter to the data set through the Filters collection. Each individual Filter element contains a collection of FilterExpression, Operator, and FilterValues. Basically, for every row in the data set, the report processing engine is responsible for evaluating the expression against that row and using the operator to compare it to the list of values. Depending on the expression, this can be time consuming.

The following code listing displays an example of the Query and Filter elements.

```
<DataSets>
  <DataSet Name="AdventureWorks">
    <Query>
      <CommandText>SELECT     ProductID, Name
OM          Production.Product</CommandText>
      <DataSourceName>DataSource1</DataSourceName>
    </Query>
```

```
    <Filters>
      <Filter>
        <Operator>Equal</Operator>
        <FilterValues>
          <FilterValue>=Cint("866")</FilterValue>
        </FilterValues>
        <FilterExpression>=Fields!ProductID.Value</FilterExpression>
      </Filter>
    </Filters>
    <Fields>
      <Field Name="ProductID">
        <rd:TypeName>System.Int32</rd:TypeName>
        <DataField>ProductID</DataField>
      </Field>
      <Field Name="Name">
        <rd:TypeName>System.String</rd:TypeName>
        <DataField>Name</DataField>
      </Field>
    </Fields>
  </DataSet>
</DataSets>
```

TABLE 7.2 DataSet Elements

Name	Required/Optional/ or Multiple	Type	Description
Name	Required	String	Unique name given to the data set. This cannot be the same name given to any data region or grouping.
Fields	Optional	Element	List of fields that are included in the data set. They can map to columns in the data set.
Field	1-N	Element	The name of the field as it is referred to within the report.
Query	Required	Element	Information used to gather data from the data source. This parameter includes connection information, query text, query parameters, and so on required to get the data from the data source.

Report Items

Report items define the contents of the report. They are under the PageHeader, Body, and PageFooter elements. Report items contain user interface elements, such as Tables, Matrixes, Images, Lines, SubReports, Lists, and Rectangles. Because SSRS allows you to nest controls, report items can also be found within other report items. Each report item must contain at least one child element.

Because many elements inherit from a report item, it is advantageous to be familiar with the shared properties. These are mostly related to presentation. Height, width, ZIndex, top, and left are all used to size and position an item. Each report item can have its own style section. The Action, Visibility, and Drill Through elements all aid in reporting interactivity. Generic RDL of a report item that contains some common elements is shown in the following code listing. `{REPORT ITEM}` abbreviates any report item, such as Textbox, Table, and so on.

```
<ReportItems>
       ...
        <{REPORT ITEM} Name="...">
              <Style>...</Style>
              <Top>...</Top>
              <Left>...</Left>
              <Height>...</Height>
              <Width>...</Width>
              <ZIndex>...</ZIndex>
              <Visibility>...</Visibility>
              <ToolTip>...</ToolTip>
              <Bookmark>...</Bookmark>
              <RepeatWith>...</RepeatWith>
              <Custom>...</Custom>
              <ReportItems>...</ReportItems>
              <PageBreakAtStart>...</PageBreakAtStart>
              <PageBreakAtEnd>...</PageBreakAtEnd>
        </{REPORT ITEM}>
       ...
</ReportItems>
```

Table 7.3 shows explanations and types of common ReportItem elements.

TABLE 7.3 Common ReportItem Elements

Name	Required/ Optional	Type	Description
Name	Required	String	The unique name given to the report item.
Style	Optional	Element	The style information, such as padding, color, font, and so on for the element.

TABLE 7.3 Continued

Name	Required/ Optional	Type	Description
Action	Optional	Element	An action such as a bookmark link or a drillthrough action that is associated with the ReportItem. This aids in making reports interactive.
Top	Optional	Size	The distance of the report item to the top of the containing object. If excluded, the value becomes 0 in.
Left	Optional	Size	The distance of the report item to the left of the containing object. If excluded, the value becomes 0 in.
Height	Optional	Size	The vertical size of the item. If omitted, the value defaults to the height of the containing object minus Top value.
Width	Optional	Size	The lateral size of the item. If omitted, the value defaults to the width of the containing object minus Left value.
PageBreakAtStart	Optional	Boolean	The instruction to the Report Server to put a page break before a report item.
PageBreakAtEnd	Optional	Boolean	The instruction to the Report Server to put a page break after a report item.
Visibility	Optional	Element	An action to specify initial visibility of an item and a toggle trigger item for the Visibility.

You can find additional information, including more discussion about RDL, in Chapter 11, "Working with Report Items."

Data Regions

Data regions are the primary mechanism used to display data and a base class of controls that generate repeating content based on a data in a data set. Four basic elements inherit from a data region: Chart, Table, List, and Matrix. Each data region is unique in its own way and, as such, has many of its own specialized elements and attributes. Because all of the data regions display data, all have the `<DataSetName>` tag. For more information on the specifics of data regions, please see Chapter 11.

Summary

This chapter covered why and how Microsoft chose to use XML in SSRS. It also covered the programming model that arose as a result, and explained some of the key elements and their derivations.

The following chapters build on this information, some indirectly and some in a more direct way. Report Builder and Report Designer are nothing more than fancy RDL generators. As such, this chapter provides a cursory look at what they generate. The following chapters really do nothing more than show how to use them to build bigger and better reports by generating more advanced RDL. Chapter 11 incorporates additional RDL discussion around report items and data regions.

Expressions

CHAPTER 8

IN THIS CHAPTER

- What Is an Expression?
- Expression Syntax
- Adding Expressions
- Collections
- Using Functions
- Other Functions
- Using Expressions to Change Report Item Properties and Behavior
- Example: Placing Emphasis on Certain Values

This might come as a bit of a shock, but everything you have done up to this point has been done using expressions. Expressions are central to SSRS. In fact, they are so central, that just about everything depends on them. Every property on every report item is an expression. The designer just sets them to predefined values, instead of making them dynamic. This chapter covers making these properties dynamic, and how to use SSRS's built-in tools to help you do so.

What Is an Expression?

Expressions are a VB.NET statement that resolves to a single value of a .NET type, such as Integer, String, and so on. Much like VB.NET statements, expressions can be composed of constants, variables, functions, and operators. Most expressions are nothing more than simple strings or VBA constants. For example, the `FontWeight` property of a text box can be set to a number of values, including `Bold`, `Normal`, and `Extra Light`. Other expressions are strings, such as the `Height` and `Width` properties.

Report Designer aids us by setting property values to predefined constants. They remain constant while the report is being rendered.

The real power of expressions comes when these formerly static values can be changed while the report is processing to give the report a level of dynamism that it otherwise would not have had.

Suppose, for example, that you are generating a report of products and their profit and loss. One of the requirements of the report is to show the products that are losing money in big, bold, red letters.

Profitability information is known in advance, not until a report pulls data from a data source. After data is retrieved, the report can use a simple expression logic `=iif(Fields!ProductProfit.Value < 0, "Red", "Black")` in the `Color` property of a text box to highlight negative values in `Red`.

Now on to the world of expressions...

Expression Syntax

Expressions are preceded by an "=" sign, which tells the report-processing engine that the statement following this sign has to be evaluated. It is certainly possible to turn even a constant to an expression. For example, the `VerticalAlign` property can have constant values: `Top`, `Middle`, and `Bottom`, or, alternatively, a developer can express those constants as expressions `="Top"`, `="Middle"`, or `="Bottom"`.

If you are more familiar with Microsoft Excel than VB.NET, expressions are similar to VBA expressions in Excel. Starting an expression with an "=" sign only increases the resemblance.

Expressions can be used to achieve several goals: display the values on a report and calculate values for style and formatting properties.

Style change can include variation of colors, highlights, and shapes of displayed data. To accomplish those goals, expressions are used in properties of reporting items. Most properties of the reporting items support expressions, and few (such as `Name`) do not. Most of the expressions in properties are strings, few are VBA constants, such as `True` or `False`, and a few have numeric values.

Let's start our examination by taking a look at a simple yet common expression:

```
=Fields!FirstName.Value
```

This is a common expression for retrieving values from a data set. As expected, the expression starts with an equal sign. Next is the keyword "`Fields`." This is in reference to the `Fields` collection of the parent data set. The next piece (`!FirstName.Value`) makes reference to the `FirstName` field in the `Fields` collections, and gets its value. It is also possible to use functions around fields to achieve a desired result. For example:

```
=Sum(Fields!Price.Value)
```

Expressions can contain one or more of the following:

- **Constants**—Constants can be static expressions, (such as static text `="Text"` or numeric `=5`) or predefined (such as color, text alignment, and font family). Most of the properties accept predefined constants. For example, `TextAlign` can have one of the following values: `General`, `Left`, `Center`, and `Right`.

- **Collections**—Items of all collections are **read-only**. The item can belong to one of the following collections:
  - `Parameters` (see Chapter 10, "Report Parameters," for a `Parameters` collection discussion)
  - `Fields`
  - Data sets
  - Report items
  - `Users`
  - Globals
- **Operators**—Operators include the programmatic symbols used for common mathematical operations such as addition, subtraction, power, modulo, and so on, as well as operations on strings such as string concatenation.
  - Arithmetic operators include ^, *, /, \, Mod, +, and-.
  - Comparison operators include `<`, `>`, `<=`, `>=`, `=`, `<>`, `Like` (compares two strings), and `Is` (compares two object reference variables).
  - Concatenation operators include `&` and `+`. Use the `&` operator for concatenation of two strings to avoid confusion with adding two numbers.
  - Logical/Bitwise operators include `And`, `Not`, `Or`, `Xor` (logical exclusion operation), `AndAlso` (performs short-circuiting logical conjunction on two expressions), and `OrElse` (short-circuiting logical disjunction on two expressions).
  - Bit Shift operators include `<<` and `>>`.
- **Visual Basic runtime functions**—Keep in mind that the Expression Editor will provide only the most common functions from the VB runtime library such as Right, Left, InStr, Format, and so on.
- **Custom functions**—See Chapter 22, "Implementing Custom Embedded Functions," for more details.

TIP

If you use an expression for the value of a property and you either receive an error or are not able to achieve the desired result (for example, text alignment does not work properly), you need to make sure that the type of the expression value is appropriate for the property. For example, if you use the following expression for the `VerticalAlign` property `=IIF(1=1,Top,Bottom)`, SSRS returns a runtime error: `The VerticalAlign expression for the text box '<textbox name>' contains an error: [BC30451] Name 'Top' is not declared.`

The proper expression is: `=IIF(1=1,"Top","Bottom")`.

Alternatively, if you enter `=IIF(1=1,10,0)` in the `BorderWidth` property, there is no runtime error, and SSRS is not going to provide an expected width, because the property expects a string (`"10pt"`) as opposed to a numeric value.

Adding Expressions

There are two ways to add an expression:

- Type an expression in a property value either in the Properties window (by default docked at the lower-right corner of the Report Designer interface) or in the `Value` box of the `Properties` property pages dialog box (you can open this dialog by right-clicking on a control and selecting Properties from the shortcut menu).
- Compose an expression with the Expression Editor.

An Expression Editor provides a very convenient way of entering expressions, including Intellisense, a list of common VB and SSRS functions, operators, and collections that a developer can copy to an expression.

To start an Expression Editor, use one of the following methods (see Figure 8.1):

- Click on the drop-down on the right of the property in the Properties window.
- Right-click on the item and select `fx Expression` from the drop-down (only works for text box items).
- Click on the *fx* button on the right of the expression box. This is available from the properties dialog box only.

Any of the preceding methods will display the Expression Editor window, shown in Figure 8.2. Expression Editor consists of an Intellisense-enabled editing area (1), category browser (2), category member list (3), and multipurpose area (4).

The multipurpose area works in a couple of capacities: When the category is a collection (such as Parameters), this area displays the collection member browser; when the category is a constant, it displays a list of available constants.

Depending on the property being edited, the Expression Editor only displays constants available for this specific property. When the category is neither collections nor constants, the multipurpose area carries a description.

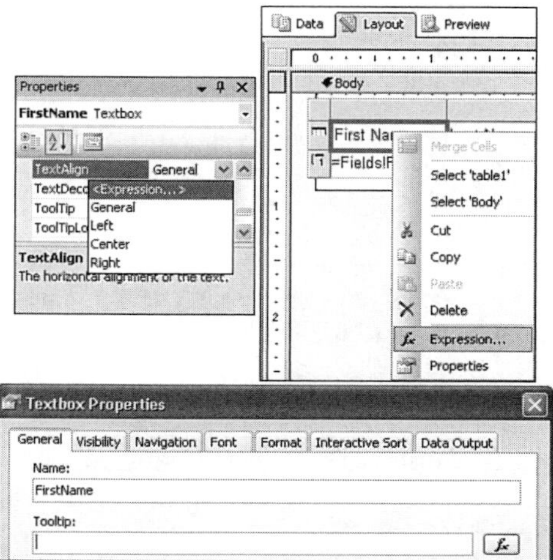

FIGURE 8.1 Various methods of accessing the Expression Editor.

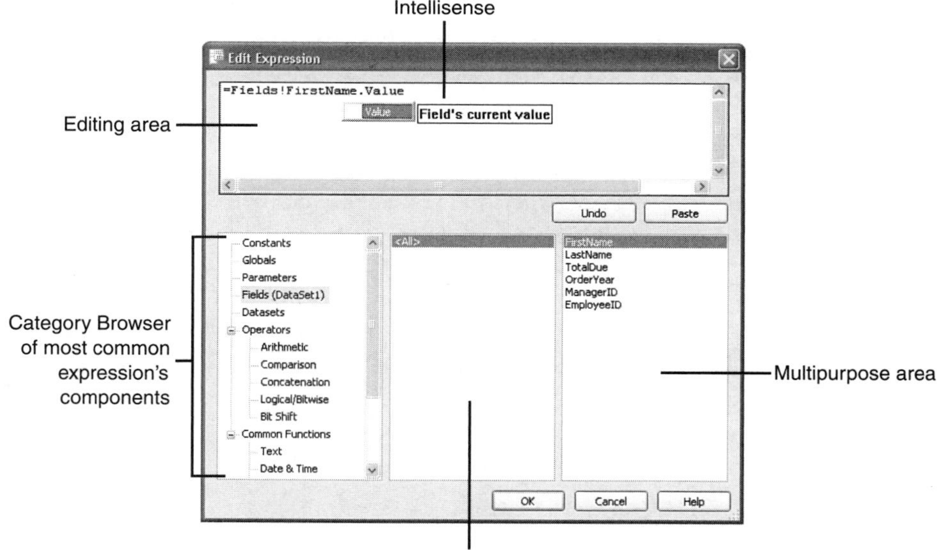

FIGURE 8.2 Edit Expression window also known as Expression Editor.

Collections

SSRS provides five read-only global collections to draw information from as it processes reports. There are four valid ways to access collection items:

```
=Collection!{ItemName}.Value
=Collection.Item("{ItemName}") .Value
```

```
=Collection.ObjectName
=Collection("!{ItemName}") .Value
```

Thus `=Fields.("FirstName").Value` is the same as `=Fields!FirstName.Value` and the same as `=Fields.Item("FirstName").Value`.

NOTE

All objects in the SSRS object model are read-only. Thus, it is not possible to assign a value to a parameter, for example, during report processing.

ReportItems

The `ReportItems` collection is simply a list of text boxes on the report. Only the `Value` property of a text box can be accessed. By accessing these values, developers can use them in calculating derived values.

NOTE

Keep in mind that text boxes can be hidden from the user. By using invisible text boxes, you can acquire data at runtime and use them to process values for other visible items.

For example, the value of `textbox1` can be accessed with the following expression using the `ReportItems` collection:

```
=ReportIems!Textbox1.Value
```

The use of `ReportItems` enabled developers to create page summaries. For example, the following expression creates a summary of values displayed in `textbox1`:

```
=Sum(ReportItems!textbox1.Value)
```

In addition, `ReportItems` can be used in complex expressions involving several items. `ReportItems` can also be passed to and used in a code, such as in the following example:

```
Function Incr(ReportItems As Object) '***This function increments passed parameter
    return ReportItems("textbox1").Value+1
End Function
```

Although a `ReportItems` item can be used to access data from any text box in the report, to access the value of the current text box, use `Me.Value` or simply `Value`.

The need to use `Value` might arise, for example, for conditional formatting. The following expression could be used in the property `BackgroundColor`:

```
=IIF(Value < 0, "Red", "White")
```

Fields

The `Fields` collection contains references to fields within a data set. The most typical use of the `Fields` collection is to display data in text boxes; however, they can be used in calculating formulas for other properties and functions.

All fields have names. When a data set is created, Report Designer executes a query and retrieves column metadata, including names and a populated `Fields` collection for this data set with names retrieved. `Fields` can be either mapped to columns of a query or calculated by SSRS. Calculated fields are expressions (such as adding two database fields together) and are often used when it either adds elegance to a report or the query language is not powerful enough to retrieve calculated fields (infrequent occurrence with modern enterprise databases).

Report Designer allows one to subsequently add new fields (right-click on a data set where you want to add fields and select Add from the shortcut menu) or modify/delete existing fields (right-click on the field to modify and select Edit or Delete from the shortcut menu). The preceding steps assume that the Datasets window is visible; to open it from a main menu, navigate to View, Datasets.

Report Designer allows one to drag fields from the Datasets window to a report. If the report creator drops a field to a table or matrix, a corresponding cell is filled with an expression, based on the field. If a field is dropped outside of the matrix or table, a text box is created.

Recall that the RDL schema allows each data set to have its own set of fields. The result of this is that while authoring reports, you will have multiple sets of Fields collections. The important thing to remember is that each data region can only have a reference to one data set, and, hence, one set of fields that belongs to that data set. The data set name that the Fields collection refers to is actually a property of the data region, and not of the Fields collections.

SSRS must be able to match {`FieldName`} to an appropriate data set or the scope has to be explicitly defined. For example, if a report has a single data set, using an expression like `=First(Fields!FirstName.Value)` is acceptable in an independent text box. However, if the report has multiple data sets, an expression `=First(Fields!FirstName.Value, "DataSet1")` is required. Because data regions have an associated data set, this association provides scope resolution for fields within a data region. The downside of being tied to a data region is that the `Fields` collection is only accessible within data regions. This means that you cannot derive values from data sets for anything that does not or cannot contain a data region, such as page headers and footers.

Each field in the `Fields` collection has only two properties. The first one is `Value`. The value is actually what it says it is—the value of the field from the data set. The second property is `IsMissing`. This property tells you if the field actually exists in the data set. Although this might seem strange, this might prove to be very helpful if there is no way to be certain of the name of the fields being returned from a particular data set. `IsMissing` also helps if you have misspelled a field's name.

Parameters

The `Parameters` collection contains the list of parameters in the report. The parameters collection only has two properties: `Value` and `Label`. The `Value` is the value of the parameter. The `Label` is the friendly name of the parameter from the prompt property of the parameter.

The `Parameters` collection is similar to the `Fields` collection in that it can be used in any number of properties or functions. Unlike the `Fields` collection, the `Parameters` collection is global in scope. This means that the parameter can be accessed anywhere in the report, including page headers and footers.

Globals

The `Globals` collection is also fairly straightforward and has a predefined, fixed number of items. It is simply a list of global variables that are accessible while rendering the report.

Table 8.1 shows the properties available via the `Globals` collection.

TABLE 8.1 Globals Collection Items

Member	Type	Description
ExecutionTime	DateTime	The date and time that the rendering engine began processing the report.
PageNumber	Integer	The page number of the current page. This parameter can only be used in headers and footers.
ReportFolder	String	The virtual path to the folder containing the report. This does not include the ReportServerName.
ReportName	String	The name of the report from the Report Server's catalog.
ReportServerUrl	String	The URL of the Report Server from which the report is being processed.
TotalPages	Integer	The value for the total number of pages in a report. This parameter can only be used in headers and footers.

One of the most frequent uses of the `Globals` collection is to display a page number in the report's footer, such as in the following expression, which can be placed in a text box in the report's footer:

```
=Globals.PageNumber & " of " & Globals.TotalPages.
```

User

The `User` collection is the simplest of collections. It only contains two properties related to the user running the report, and both properties are strings. The first item is `UserId`, and the second item is `Language`. The `UserId` is the user identity of the person running the report. By default, SSRS uses Windows Authentication, which supplied the `UserId` in the form `<DomainName>/<User Name>`. The `LanguageId` is the language identifier (used in localization) for the user. In the case of US localization this value is "`en-US`".

NOTE

When using Expression Editor, please, keep in mind that members of `User` collection (`UserID` and `Language`) are both located under `Globals` branch of the category member list. Please refer to Figure 8.2.

Report designers can use the `User` collection to provide user-dependent formatting customization of a report. To do that, a report developer can create a parameter with the following properties:

```
Name: User
Internal: Checked (this eliminates prompt to a report user)
Available Values: Leave empty
Default Values: Non Queried with expression =User!UserID
```

Then, the report developer can use such parameters to conditionally format report items or to pass the parameter to a query. The benefit of using the parameter versus using `=User!UserID` directly (which is also an option) is an ability to modify the parameter's value. The parameter can be, for example, modified through users, while in turn `=User!UserID` is read-only.

Using Functions

Functions are really what make expressions so powerful. If SSRS did not have functions, developers would not be able to manipulate data in any of the collections.

SSRS comes with two generic types of built-in functions. The first are the functions used for aggregations of data. The rest are functions having to do with scope.

SSRS also allows you to reference any of the standard or custom assemblies that come with the Common Language Runtime. In fact, three of them are already referenced for you: `Microsoft.VisualBasic`, `System.Math`, and `System.Convert`.

Lastly, SSRS gives you the ability to write your own functions using custom code blocks (in VB.NET).

Visual Basic Runtime Functions

Runtime functions are provided through Microsoft .NET library's namespaces: `Microsoft.VisualBasic`, `System.Math`, and `System.Convert`.

Note that the Visual Basic namespace adds a couple of functions to `System.Math`; one of those functions is the random number generator, `Rnd`. The functions fall in the following categories: Conversion (for example, `Str`), `DateAndTime` (for example, `DateAdd`), Financial (for example, NPV [net present value] calculation), Inspection (for example, `IsNull`), Interaction (for example, `IIF`; Expression Editor includes this in the Program Flow group), Strings (for example, Len), and Mathematical (for example, Ceiling). Expression Editor displays a subset of all available functions. However, Intellisense recognizes all available functions and provides signature information. One of the functions that is not available for selection inside Expression Editor is `Partition(Input, RangeStart, RangeEnd, Interval)`. This function evaluates an `Input` expression and returns string `"#:#"` that represents a partition where number is located. For example, `Partition(56, 0, 100, 5)` returns the string "55:59". This function can be used to group expressions within a range of values.

The set of functions outlined in this chapter is the set that SSRS allows to execute by default. By default, all reports run with `ExecuteOnly` permission. This means, for example, that functions such as `Dir` that access file system functionality will not execute by default. However, an administrator can give report processing additional permissions by editing the CAS policy file, but this would be applied to **all** reports on the server. In this case, the report publishing right **must** be restricted to the trusted personnel. This is because anybody who has the right to publish will be able to execute any method, which can result in security-related issues.

Table 8.2 provides a comprehensive list of available functions, categorized by their most likely usage.

TABLE 8.2 Available Script Functions

Conversion Functions

Action	Functions
ANSI value to string	`Chr`, `ChrW`
String to lowercase or uppercase	`Format`, `LCase`, `UCase`
Date to serial number	`DateSerial`, `DateValue`
Decimal number to other bases	`Hex`, `Oct`
Number to string	`Format`, `Str`
One data type to another	`CBool`, `CByte`, `CDate`, `CDbl`, `CDec`, `CInt`, `CLng`, `CSng`, `CShort`, `CStr`, `CType`, `Fix`, `Int`
Date to day, month, weekday, or year	`Day`, `Month`, `Weekday`, `Year`
Time to hour, minute, or second	`Hour`, `Minute`, `Second`
String to ASCII value	`Asc`, `AscW`
String to number	`Val`
Time to serial number	`TimeSerial`, `TimeValue`
Partition where parameter is located	`Partition`

Date and Time Functions

Action	Functions
Get the current date or time.	`Now`, `Today`, `TimeOfDay`
Perform date calculations.	`DateAdd`, `DateDiff`, `DatePart`
Return a date.	`DateSerial`, `DateValue`, `MonthName`, `WeekDayName`
Return a time.	`TimeSerial`, `TimeValue`
Set the date or time.	`DateString`, `TimeOfDay`, `TimeString`, `Today`
Time a process.	`Timer`

TABLE 8.2 Continued

String Manipulation Functions

Action	Functions
Compare two strings.	`StrComp`
Convert strings.	`StrConv`
Reverse a string.	`InStrRev`, `StrReverse`
Convert to lowercase or uppercase.	`Format`, `LCase`, `UCase`
Create a string of repeating characters.	`Space`, `StrDup`
Find the length of a string.	`Len`
Format a string.	`Format`, `FormatCurrency`, `FormatDateTime`, `FormatNumber`, `FormatPercent`
Manipulate strings.	`InStr`, `Left`, `LTrim`, `Mid`, `Right`, `RTrim`, `Trim`
Work with ASCII and ANSI values.	`Asc`, `AscW`, `Chr`, `ChrW`
Replace a specified substring.	`Replace`
Return a filter-based string array.	`Filter`
Return a specified number of substrings.	`Split`, `Join`

Financial Functions

Action	Functions
Depreciation	`DDB`, `SLN`, `SYD`
Future value	`FV`
Interest rate	`Rate`
Internal rate of return	`IRR`, `MIRR`
Number of periods	`NPer`
Payments	`IPmt`, `Pmt`, `PPmt`
Present value	`NPV`, `PV`

Math Functions

Action	Functions
Random number generation.	`Randomize`, `Rnd`
Absolute value and sign of a specified number.	`Abs`, `Sign`
Reverse trigonometric functions. For example, Acos returns an angle for a specified Cos value.	`Acos`, `Asin`, `Atan`, `Atan2`
Produce the full product of two 32-bit numbers. Multiplies two big numbers.	`BigMul`
Smallest/Largest/Nearest whole number greater/less than or equal to the specified number.	`Ceiling/Floor/Round`

TABLE 8.2 Continued

Math Functions

Action	Functions
Trigonometric functions	`Cos, Cosh, Sin, Sinh, Tan, Tanh`
Quotient (division result) of two numbers, also passing the remainder as an output parameter.	`DivRem`
Result of e raised to the specified power.	`Exp`
Remainder resulting from the division of a specified number by another specified number.	`IEEERemainder`
Logarithm and Base 10 Log of a specified number.	`Log, Log10`
Larger and smallest of two specified numbers.	`Max, Min`
Result of specified number raised to the specified power.	`Pow`
Square root of a specified number.	`Sqrt`

Information Functions

Action	Functions
Check if the parameter of the specified type.	`IsNothing` (or `IS Nothing`), `IsDate, IsNumeric, IsError, IsArray, IsReference`
Examine array bounds.	`LBound, UBound`
Examine the type of the expression, return the string name of the type.	`TypeName`

Function `IsNothing` can be used to check for the `Null` values; for example, an expression `=IsNothing(Fields!SalesPersonId.Value)` checks if `SalesPersonId` is equal to `Null`. This expression is equivalent to `=Fields!SalesPersonId.Value IS Nothing` (that is, comparison to the keyword `Nothing`). Do not use `IsDBNull` in your expressions; this function does not have useful applications in SSRS expressions.

Table 8.3 lists the functions related to program flow. These functions help with programmatic decision making.

TABLE 8.3 Program Flow Functions

Function	Description	Example
Choose	Selects and returns a value from a list of arguments.	`= CStr(Choose(Value, "Red", "Yellow", " Green "))` returns color depending on the Value (1-3). This example can be used to control "traffic light" highlight.
IIf	Selects and returns one of two objects, depending on the evaluation of an expression.	`= IIf(TestMe < 0, "Red", "Green")` returns color, depending on the value. This example can be used to highlight negative values.

TABLE 8.3 Continued

Function	Description	Example
Switch	Evaluates a list of expressions and returns an Object value of an expression associated with the first expression in the list that is True.	`=Switch(Fields!City.Value = "London", "English (United Kingdom)", Fields!City.Value = "Rome", "Italian (Italy)", Fields!City.Value = "Paris", "French (France)")`. Returns locale depending on the city. Can be used in the `Language` property to provide appropriate format defaults.

Aggregate Functions

Aggregate functions are used to aggregate data over a certain scope. Some examples of these types of operations are `Sum` and `Average`.

Aggregate functions are very simple to use. The big trick to them is scope. All aggregate functions contain scope as a parameter. If scope is not entered, it defaults based on a number of criteria. Because of this defaulting, you will usually see aggregates used without a reference to scope. For example, with a sum in a table or a matrix, the scope is assumed to be the innermost grouping within the table or matrix.

Outside of a data region, the scope is simply the name of the data set. For example, if you had a text box outside a table in which you intended to put a total sales value, you would put the following expression inside the text box value property:

```
=Sum(Fields!Sales.Value,"SalesDataset")
```

If a report has only one data set, the scope parameter does not need to be specified.

If you are in a data region, and you want to override the default group for an aggregate, simply give the group name you want or `Nothing` to specify the outermost grouping available.

With that out of the way, Table 8.4 provides a list of available aggregate functions.

TABLE 8.4 Aggregate Functions

Function Signature	Expression Type	Return Type	Description
`Aggregate (Expression, [Scope])`			Returns a custom aggregate of the specified expression, as defined by the data provider
`Avg(Expression, [Scope, [Recursive]])`	Float	Float	Returns the average of all nonnull values from the specified expression

TABLE 8.4 Continued

Function Signature	Expression Type	Return Type	Description
`Count(Expression, [Scope, [Recursive]])`	Object	Integer	Returns a count of all nonnull values of the specified expression
`CountDistinct(Expression, [Scope, [Recursive]])`	Object	Integer	Returns a count of all distinct values from the specified expression
`CountRows([Scope], [Recursive])`	N/A	Integer	Returns a count of rows within the specified scope
`First(Expression, [Scope])`	Object	Same as type of Expression	Returns the first value from the specified expression after all sorting has been applied to the data
`Last(Expression, [Scope])`	Object	Same as type of Expression	Returns the last value from the specified expression after all sorting has been applied to the data
`Max(Expression, [Scope, [Recursive]])`	Object	Same as type of Expression	Returns the maximum value from all nonnull values of the specified expression
`Min(Expression, [Scope, [Recursive]])`	Object	Same as type of Expression	Returns the minimum value from all nonnull values of the specified expression
`StDev(Expression, [Scope, [Recursive]])`	Integer or Float	Float	Returns the standard deviation of all nonnull values of the specified expression
`StDevP(Expression, [Scope, [Recursive]])`	Integer or Float	Float	Returns the population standard deviation of all nonnull values of the specified expression
`Sum(Expression, [Scope, [Recursive]])`	Integer or Float	Float, Decimal, or Double [1]	Returns a sum of the values of the specified expression
`Var(Expression, [Scope, [Recursive]])`	Integer or Float	Float, Decimal, or Double [1]	Returns the variance of all nonnull values of the specified expression
`VarP(Expression, [Scope, [Recursive]])`	Integer or Float	Float, Decimal, or Double [1]	Returns the population variance of all nonnull values of the specified expression

[1] *Depending on the type of expression*

An aggregate function can be used in expressions for any report item. Call syntax for the majority of aggregate functions is:

```
=Function(Expression,[Scope, [Recursive]])
```

This syntax indicates that both Scope and Recursive parameters can be omitted, but if Recursive is specified, then scope also has to be present. Aggregate functions cannot call other aggregate functions.

- **Expression**—A valid SSRS expression on which to perform the aggregation. The expression cannot contain aggregate functions.
- **Function**—A name of an aggregate function.
- **Recursive**—A modifier directing aggregate function to include aggregations from lower levels plus aggregation of the current level.
- **Scope**—String, the name of a dataset, grouping, or data region to which an aggregate function is applied.

Other Functions

Table 8.5 outlines additional scripting functions offered by SSRS. These functions don't directly aggregate or perform any other calculations on values.

TABLE 8.5 Additional Scripting Functions

Function Signature	Expression Type	Return Type	Description
`Previous(Expression, [Scope])`	Object	Same as type of Expression	Returns the previous instance (value) of the expression within specified scope.
`RowNumber(Scope)`	N/A	Integer	Returns a running count of all rows in the specified scope. Scope controls reset of the running value, when scope is equal to: Dataset—Running value is not reset throughout the entire data set. Group—Running value is reset on group expression change. Data region—Running value is reset for each new instance of the data region.
`RunningValue Expression, Function, [Scope])`	Determined by `Function` parameter	Determined by `Function` parameter	Uses a specified function to return a running aggregate of the specified expression. Same running value reset rules as for `RowNumber()` function. The expression cannot contain aggregate functions.

The RowNumber function can be used to change the background color of a table row: =IIf(RowNumber("DataSet1") Mod 2,"White","Gray").

This book covers two additional built-in functions InScope and Level in Chapter 12, "Grouping, Sorting, and Aggregating Data, Working with Scope."

Remember that in addition to built-in functions, developers can always write their own functions with custom code. If custom functions are used, the way to access the custom functions is by preceding the function name with "Code," for example, =Code.MyFunctionName().

Custom functions and assemblies are covered in Chapter 22.

Using Expressions to Change Report Item Properties and Behavior

Expressions are pretty basic in concept and exceptionally simple in implementation. They are the Swiss army knife in the report developer's toolbox. With the basics out of the way, it's time to create another report.

1. Open the AdventureWorks solution.
2. Add a new report called "Top SalesPeople."
3. Using the shared data source, create a data set using the following query:

```
SELECT TOP 5 C.LastName, C.FirstName, E.EmployeeID, SUM(SOH.SubTotal) AS SaleAmount
FROM         Sales.SalesPerson SP INNER JOIN
             HumanResources.Employee E ON SP.SalesPersonID = E.EmployeeID INNER JOIN
             Person.Contact C ON E.ContactID = C.ContactID INNER JOIN
             Sales.SalesOrderHeader SOH ON SP.SalesPersonID = SOH.SalesPersonID
➥INNER JOIN
             Sales.SalesOrderDetail SOD ON SOH.SalesOrderID = SOD.SalesOrderID
➥INNER JOIN
             Production.Product P ON SOD.ProductID = P.ProductID INNER JOIN
             Production.ProductSubcategory PS ON P.ProductSubcategoryID =
PS.ProductSubcategoryID INNER JOIN
             Production.ProductCategory PC ON PS.ProductCategoryID =
➥PC.ProductCategoryID
Group by  C.LastName, C.FirstName, E.EmployeeID
```

4. Name the data SalesDS.
5. In the layout section, add a table to the report and drop the last column. You should have two columns.
6. Drag the last name from the `Fields` collection in the toolbox, and drag the `SalesAmount` field from the data set onto the second column. Format the `SalesAmount` text box with the format string `c0`.
7. Change the header color to Red and text color to White. Make the font Bold.

This should give us a good starting point; see Figure 8.3.

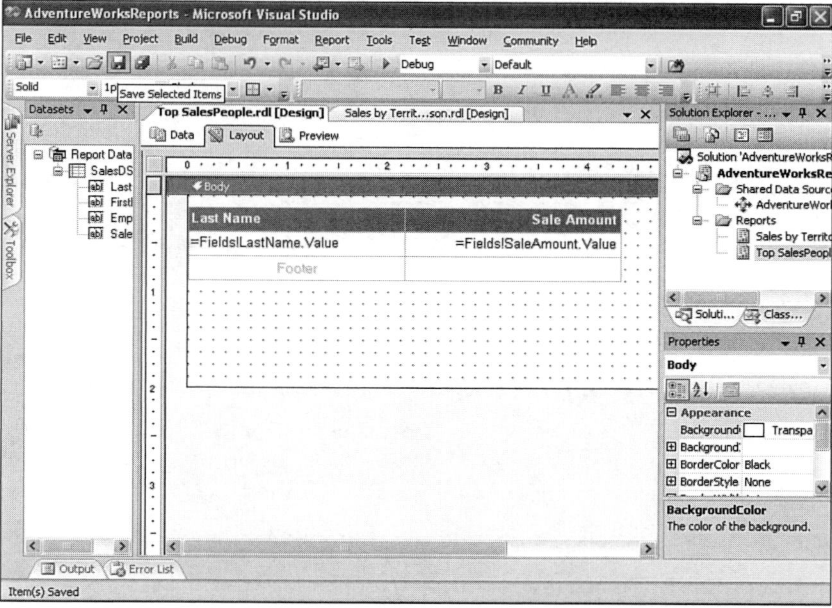

FIGURE 8.3 Layout view of Top SalesPeople report.

Select the table details row. On the `BackgroundColor` property, enter the following expression:

```
=iif(RowNumber("SalesDS") Mod 2,"Gray","White")
```

You should now be able to preview the alternating colors on each detail row, such as in Figure 8.4.

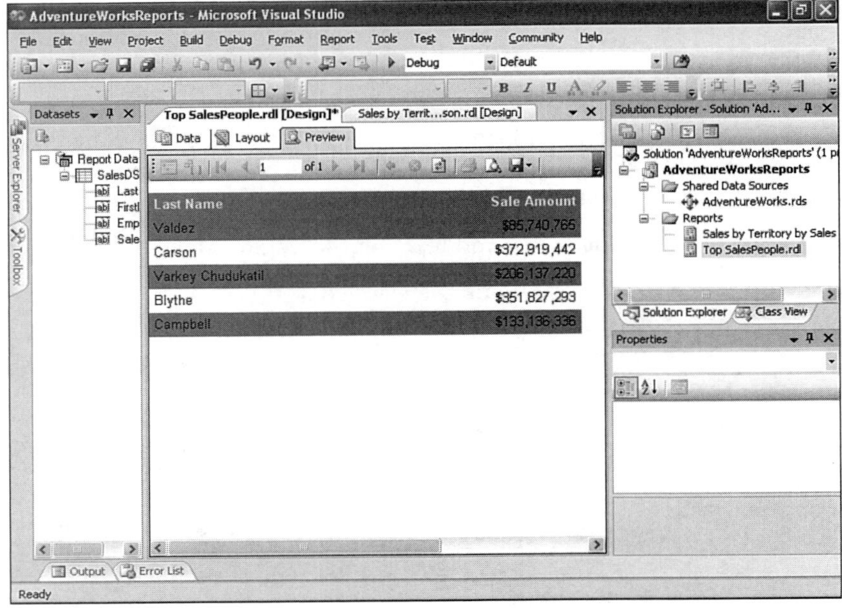

FIGURE 8.4 Resulting output after background color change.

Example: Placing Emphasis on Certain Values

Now suppose that you want to recognize salespeople with over $250,000 in sales. First, you need to sort the data. Next, you need to put emphasis on the people by changing the font color. The following steps allow you to do these things:

1. Select the table, right-click on it, and select Properties.
2. On the Sorting tab, place the following expression `=Fields!SaleAmount.Value` in the list box labeled "Sort On" underneath the Expression heading.
3. In the same list box, select Descending as the sort direction underneath the Direction heading.
4. Click OK.
5. Select the detail row on the table.
6. On the Color properties of the selected table row, place the following expressions `=IIf(Fields!SaleAmount.Value>=250000000,"Green","Black")`
7. Preview the report.

Summary

Expressions are one of the major components that make SSRS flexible, yet powerful. Using them, you can make decisions at runtime and base decisions on the data being returned. Expressions are derivatives of VB.NET, or they can be constants.

Expressions contain constants, variables, operators, collection members, and functions.

There are five major collections: `Globals`, `Fields`, `Parameters`, `ReportItems`, and `User`.

By combining these collections with either aggregate functions or any other kind of function, you can make powerful expressions that help to add a level of dynamism to reports.

Accessing Data

CHAPTER 9

IN THIS CHAPTER

- Data-Processing Extensions
- Types of Data Sources
- Connection Strings
- Querying Data
- Adding a Data Source

Chapters 9 and 10 look more closely at data sets, and takes a look at report parameters. The combination of these two items helps to add incredible flexibility to SSRS.

Parameters are values you can pass into the report to help make rendering decisions at runtime. Users can get prompted to input parameters at runtime. In combination with data sets, you can draw a list of valid values from your data sources. You can even make parameters dependent on each other in such a way that the lists of values for Parameter `B` are derived as a function of Parameter `A`.

As you have already seen, data sets contain the data that reports use, and they are critical to report processing. Data sets contain data sources that are pointers to the actual data store. They also contain the query that the data source will process. The end result of this is a list of fields that result from the processing of the query. To this, you can add your own calculated fields and apply filters. The result of this is a single set of rows and columns that is used in processing the report, or as a list of parameter values.

Data-Processing Extensions

The first thing created during the report development process is, usually, a data set. With that, a developer would select a source of data, create a query, and evaluate the quality of the data returned by the data set.

Data quality is something you, as the developer, must evaluate; however, the open-ended nature of SSRS helps tremendously by not putting any hard limits on the type of data you can use.

SSRS comes with the ability to connect to SQL Server, Analysis Services, Integration Services, Oracle, ODBC, OLE DB, and XML.

If these choices are not enough, it is possible to extend SSRS by writing a custom data-processing extension to be used within a data source. Extensions are covered in Chapter 26, "Writing Custom Reporting Services Extensions."

NOTE

To connect to SQL Server 6.5, use OLEDB.

Types of Data Sources

There are three types of data sources. The first type of data source is the embedded data source. This type is kept within the report, and cannot be accessed by other reports. In the SSRS documentation, this is referred to as a report-specific data source.

The second type of data source is the shared data source. The largest difference between the two data sources is location. A shared data source lives on the Report Server as a separate entity from the reports, whereas the definition for a report-specific data source is stored within the report itself.

This allows other reports to use them for their data sources.

The third type of data source is an expression that is used to dynamically choose the data source at runtime. This is called a data source expression. Remember that just about every property can be modified by an expression. Data sources are no different.

Report-Specific Data Source

The report-specific data source should only be used when the data needed to process a report should be restricted to that report. If multiple reports need to access the same data source with the same credentials, you should use a shared data source. This is because maintaining lots of embedded data sources can be cumbersome. After the report has been published to the Report Server, the embedded data source has to be maintained as part of that report. Then, you can change it to reference a shared data source.

Shared Data Source

A shared data source exists on the Report Server as a separate entity. Report developers can define a shared data source in Visual Studio, but it does not overwrite an existing data source by default in the same manner that it overwrites reports.

A shared data source is useful when

- Many reports use data from the same location with the same credentials.
- An administrator needs to have an easy way to change the location of a data source for several reports. This is the case, for example, when moving reports from development to production.

Data Source Expressions

An expression can be used to define the connection at runtime. A classic case is the difference between an active OLTP database and historical data or a data warehouse. Many companies store historical data that is more than six months old in a data warehouse. You would have to determine an appropriate connection from some report-level parameter.

Like all expressions, a data source expression would have to be written in Visual Basic.NET and preceded by an "=" sign.

To define data source expressions, consider the following guidelines:

- Do not use a shared data source. You cannot use a data source expression in a shared data source. You must define a report-specific data source for the report instead.
- Design the reports using a static connection string.
- Use a report parameter to specify the values to be passed to the expression. The parameter can pull from a list of valid values from a query using a separate data source. Later in this chapter, you will see how to set up parameter dependencies that allow you to do this.
- Make sure all the data sources implement the same schema.
- Before publishing the report, replace the static connection string with an expression.

It is easiest to use Windows authentication. This is because the Report Server stores data source credentials separately from the data sources themselves. Another option is to hard-code the credentials, or prompt a user for login credentials.

The following is an example of an expression-based data source for SQL Server:

```
="Data Source=" &Parameters!DBServer.Value & ";Initial Catalog=NorthWind
```

The preceding example assumes that there is a parameter called `DBServer`.

Connection Strings

Connection strings vary wildly by the type of processing extensions used in the data set. For example, if you use the OLEDB or ODBC process, you must specify the driver. For SQL Server, you should specify a database name, whereas for Oracle the database name is not required. For XML, just point it to the source by entering a URL in the connection string. In all cases, you should not specify the credentials used in accessing the data source inside the connection string. SSRS stores data source credentials separately.

NOTE

If you are developing with a fixed user ID and password for your data source credentials and you happen to use an embedded data source, the user ID and password will not carry over to the Report Server. This is because your machine and the Report Server will undoubtedly have different encryption keys.

The following are some common connection strings:

- SQL Server 2000 and above

```
Data source=MyServer\MyInstance,1433;Initial Catalog=Pubs
```

- Analysis Services (SQL 2005)

```
Data Source= MyServer\MyInstance,1433;initial catalog=AdventureWorksDW
```

- Analysis Services

```
provider=MSOLAP.2;data source=MyOLAP;initial catalog=AdventureWorksDW
```

- Oracle

```
Data Source=OracleSID
```

- XML via URL

```
URL="http://MyWebServer.com/Queryresults.aspx"
```

- XML via Web Service

```
URL=<url>; SOAPAction=<method-uri>[#¦/]<method-name>

URL=http://MyReportServer/reportserver/reportservice.asmx;
SOAPAction="http://schemas.microsoft.com/sqlserver/2004/05/reporting/
reportservices/ListChildren"
```

NOTE

When specifying XML as a data source, the credentials should be set to integrated security or "No credentials" for anonymous access. Anything else is ignored.

- SSIS Package

```
-f c:\packagename.dtsx
```

- SAP Connector

```
ashost=SAPAppServer client=000 snc_mode=1 sysnr=00 type=3 user=SAPDOTNET
snc_partnername=\"p:SAPAppServerServiceUser@adventureworks.com\";
```

NOTE

SAP Connector allows SSRS to connect and communicate with SAP Business Objects. SAP Connector is a separate download. Additional information can be found at http://www.microsoft-sap.com/overview_sap_connector.html and http://msdn2.microsoft.com/en-us/library/ms345256.aspx.

Querying Data

After a connection is established, your next step is to query the data source for the data intended. For most relational databases, this involves executing some type of SQL query against the catalog. In the case of Analysis Services, you use Multidimensional Expressions (MDX) queries, and for Data Mining, you use Data Mining Extensions (DMX) queries.

The Graphical Query Designer that comes with Report Designer aids developers in developing queries in any of the preceding languages. For more advanced queries, or in cases when the data source is not an RDBMS, the Generic Query Designer can be used.

Graphical Query Designer

The Graphical Query Designer is a tool to aid in the development of the query. Behind the scenes, it connects to the data store to pull tables and views. All you have to do is right-click on the top pane to add the table you want and select the columns. If the database has referential integrity, the Graphical Query Designer picks that up as well, and makes the necessary joins automatically. You can also join the tables by dragging columns from one table to the other.

Table 9.1 outlines the four panes in the Graphical Query Designer.

TABLE 9.1 Panes of Graphical Query Designer

Pane	Function
Diagram	Displays graphic representations of the tables in the query. Use this pane to select fields and define relationships between tables.
Grid	Displays a list of fields returned by the query. Use this pane to define aliases, sorting, filtering, grouping, and parameters.
SQL	Displays the Transact-SQL query represented by the Diagram and Grid panes. Use this pane to write or update a query using Transact-SQL query language.
Result	Displays the results of the query. To run the query, right-click in any pane, and then click Run.

Changing the diagram or grid affects the SQL and Results panes. For example, when you add a table to the diagram, it actually adds the table to the SQL query as it is being generated. This is a good way for users to actually learn SQL. Figure 9.1 shows the Graphical Query Designer.

Generic Query Designer

The Generic Query Designer is open ended. It is for times when you need more flexibility than the Graphical Query Designer allows. This is especially good for running multiple SQL statements to perform some preprocessing, or dynamic statements based on parameters or custom code. The Generic Query Designer is shown in Figure 9.2.

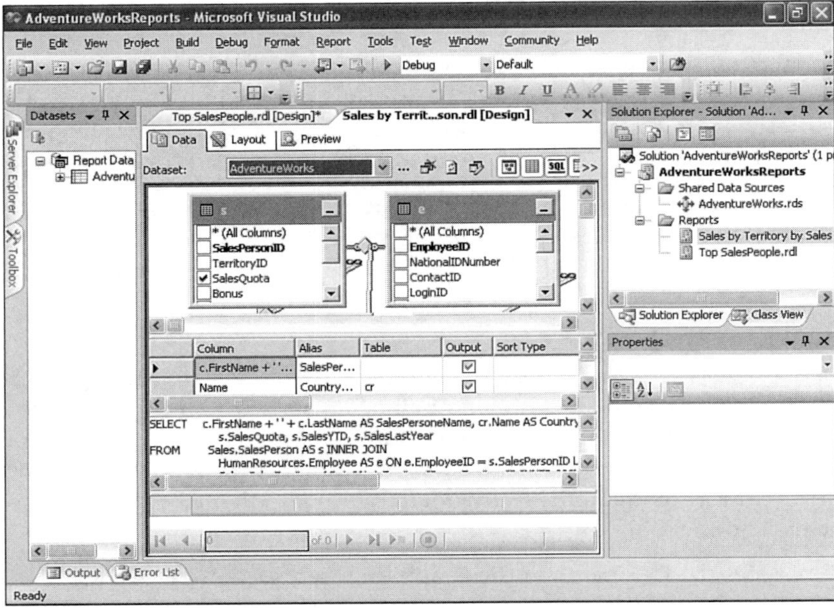

FIGURE 9.1 Graphical Query Designer.

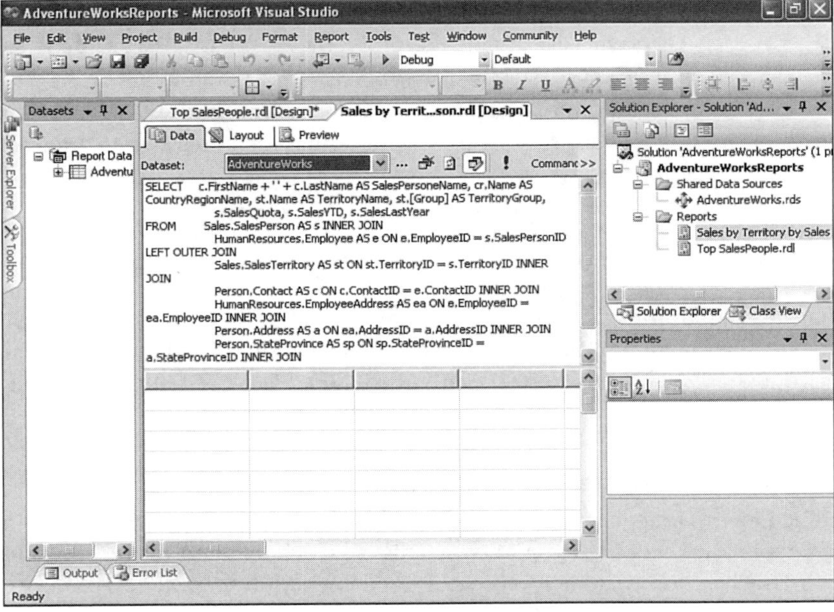

FIGURE 9.2 Generic Query Designer.

The data set contains a couple of properties of which developers should be mindful. They are as follows:

- The Name of the data set
- The Data Source or a pointer to a shared data source
- The Query String, which represents a query that retrieves data from the data source
- The Fields collections, which includes fields retrieved by the query and calculated fields
- The Query parameters (a parameter in a query string, such as `SELECT * FROM Address WHERE City = @City`) and Dataset/Parameters, which are used to limit selected data and must have matching parameters in each for proper report processing
- The Filters collection, which further filters result of the query inside of a Report Server after a data set returns data

Command Type

Command type is similar to the ADO.NET command type. It indicates the type of query that is contained in the query string and corresponding `CommandText` element of RDL. There are three values: `TableDirect`, `Text`, and `Stored Procedure`. `Text` provides for execution of a free-form (but, of course, valid) dynamic query. `Stored Procedure` corresponds to a stored procedure call. Finally `TableDirect` indicates that the value is the name of a table from which to retrieve data. All data from the table is returned.

NOTE

Not all the providers support all three values. For example, whereas OLEDB supports the `TableDirect` command type, the `Microsoft SQL Server (SqlClient)` provider does not. Thus, `TableDirect` is not shown as one of the choices for the `Microsoft SQL Server (SqlClient)` provider. Of course, `SELECT * FROM <Table>` would work just the same in the case of either provider.

Queries and Data Parameters

Most queries and stored procedures require inputting some type of parameter to return data. Take the following example:

```
Select * from Test_Table where Id = @Id
```

This is an example of a parameterized SQL on a fictitious table. Input parameters to stored procedures are another good example. So how does the data set give us this functionality?

The answer is in the Parameters collection. To be clear, this is separate from report parameters. Query parameters are used during the processing of the query, or select statement.

If a query parameter is specified, a value must be given to the parameter for the query to process. A report parameter is used during report processing to show different aspects of the data that can include, but are not limited to, query processing. If a T-SQL query includes query parameters, the parameters are created in a report automatically, and the values specified in the report parameters are passed along to the query parameter.

In the case of stored procedures, they are usually the inputs to them; see Figure 9.3. For plain SQL, they could be any variable.

FIGURE 9.3 An example of how the designer prompts you for the parameters.

The Report Designer automatically creates a report parameter with the same name as the query parameter. If there is already a parameter with the same name, it associates the two parameters. Figure 9.4 shows the association and where it is located in the UI.

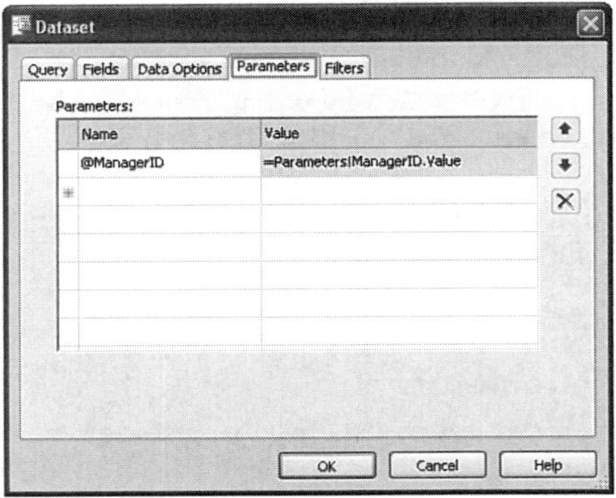

FIGURE 9.4 SQL and Report Parameter Association.

Stored procedures can be executed by changing the command type to `Stored Procedure` and entering the SQL statement. There is no reason for the `exec` clause. If a stored procedure has default values, that value can be passed through to the procedure by passing the query parameter the keyword `DEFAULT`.

The `Timeout` property sets a limit as to the amount of time the query can run. If left empty, the query can run indefinitely.

Querying XML *NEW IN 2005*

The ability to directly query XML as a data source is a new feature for SSRS 2005. Because querying XML is a little different than querying, it is worth noting some special requirements that are unique to using XML as a data source. They are as follows:

- Set XML as the data source type.
- Use a connection string that points to either the URL of a web services, web-based application, or XML document. XML documents from inside SQL Server cannot be used. Instead use xquery or xpath as a part of the query with SQL Server as the data source type.
- Use either Windows integrated security or no credentials. No other type of credentials are supported.
- Define the XML query using either element path, query element, or leave it empty.

The Generic Query Designer is the only way to create queries against XML. The Graphical Query Designer will not work. The good news is that developers can specify one of three types, as shown in Table 9.2.

TABLE 9.2 XML Query Types

XML Query Type	Description and Syntax
Element path	The element path specifies the path to the data to return without including namespaces. Syntax: ElementPath = XMLElementName [/ElementPath] XMLElementName = [NamespacePrefix:]XMLLocalName
Query element	The query element is similar to the element path, but it helps to define namespaces for the element path. Syntax: <Query xmlns:es="http://schemas.microsoft.com/StandardSchemas/ExtendedSales"> <ElementPath>/Customers/Customer/Orders/Order/es:LineItems/es:LineItem</ElementPath> </Query>
Empty	No query. It takes the first element path to a leaf node and applies it to the whole document. In the following document an empty query will default to: /Custs/Cust/Orders/Order: <Custs> <Cust ID=1>

TABLE 9.2 Continued

XML Query Type	Description and Syntax
Empty (continued)	<Name>Bob</Name> <Orders> <Order ID=1 Qty=6>Chair</Order> <Order ID=2 Qty=1>Table</Order> </Orders> <Returns> <Return ID=1 Qty=2>Chair</Order> </Returns> </Cust> <Cust ID=2> Name>Aaron</Name> </Cust> </Custs>

Fields

The result of processing the query is the Fields collection. As you run statements, you can click on the Refresh Fields button to update the fields in the data set.

There are two types of fields. The first and most obvious is the database fields. Database fields are the direct result of running the query. As you might have noticed, the field name automatically gets set to the field name as expressed by the query.

The second type of field is a calculated field. This is the result of using expressions or custom code to derive a value based on one of the database fields. For example, suppose you want to determine the percent of a quota a salesperson has met.

You can add a field to the data set and plug in this expression (see Figure 9.5):

```
=SalesYTD/SalesQuota * 100
```

A word of caution on calculated fields. The calculation is performed for every row brought back from the data set. If it is a large data set, this can be rather time consuming.

Fields and XML

In dealing with XML, every element along the element path and every attribute is returned as a field. All the fields are `String` data types. Some fields even include embedded XML.

Filters

At first, it might seem strange that you would need a filter at the data set level. After all, why would you need them, if you can simply modify the `WHERE` clause in the SQL? The dilemma comes when you need to run canned queries, such as stored procedures, or if you cannot pass in the appropriate value to filter inside the SQL.

A word of caution comes with this as well. It is much easier to filter at the database level than at the client level. Returning large data sets simply to filter it down to one or two rows on the Report Server is possible, but it might be an inefficient use of system resources.

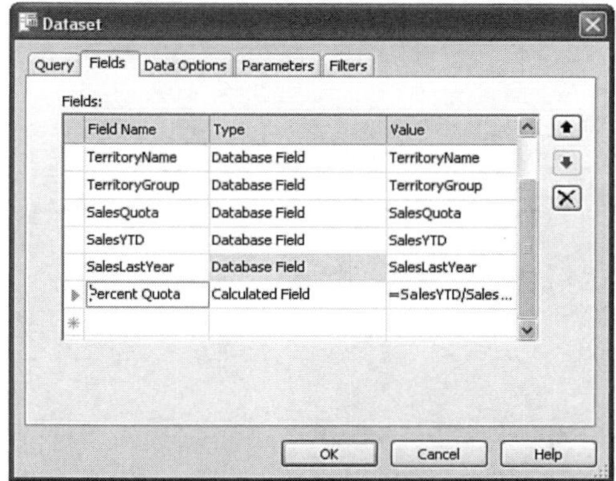

FIGURE 9.5 Adding a calculated field to a data set.

Adding a Data Source

If you have closed the AdventureWorksReport solution, reopen it. To create a data source, complete the following steps:

1. From Solution Explorer, click on the AdventureWorksReports project.
2. From the Project menu, select Add New Item.
3. In the Project Items list box that appears, select Data Source.
4. For the name, type "MyDS".
5. Select Microsoft SQL Server. By now, your screen should resemble Figure 9.6.
6. Enter the following connection string:

```
Data Source=(localhost);Initial Catalog=AdventureWorks
```

7. On the Credentials tab, select the Use Windows Authentication (Integrated Security) option, if necessary.
8. Click OK.

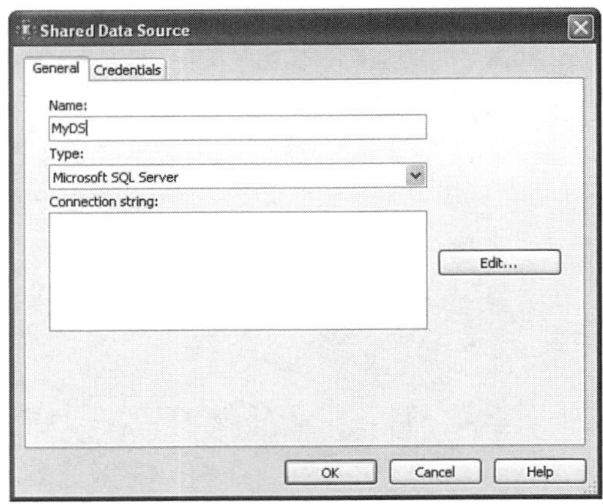

FIGURE 9.6 Creating a shared data source.

Summary

Data sources provide the report with a connection to the data. Data sets use the data source along with a query of some kind to produce a resultset that the rendering engine takes and uses to process the report.

Data sources can be either specific to a report or shared among many reports. SSRS can natively hook into SQL Server, Analysis Services, Integration Services, and Oracle. A number of other providers are supported through ADO.NET, and if a provider is not available, one can be custom developed. It is helpful from an administration point of view to use a shared data source whenever possible. An exception to this is when a data source needs specific credentials or elevated security.

Visual Studio offers two query designers—the Graphical Query Designer and the Generic Query Designer. SSRS leaves the processing of the query to the data source. After the data source is finished processing the data, it generates a data set, which is a collection of fields inside of rows. Calculated fields can be added to the data set at design time to augment the returned results. Filters can also be applied to the resulting data sets. Both filters and fields are applied on a row-by-row basis and, if not used carefully, can lead to performance problems.

Parameters can either be static or bound to data sets. The value of certain parameters can also be passed in as input to a query. The output of that query can be used as the list of values for a parameter, in effect creating a dependency between parameters and data sets. This dependency can be used in many different ways to affect the data used in the final data set processed.

CHAPTER 10

Report Parameters

IN THIS CHAPTER

- Setting Up Parameters
- Parameter Properties
- Data-Driven Parameters
- Parameters and Data Sources
- Expressions with Parameters
- Dynamic SQL with Parameters
- Parameter Dependencies
- Example Using MultiSelect

Report-level parameters can serve a number of functions, including the following:

- Manipulating report data
- Connecting related reports together
- Varying report layout and presentation

Parameters are used to pass information to a report to influence report processing. For example, a parameter can serve as a condition in a `WHERE` of a query that generates the report's data set. Parameters are relatively easy to set up and are very flexible.

Report parameters can be presented to the user in four ways, as shown in Table 10.1.

Parameters can also be hidden from the user. Although this might sound strange at first, hidden parameters can be used to alter report processing based on the input from other parameters, or based on the result from a data set.

TABLE 10.1 Parameter Presentation Options

Control	Number of Values	Control over Values
Text box	1	No
Drop-down	1	Yes
Multiselect	1-N	Yes
Radio list	1	Yes (for Boolean parameters only)

Setting Up Parameters

You can set up parameters from the Report Designer by selecting Report and then Report Parameters from the menu. The initial screen looks similar to Figure 10.1.

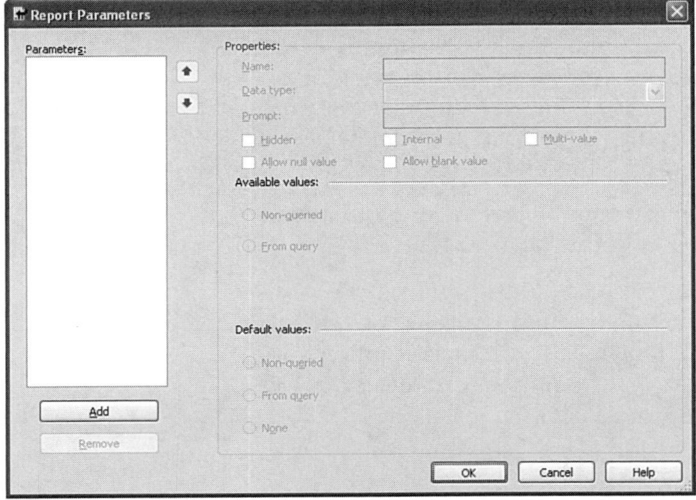

FIGURE 10.1 Report parameters.

Parameter Properties

Table 10.2 outlines several properties of parameters.

TABLE 10.2 Parameter Properties

Property Name	Expected Value	Description
Name	String	The actual and unique name of the parameter within the scope of the report. This is what the parameter is referred to when referencing it in the Globals collection.

TABLE 10.2 Continued

Property Name	Expected Value	Description
Parameter Type	Enum : String (default), Integer, DateTime, Boolean, Float	The data type in which to expect the parameter. It defaults to string, but you can choose a different data type from the drop-down list. If the report parameter values come from a query, the return type for the query must match the type specified here. Because .NET CLR is a strongly typed system, SSRS is as well. It returns an error if a string is passed in for what is supposed to be a number value. For a Boolean value, the Report Server simply creates a radio button list with true/false as the only options.
Prompt	String	A friendly message to pass to the user who enters the parameter data. If it is left empty, and a default value is specified for the parameter, the user is not asked to input the value because the report will use the defaulted value. If the prompt is empty, and no default value is specified, the report will not run.
MultiValue	Boolean	New in SSRS 2005; this option allows you to select multiple values by checking check boxes in a drop-down list, instead of displaying a single text box or drop-down list.
Hidden	Boolean	The value of this should not appear in the report, but it can still be set at runtime.
Internal	Boolean	A parameter that cannot be changed at runtime. A consumer of a published report will never see this as a parameter.
Allow Null	Boolean	A parameter that can have a null value.
Allow Empty string	Boolean	An empty string is a valid value.

Later on in the chapter, you will walk through creating report parameters. For now, all you need to know is that to create parameters, simply click the Add button in the Report Parameters dialog box and simply fill in the values.

Data-Driven Parameters

Report parameter values can be driven from a list of valid values. This list can come from a data set. Under Available Values, simply add a list of values for the values to remain hard-coded in the RDL. If you want to drive them from a data source, select From Query. The screen should look similar to Figure 10.2.

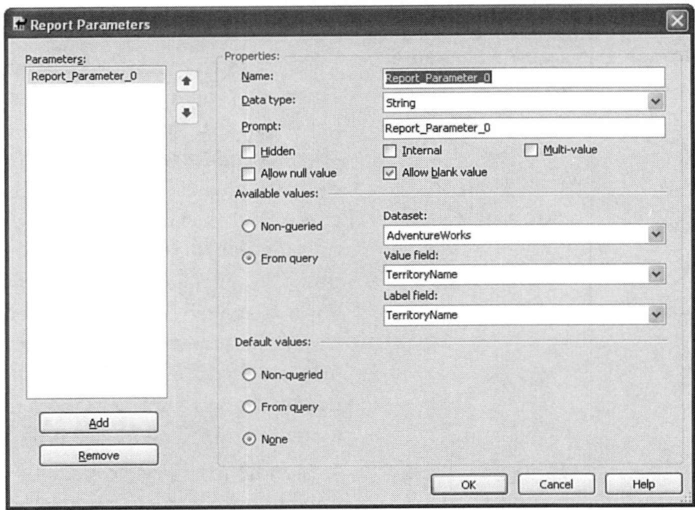

FIGURE 10.2 Query parameter values.

The same holds true for the default values. They can be either data-driven through the same mechanism or hard-coded within the RDL.

The label is the value displayed to the user, whereas the value is the value passed back to the Report Server. For example, this is useful in a query parameter in which you want the user to select a familiar name from a drop-down list, yet the query expects the ID.

Parameters and Data Sources

If a data source is set to prompt the user for an ID and password, two more parameters are created at runtime for the data source. Because they are created at runtime, they do not show up in the Report Parameters dialog box. The only way to find the names is by making a web service call to the Report Server. Report Server web service calls are explained in more detail in Chapter 25, "How to Use Reporting Services Web Services." This does not preclude them from being passed in via a URL; however, this is not recommended because the user ID and password would be in clear text.

Expressions with Parameters

Up to this point, we have only talked about parameters within queries or queries being used as a source for data in parameters. Because the parameter collection is part of the Globals collection, you can use a parameter anywhere in the report.

For example, suppose you have a parameter called `Emphasis`. Its values come from a predefined list of controls within the report. The intention is to change the font style from normal to bold if the value of the parameter is set to the name of the control.

The following expression on the bold property of a fictitious `Location` control does exactly that:

```
=IIF(Parameters!Emaphasis.Value="Location",True,False)
```

Taking this a step further, you can change the visible property or any of the other properties in any report item. This allows you to use parameters in all sorts of ways not necessarily related to the data retrieved for a report.

Dynamic SQL with Parameters

So far, you have seen how parameters can be passed onto query values, but can you rearrange the whole query with parameters? The answer is yes.

Believe it or not, the query is just an expression like any other expression. By default, it is evaluated as a constant string, but with the use of parameters and custom code blocks, you can make the query behind the report dynamic. There is a catch to all that flexibility. You must return the same number of columns with the same names no matter what the query.

A good example of this is in the `ORDER BY` or `GROUP BY` clause within a query. Although any of the controls can sort or group the results of a data set by any column, they are limited in speed and capacity of the Report Server. By contrast, most databases are built for exactly this sort of thing, and with the effective use of indexes, a lot of spare CPU cycles can be recovered.

To make a dynamic query, open the Generic Query Designer and type in an expression that evaluates to a query. The following is an example that uses the `Emphasis` parameter used previously:

```
="select * from test_tb order by " & Parameters!Emaphasis.Value
```

You could also declare this in a custom code block:

```
Function fnGetSql(Byval parameter as String) as String
Return "select * from test_tb order by " & Parameters!Emaphasis.Value
End Function
```

And call it like this:

```
=Code.fnGetSql(Parameters!Emaphasis.Value)
```

Parameter Dependencies

You can make parameter values dependent on other parameters. The trick to doing this is to derive the list of values from a data set. That data set must use the parent parameter to get its data.

For example, suppose you have two parameters `A` and `B`. Parameter `B`'s values are queried from `DataSetB`. `DataSetB` needs a value from Parameter `A` to process. From the user's perspective, the second parameter (Parameter `B`) does not display until a value is passed in from Parameter `A` and `DataSetB` gets processed.

Example Using MultiValue *NEW in 2005*

Let's use a parameter to modify the `Top SalesPeople.rdl` report to include product categories and subcategories. First create a new report called "Top SalesPeople by Category."

1. Add the following data sets using the AdventureWorks data source.
2. Name the data set TopEmployees.
3. Use the following query:

```
SELECT TOP 5 C.LastName, C.FirstName, E.EmployeeID, SUM(SOH.SubTotal) AS SaleAmount
FROM         Sales.SalesPerson SP INNER JOIN
             HumanResources.Employee E ON SP.SalesPersonID = E.EmployeeID INNER JOIN
             Person.Contact C ON E.ContactID = C.ContactID INNER JOIN
             Sales.SalesOrderHeader SOH ON SP.SalesPersonID = SOH.SalesPersonID
➥ INNER JOIN
             Sales.SalesOrderDetail SOD ON SOH.SalesOrderID = SOD.SalesOrderID
➥ INNER JOIN
             Production.Product P ON SOD.ProductID = P.ProductID INNER JOIN
             Production.ProductSubcategory PS ON P.ProductSubcategoryID =
➥ PS.ProductSubcategoryID INNER JOIN
             Production.ProductCategory PC ON PS.ProductCategoryID =
➥ PC.ProductCategoryID
WHERE        PC.ProductCategoryID in (@ProductCategory) AND
➥ PS.ProductSubcategoryID in (@ProductSubcategory)
GROUP BY     C.LastName, C.FirstName, E.EmployeeID, PC.ProductCategoryID,
➥ PS.ProductSubcategoryID
order by SUM(SOH.SubTotal) desc
```

4. Create two more data sets from the following:
   - Data Set Name: ProductCategory
   - Query:

     ```
     SELECT DISTINCT ProductCategoryID, Name
     FROM         Production.ProductCategory
     ORDER BY     Name
     ```

   - DataSet Name: SubCategory

- Query:

```
SELECT      ProductSubcategoryID, ProductCategoryID, Name
FROM        Production.ProductSubcategory
WHERE       ProductCategoryID in (@ProductCategory)
```

These two data sets will not return any data without specifying the values for the query parameters. This should not stop the field list from displaying the Datasets window.

5. Switch to Layout view.
6. Drag a table control from the toolbox over to the report's Layout window.
7. From the Datasets tab in the toolbox, drag LastName, FirstName, and SaleAmount from the TopEmployees data set into the table columns.
8. Format SaleAmount with the format string c0.
9. Go to the Report menu and select Report Parameters.
10. There should be two parameters. Change the prompt on ProductCategory to Category and change the data type to Integer. Check the Multi-value option.
11. Under Available Values, check the From Query option.
12. Select Product Category for the data set.
13. Change the Value field to ProductCategoryID and the Label field to Name.
14. Select the ProductSubcategory parameter.
15. Change the data type to Integer.
16. Change the prompt to Subcategory, and check the Multi-value option.
17. Under Available Values, check the From Query option.
18. Select the Subcategory data set. Enter SubCategoryId for the value and Name for the label.
19. Click OK.
20. Preview the report by clicking the Preview tab of the Report Designer.

NOTE

As you have probably noticed, the report-processing engine was clever enough to properly place comma-separated multiple parameter values in the `WHERE` clause. If you are writing expressions, the multivalue parameters can be accessed like an array: `=Parameters!ProductCategory.Value(0)` .

Summary

Over the course of this chapter, you have learned what report parameters are and how they can be used. This includes their use in queries or in expressions that can be used throughout the report.

Parameters allow for dynamism by adding user input to the report-rendering process. A number of parameter options as well as a number of ways SSRS prompts the user are available using familiar controls. Parameters can be data-driven, or they can have a static list of valid values.

After being entered, a parameter can be used as a parameter for a data set's query or anywhere within the report as a part of an expression.

SSRS 2005 adds multivalued parameters that can be used in the `WHERE` clause of a data set query (`WHERE PC.ProductCategoryID in (@ProductCategory)`) or within an expression (`=Parameters!ProductCategory.Value(0)`).

Working with Report Items

CHAPTER 11

IN THIS CHAPTER

- Data Regions, Containers, and Independent Report Items
- Report Designer's Toolbox
- Line Report Item
- Rectangle Report Item
- Image Report Item
- Textbox Report Item
- Table Report Item
- List Report Item
- Practical Application of Report Items
- Matrix Report Item
- Chart Report Item
- Practical Application of Chart and Matrix
- Report Body Versus Page Header/Footer

Now that the book has covered what is necessary to retrieve data, let's move on to designing reports. This chapter goes into the Toolbox (literally and figuratively) and discusses the various controls used for building reports and the resulting RDL. Toward the end of the chapter, we will generate a couple of reports.

Presentation elements in SSRS are called report items. These include: Table, Matrix, List, Chart, Textbox, Image, Line, Rectangle, and Subreport.

Report items are very similar to visual controls available in Visual Studio languages, such as Visual Basic or C#. This book introduced you to report items in Chapter 2, "Reporting Services Capabilities: Presentation, Navigation, and Programmability." This chapter provides more details on each of these items.

You might have noticed that the set of report items did not change in SSRS 2005. However, Microsoft has expanded the capabilities of report items, and some items can now do more. For example, the Textbox in SSRS 2005 provides interactive sorting capabilities.

Data Regions, Containers, and Independent Report Items

Report items (or presentation elements) in SSRS can be categorized as data regions (items that must be associated with data sets), containers (items that can contain other items), and independent report items. Some items can belong to more than one category.

Independent report items are items other than data regions. Textbox, Image, Line, Rectangle, and Subreport are independent report items. Independent report items do not have to be associated with any data sources.

Data regions function as a repetitive display of rows, groups of rows, or columns from a data set associated with a region. Table, Matrix, List, and Chart are data regions. In addition, data regions support grouping and sorting of displayed information. For more details of grouping and sorting, see Chapter 12, "Grouping, Sorting, and Aggregating Data, Working with Scope." All of the data regions, except Chart are also containers.

Containers, as the name implies, can contain any reporting items, including containers and data regions. Table, Matrix, List, Rectangle, Report Body, Page Header, and Page Footer are containers. Items placed in a container become the container's children and the container becomes the parent. As a result, the `Parent` property of each child item is populated with the name of a container. All children move together with the container when the container is moved. When the container is deleted, all children are deleted. The container is fixed when the position of a report item within this container is fixed. For example, a Table is a fixed container because the position of each cell is fixed. Most, but not all, of the containers are also data regions. Thus, data regions can be nested within other data regions.

TIP

If you delete a container by mistake, you can easily undo this action using the Edit, Undo menu or by using the Ctrl+Z keyboard shortcut. For the shortcut to work properly, the focus of the action should be the `ReportName.rdl[Design]` (Data or Layout tabs) or `ReportName.rdl[XML]` window.

From the perspective of RDL, the container has a `<ReportItems>` section, which is used to specify the beginning of a container for report items.

For example, Table 11.1 shows the RDL of a Rectangle that contains a single Line. The graphical presentation of this RDL is shown in Figure 11.1.

TABLE 11.1 Rectangle's RDL Explained

RDL Fragment	Explanation
`<Rectangle Name="rectangle1">`	Opening RDL/XML tag indicating beginning of the Rectangle item.

`<Left>0.375in</Left>`
`<Height>1in</Height>`
`<Top>0.25in</Top>`
`<Width>2in</Width>`
`<ZIndex>1</ZIndex>`
	`Left` and `Top`—Coordinates of the left end of an item. `Width` and `Height`—Relative position of the right end of an item. `Height=0in` or not included indicates horizontal line. `Width=0in` or not included indicates vertical line. `ZIndex`—Drawing order. In case of overlapping items, an item with a higher number covers an item with a lower number.
	`ZIndex`, `Left`, `Top`, `Width`, and `Height` are abbreviated as `{POSITION}` in the future discussion.

LISTING 11.1 Continued

RDL Fragment	Explanation
<ReportItems>	Beginning of a container for report items. To simplify further discussion, one or many items in the <ReportItems> section are abbreviated as {ITEMS}.
<Line Name="line1">	Beginning of the line item.
<Left>0.5in</Left> <Top>0.25in</Top> <Width>1in</Width><Height> 0.5in</Height> <ZIndex>1</ZIndex>	{POSITION} see explanation above. Note: ZIndex numbering starts anew within each container. The ZIndex tag is not shown in the future RDL code samples unless attempting to pinpoint an explicit element of the style.
<Style> <BorderColor> <Default>Blue</Default> </BorderColor> <BorderWidth> <Default>5pt</Default> </BorderWidth> <BorderStyle> <Default>Solid</Default> </BorderStyle> </Style>	Style—Style of an item, such as color and width. More details on style are in Chapter 13, "Advanced Report Formatting." Report Designer inserts an empty tag, even if no style is specified. The style tag is not shown in the future RDL code samples unless attempting to pinpoint an explicit element of the style.
</Line>	Closing tag indicating the end of the Line item.
</ReportItems>	Closing tag indicating the end of the container.
<Style> <BorderStyle> <Default>Solid</Default> </BorderStyle> </Style>	
</Rectangle>	Closing tag indicating the end of the Rectangle item.

Report Designer's Toolbox

The Toolbox window provides a convenient drag-and-drop interface for all report items. The Toolbox can be opened, closed, hidden, docked, or can float within Report Designer. If the Toolbox is closed, it can be opened through the View, Toolbox menu or by pressing the Ctrl+Alt+X keyboard combination.

If the Toolbox is hidden, the designer can click the Toolbox tab on the left of the BI Studio interface or mouse over the tab.

To add a report item to a report using the Report Designer, you can either drag and drop a report item from the Toolbox or copy a report item from the same or another report. Another method is to right-click on any report item in the Toolbox, and then click on the report body on the Layout tab. A less-common approach is to edit the RDL file by hand, but this is not recommended by Microsoft within the context of Report Designer.

Line Report Item

Line is, perhaps, the simplest report item and can be placed anywhere on a report. Line does not display any data values and serves as a decoration and navigation item. When used for navigation, a line can carry a bookmark or a label. Navigation is discussed in more detail in Chapter 14, "Report Navigation."

The RDL of the line is defined with the `<Line>` tag. Figure 11.1 demonstrates Line and Rectangle items.

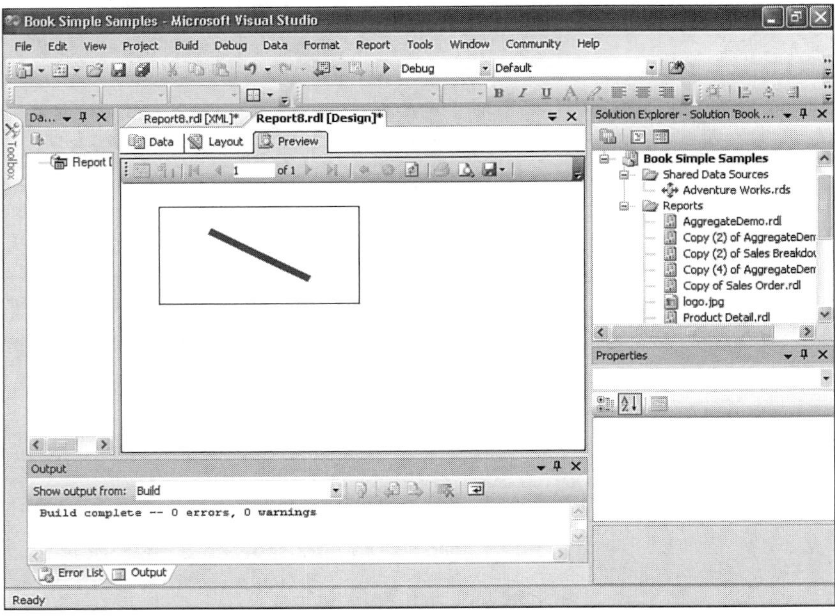

FIGURE 11.1 Line and Rectangle items.

Rectangle Report Item

Rectangle is a graphical element that can provide three functions: decoration, container, and navigation. When used for navigation, a line can carry a bookmark or a label.

Rectangle by itself is not able to display any data values and can be placed anywhere on a report. Because the Rectangle is a container, it can contain other report items, including other containers and data regions. The RDL of the Rectangle is defined with the `<Rectangle>` tag.

Image Report Item

Image report item, as the name implies, is designed to display an image. SSRS supports `.bmp`, `.jpg`, `.jpe`, `.gif`, and `.png` image formats. An image can be embedded in a report, stored as a part of the project, stored in a database, or loaded from a URL.

You can add an image to a report in several ways. The most common is to drag an Image report item from the Toolbox and drop it onto a report (or generally on any container item). Report Designer displays the Image Wizard with the window shown in Figure 11.2. To see the window, click the Next button on the Welcome screen at the drop completion.

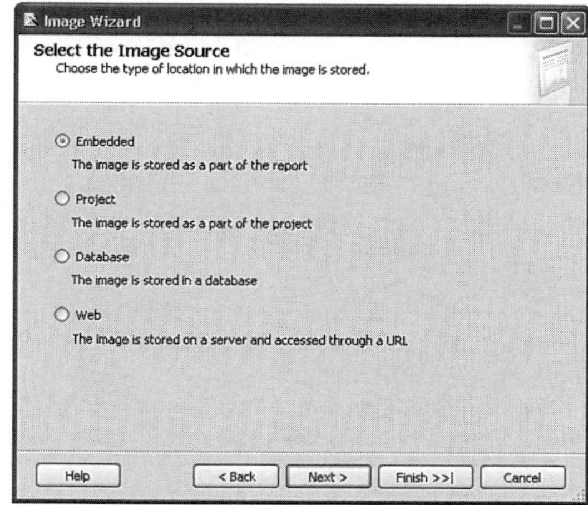

FIGURE 11.2 Selecting the Image Source window.

The Image Source window, as the name implies, allows you to select the source of the image. If you select Embedded or Project, Report Designer shows a window similar to Figure 11.3.

Report Designer assigns the name `logo` to an image with the filename `logo.jpg`. You can change the name, if you want, just make sure to click on a cell different from the one that contains the name of the image to commit the change.

Understanding the underlying difference between embedded and project images will help you to understand differences in the handling of those images. An embedded image is actually a MIME-encoded image, stored as text in the report definition file.

An embedded image is stored in the RDL file and rendered during the render process.

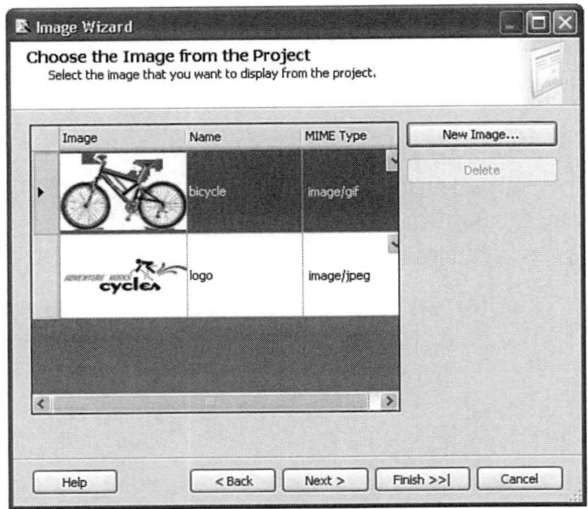

FIGURE 11.3 Choosing the image from the project.

A project image is a file that first gets added as an item to a project (and copied as a file to the project's directory from an original location) and then gets published as a resource file to a Report Server.

NOTE

In addition to using the Image Wizard described previously, you can add a project image by dragging and dropping a graphical file on the project in Solution Explorer or by adding an image from the Add Existing Item menu. You can access the Add Existing Item menu from the Project menu or from the drop-down Add menu in Solution Explorer.

Both embedded and project image selection dialog boxes allow adding several images with the same name.

For example, for images from the file `logo.jpg`, Report Designer adds images **`logo`**, **`logo_1`**, and so on. Report Designer does not compare encoded images in a report to determine if there is a duplication, thus Report Designer adds more embedded images with the same content, automatically incrementing the name.

The Project image selection dialog box behaves similarly until you save changes. When saving changes, Report Designer eliminates duplicates and adds only a single file `logo.jpg` to a project.

Technically, there is no reason to keep duplicates whether the image is embedded or project-level. Because the project-level image is saved as a file, there could be only one file with the specific name.

NOTE

As you are using the Image Wizard (starts when you drag and drop an Image control on a report), please note image's `Source` and `Value` properties.

You can modify `Source` and `Value` properties to change the source of an image.

The Delete button in the Image Selection dialog box of the Image Wizard is disabled for the existing embedded or project-level images. The Delete button is available only for new (added during the wizard's session) images before the addition is finalized.

You can delete or rename project-level images through Solution Explorer.

You can add, delete, or rename embedded images through the Embedded Images dialog box, which can be accessed through the Report, Embedded Images menu. Alternatively, you can edit an RDL file of a report to delete or rename embedded images.

Embedded images insert character-encoded information in the RDL file. `{MIME}` indicates graphical format of the image, for example `image/jpg`.

```
<EmbeddedImages>
    <EmbeddedImage Name="logo">
      <ImageData>{Character encoded binary Data}</ImageData>
       <MIMEType>{MIME}</MIMEType>
    </EmbeddedImage>
</EmbeddedImages>
```

The RDL for an Image can be broken down into the sections shown in Table 11.2.

TABLE 11.2 Image's RDL Explained

Element	Explanation
`<Image Name="image1"> {POSITION}`	Open tag and image's position on a report.
`<Source>{SOURCE}</Source>` `<MIMEType>{MIME}</MIMEType>`	`{SOURCE}`—The location of the image on a report. `{SOURCE}` can be `Embedded`, `Database`, or `External` (this is for either `Project` or `Web` images). `{MIME}`—A graphical format of the image.
`<Value>{EXPRESSION}</Value>`	`{EXPRESSION}`—An expression that evaluates to an image name or a constant. For example, an `{EXPRESSION}` could be `logo` for an embedded image, `logo.gif` for a project-level image, `=Fields!ProductImage. Value` for a database image, or URL http://sc.msn.com/ global/c/lgpos/ MSFT_pos.gif for a web-based image.
`</Image>`	Closing tag.

Textbox Report Item

Textbox displays all text, including textual representation of numeric data on the report. A standalone text box should always be used to display a single expression. The name of a report is an example of such an expression. The expression in this case is a constant string.

An individual text box can be placed anywhere on a report and can include almost any expression. However, expressions that will work in a text box can be limited by a container. For example, a report's page footer does not allow the Fields collection and, thus, expressions that use the Fields collection cannot be used within a text box located in the page footer.

If the data set associated with a report contains multiple rows and the following expression is used, only the last value is displayed. For example, the following expression will display the last product name in the data set:

```
=Fields!ProductName.Value
```

Aggregate functions, such as `First`, `Maximum`, `Minimum`, and `Average`, can be used to access other values. More information about aggregate functions can be found in Chapter 12. In addition, conditional functions can be used to display a value matching a certain condition. However, default SSRS functionality does not allow you to access the data set's fields by index.

Textbox is denoted by the `<Textbox>` tag and in a simple case has the following RDL:

```
<Textbox Name="textbox1">
   {POSITION}
   <Value>=Fields!ProductName.Value</Value>
</Textbox>
```

The `<Value>` tag needs to be present for a text box's RDL to be valid; it can also be empty, such as `<Value />` or `<Value></Value>`.

Table Report Item

Table presents data with static columns and expands row by row. Table allows you to group (a table can have multiple groups) and sort rows of data. See Chapter 12 for more details.

Table has the best performance of all data regions. A cell in a table is a text box by default, but can be replaced with any other SSRS item, such as an image. A default table placed on a report contains three rows and three columns.

You can interact with row, group, and column handles within the Report Designer interface to adjust table layout. If handles on the designer window are not visible, click on any cell within the table. Adjustment is very similar to that in Microsoft Excel and can be done by dragging adjustor lines or specifying `Height` and `Width` properties. See Figure 11.4 for design-time view of a table in Report Designer.

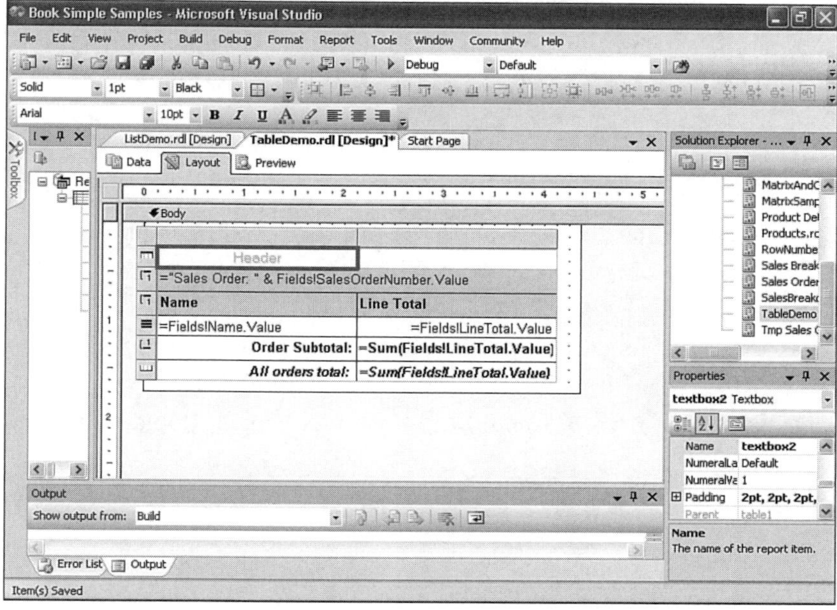

FIGURE 11.4 Design-time view of a table.

Each row on a table can be deleted or an additional row of the same type can be inserted. For example, a table can have multiple table detail, table header, table footer, group header, and group footer rows.

To add an additional group header row, click on a row handle and select `Insert Row Above` or `Insert Row Below` from the drop-down menu. You can delete a row in a similar fashion. For example, Figure 11.4 demonstrates an empty space created by a retained table header row. To remove a row, right-click on the row handle and select Delete Rows from the shortcut menu.

It is possible to first delete all rows of a certain type, such as table header. To reverse this operation, consult the following list, which shows a set of procedures for different types of rows:

- For table header, footer, or detail rows, right-click on any row handle and select Table Header, Table Footer, or Table Detail from the shortcut menu.
- For a group that has at least one group header or group footer left, right-click on any header or footer row and select Edit Group from the shortcut menu. When the Grouping and Sorting Properties dialog box is displayed, check an appropriate text box to include a group header or footer or both. This book discusses more details about grouping in Chapter 12.
- For a group that does not have any rows left on a table (yes, it is possible to have a group that has no rows displayed), click on the table's corner handle and then

right-click on the table to bring up the Table Properties dialog box. Select the Groups tab. Select and edit the group to bring up the Grouping and Sorting Properties dialog box. Check an appropriate text box to include a group header or footer or both.

To add data to a table in a simple scenario, you can drag and drop to a table's cell field from the Datasets window (which, in turn, drops a text box) or any report item to a cell. When the first field is dropped on a table, Report Designer sets the table's Dataset property to match the name of the data set from which the field came.

As you can see in Figure 11.4, a row that displays subtotal information is the group footer. This book discusses more details of grouping in Chapter 12. In addition to subtotals, a table has header and footer rows for calculation of total numbers.

A simple one-cell Table RDL is broken down into components in Table 11.3.

TABLE 11.3 Table's RDL Explained

Element	Explanation
<Table Name="table1"> {POSITION}	Opening tag and table's position on a report.
{ROW TYPE TAG}	Type of a row. Depending on the type of the row (see design picture), this could be either <Details>, <Header>, or <Footer>.
<TableRows>	Table can contain multiple rows of each type.
<TableRow> <Height>0.25in</Height>	Row definition. If the table has a single row, the height is equal to the height of the table. If the developer specified a value for this table's Height property, the entire table is sized, proportionally reducing or increasing the height of each row.
<TableCells> <TableCell> {ITEMS} </TableCell> </TableCells>	Cell definition. Each table cell could be any report item.
</TableRow> </TableRows> {CLOSING ROW TYPE TAG} <Style />	Closing tags. {CLOSING ROW TYPE TAG} could be either </Details>, </Header>, or </Footer>.
<TableColumns> <TableColumn> <Width>2.16667in</Width> </TableColumn> </TableColumns> </Table>	Collection of columns. If the table has a single column, this is equal to the width of the table.

TIP

When possible, use a table for best report performance.

Multiple adjacent table cells can be merged horizontally into a single cell across multiple columns. Unlike Excel or Microsoft Word, SSRS table cells cannot be merged vertically even across the same type of rows, such as a detail row. Report Designer only preserves data from the first cell. Data in other merged cells is discarded. Report Designer allows you to split back to the original columns.

To merge or split cells, select the cells, right-click the selection, and then select Merge Cells or Split Cells, respectively, from the shortcut menu (see Figure 11.5). Alternatively, Report Designer provides a toolbar button to perform this operation. The toolbar button icon is the same as the icon on the menu.

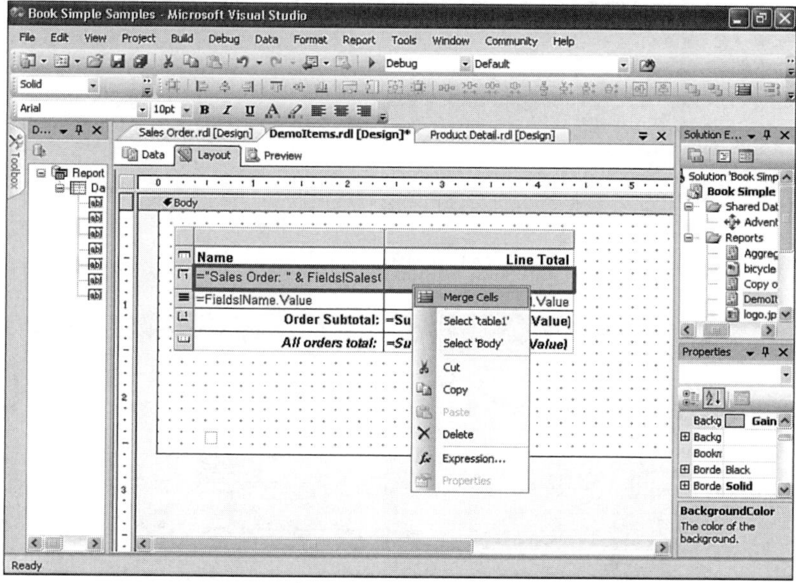

FIGURE 11.5 Merging table cells.

List Report Item

List is designed to present data in a free-form fashion for complex repeating areas. List repeats items for each row of the associated data set. List allows you to group and sort rows of data. A single list can have only a single group, but lists can be nested within each other to provide multiple grouping.

A list or, more precisely, a nested set of lists has the same overall capabilities as a table. Examples `TableDemo` and `ListDemo` that are included in the samples for this book demonstrate how both a table and a list can produce the identical rendered result. However,

Table report item has better performance and you should almost always choose a table when possible.

In some cases, report developers might find List to be very useful for complex formatting. In such cases, using a table might no longer provide an elegant solution. One of the examples in which List can be used is check printing. List allows you to position items in a free-form fashion and allows for an elegant design.

List is described with the following RDL. This RDL contains an optional group expression: `=Fields!SalesOrderNumber.Value`.

```
<List Name="list1">
{POSITION}
{ITEMS}
  <DataSetName>DataSet1</DataSetName>
  <Style />
  <Grouping Name="list1_Details_Group">
    <GroupExpressions>
      <GroupExpression>
=Fields!SalesOrderNumber.Value</GroupExpression>
    </GroupExpressions>
  </Grouping>
</List>
```

An example of a list is shown in Figure 11.6.

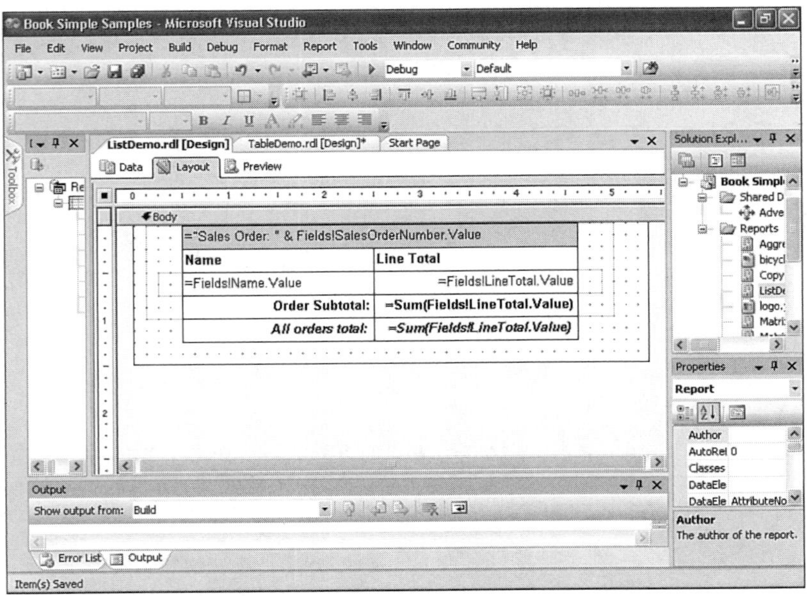

FIGURE 11.6 Design-time picture of a list.

When deciding whether to use Rectangle or List as a container for other nonrepetitive controls, you should consider the number of data sets defined for a report. If there are multiple data sets, List can provide a better choice from a perspective of scope resolution for a Fields collection. In this case, all the controls contained in a List can benefit from the `DataSetName` property of a List. This allows you to use a simplified expression, such as

```
=Fields!Name.Value
```

as opposed to an expression with specified scope resolution, such as

```
=First(Fields!Name.Value, "DatasetName").
```

Scope resolution will be required for an expression contained within a Rectangle.

Practical Application of Report Items

It is time to put your knowledge to practical use. By now, you have sufficient knowledge to put fairly complex reports together. Let's start with a Sales Order summary report.

Adventure Works' management requested a report that displays selected properties of an order header (ship and bill to addresses, contact information, and billing summary) and selected properties of an order's line items (product name, unit price, order quantity, and line total). Adventure Works requires each report to have a company logo.

1. Create a new report with two data sets: `Order_Header` (data selected from join between `SalesOrderHeader`, `Address`, and `StateProvince` tables) and `Order_Detail` (data selected from join between `SalesOrderHeader`, `SalesOrderDetail`, and `Product` tables). To retrieve a specific order, you will use parameter `@SalesOrderNumber` in the `WHERE` clause of both data sets: `WHERE SalesOrderHeader.SalesOrderNumber = @SalesOrderNumber`).
2. To have a more complete picture of an order and include both shipping and billing addresses, you need to include `Address` and `StateProvince` tables twice in the `Order_Header` data set. Create aliases for the first set of `Address` and `StateProvince` tables as `BillToAddress` and `StateProvinceBill`, use `ShipToAddress` and `StateProvinceShip` aliases for the second set of tables. To create an alias for a table, right-click a table in a Graphical Query Designer, select Properties from the shortcut menu, and fill the Alias field as needed. Alternatively, you can edit the query text directly.
3. Create an alias for each field you want to include on a report. You can prefix fields with `Ship` or `Bill` for tables related to shipping and billing addresses, respectively.
4. Add the company logo image report item. From the Toolbox, drag the image item and drop it onto the report body. Click Next to skip the Welcome screen of the Image Wizard. Select Embedded on the Select the Image Source dialog box (refer to Figure 11.2).

5. If the image is already embedded, select it from the Choose the Embedded Image dialog box; otherwise, select New Image and browse for the image or type its location. For images stored in the project, the process is similar. For the images stored in the database, you need to select `Dataset`, `Image Field`, and `MIME Type` properties. A web image requires you to specify a URL.

6. Add a List by dragging a List item from the Toolbox. As was noted previously, you can take advantage of the `Dataset` property of the List item. As an experiment, drag and drop the `FirstName` field of `Order_Header` outside of the list.

7. Note the value of the created text box is `=First(Fields!FirstName.Value, "Order_Header")`. As a comparison, drag and drop the `FirstName` field on the list. Note the value of the created text box is `=Fields!FirstName.Value`. Also note that the `Dataset` property of the List item is now set to `Order_Header` and it was blank prior.

8. Add a report heading. Drag and drop a text box from the Toolbox. Enter the following expression as a value: `="Sales Order Number" & " - " & Fields!SalesOrderNumber.Value`. This expression concatenates the constant `"Sales Order Number - "` and the value of the `SalesOrderNumber` field. To highlight the heading of the report, increase the font size and change the text box background.

9. Add and arrange data fields in the page header by dragging and dropping data set fields on the list: `Street`, `City`, `State`, and `Zip` from both billing and shipping addresses. Second, add contact information and billing summary fields. Add text box items to denote values that were added. Change the heading for information sections to bold font.

10. Add lines to help separate informational pieces. Note that not all the web browsers support overlapping controls, such as lines. In your particular case, you might need to have several lines bordering each other as opposed to crossed lines as on a sample report.

11. Add a table to display details of an order. Drag and drop a Table item from the Toolbox. The default table has three rows and three columns. Right-click on the header of the rightmost column and select Add Columns to the Right from the shortcut menu. Drag and drop `Order_Detail` fields to the Detail area of the table, and note how the heading is changed to the name of the field.

12. To summarize line item charges, drag and drop the `LineTotal` field from the `Order_Detail` data set to the footer of the table, and note that SSRS inserted the aggregation function `Sum()` and the value of the footer cell is now `=Sum(Fields!LineTotal.Value)`.

The resulting design-time view of the report should look similar to Figure 11.7. The complete report can be found in samples that accompany this book at `CodeSamples\part2.relationaldbsamplereports\part2_simple_samples\Sales Order.rdl`.

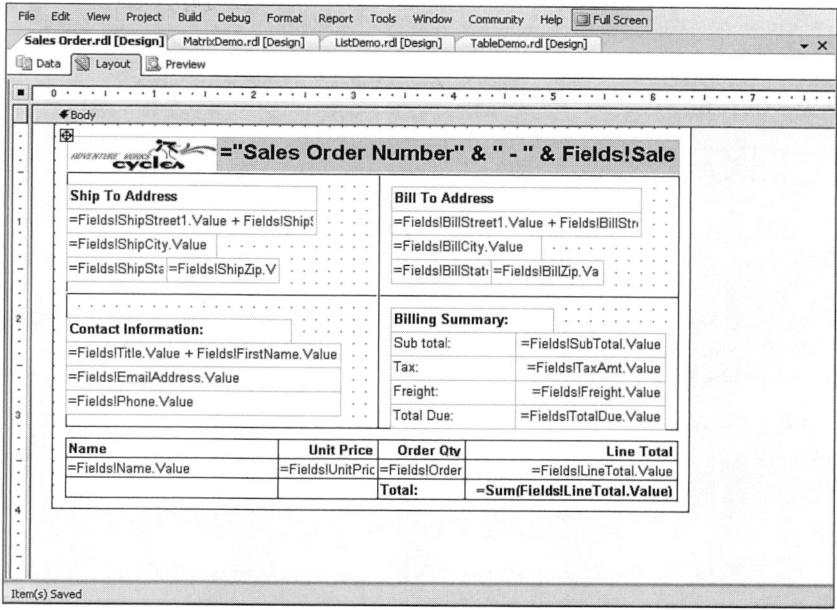

FIGURE 11.7 Design-time picture of an Order Detail report.

Matrix Report Item

The Matrix report item is also known as a cross-tab or pivot table. Matrix is capable of having a dynamic number of rows and columns and expands row by row and column by column. Matrix can act like a Table (fixed columns, dynamic rows) or like a pivot table (fixed rows, dynamic columns) to transpose data (turn rows into columns of data). Matrix allows you to group and sort rows and columns of data and can have multiple groups of rows or columns.

Just like a table, each cell in a matrix contains a text box by default. Matrix also requires at least one row and one column group. Because of this requirement, the RDL of a matrix carries a <Grouping> section:

```
<Grouping Name="matrix1_RowGroup1">
  <GroupExpressions>
    <GroupExpression />
  </GroupExpressions>
</Grouping>
```

This book uses a {GROUPING:{expression}} shortcut to abbreviate the appearance of this RDL. In turn, the {GROUPING} section is included in <RowGroupings> or <ColumnGrouping> sections, such as

```
<RowGroupings>                     <ColumnGroupings>
  <RowGrouping>                     <ColumnGrouping>
    <Width>1in</Width>                 <Height>0.25in</Height>
    <DynamicRows>                      <DynamicColumns>
      {GROUPING}                         {GROUPING}
      {ITEMS}                            {ITEMS}
    </DynamicRows>                     </DynamicColumns>
  </RowGrouping>                     </ColumnGrouping>
</RowGroupings>                    </ColumnGroupings>
```

Later in the book, `<RowGroupings>` and `<ColumnGroupings>` sections are abbreviated as `{ROWGROUPINGS}` and `{COLUMNGROUPINGS}`, respectively.

A simple matrix carries the following RDL. Note that `DataSetName` is for data regions during runtime.

```
<Matrix Name="matrix1">
{POSITION}
<MatrixColumns>
  <MatrixColumn>
    <Width>1in</Width>
  </MatrixColumn>
</MatrixColumns>
{ROWGROUPINGS}
{COLUMNGROUPINGS}
<DataSetName>DataSet1</DataSetName>
<Corner>
  {ITEMS}
</Corner>
<MatrixRows>
  <MatrixRow>
    <Height>0.25in</Height>
    <MatrixCells>
      <MatrixCell>
        {ITEMS}
      </MatrixCell>
    </MatrixCells>
  </MatrixRow>
</MatrixRows>
</Matrix>
```

Figure 11.8 demonstrates the design-time view of a matrix.

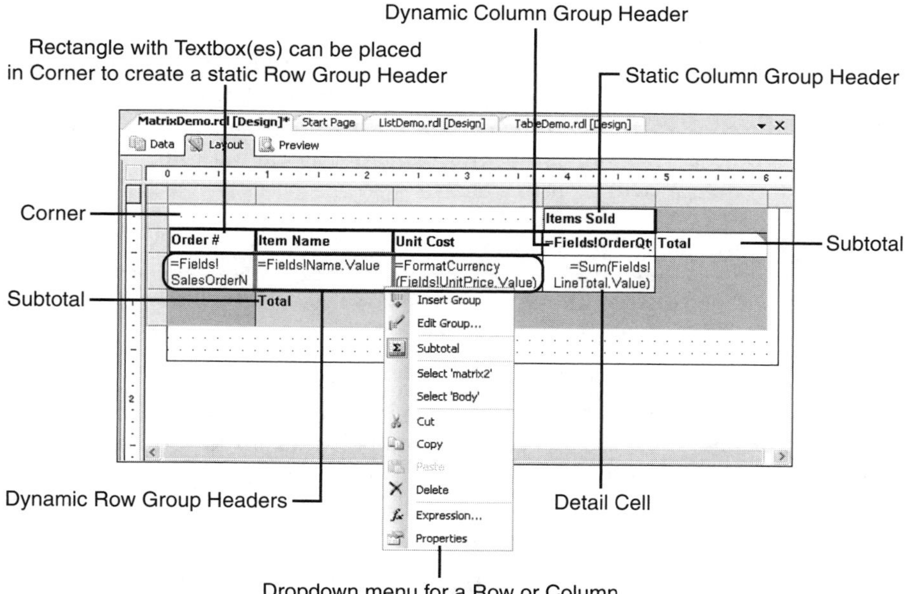

FIGURE 11.8 Design-time picture of a matrix.

You should note a couple of items related to Figure 11.8 (this book provides additional information on grouping in Chapter 12):

- To create a subtotal for each group, right-click on a group header (row or column) and select Subtotal from the shortcut menu. Use the same menu to toggle `Subtotal` on and off.
- A static group is created by using constant as a grouping expression.
- To create a static row header, you can place a Rectangle item in the corner of the matrix and lay out some text boxes inside.
- To properly color the entire `Subtotal` row, you can use the following expression in the `BackgroundColor` property of the `Detail` cell. This book provides more information about the `InScope()` function in Chapter 12.

```
=IIF(Not InScope("matrix2_RowGroup1"), "LightGrey", "White")
```

Chart Report Item

A Chart report delivers a graphic presentation of data. Chart has comprehensive functionality and is very similar by capabilities to an Excel chart, including a variety of chart types, 3D effects, and more. Unlike an Excel chart, the SSRS Chart does not build a trend line internally; however, this limit can be overcome by calculating values for a trend line in the data set and then providing it to a chart.

NOTE

For examples and explanations about charts, this book uses `Chart type = Column chart`**. This is the default type of chart that Report Designer adds to a report.**

The Chart control used in this release of Reporting Services is licensed from Dundas Software (www.dundas.com). You can obtain an add-on pack for Reporting Services from Dundas Software. Figure 11.9 shows a design-time view of a chart.

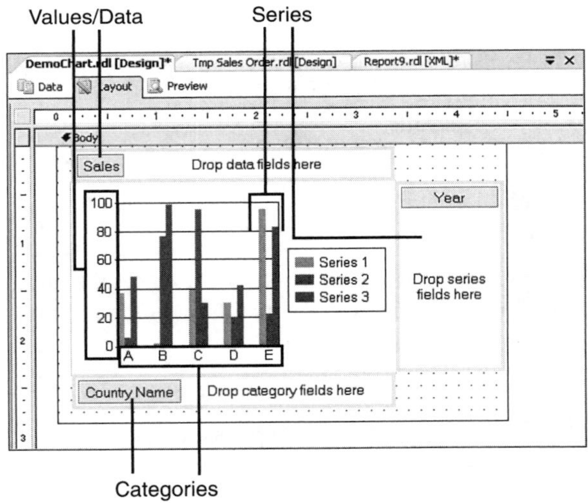

FIGURE 11.9 Design-time picture of a chart.

The Chart Properties dialog box (see Figure 11.10) provides an interface to access chart properties. To access this dialog box, right-click on a chart and select Properties from the shortcut menu.

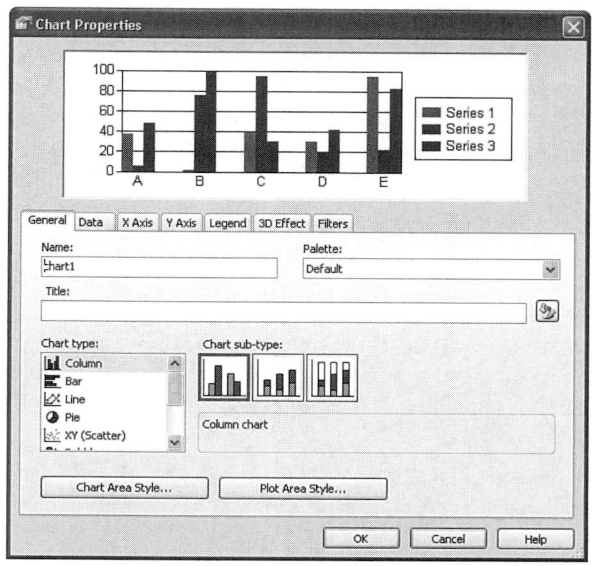

FIGURE 11.10 Chart Properties dialog box.

TIP

You might have noticed that it is not possible to control label orientation. The x-axis label orientation is determined automatically by the chart control based on the available space. You can try to adjust the dimensions of a chart to achieve the desired result. Alternatively, for example in a case of a column chart, you can try to achieve the desired orientation with a matrix aligned to a chart's.

Chart Data (Value)

Chart requires at least one set of data values associated with it. You can simply drag and drop a field to the Drop Data Fields Here area of a chart. The data determines the size of a chart element for each type of chart. For example, for a column chart, the data determines the height of a column on a chart.

Data is considered static. For a Column chart, it means that a single data file added to a chart (and no series) results in a single column providing a sum of all values and a single legend. If you add one more data field to a chart, SSRS shows a second column and adds a second legend.

Most charts group data by a series or a category. In this case, you must use an aggregate expression for a data value. This is similar to grouping in a table or matrix where non-aggregate expressions are syntactically allowed. However, the result contains the last value of a field instead of a summary value for a group and, thus, produces an unexpected result. Report Designer automatically adds an aggregate function, but changes are allowed. To verify or change the data value expression, you can either edit the RDL or access this expression from the Data tab of the Chart Properties dialog box. Following is the RDL that describes the data value. From this point forward in this book, the section surrounded by the <ChartData> tag is abbreviated as {CHART DATA}.

```
<ChartData>
  <ChartSeries>
    <DataPoints>
      <DataPoint>
        <DataValues>
          <DataValue>
            <Value>=Sum(Fields!LineTotal.Value)</Value>
          </DataValue>
        </DataValues>
        <DataLabel />
        <Marker />
      </DataPoint>
    </DataPoints>
  </ChartSeries>
</ChartData>
```

Chart Series Groups

Optional series groups allow adding more dimensions of data to a report. Series group labels are placed in the legend of the chart. Series groups are dynamic. A chart that uses series groups displays a chart element for each series group for each category. For example, a column chart with sales data displays a column for each year returned by a series group expression.

Following is the RDL that describes a series. From this point forward, the section surrounded by the <SeriesGroupings> tag is abbreviated as {SERIES GROUPS}.

```
<SeriesGroupings>
  <SeriesGrouping>
    <DynamicSeries>
      <Grouping Name="chart1_SeriesGroup1">
        <GroupExpressions>
          <GroupExpression>=Fields!OrderQty.Value</GroupExpression>
        </GroupExpressions>
      </Grouping>
      <Label>=Fields!OrderQty.Value</Label>
    </DynamicSeries>
  </SeriesGrouping>
</SeriesGroupings>
```

Chart Category Groups

Chart Category Groups is the optional mechanism of grouping data that provides the labels for chart elements.

For example, in a column chart, `Country Name` fields placed in the Category region generate country labels for x-axes (United States, Italy, and so forth).

You can nest categories. Multiple categories nest x-axes labels. For example, in a column chart with sales data, the first category group could be a county, and the second category group could be TerritoryId. The column chart would display groupings of products by TerritoryId on the x-axis.

Following is the RDL that describes a Category grouping. From this point forward, the section surrounded by the `<CategoryGroupings>` tag is abbreviated as `{CATEGORY GROUPS}`.

```
<CategoryGroupings>
  <CategoryGrouping>
    <DynamicCategories>
      <Grouping Name="chart1_CategoryGroup1">
        <GroupExpressions>
          <GroupExpression>=Fields!SalesOrderNumber.Value</GroupExpression>
        </GroupExpressions>
      </Grouping>
      <Label>=Fields!SalesOrderNumber.Value</Label>
    </DynamicCategories>
  </CategoryGrouping>
</CategoryGroupings>
```

Chart's RDL

A rudimentary chart is described by the following RDL:

```
Chart Name="chart1">
        {POSITION}
        <DataSetName>DataSet1</DataSetName>
        {SERIES GROUPS}
        {CATEGORY GROUPS}
        {CHART DATA}
</Chart>
```

A real-life chart has additional elements in its RDL, such as sections for Axis, Gridlines, Plot Area, and Legend. These elements describe graphical presentation details for a chart.

Reporting Services supports the following chart types: Column, Bar, Line, Pie, Scatter, Bubble, Area, Doughnut, and Stock. Table 11.4 provides a description of each type.

TABLE 11.4 Chart Types

Chart Type	Description
Column	Displays data as sets of vertical columns. Includes information about hybrid column/line charts.
Bar	Displays data as sets of horizontal bars.
Line	Displays data as a set of points connected by a line.
Pie	Displays data as percentages of the whole.
XY (Scatter)	Displays data as a set of points in space.
Bubble	Displays a set of symbols whose position and size are based on the data in the chart.
Area	Displays data as a set of points connected by a line, with a filled-in area below the line.
Doughnut	Displays data as percentages of the whole.
Stock	Displays data as a set of lines with markers for high, low, close, and open values.

You can select a chart's type by either right-clicking on a chart and selecting Chart Type from the shortcut menu or by selecting Properties from the same shortcut menu and working with the Chart Properties dialog box on the General tab.

Practical Application of Chart and Matrix

Let's apply the knowledge from this chapter to create a report.

Create a report that displays sales by country and by year, including graphical presentation of sales data using the following steps.

1. Add a new report with data set, based on the following query:

```
SELECT SUM(SOH.TotalDue) AS Sales, DATENAME(yyyy, SOH.OrderDate) AS Year, 'Q' +
DATENAME(qq, SOH.OrderDate) AS Quarter, Person.CountryRegion.Name AS CountryName
FROM Sales.SalesOrderHeader AS SOH INNER JOIN Sales.SalesTerritory AS ST ON
SOH.TerritoryID = ST.TerritoryID INNER JOIN Person.CountryRegion
➥ ON ST.CountryRegionCode =
Person.CountryRegion.CountryRegionCode
GROUP BY ST.Name, DATENAME(yyyy, SOH.OrderDate), 'Q' + DATENAME(qq, SOH.OrderDate),
Person.CountryRegion.Name
ORDER BY ST.Name, DATENAME(yyyy, SOH.OrderDate), 'Q' + DATENAME(qq, SOH.OrderDate)
```

2. Include the AdventureWorks logo and title of the report (Sales By Country).
3. Drag and drop a Chart item onto a report. Note the drop areas: Drop Data Fields Here, Drop Category Fields Here, and Drop Series Fields Here. Drag and drop the `Sales` field on the data area, `CountryName` on the category area, and `Year` on the series area.

4. Drag and drop a Matrix item on the report. Drag and drop the `Sales` field on the data area of the matrix, `CountryName` on the columns area, and `Quarter` and `Year` field on the row area.

Figure 11.11 provides resulting design and runtime views of the report. Final report can be found in the samples for this book at `CodeSamples\part2.relationaldbsamplereports\part2_simple_samples\ Matrix and Chart -- SalesByCountry.rdl`.

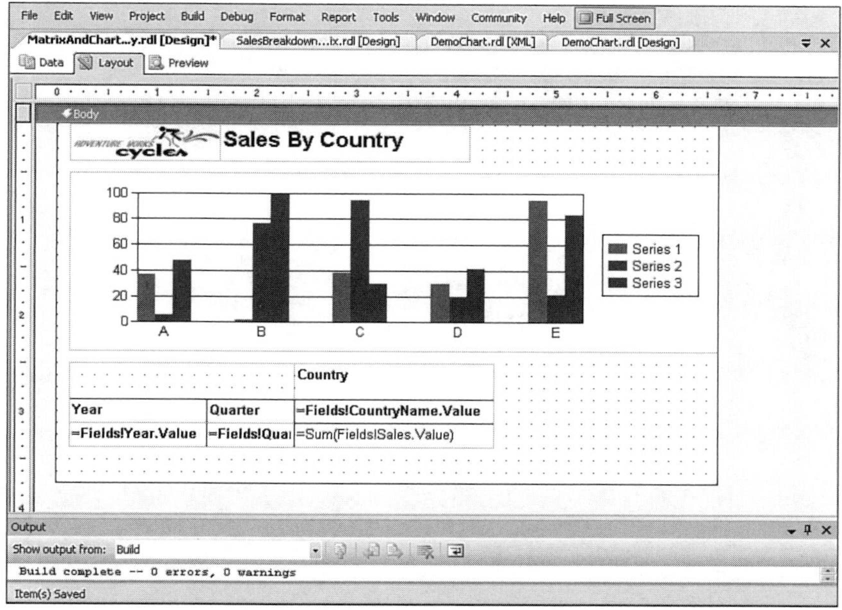

FIGURE 11.11 Chart and matrix items at work.

Report Body Versus Page Header/Footer

The report body can contain any SSRS items, including data regions. The page header and footer can only contain independent report items, such as Textbox, Line, and Rectangle. More complex page header and footer functionality can be implemented with Table or Matrix and the `RepeatOnNewPage` property. Some limited paging functionality can be implemented with List.

Summary

Report items are the presentation elements within SSRS.

Data regions function as a repetitive display of rows, groups of rows, or columns from a data set associated with a region. Data regions include Table, Matix, Chart, and List. Data regions cannot be included in page headers or page footers.

Other report items are used for display purposes and are commonly called independent report items. These items include Line, Rectangle, Textbox, and Image.

Data regions and independent report items support navigation; please see Chapter 14 for more details.

Containers can include other reporting items. Items placed in a container become the container's children and the container becomes the parent. Table, Matrix, List, Rectangle, Report Body, Page Header, and Page Footer are containers.

In the following chapter, you will build on this knowledge by learning how to group, sort, and aggregate data within a given scope of a data region. By learning how to use report items and group data effectively, you will be able to create advanced reports in no time.

CHAPTER 12

Grouping, Sorting, and Aggregating Data, Working with Scope

IN THIS CHAPTER

- Grouping Data on a Report
- Sorting, Including Interactive User Sorting
- Scope of an Aggregate Function
- Level and InScope Functions

Grouping and sorting functionality provides some of the key motivators for purchasing reporting tools. Although every enterprise DBMS has the ability to group and sort data, reports presented to business users usually have multiple levels of grouping inside of them, not to mention lots of pretty pictures, complex layouts, and graphs. A simple query tool is inadequate for this task. This chapter discusses grouping and sorting as well as when it is appropriate to do it in SSRS versus the DBMS. In SSRS, grouping and sorting is available within data regions.

Grouping Data on a Report

Grouping allows you to aggregate items within a group and, in turn, to generate reports with complex formatting. Chapter 8, "Expressions," covered a set of aggregation functions. Aggregation functions help grouping scenarios by providing totals for groups and subtotals for subgroups. The relationship between an aggregation function and group is controlled by scope. This relationship becomes useful when, for example, a user needs to see what percentage of a total a particular line item is.

In the examples from previous chapters, you have seen summarizations that can be done in data regions, such as the Table, Matrix, Chart, and List data regions.

Most scenarios employ grouping in SSRS to aggregate data and generate summary information. Concepts applicable to aggregation in SSRS are very similar to those applicable to the `GROUP BY` expression in SQL. However, unlike a query, which allows for very limited formatting, SSRS is practically unlimited in its formatting capabilities.

As in many cases in software development, choosing a particular approach is based on several key factors: performance, scalability, elegance, and development time. This is a "magic" formula. The complex part of this is to find the best balance that can solve this "magic." The best solution is to experiment with various approaches and find the best for a particular application.

In almost all cases, using SQL for grouping provides the best performance. However, a static SQL statement is not very flexible.

The SQL statement might be too complex, lose its elegance, and, especially, not provide required formatting. It might be hard for a developer, who just started working on a newly developed reporting system, to determine what a complex query is doing and why it is not producing the correct result.

The following are some tips to help strike a balance between SSRS' ability to group and SQL:

- Ideally, use single query with `GROUP BY`.
- Use query grouping (`GROUP BY`) with `WHERE` and `HAVING` clauses if it allows you to reduce the amount of data received by SSRS.
- Do not format or convert data in a query, unless needed for `GROUP BY`.

For example, the following query to retrieve a summary of all line items for each order with the result displayed in a Table report item will execute several times faster than using a Table report item to accomplish the same grouping.

```
SELECT     Sales.SalesOrderHeader.SalesOrderNumber,
➥ SUM(Sales.SalesOrderDetail.LineTotal) AS SumOfDetails,
➥ SUM(Sales.SalesOrderHeader.SubTotal) AS OrderSubTotal
FROM  Sales.SalesOrderDetail INNER JOIN
        Sales.SalesOrderHeader ON Sales.SalesOrderDetail.SalesOrderID =
        ➥ Sales.SalesOrderHeader.SalesOrderID
GROUP BY Sales.SalesOrderHeader.SalesOrderNumber
```

The Grouping and Sorting Properties dialog box provides an interface to edit groups for Matrix, Table, List, and Chart.

See Figure 12.1 to view the Grouping and Sorting Properties dialog box for a Table Group.

The Grouping and Sorting Properties dialog box will vary slightly in check boxes at the bottom, depending on the report item. For example, List only has Page Break at Start and Page Break at End check boxes.

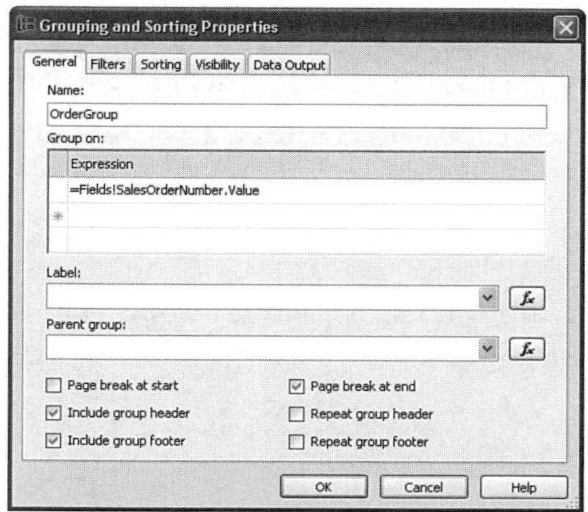

FIGURE 12.1 Grouping and Sorting Properties dialog box.

The following are procedures to display grouping properties:

- **List**—Right-click on a list, select Properties from the shortcut menu, and click the Edit Details Group button.
- **Table Detail**—Right-click the detail handler and select Edit Group from the shortcut menu. This group is not very frequently used as it only allows you to group details and does not provide functionality to calculate subtotals.
- **Table Group**—On an existing group, right-click a group header or footer handler and select Edit Group from the shortcut menu.

  This is a frequently used group and provides functionality to calculate subtotals and pagination functionality for a group.
- **Matrix**—Right-click a row or column group and select Edit Group from the shortcut menu.
- **Chart**—Right-click on a chart, select Properties from the shortcut menu, click on the Data tab, and select Edit on either the Series or Category groups.

The number of available grouping properties varies, but `Name`, `Group on Expression` (allows for multiple expressions), `Document Map Label` (or simply label in the case of a Chart item), and `Parent Group` are always available. The RDL that describes grouping is as follows:

```
<Grouping Name="OrderGroup">
  <GroupExpressions>
    <GroupExpression>=Fields!SalesOrderNumber.Value</GroupExpression>
  </GroupExpressions>
</Grouping>
```

Sorting, Including Interactive User Sorting

In SSRS 2005, three options are available to sort results on a report:

- Make the data source (database) sort data on data retrieval by using an `ORDER BY` clause.
- Make SSRS sort data during report generation. SSRS sorts items that have the `Sorting` property defined.
- Use the new, interactive sort functionality for HTML-rendered reports only. This functionality makes SSRS regenerate a report with a new direction: ascending or descending.

The RDL that describes sorting is as follows:

```
<Sorting>
 <SortBy>
   <SortExpression>=Fields!Name.Value</SortExpression>
   <Direction>Ascending</Direction>
 </SortBy>
</Sorting>
```

Interactive Sorting *NEW in 2005*

SSRS 2005 adds a new, interactive sort action that allows users to sort an HTML-rendered report.

The RDL that describes interactive sorting is as follows:

```
<UserSort>
  <SortExpression>=Fields!Name.Value</SortExpression>
</UserSort>
```

A developer can set up this type of sorting though a text box's property `UserSort` or through the Interactive Sort tab of a text box's property sheet (see Figure 12.2).

To determine the proper position of an interactive sorting control, visualize the output and decide what location makes sense for the interaction to occur. For example, to sort values within a group, a cell in a group header should contain an interactive sort control.

The following are the components of an interactive sort:

- **Sort expression (required)**—Normally, is a column expression for the column to be sorted. For example, if the designer needs to sort a column that contains the expression `=Fields!FirstName.Value`, the same expression is used for sorting. In a few cases, the designer might choose to use different expressions for sorting; for example, the designer might decide to use `=Fields!UserId.Value` if `UserId` is sequenced in the same sort order as `FirstName`.

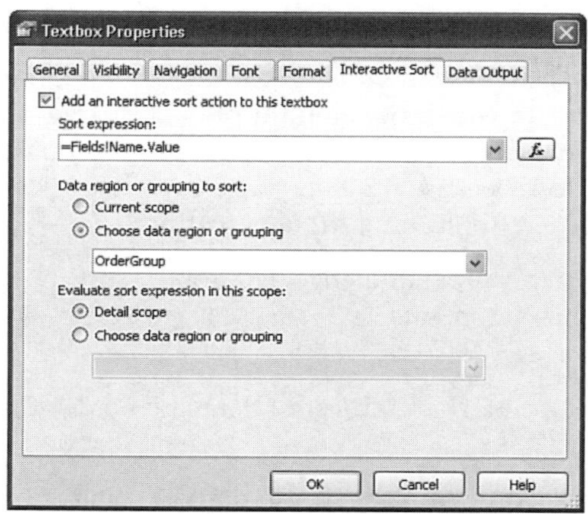

FIGURE 12.2 Interactive sorting.

- **In data region or grouping to sort current scope**—Enables sorting on the repeated rows in the data region that contains the sort item. The scope must be the current scope, a peer scope that is a data region, or an ancestor scope. The Choose Data Region or Grouping option allows you to select a specific data region or group (for example, if a developer wants the sort to affect additional data regions or data regions other than the one that contains the sortable item).
- **Evaluate sort expression in this scope**—Specifies which data regions or groups are sorted. Setting these options is useful if you are targeting a specific data region and want to further specify where sorting occurs within that data region.
- **Detail scope**—Sorts only the repeated rows of the selected data region.
- **Data region or grouping**—Selects a specific data region or group on which to sort.

There is nothing magical about interactive sorting behind the scenes. If you look at the rendered report's source, you will notice the following pieces of the puzzle were added to your field to be sorted:

```
<a style="cursor:hand;" onclick="return
➥ClientReportctl00.ActionHandler('Sort','18_A');">
<IMG SRC="<ReportViewerControlURL><DisplayImageReportViewerCommnand><ImageName>"/>
```

`ImageName` is initially `unsorted.gif` and changes to `sortAsc.gif` or `sortDesc.gif`, depending on the direction of the sort. This is internal functionality to SSRS and you do not want to mess with it. It reveals that the "magic" is simply scripting. You can further explore this functionality by adding more interactive sort fields and observing changes in rendered HTML and the report's URL.

Data Source Sorting

A designer can use the ORDER BY clause in a query. In this case, the database performs sorting. Especially in cases in which the amount of data is large, this provides the best performance. In this case, a developer needs to consider performance implications for the database server. In addition, because the query approach has a scope of an entire data set, it might not provide needed fine-tuning for data sorting.

When necessary, a designer can parameterize data source sorting by using the following expression used as the query in a data set: ="SELECT {fields} FROM {table} ORDER BY " & Parameters!MySort.Value.

Parameter MySort should contain a valid list of database fields or numbers corresponding to the fields to use in ORDER BY.

For example, to retrieve a list of employees, use the following expression:

```
="SELECT FirstName, LastName, Title FROM Employee ORDER BY " & Parameters!MySort.
➥Value
```

In this example, MySort could be set to a nonqueried parameter with the values FirstName and LastName or values 1 and 2. For more details about parameters, including information on how to pass a parameter value to a report, refer to Chapter 10, "Report Parameters."

For dynamic query expressions, developers need to make sure that Parameters!MySort.Value properly corresponds to a database field or fields. In addition, a dynamic query expression has to return a valid query. Each properly placed space is crucial, such as the space between ORDER BY and a parameter.

Query design has to follow best practices to avoid SQL injection. Here is a good article on avoiding SQL injection attacks: http://msdn.microsoft.com/msdnmag/issues/04/09/SQLInjection/.

Data Region and Group Sorting

A designer can implement sorting for a group or a data region by providing one or many expressions for the Sorting property of each, as shown in Figure 12.3.

Similar to data source sorting, an expression can, for example, sort by FirstName and LastName. Of course, fields used in expressions in this case will belong to the Fields collection. That is, the sorting expressions will have the form of =Fields!FirstName.Value and =Fields!LastName.Value. FirstName and LastName by default have the same name as fields retrieved by the data source (or database field names), but could be changed to different names. Similar to data source sorting, sort expressions can take advantage of parameters. For more details about parameters, including information on how to pass a parameter value to a report, refer to Chapter 10. The expression that incorporates parameters has a form of =Fields(Parameters!{ParameterName}.Value).Value. For example, if the parameter MySort is used, the expression will be =Fields(Parameters!MySort.Value).Value. In addition, expressions can include flow control functions, such as IIF().

Sorting is performed in the scope where the sort is specified. For example, if you have a table that contains a group, sorting expressions specified for a table will not affect the data sort in the group.

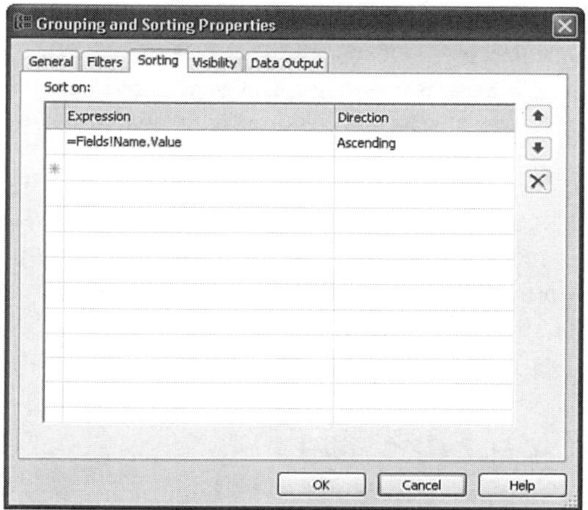

FIGURE 12.3 Sorting expressions.

Scope of an Aggregate Function

The `Scope` parameter defines the scope in which the aggregate function is performed. A valid scope could be

- A string name of data set.
- String name of containing grouping.
- String name of containing data region. Within the data region, `Scope` is optional for all aggregate functions except `RowNumber()`.
- Omitted, when optional. In this case, the scope of the aggregate is the innermost data region or grouping to which the report item belongs. If the item is outside of a data region and there is a single data set, `Scope` refers to this single data set. If there are multiple data sets, `Scope` cannot be omitted. In the case of multiple data sets, SSRS provides an explicit reference if the designer drags and drops a field outside of the data region.
- A keyword set to `Nothing`. This is only allowed inside of data regions. In this case, the scope of the aggregate is the outermost data region or grouping to which the report item belongs.

TIP

`Scope` **is a context-sensitive string, thus** `Dataset1` **and** `dataset1` **are different** `Scope` **values.**

If the containing group or data region is not used as scope, then SSRS throws an error:

"The Value expression for the <Item> '<Item Name>' has a scope parameter that is not valid for an aggregate function. The scope parameter must be set to a string constant that is equal to either the name of a containing group, the name of a containing data region, or the name of a data set."

The `Scope` parameter cannot be used in page headers or footers.

For `RowNumber` to generate expected results, the expression containing this function has to be in the "detail" row and not on the "summary" row like a group header or footer.

Table and Matrix report items can have multiple defined scopes. Table can have multiple row scopes. Table with a single group has three scopes: entire data set, entire Table for detail rows, and one for a group. Matrix can have multiple scopes defined on rows and columns. Because Matrix requires at least one row and at least one column group, it has at least four scopes: entire data set, Matrix for details, scope, and one for each of the groups.

Level and InScope Functions

`Level([Scope])` returns a zero-based (top level in a hierarchy is 0) Integer—the current level of depth in a recursive hierarchy.

If `Scope` specifies a grouping with no `Parent` element, data set, or data region, `Level` returns `0`. Child group, which specifies Parent, can only have a single group expression. If Scope is omitted, it returns the level of the current scope.

`Level` can be useful to provide indentation, for example, a hierarchy of employees in a sales department. To provide indentation, a designer needs to

- Retrieve `EmployeeId` and `ManagerID` from a database.
- Specify the hierarchy by setting the Parent of a group to `ManagerId`.
- Specify padding as `Padding.Left = (2 + Level()*20) & "pt"`.

The `InScope(Scope)` function returns `True` if the current instance of an item is within the specified scope. Practical usability of `InScope()` is mostly limited to data regions that have dynamic scoping, such as Matrix and Chart.

To illustrate how scope works, let's capitalize on the example used previously for Matrix and change the detail cell to the following expression:

```
= "Scope ="
+ IIF(InScope("RG_SalesOrderNumber"), "RG_SalesOrderNumber,",  "")
+ IIF(InScope("RG_ItemName"), "RG_ItemName,", "")
+ IIF(InScope("RG_static"), "RG_static,", "")
+ IIF(InScope("CG_OrderQty"), "CG_OrderQty,", "")
+ IIF(InScope("CG_static"), "CG_static,", "")
```

```
+ IIF(InScope("matrix2"), "matrix,", "")
+ IIF(InScope("DataSet1"), "DataSet1,", "")
+ ")"
```

Remember there are several groups in that example that denoted `"RG"` for row group and `"CG"` for column group. The same example also has the Matrix item and a data set.

You will see the resulting output similar to the following.

Scope = RG_SalesOrderNumber, RG_ItemName, RG_static, CG_OrderQty, CG_static, matrix, DataSet1	Scope = RG_SalesOrderNumber, RG_ItemName, RG_static, ~~CG_OrderQty,~~ CG_static, matrix, DataSet1
Scope = RG_SalesOrderNumber, ~~RG_ItemName,~~ CG_OrderQty, CG_static, matrix, DataSet1	Scope = RG_SalesOrderNumber, ~~RG_ItemName,~~ ~~CG_OrderQty,~~ CG_static, matrix, DataSet1

We have used strikethrough text to indicate information that is not presented on the actual output.

This example provides insight on Scope information and clearly identifies each type of cell on a Matrix. Table 12.1 presents a summary of the `Scope`.

TABLE 12.1 Scope of Cells in Matrix

Matrix's Element	Scope Inclusion
Dynamic row/column	Is included in each scope
Row subtotal	Is not included in `CG_OrderQty` scope
Column subtotal	Is not included in `RG_ItemName`
Total sum of all row subtotal or column subtotal	Is not included in `RG_ItemName` and `CG_OrderQty` scope

This knowledge allows developers to implement advanced formatting. For example, `InScope()` can be used to highlight rows with subtotals or to create a drill-through link with capabilities to access different reports, depending on the clicked cell.

Type a drill-through link expression in `BackgroundColor` of a Matrix's cell. This highlights the last row for an order:

```
=IIF(Not InScope("RG_ItemName"), "LightGrey", "White")
```

Summary

Grouping and Sorting is a separate reporting tool from a simple query tool. Matrix and Table both have the capability to perform multiple levels of grouping. Matrix provides the ability to group across multiple columns as well as rows. Although List can only contain a single grouping, nesting a list creates the same effect as multiple grouping.

SSRS provided multiple ways to allow for sorting. Data regions can sort data statically, as well as provide an interactive sort. Using query parameters and expressions, it is also possible to make Dynamic SQL to do sorting within the database.

`Scope` is another critical aspect of sorting and grouping. In most cases, scope is handled effortlessly by default. In the cases in which scope is dynamic, SSRS provides an `InScope` function to check and see if a scope is valid.

Advanced Report Formatting

CHAPTER 13

IN THIS CHAPTER

- Formatting-Related Report Item Properties
- Formatting Numeric and Date/Time Values
- Creating Alternating Colors for the Lines on a Report
- Paging Report

Thus far, this book has discussed some basic formatting, such as highlighting text in bold, changing background color, and adjusting report layout. This chapter provides a broader view on formatting.

TIP

Try to preview a report (click on the Preview tab of Report Designer) to verify if the formatting is satisfactory.

`Me.Value` **or simply** `Value` **provides access to the value property of a SSRS item and simplifies formatting expressions. Instead of using the same expression that was used to set the value property, you can access the value of this expression through** `Me.Value`. **For example, to display negative values in red, the property** `Color` **can be an expression** `=IIF(Fields!TotalDue.Value >= 0, "Black", "Red")`. **Alternatively, you can use** `=IIF(Value >= 0, "Black", "Red")` **and achieve the same result.**

Report Formatting, Report Border, and Layout toolbars (see Figure 13.1) are conveniently available to do some design-time formatting.

The Item Properties window and Property Pages dialog box shown in Figure 13.2 provide access to a full set of formatting properties, including runtime formatting.

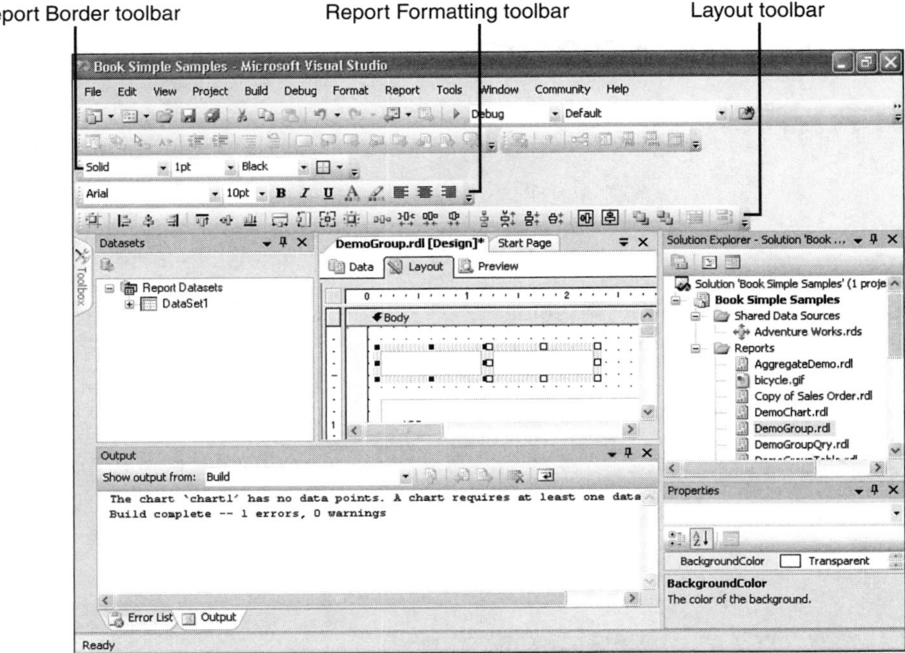

FIGURE 13.1 Report formatting related toolbars.

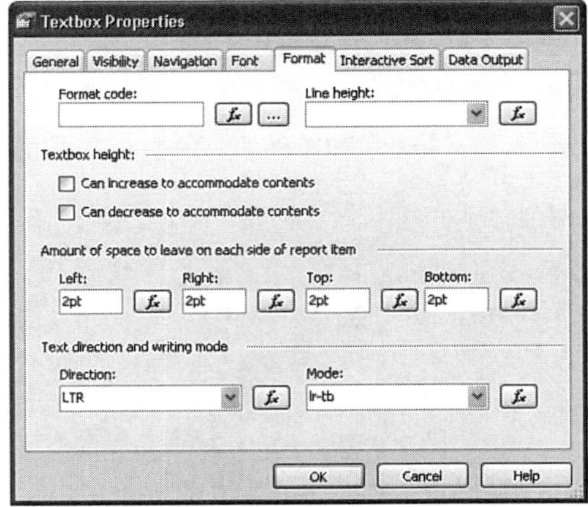

FIGURE 13.2 Item Properties window and Property Pages dialog box.

Formatting-Related Report Item Properties

Formatting properties can be subdivided into three categories:

- **Background-control properties**—Designed to control background, such as background color, of data presented on a report. These properties are shown in Table 13.1.
- **Output text control properties**—Designed to control textual (string, numeric, and date) output, such as color, font, currency, and date formatting. These properties are shown in Table 13.2.
- **Border appearance control properties**—Designed to control a border surrounding output. All report items, except Line have a border. These properties are shown in Table 13.2.

Formatting properties accept expressions to provide dynamism of representation, based, for example, on the retrieved data or parameters. Please refer to Chapter 8, "Expressions," for more details about expressions.

NOTE

Note, for example, that a value `Red` is valid when used as a property value by itself, whereas an expression must evaluate to a string "`Red`".

TABLE 13.1 Background-Related Report Item Formatting Properties

Property	Description
BackgroundColor	The color of the background of the item. This property could be a name of the color, such as `Red` or the HTML color string in the form `#RRGGBB`. Letters `R`, `G`, and `B` provide hexadecimal representation for red, green, and blue color intensity. For example, `#FF0000` is red. If this property is omitted, the background becomes transparent. This property is not available for Line, Subreport, and Image report items.
BackgroundGradientType	The direction in which the background gradient is displayed: `None, LeftRight, TopBottom, Center, DiagonalLeft, DiagonalRight, HorizontalCenter, VerticalCenter.` This property is only available for a chart's areas (plot, chart, and legend).
BackgroundGradientEndColor	The end color of the background gradient. If omitted, the item has no background gradient. This property is only available for a chart's areas (plot, chart, and legend).

TABLE 13.1 Continued

Property	Description
BackgroundImage	An image to display as the background of the item. This property applies to rectangle, text box, list, matrix, table, body, page header and footer, subtotal, and the chart's plot area (settable through the properties dialog box). `BackgroundImage` does not apply to line, image, subreport, and the chart's legend and chart areas.

Other formatting properties (Table 13.2) control the appearance of text displayed in the item (font, color, international properties, alignment, and so on) and appearance of the border (color, width).

TABLE 13.2 Other Formatting Properties

Property Type	Properties	Description
Border formatting	BorderColor BorderStyle BorderWidth	The color of the border of the item: `Bottom`, `Default`, `Left`, `Right`, `Top`. The style of the border of the item: `Dotted`, `Dashed`, `Solid`, and so on. The width of the border of the item. All border formatting properties have child elements to format the corresponding location of a border: `Bottom`, `Default`, `Left`, `Right`, `Top`.
General formatting	Format Calendar	The Microsoft .NET Framework formatting string to apply to the item. For example, `C` for currency. The calendar to use to format dates. Used in conjunction with the `Language` property.
Text formatting	Color Direction FontFamily FontSize FontStyle FontWeight TextDecoration WritingMode	The color (`Red`), direction, font family name (such as `Arial`), size in points (`1pt`), style (such as `Italic`), weight (thickness, such as `Bold`), special effect to apply to the font for the text in the item (such as `Underline`), and the direction of the text.
Locale control	Language NumeralLanguage NumeralVariant	The primary language of the text. The digit format to use based on the `Language` property. Used for locale formatting. For example, "`English (United Kingdom)`" changes formatting to United Kingdom locale. For example, currency formatting changes from `$` to `£` and date changes from `mm/dd/yy` to `dd/mm/yy`. `NumeralLanguage` and `NumeralVariant` control numeric presentation of text.

TABLE 13.2 Continued

Property Type	Properties	Description
LineHeight		The height of a line of text. If not specified, the height is based on the font size.
Padding	Bottom/Left/Right/Top	The amount of space to insert between the bottom/left/right/top edge of the item and the text or image in the item.
Text Alignment	TextAlign and VerticalAlign	The horizontal (left, right, or center) and vertical (top, middle, or bottom) alignment of the text in the item.
UnicodeBiDi		The level of bidirectional embedding. Essentially, this property controls left to right (English language) or right to left (Hebrew language) order of characters. More information about this property can be found at http://www.w3.org/TR/REC-CSS2/visuren.html#direction.

Formatting Numeric and Date/Time Values

Both numeric and date/time values allow for standard and custom formatting strings. A standard formatting string refers to a single character that specifies the desired output format for a value.

Any numeric format string that does not fit the definition of a standard format string (either numeric or date/time) is interpreted as a custom format string. For example, format string "`d!`" is interpreted as a custom format string because it contains two alphabetic characters, even though the character "`d`" is a standard date/time format specifier. This is true even if the extra characters are white spaces. Similarly, character "`h`" is interpreted as a custom format because it does not match any standard format specifiers.

In addition, developers can exercise greater control over how values are formatted by using custom format specifiers.

Resulting output strings are influenced by the settings in the Regional Options control panel and locale control properties: `Language`, `NumeralLanguage`, and `NumeralVariant`. Computers with different locale-specific settings generate different formatting for numbers and dates.

For example, `February 4, 2006` returns `2/4/2006` when run with the `United States English (en-US)` locale, but it returns `04.02.2006` when run with the `German (de-DE)` locale.

You can learn more about globalization and locale options at http://www.microsoft.com/globaldev/getWR/steps/WRG_lclmdl.mspx.

Standard Numeric Format Strings

Numeric format strings are used to format common numeric types. A standard format string takes the form Axx, where A is a single alphabetic character called the format specifier, and xx is an optional integer called the precision specifier. The format specifier must be one of the built-in format characters (see Table 13.3). The precision specifier ranges from 0 to 99 and controls the number of significant digits or zeros to the right of a decimal. The format string cannot contain white spaces.

If the format string does not contain one of the standard format specifiers, the format string is ignored.

The following abbreviations are used: letter 'd' indicates a digit (0-9), letter 'E' or 'e' denotes an exponent, '±' indicates that you can use either the plus or minus sign in the expression. The exponent always consists of a plus or minus sign and a minimum of three digits. By default, SSRS prefixes negative numbers with a minus sign.

The precision specifier indicates the minimum number of digits desired. If required, the number is padded with zeros to produce the number of digits given by the precision specifier. The number is padded to its left for integer types formatted with Decimal or Hexadecimal specifiers and in digits after the decimal point for other specifiers. Padding is ignored for the 'R' format specifier.

TABLE 13.3 Standard Numeric Format Strings

Format Specifier	Name	Description	Example
C or c	Currency	The number is converted to a string that represents a currency amount. The conversion is controlled by the Language property. The precision specifier indicates the desired number of decimal places; if omitted, the default currency precision is controlled by the Language property.	Value=1234.567 Language=default Output=$1,234.57 Language= "English (United Kingdom)" Output=£1,234.57
D or d	Decimal	This format is supported for integer types only. The number is converted to a string of decimal digits (0-9).	Value=1234 Output=1234
E or e	Scientific (exponential)	The number is converted to a string of the form d.ddd...E±ddd or d.ddd...e±ddd. One digit always precedes the decimal point, a minimum of three digits follow the ± sign, and the case determines the prefix of the exponent ('E' or an 'e'). If the precision specifier is omitted, a default of 'E6' is used.	Value=1234.567 Output= 1.234567+E003

TABLE 13.3 Continued

Format Specifier	Name	Description	Example
F or f	Fixed-point	The number is converted to a string of the form `ddd.ddd...`. If the precision specifier is omitted, the default numeric precision given by the `Language` property is used.	Value=1234.567 Output=1234.57
G or g	General	The number is converted to the most compact of either fixed-point or scientific notation, depending on the type of number and whether a precision specifier is present. If the precision specifier is omitted or zero, the type of the number determines the default precision.	Value=1234.567 Output=1234.567
N or n	Number	The number is converted to a string of the form `d,ddd,ddd.ddd...`. Thousand separators are inserted between each group of three digits to the left of the decimal point. If the precision specifier is omitted, the precision is guided by the `Language` property.	Value=1234.567 Output=1,234.567
P or p	Percent	The number is converted to a string where the value is multiplied by 100% and presented with a percentage sign. If the precision specifier is omitted, the precision is guided by the `Language` property.	Value=123.4567 Output=12,345.67
R or r	Round-trip	The round-trip specifier guarantees that a numeric value converted to a string will be parsed back into the same numeric value. SSRS examines data for the best output to accomplish this.	Value=1234.567 Output=1234.567
X or x	Hexadecimal	The number is converted to a string of hexadecimal digits. 'X' produces uppercase ("ABCDEF") for digits greater than 9, 'x' produces "abcdef". Decimal number '123' is correspondingly converted to hexadecimal '7b'. This format is supported for integer types only.	Value=1234 Output=4D2

Additional information about standard numeric format strings can be found in the .NET Framework Developer's Guide at http://msdn.microsoft.com/library/default.asp?url=/library/en-us/cpguide/html/cpconstandardnumericformatstrings.asp.

Custom Numeric Format Strings

Table 13.4 shows custom numeric format strings, descriptions, and output examples. You can exercise greater control over how values are formatted by using custom format specifiers.

TABLE 13.4 Custom Numeric Format Strings

Format Specifier	Name	Description	Example
0	Zero placeholder	In the position where the '0' appears in the format string, copy the digit of the value to the result string. Number of 0s before and after the decimal point determines exact number of digits. The number is rounded to the nearest decimal position.	Value=012.3 Format=000.00 Output=012.30 Format=000. Output=012
#	Digit placeholder	In the position where the '#' appears in the format string, copy the digit of the value to the result string. This specifier never displays '0' character if it is not a significant digit, even if '0' is the only digit in the string.	Value=012.30 Format=###.## Output=12.3 Format phone number Value=1234567890 Format(###) ###-#### Output=(123)456-7890
.	Decimal point	The first '.' character in the format string determines the location of the decimal separator in the formatted value; any additional '.' characters are ignored. The actual character used as the decimal separator is determined by the `Language` property. For example, the French decimal point is actually a comma ','.	Value=12.34 Format=###.## Language="French" Output=12,3
,	Thousand separator and number scaling	First occurrence of ',' when used in conjunction with '0' and '#' placeholders inserts thousand separators between each group of three digits to the left of the decimal separator. The actual character used as the decimal separator is determined by the `Language` property.	Value=10000000.5 Format=#,###,. Output=10,000

TABLE 13.4 Continued

Format Specifier	Name	Description	Example
%	Percentage placeholder	Multiply the value by 100 and insert the % sign. The percent character used is dependent on the current `Language`.	Value=10.5 Format=###% Output=1050
E0 E±0 e0 e±0	Scientific notation	Format using scientific notation. The number of '0's determines the minimum number of digits to output for the exponent. The "E+" and "e+" formats indicate that a sign character (plus or minus) should always precede the exponent. The "E", "E-", "e", or "e-" formats indicate that a sign character should only precede negative exponents.	Value=12000 Format= 0.###E+000 Output= 12E+004
'ABC' "ABC"	Literal string	Characters enclosed in single or double quotes are copied to the result string literally, and do not affect formatting.	Value=12 Format= F "AB"00.00 Output= AB12.00
;	Section separator	The ';' character is used to apply separate formatting for positive, negative, and zero numbers in the format string. If there are two sections and the result is zero, it is formatted per the first section. If the second section is skipped, such as `##;;0`, then 0 is formatted according to the third section.	Value=-123 Format=##;(##) Output=(123)
\c	Escape character	Where *c* is any character, the escape character displays the next character as a literal. In this context, the escape character cannot be used to create an escape sequence (such as "\n" for newline).	Value=-123 Format= \z0000 Output=-z0123
Other	All other characters	All other characters are copied to the result string as literals in the position they appear.	

Numbers are rounded to as many decimal places as there are digit placeholders to the right of the decimal point. If the format string does not contain a decimal point, the number is rounded to the nearest integer. If the number has more digits than there are digit placeholders to the left of the decimal point, the extra digits are copied to the result string immediately before the first digit placeholder.

Additional information about custom numeric format strings can be found in the .NET Framework Developer's Guide at http://msdn.microsoft.com/library/default.asp?url=/library/en-us/cpguide/html/cpconcustomnumericformatstrings.asp.

Standard Date/Time Format Strings

A standard Date/Time format string consists of a **single** character format specifier character from Table 13.5.

TABLE 13.5 Standard Date/Time Format Strings

Format Specifier	Name/Note	Output of Value= CDate("1/2/2003 23:59:11.15")
d	Short date pattern	02/01/2003
D	Long date pattern	02 January 2003
t	Short time pattern	23:59
T	Long time pattern	23:59:11
f	Full date/time pattern (short time)	02 January 2003 23:59
F	Full date/time pattern (long time)	02 January 2003 23:59:11
g	General date/time pattern (short time)	02/01/2003 23:59
G	General date/time pattern (long time)	02/01/2003 23:59:11
M or m	Month day pattern	02 January
R or r	RFC1123 pattern is the same as custom pattern `ddd, dd MMM yyyy HH:mm:ss G\MT`	Thu, 02 Jan 2003 23:59:11 GMT
s	Sortable date/time pattern; conforms to ISO 8601 and is the same as custom pattern `yyyy-MM-ddTHH:mm:ss`	2003-01-02T23:59:11
u	Universal storable date/time pattern—same as custom pattern `yyyy-MM-dd HH:mm:ssZ`; does not do time zone conversion	2003-01-02 23:59:11Z
U	Universal sortable date/time pattern—displays universal, rather than local time	02 January 2003 05:59:11
Y or y	Year month pattern	January 2003
Any other single character=	Unknown specifier; SSRS uses default	02/01/2003 23:59:11

Additional information about standard date/time format strings can be found in the .NET Framework Developer's Guide at http://msdn.microsoft.com/library/default.asp?url=/library/en-us/cpguide/html/cpconstandarddatetimeformatstrings.asp.

Custom Date/Time Formatting

Table 13.6 describes the custom format specifiers and examples of output. Note how the percent sign (`%`) converts standard to custom specifiers. For example, `d` specifies short date pattern, but `%d` specifies day of the month. When `%` is used with a character not reserved for custom formatting, the character displayed is literal. For example, a format string `%n` results in the output `n`.

TABLE 13.6 Custom Date/Time Formatting

Format Specifier	Description	Output of Value= CDate("1/2/2003 23:59:11.15")
%d	Displays the current day of the month, measured as a number between 1 and 31, inclusive. Single digit only (1-9) displayed as a single digit.	2
dd	Displays the current day of the month, measured as a number between 1 and 31, inclusive. Single digit only (1-9) is prefixed with a preceding 0 (01-09).	02
ddd	Displays the abbreviated name of the day specified.	Thu
dddd (plus any number of additional "d" characters)	Displays the full name of the day specified.	Thursday
f to fffffff	Displays seconds fractions represented in one to seven digits.	1 to 1500000
g or gg or any number of additional "g" characters	Displays the era (A.D., for example).	A.D.
%h	Displays the hour for the specified value in 12-hour format (undistinguished AM/PM, range 1-12). No rounding occurs; that is, a value of 4:45 returns 4.	11
hh plus any number of additional "h" characters	Same as above, but a single digit hour (1-9) is preceded with 0 (01-09).	11
%H	Displays the hour for the specified value in 24-hour format (the range 0-23). The hour represents whole hours passed since midnight (displayed as 0). If the hour is a single digit (0-9), it is displayed as a single digit.	23

TABLE 13.6 Continued

Format Specifier	Description	Output of Value= CDate("1/2/2003 23:59:11.15")
HH, HH (plus any number of additional "H" characters)	Same as above, but a single digit hour (1-9) is preceded with 0 (01-09).	23
%m	Displays the minute for the specified value in the range 0-59. The minute represents whole minutes passed since the last hour. If the minute is a single digit (0-9), it is displayed as a single digit.	59
mm, mm (plus any number of dditional "m" characters)	Same as above. A single digit minute (0-9) is formatted with a preceding 0 (01-09).	59
%M	Displays the month, measured as a number between 1 and 12, inclusive. If the month is a single digit (1-9), it is displayed as a single digit.	1
MM	Same as above. A single digit month (1-9) is formatted with a preceding 0 (01-09).	01
MMM	Displays the abbreviated name of the month for the specified value.	Jan
MMMM	Displays the full name of the month for the specified value.	January
%s	Displays the seconds for the specified value in the range 0-59. The second represents whole seconds passed since the last minute. If the second is a single digit (0-9), it is displayed as a single digit only.	11
ss, ss (plus any number of additional "s" characters)	Same as above. A single digit second (0-9) is formatted with a preceding 0 (01-09).	11
%t	Displays the first character of the A.M./P.M. designator for the specified value.	P
tt, tt (plus any number of additional "t" characters)	Displays the A.M./P.M. designator for the specified value.	PM

TABLE 13.6 Continued

Format Specifier	Description	Output of Value= CDate("1/2/2003 23:59:11.15")
%y	Displays the year for the specified value as a maximum two-digit number. The first two digits of the year are omitted. If the year is a single digit (1-9), it is displayed as a single digit.	3
yy	Same as above. A single digit year (1-9) is formatted with a preceding 0 (01-09).	03
yyyy	Displays the year for the specified value, including the century. If the year is less than four digits, 0s are added to the left to display four digits.	2003
%z	Displays the time zone offset for the system's current time zone in whole hours only. The offset is always displayed with a leading sign, which indicates hours ahead of Greenwich mean time (+) or behind Greenwich mean time (-). The range of values is –12 to +13. Value is affected by daylight savings time.	–6 Note: –6 offset is for central standard time.
zz	Same as above. Single digit is formatted with a preceding 0 (00-09).	–06
zzz, zzz (plus any number of additional "z" characters)	Same as above, but displays hours and minutes. The range of values is –12:00 to +13:00. Single digit offset (0-9) is formatted with a preceding 0 (00-09).	–06:00
:	Displays time separator.	
/	Displays date separator.	
" " or ' '	Displays the literal value of a string enclosed.	
\	Displays the next character as a literal. Cannot be used to create an escape sequence.	

Additional information about custom date/time format strings can be found in the .NET Framework Developer's Guide at http://msdn.microsoft.com/library/default.asp?url=/library/en-us/cpguide/html/cpconcustomdatetimeformatstrings.asp.

Creating Alternating Colors for the Lines on a Report

To alternate color of the lines in the table, you can use the function `RowNumber()`.

To generate alternating colors for a table's `Detail` row, similar to those displayed in Table 13.7, you can set the `BackgroundColor` property of all columns and the table's `Detail` row to the expression `=IIF((RowNumber("MyTable") Mod 2) = 0, "LightGrey", "White")`.

TABLE 13.7 Alternating Table Row Colors

Row Number ("MyTable")	Product Name
1	Adjustable Race
2	All-Purpose Bike Stand
3	AWC Logo Cap

What if alternating colors need to be set for the group header (or footer)? In this case, you can employ the `RunningValue()` function to return a row number of a group's header.

If you have a table with a single group that uses `=Fields!ProductId.Value` as a group expression and you only display the group's header in the result, you can set the `BackgroundColor` property for all columns in the group's header equal to the expression `=IIF(RunningValue(Fields!Name.Value, CountDistinct, Nothing) Mod 2=0,"Gainsboro", "White")` to generate alternating colors, similar to Table 13.8.

TABLE 13.8 Design of Alternating Colors for the Group Header

TH→	Row Number (RunningValue)	Product Name	Items Sold
G1→	=RunningValue(Fields!Name.Value, CountDistinct, Nothing)	=Fields!Name.Value	=RowNumber("G1")

TH—Table header row

G1—Header of a single table group (named "G1") with the group expression `=Fields!Name.Value`

The resulting output is presented in Table 13.9. Note the number of items displayed in the Items Sold column. Although each group contains more than one hundred rows—each group's header is displayed only once, thus Items Sold displays aggregate number of rows in a group.

TABLE 13.9 Presentation of Alternating Colors for the Group Header/Footer

Row Number (RunningValue)	Product Name	Items Sold
1	Adjustable Race	1
2	All-Purpose Bike Stand	249
3	AWC Logo Cap	3382

Similarly to a single group, to display alternating colors when there is more than one table group, you can use `RunningValue()` on the combination of all group expressions, like this:

```
=RunningValue(CStr(Fields!ProductId.Value) & CStr(Fields!InnerGrouping.Value),
CountDistinct, Nothing)
```

NOTE

The `Demo Alternating Colors.rdl` **sample illustrates concepts discussed in this section.**

Paging Report

Pagination support depends on a rendering extension. PDF and TIFF (Image) formats are page oriented and allow you to precisely set page properties. HTML and Microsoft Excel are not page oriented. CSV and XML do not support pagination and ignore pagination properties.

SSRS provides several properties to support pagination: `PageBreakAtEnd`, `PageBreakAtStart`, `PageHeight`, `PageWidth`, `InteractiveHeight`, and `InteractiveWidth`.

PageHeight and PageWidth

These properties are used to control physical page sizing for PDF- and image-rendering extensions to insert page breaks based on the value of those properties. These properties accept strings in the format `{FloatingNumber}.{unit designator}`, where a unit designator could be: `in`, `mm`, `cm`, `pt`, and `pc`.

InteractiveHeight and InteractiveWidth

These properties are used for logical page sizing by the HTML- and Excel-rendering extensions. HTML allows specifying interactive page size that creates interactive breaks and allows navigating through pages, using a toolbar. Excel-rendering extensions insert "soft" page breaks into the resulting spreadsheet (can be seen through the Excel menu View Page Breaks). Both HTML and Excel pages are based on approximate page size and provide less precise page breaks than page-oriented formats. These properties are similar in format to `PageHeight/Width`. You can disable soft page breaks by setting `InteractiveHeight` to 0. However, if the report contains a large amount of data, this might negatively impact perceived performance—the user will not see a report until rendering of all data is complete.

PageBreakAtEnd and PageBreakAtStart

Setting these properties to `True` allows report designers to add page breaks at the beginning or the end of a rectangle, table, matrix, list, chart, or group. To take advantage of these properties, the following approach is often used:

- Create a group with the grouping expression `=System.Math.Ceiling(RowNumber(Nothing)/{Number of Rows per page})`
- Set `PageBreakAtEndProperty = True`
- Repeat table column headers by setting the table property
- Set `RepeatHeaderOnNewPage = True`

To dynamically adjust the number of rows in a page, a developer can pass a report parameter and use the following group expression:

```
=System.Math.Floor(RowNumber(Nothing)/(Parameters!RowsPerPage.Value)).
```

For physical page formatting, the `PageBreak` property adds page breaks in addition to those controlled by `PageHeight` and `PageWidth`. For example, when a report is rendered to Excel, this property breaks down the report to individual sheets. For HTML rendering, if `PageBreakAtEnd` and `PageBreakAtStart` are supplied, Interactive Height and Weight are ignored.

There are differences between different renderers on the amount of data included in a rendered report. For example, if a designer uses the toggle action, the PDF report renderer does not include a collapsed section, whereas the Excel renderer includes all sections, including collapsed ones, and provides an interface similar to the toggle action.

HTML pagination is based on current visibility. If a part of a report is collapsed, it will be included on the page if it fits in a collapsed state, even though expanding this section will take its size outside of the intended page size.

Pagination might improve perceived performance of a report—the first page will be rendered and presented to a user while SSRS continues rendering the remaining pages.

To access a particular page of a report, add the following to the URL: `&rc:Section={PageNumber}`.

Summary

SSRS supports a comprehensive set of formatting capabilities through the report item's properties, which control output appearance.

Some of the key properties are as follows:

- `BackgroundColor`—Controls background color of the item. When a report requires alternating colors for rows of output, this property can be used in conjunction with functions `RowNumber()` and `RunningValue`.
- `Color`—Controls the color of the text.

- `Format`—.NET Framework formatting string to apply to the item. The following are examples of format strings:
  - `###.##` formats a value of 012.30 to the following output 12.3
  - `(###)###-####` formats a value of `1234567890` to the output `(123)456-7890`, which is typical presentation of a phone number
  - `C` formats a value of `1234.56` to typical presentation of currency `$1,234.56`
  - `yyyy-MM-dd HH:mm` formats `11:59PM on 1/2/2006` to `2003-01-02 23:59`
- `Language`—Controls locale formatting. For example, when set to "`English (United Kingdom)`" currency sign in formatting changes from `$` to `£`.
- `PageBreakAtEnd` and `PageBreakAtStart`—Control pagination before and after an item.
- `PageHeight` and `PageWidth`—Control physical page sizing for PDF- and image-rendering extensions.

The following chapter discusses functionality that SSRS provides to simplify navigation in large reports and within the hierarchy of reports.

Report Navigation

CHAPTER 14

IN THIS CHAPTER

- Hyperlink (Jump to URL) Navigation
- BookmarkLink (Jump to Bookmark) Navigation
- Document Map
- Drillthrough (Jump to Report) Navigation
- Hiding Items and Toggle Items
- Practical Application of Action Items

One of the main uses for navigation functionality is to simplify navigation of large reports and hierarchies of reports. Report developers can add hyperlink actions (or simply actions) to a report. Reporting Services supports three types of actions:

- **`Drillthrough`** (`Jump to report`)—Jump to other reports. This action also provides an opportunity to provide parameters for the target report as well as the ability to jump to the same report with different parameters. This action is denoted with the `<Drillthrough>` element in a report's RDL.
- **`BookmarkLink`** (`Jump to bookmark`)—Jump to other areas (bookmarked) within the report. This action is denoted with the `<BookmarkLink>` element in a report's RDL.
- **`Hyperlink`** (`Jump to URL`)—Jump to web pages and other HREF constructs, such as mail and news. This action is denoted with the `<Hyperlink>` element in a report's RDL.

Expressions can be used as a value for any action. Developers can add an action from either the Properties dialog box (right-click on a report item, select Properties from the shortcut menu, and click the Navigation tab) or from the `Action` property (click the ellipses in the `Action` property of the control). See Figure 14.1 for more details.

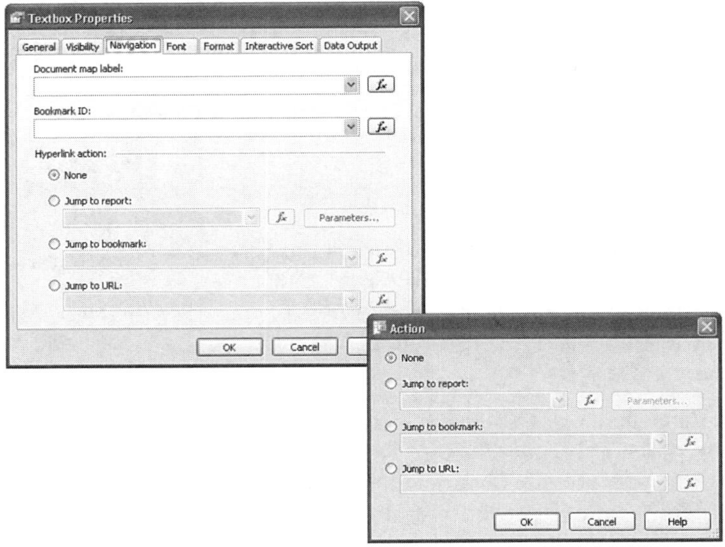

FIGURE 14.1 Two methods of adding actions to a report.

Actions can be added to a Textbox or an Image item, which, in turn, provides actionable items for List, Table, and Matrix. Any Reporting Services item can have a single action and either one or both of the `Bookmark` and `Document Map` labels associated with it. Multiple actions can point to a single bookmark link. This is similar to a reference to a particular topic in a book, in that multiple pages can point to a single topic.

TIP

Highlight an actionable item so it is intuitive to a user that the item can be clicked. Blue in color and underlined text items, usually, provide good highlights.

Hyperlink (Jump to URL) Navigation

When a report developer adds `Hyperlink` action, SSRS generates `HREF` to create a navigatable HTML link. For example, when a developer enters http://www.microsoft.com into a Textbox's `Jump to URL` action field and sets the value of `Textbox.Value` equal to "Visit Microsoft," the following is the link generated by SSRS when it renders the report to HTML format:

```
<a href="http://www.microsoft.com/" style="text-decoration:none;color:Black"
TARGET="_top">Visit Micorosft</a>
```

Reporting Services allows navigation using other constructs valid for the `HREF` tag. For example, `javascript:history.back()` allows you to emulate a browser's Back button. This particular construct relies on Java support by browser (Netscape 2 or higher and MSIE 3 or higher) and enabled JavaScript. Another valid construct is `mailto:support@adventureworks.com`, which allows creating a link that launches an email editor and places `support@adventureworks.com` on the `To` line. Other valid constructs include the following: ftp://www.microsoft.com to launch a FTP download or news:www.microsoft.com to get to a newsreader.

NOTE

Not all `HREF` constructs function in `Preview` mode. For example, `javascript:history.back()` will not deliver the action in `Preview` mode; also this construct will function after the report is deployed to a Report Server.

To create a `Hyperlink (Jump To URL)` action, enter a valid (such as http://www.microsoft.com or other described previously) `HREF` construct in the `Jump To URL` action field. Figure 14.1 shows two dialogs that allow you to input `Jump To URL` action field for a Textbox or Image report item. Action has the following corresponding RDL.

```
<Action>
  <Hyperlink>http://www.microsoft.com</Hyperlink>
</Action>
```

or

```
<Action>
  <Hyperlink>={Expression}</Hyperlink>
</Action>
```

In the preceding code fragment, an `{Expression}` is any expression that evaluates to a valid `HREF` construct as described previously, such as http://www.microsoft.com.

BookmarkLink (Jump to Bookmark) Navigation

`BookmarkLink (Jump to bookmark)` simplifies navigation for large reports. This action allows navigation to a bookmarked line or page of the report.

To create a `BookmarkLink` navigation, the first step is to set a bookmark. A bookmark can be set for any report item using the following:

- **Properties window**—The Properties window is normally docked in the lower-right corner of Report Designer. If you do not see this window, press F4 or use the View, Properties Window menu.
- **Navigation tab of an item's Properties dialog box**—The Properties dialog box can by accessed by right-clicking on a report item and selecting Properties from the shortcut menu. The Navigation tab of an item's Properties dialog box is shown in Figure 14.1.

An example of a bookmark is included in the `Actions -- Bookmark-Toggle-Document Map -- Products.rdl` sample for this book. After `Bookmark` is set, Report Designer adds the following RDL:

```
<Bookmark>
   ={Expression}
</Bookmark>
```

The next step is to create a `BookmarkLink` action, which performs the navigation to the bookmark set in the previous step. The `BookmarkLink` action can be created only for Textbox and Image report items. To create a `BookmarkLink` action, enter the `Jump to bookmark` expression on either of the following:

- **Action dialog box**—The Action dialog box can be accessed by clicking the ellipses "`(...)`" next to the `Action` property in the Properties window.
- **Navigation tab of an item's `Properties` dialog box**—The previous step describes how to access the Navigation tab.

After the `BookmarkLink` action is set, Report Designer adds the following RDL:

```
<Action>
   <BookmarkLink>
      ={Expression}
   </BookmarkLink>
</Action>
```

Document Map

Much like bookmarks, the document map is designed to simplify navigation for large reports. A document map is intended for interactive (HTML rendering) report viewing and is displayed as a side panel on a report.

PDF and Excel rendering extensions have a different way of articulating a document map. Excel rendering extensions create a separate worksheet with the name "Document map," which provides links to a worksheet with the report's data. PDF displays the document map in the `Bookmarks` Navigation tab.

Document map labels are set similarly to bookmarks as they relate to report items. To create a document map label for a report, you just fill the Document Map Label entry on the Navigation tab of an item's Properties dialog box, or enter the `Label` property in the Properties window.

After the document map labels are created, Reporting Services automatically generates a document map and renders a treelike structure containing navigational items. SSRS builds a document map entry when it sees the following RDL:

```
<Label>={Expression}</Label>
```

Document map labels defined for report items are displayed on the same level (next after the root level) and ordered in the order of the report item's appearance on a report. Order is based first on the position of the top side (vertical ordering) and second on the position of left side (horizontal ordering) of the item.

The document map also supports a hierarchical display of labels. SSRS creates a hierarchical view on a document map when you set Document Map Label and Parent Group expressions using the Grouping and Sorting Properties dialog box. The Grouping and Sorting Properties dialog box was discussed in Chapter 12, "Grouping, Sorting, and Aggregating Data, Working with Scope." The hierarchical view is not supported in PDF. Instead, PDF shows labels of a document map as a single level in the `Bookmarks` Navigation tab.

The document map has the same name as the name of the report. This name is used for the root node of a document map. There are no options that allow changing the name of a document map. Only one document map is allowed for a report.

NOTE

An example of a document map is included in the `Actions -- Bookmark-Toggle-Document Map -- Products.rdl` sample for this book.

Drillthrough (Jump to Report) Navigation

This type of action is usually employed when there is a need to design master (parent) and detail (child) reports. An action, which takes users to a detail report, is created on the master report.

To create a `Drillthrough` navigation (action) you need to set `Jump to report` expression on either the Action dialog box or on the Navigation tab of the item's Properties dialog box. The `Jump to report` expression needs to evaluate to a name of a report.

You can also specify parameters to pass to a report by clicking the Parameters button next to the `Jump to report` expression. The Parameters dialog box allows you to enter a constant name of a parameter and an expression that will assign a value to the parameter.

The following is an example of RDL for the `Drillthrough` action:

```
<Action>
  <Drillthrough>
    <ReportName>Product Detail</ReportName>
    <Parameters>
      <Parameter Name="ProductNumber">
        <Value>=Fields!Name.Value</Value>
      </Parameter>
    </Parameters>
  </Drillthrough>
</Action>
```

NOTE

The Back to Parent Report button on the Report Viewer's toolbar provides a convenient way to navigate back to a parent report. This button is especially handy in `Preview` mode.

An example of a `Drillthrough` **is included as a sample for this book and consists of master** (`Actions -- Drillthrough.PlusInteractiveSort -- Sales Order.rdl`) **and detail** (`Actions -- Hyperlink -- Product Detail.rdl`) **reports.**

Hiding Items and Toggle Items

Hiding and toggling items handles interactive visibility for sections of a report and allows you to dynamically expand portions of a report that you want to see. This is yet another option to simplify navigation. Hide and toggle functionality can be used, for example, to implement master/detail functionality, category/subcategory functionality, or to simply shorten a large report.

To implement this functionality, set an `InitialToggleState` property. The `InitialToggleState` property indicates an image that is displayed for a toggle item: `Collapsed`, `Expanded`, or `Expression`. Normally, toggle control is a picture of a plus or minus sign, which indicates an expanded or collapsed state, respectively. `InitialToggleState` property just defines a picture of a state image, but does not change the visibility of an item. If not specified, the default toggle state is collapsed. If a developer clears an initial state property, it reverts back to collapsed.

NOTE

Note that the toggle state is not available for groups. It is only available for individual items.

Reporting Services adds the following RDL (if the item is visible, the `<Hidden>` tag is not included):

```
<Visibility>
  <ToggleItem>{ToggleItem}</ToggleItem>
  <Hidden>={Expression}or {true}</Hidden>
</Visibility>
```

NOTE

An example of a toggling and hiding items is included as a sample report: `Actions -- Bookmark.Toggle.Document Map. -- Products.rdl.`

Practical Application of Action Items

Adventure Works Internet sales department wants to create an interactive product catalog. The initial screen of a report should not be larger than a single page. A report must provide effective navigation through products. A user must be able to navigate through the product category and subcategory hierarchies.

Implementation

A finished implementation is included as a sample for this book, as shown in `Actions -- Bookmark.Toggle.Document Map. -- Products.rdl`.

First, create a data set (you can name the data set "ProductCategories" as in the sample) with the following query using AdventureWorks data source.

```
SELECT Production.ProductCategory.Name AS CategoryName,
       Production.ProductSubcategory.Name AS SubCategoryName,
       Production.Product.Name AS ProductName,
       Production.ProductPhoto.ThumbNailPhoto,
       Production.Product.ProductNumber
FROM
Production.ProductCategory
INNER JOIN
Production.ProductSubcategory ON Production.ProductCategory.ProductCategoryID =
Production.ProductSubcategory.ProductCategoryID
INNER JOIN Production.Product ON Production.ProductSubcategory.ProductSubcategoryID
= Production.Product.ProductSubcategoryID
INNER JOIN
Production.ProductProductPhoto ON Production.Product.ProductID =
Production.ProductProductPhoto.ProductID
INNER JOIN
Production.ProductPhoto ON Production.ProductProductPhoto.ProductPhotoID =
Production.ProductPhoto.ProductPhotoID
```

Create a report layout outline, as shown in Figure 14.2. This report uses Matrix to provide category navigation.

Right-click Matrix's column group and view the Properties dialog box. On the Navigation tab (see Figure 14.3), add the following expression to the `BookmarkLink` (`Jump to bookmark`) action:

```
=Fields!CategoryName.Value
```

This allows users to access an appropriate category name on a report. Apply formatting so a user can tell that this is a clickable item.

Right-click the text box and view the Properties dialog box. On the Navigation tab, enter the following expression to the `Jump to URL` action (see Figure 14.4):

```
mailto:support@adventureworks.com
```

This action starts the user's email application and places `support@adventureworks.com` in the `To...` line.

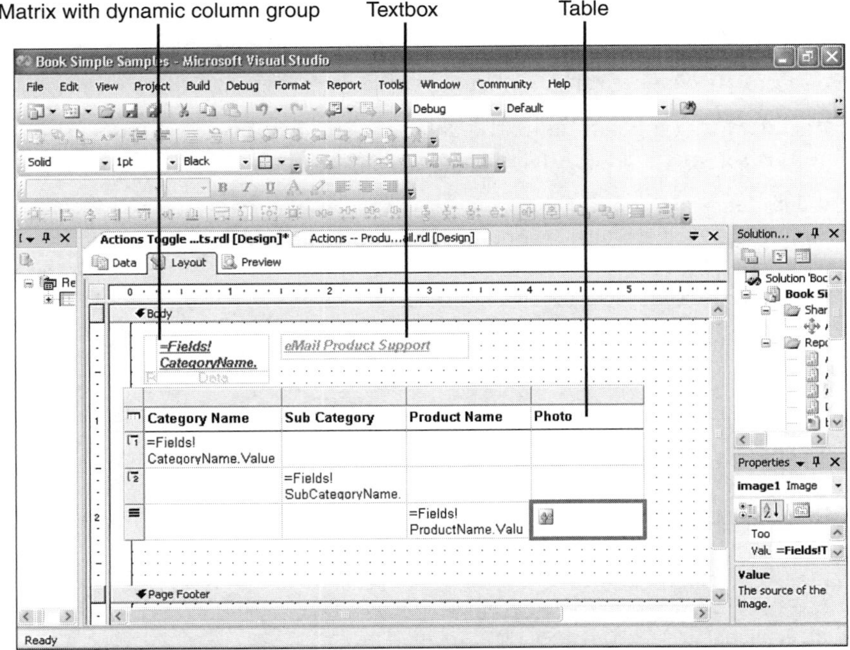

FIGURE 14.2 Navigation Report Layout view.

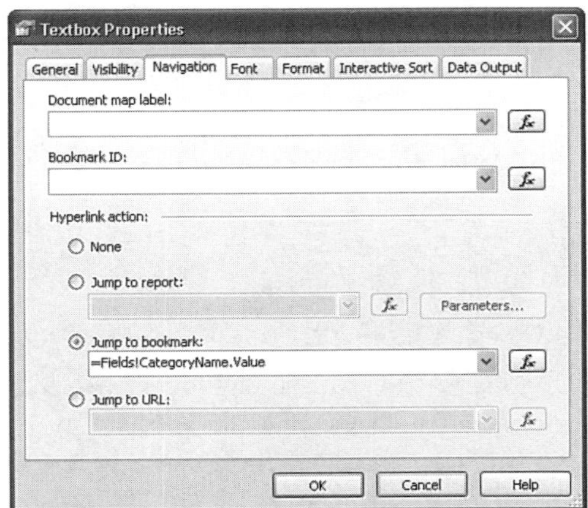

FIGURE 14.3 Jump to bookmark.

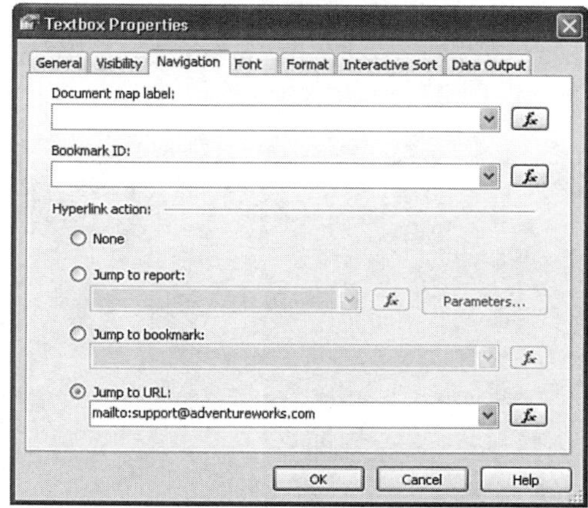

FIGURE 14.4 Jump to URL navigation.

Edit the table Subcategory group (inner group) and enter the following expression in the Document Map Label:

```
=Fields!SubCategoryName.Value
```

and the following expression in the Parent Group:

```
=Fields!CategoryName.Value
```

Note that this is a grouping expression and a document map for the outer (parent) group (see Figure 14.5). Thus, a hierarchy is formed for a document map.

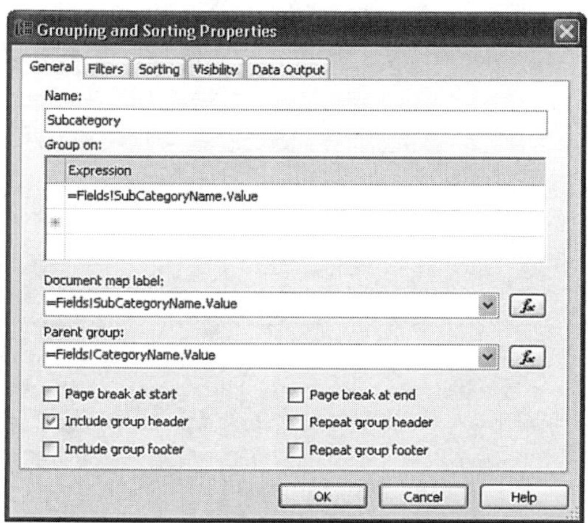

FIGURE 14.5 Document map and its hierarchy.

Click the Visibility tab. Set Initial Visibility to Hidden. Check the Visibility Can Be Toggled By Another Report Item check box, and enter CategoryName. Visibility information should look similar to Figure 14.6.

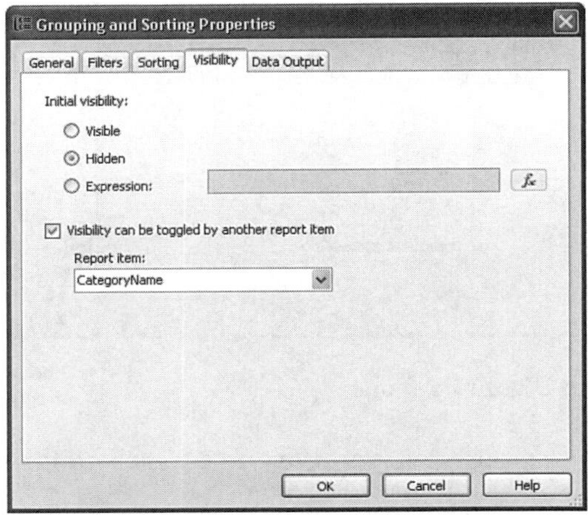

FIGURE 14.6 Setting item visibility.

In addition, set the `Visibility/Hidden` property to `True` for all detail cells and set the Visibility Can Be Toggled By Another Report Item to SubCategoryName for detail cells in the Product Name and Photo columns.

Edit the parent group to enter `=Fields!CategoryName.Value` as a grouping expression and a document map.

Access the properties of an image and add navigation to the `Actions -- Hyperlink -- Product Detail` report by filling the `Jump to report` action. Additional formatting and retrieving a picture of a product from the database should be easy. See Figure 14.7 for the final product.

An actual sample produces slightly different output and has some remarks pointing to the implemented futures.

NOTE

Note how the `Actions -- Hyperlink -- Product Detail` **report make use of the** `HideCost` **parameter. This is a hidden parameter that prevents the casual user from viewing cost information. However, when this report is accessed from** `Actions -- Drillthrough.PlusInteractiveSort -- Sales Order`**, a** `Drillthrough` **action on this report sets the** `HideCost` **parameter to** `False` **and thus reveals cost information.**

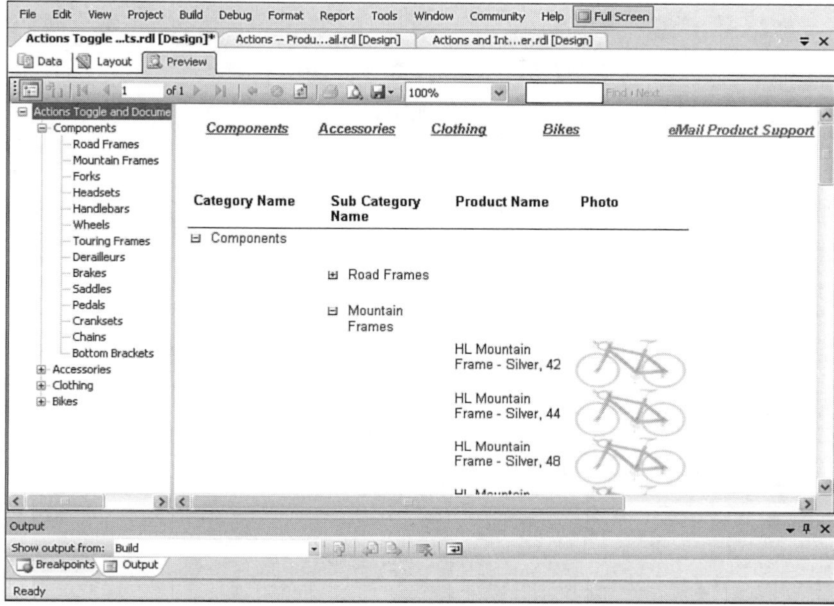

FIGURE 14.7 Sample report with navigation.

Summary

Actions, document maps, and bookmarks simplify navigation of complex reports, report hierarchies, and more. SSRS supports three types of actions: `Drillthrough` (or `Jump to report`), `BookmarkLink` (or `Jump to bookmarked` areas of a report), and `Hyperlink` (or `Jump to URL`—general web navigation).

Image and Text report items support the most complex navigation capabilities. Image and Text can contain a `Document map label` and `Bookmark ID`. `Document map label` and `Bookmark ID` mark navigation destinations on a report. Image and Text also support `Jump to ...` actions. Other SSRS items can serve as `Document map label` and `Bookmark ID` but do not by themselves support actions.

After a developer has defined document map labels, SSRS automatically renders a document map. Document map is supported by HTML, Excel, and PDF rendering extensions.

The next chapter reviews how SSRS works with multidimensional data sources and integrates with Analysis Services and Data Mining features of SQL Server 2005.

CHAPTER 15

Working with Multidimensional Data Sources

IN THIS CHAPTER

- Analysis Services Concepts
- Data-Mining Concepts
- MDX and DMX
- More In-Depth OLAP Concepts
- Creating Data-Mining Reports

Analysis Services is a large subject and deserves an entire book by itself. Although the details of Analysis Services are outside the scope of this book, discussion of basic concepts will help you to get the most out of this chapter.

Analysis Services Concepts

It is no surprise that during the course of business every company accumulates data. It is common to divide databases into two categories: transaction processing and data warehouses.

Typical transaction processing (Online Transaction Processing or OLTP) databases are used for current processing, such as online sales, customer management, employee management, production, and inventory management. Transaction processing databases are small in size, usually less than 100GB, and tend to have only a small amount of historical data that is directly relevant to ongoing transaction processing. OLTP database is tuned for fast processing of transactions, incurs many changes (volatile) throughout a day, and is normally not used for reporting. An OLTP database is typically normalized to optimize data storage and retrieval for transactions.

A data warehouse is a database that is used for reporting and data analysis. It is possible to use an OLTP database for reporting, but it often negatively impacts transactional performance and is certain to make online users unhappy. If an online purchasing transaction is slow, a user is likely going to use another site that offers better performance.

A data warehouse (DW) usually has the following attributes:

- It is large in size (it is not uncommon to have multiterabyte data warehouses) and might contain years of historical data. Part of the data might not be currently useful, but provides a view into the company's past and can be analyzed to determine why, for example, online sales were successful in a certain time frame, or how well a marketing campaign performed.
- It stores data in the matter understandable to business users as opposed to applications. In contrast, OLTP databases are designed to accommodate applications. A DW is designed to answer business questions, such as sales numbers for a particular region and time frame.
- It is updated on predetermined intervals (once daily, weekly, or monthly) from transactional databases and ideally does not change previously stored historical data.

A subset of a data warehouse is called a data mart. A data warehouse usually contains data from a variety of heterogeneous data sources. Data marts are designed to minimize the amount of data used in processing and can contain a subset of data, based, for example, on time or geography.

Unified Data Model (UDM) is a new future that is available in SQL Server 2005. UDM greatly simplifies access to data and combines the best of relational and analytical models.

UDM allows Reporting Services to get data from Analysis Services in a similar fashion as from any relational data source. One way to think about UDM is as a view on data, which allows "combining" data from various data sources (SQL Server relational and OLAP databases, Oracle, Teradata, DB2, and so on), "defining" relationships between that data, "defining" calculated fields, and mapping between original column names and newly defined names that might be more understandable to users of UDM. Several words in the previous sentence are included in double quotes (""). UDM does not really combine data, but rather creates a metadata (data describing) view. This does not affect source data itself, but allows creating a metadata view that, for example, may have a "relationship" between SQL Server and an Oracle table. Then UDM can be queried, like a database, and UDM, in turn, will access original data sources to retrieve needed data. UDM blurs the usual differentiation between OLTP and DW data. In the past, DW stored denormalized data for quick retrieval. This is standard in the industry, but with UDM, users no longer have to denormalize their data warehouses.

Analysis Services consists of two components: Online Analytical Processing (OLAP) and Data Mining (DM). OLAP is designed to summarize data and DM is designed to look for patterns and trends in data.

Let's look at the example in which a manager wants to analyze sales by country. It is certainly possible to use aggregate functions such as `SUM()` in a query or in SSRS to calculate summaries by country, but for the large amounts of data, it is not very efficient.

Depending on the amount of data, summarization could be slow, which would be unsatisfactory to online users.

Reporting Services provides caching mechanisms that allow you to prepare a summary report and then display it to a user in real time without waiting for data retrieval. However, OLAP provides a better choice when a user is looking for summarized (or aggregated) data. This is because OLAP is specially tuned to perform aggregations. One of the most useful OLAP modes is Multidimensional OLAP (MOLAP). MOLAP stores aggregated data in an Analysis Services' multidimensional structure, called cube, which is highly optimized to maximize query performance.

NOTE

This chapter discusses default OLAP aggregation mode: MOLAP. Analysis Services provides two modes in addition to MOLAP: Relational OLAP (ROLAP—does not store summaries and queries relational data for each MDX query) and Hybrid OLAP (HOLAP—is a combination of MOLAP and ROLAP). Details of various modes are outside of this book's scope.

A T-SQL query against the AdventureWorksDW database to get a summary by country would look like the following:

```
SELECT DimSalesTerritory.SalesTerritoryCountry AS [Country-Region],
     SUM(FactInternetSales.SalesAmount) AS [Internet Sales-Sales Amount]
FROM DimSalesTerritory INNER JOIN FactInternetSales ON
     DimSalesTerritory.SalesTerritoryKey = FactInternetSales.SalesTerritoryKey
GROUP BY DimSalesTerritory.SalesTerritoryCountry
```

A comparative multidimensional (or MDX—you can find more about MDX later in this chapter) query to retrieve the same result would look like the following:

```
SELECT NON EMPTY
    { [Measures].[Internet Sales Amount]} ON COLUMNS,
       NON EMPTY { [Customer].[Customer Geography].[Country]}
DIMENSION PROPERTIES
    MEMBER_CAPTION,
    MEMBER_UNIQUE_NAME ON ROWS
FROM [Adventure Works]
```

As you can see, for a simple aggregation the complexity of either query is fairly comparable. The key difference is in the underlying structures that each query accesses.

At this point, you should not be concerned if you are not familiar with MDX. SQL Server 2005 has an extremely capable visual designer that makes creation of an MDX query a fairly easy endeavor.

The result of both queries is the same and is shown in Table 15.1.

TABLE 15.1 Query Results

Country-Region	Internet Sales-Sales Amount
Australia	9061000.5844
Canada	1977844.8621
France	2644017.7143
Germany	2894312.3382
United Kingdom	3391712.2109
United States	9389789.5108

The duration of either query is not significantly different if the amount of data is small. For large amounts of data, the MDX query is going to be significantly faster, because a cube stores aggregate data. Aggregation of data can be done on multiple levels, such as country, state, and city, and can be subsequently stored in the cube; thus, MOLAP does not have to query a large DW to generate needed summaries. All that needs to be queried is the cube. MOLAP summarizes and stores data when the cube is processed.

Data-Mining Concepts

Data Mining is designed to analyze trends and patterns in the data. For example, a manager at Adventure Works wants to analyze purchasing patterns of Adventure Works customers and determine how to up-sell and cross-sell shoppers online, and how to best design a marketing (mailing) campaign. Multiple attributes of a customer can be analyzed (age, geographic location, number of cars, number of children, gender, and marital status). There are potential patterns of attributes that determine if the customer is likely to purchase a certain product. Based on determined patterns, a manager can target likely shoppers with promotions. Data Mining derives knowledge from data by examining it using mathematical models for predictions and statistical analysis.

Conversely to Data Mining, OLAP usability for trend analysis is limited. A user would have to come up with a hypothesis that he needs to verify by looking through the data and verifying if it is true. If the number of attributes that needs to be taken into account is large, some would likely be missed by an analyst. Large amounts of data increase complexity of analysis and require additional manpower to analyze the data.

A case table is one of the main constructs in Data Mining. Case encapsulates everything about an entity that is being categorized, classified, or analyzed for trends. A simple case is, for example, a Customer, who has the following attributes: Age, Martial Status, and Wealth.

Creating a Data Mining Model (DMM)

Before creating a new model, you should do the following:

- Define the problem: What columns or attributes should the model predict?

- Determine the location of the data to be analyzed. The source of data could be a SQL Server database or a cube.
- Decide the data-mining algorithm the model should use.

The Data Mining Model designed to analyze the probability of a bike purchase for a customer of a certain age could be created with the following code:

```
CREATE MINING MODEL [BikePurchasePrediction]
(
    CustomerKey LONG KEY,
    BikeBuyer DOUBLE DISCRETE PREDICT,
    Age DOUBLE CONTINUOUS
)
USING Microsoft_Decision_Trees
```

Training DMM

To train DMM, "feed" it with data for which attributes to be predicted are known. For example:

```
INSERT INTO [BikePurchasePrediction]
(
    CustomerKey,
    BikeBuyer,
    Age
)
OPENQUERY
(
   [Adventure Works DW], 'SELECT CustomerKey, BikeBuyer, Age FROM
vTargetMail'
)
```

NOTE

The first parameter for `OPENQUERY` is a named data source that exists on the Microsoft SQL Server 2005 Analysis Services (SSAS) database, such as `[Adventure Works DW]` used in example.

DMM does not, usually, store inserted data; instead, it builds a statistical model—statistical patterns that the mining algorithm detected in the data. This statistical model is stored in a truth table, which contains each possible combination of examined parameters and the probability of each combination. In a "nutshell," a truth table looks similar to Table 15.2.

TABLE 15.2 Truth Table

Age	Probability of Buying a Bike
40	70%

As needed, DMM can be retrained or incrementally refined, using `TRUNCATE TABLE` and `DROP TABLE` statements.

Querying DMM

To query a DMM, you need to have input data that you want to analyze and a trained DMM. A query maps information between input data and a DMM and needs to specify what has to be predicted.

For example:

```
SELECT
    age, PredictProbability([Bike Buyer])
FROM BikePurchasePrediction PREDICTION JOIN ProspectiveBuyer
    ON BikePurchasePrediction.age = ProspectiveBuyer.age
```

MDX and DMX

MDX is an acronym for Multidimensional Expressions. It is a statement-based scripting language used to define, manipulate, and retrieve data from multidimensional objects in Microsoft SQL Server 2005 Analysis Services (SSAS). MDX is similar in many ways to the familiar Structured Query Language (SQL) syntax typically used with relational databases, but it is not an extension of SQL.

Data Mining Extensions (DMX) is a language that you can use to create and work with data mining models in SSAS. You can use DMX to create new data mining models, to train these models, and to browse, manage, and predict using those models. DMX language is an extension of SQL, to create and work with models.

More In-Depth OLAP Concepts

First, you should understand a couple of definitions to become familiar with Analysis Services lingo. Measure or fact is a numerical value used to monitor (measure) business. Sales amount is an example of a measure. Dimension is an independent group of attributes of a measure. Each attribute within a group is called a member. Dimension has to be meaningful for business aggregations. For the member to be included in dimension, it should have a meaningful relationship to the dimension. Geography, date/time, and customer are examples of dimensions.

Measure can be analyzed by one or multiple dimensions. Table 15.1 earlier in this chapter is a simple example of aggregations or an OLAP report. In Table 15.1, Internet Sales-Sales Amount is a measure and Country-Region is a dimension. Thus, the data in Table 15.1 is analyzed and aggregated by a single dimension. Data can also be analyzed by two dimensions, such as date and geography, as shown in Table 15.3.

TABLE 15.3 Two-Dimensional Data

Internet Sales-Sales Amount			Calendar Year		
Country-Region	**2001**	**2002**	**2003**	**2004**	**Grand Total**
Australia	1,309,047	2,154,285	3,033,784	2,563,884	9,061,000
Canada	146,830	621,602	535,784	673,628	1,977,844
France	180,572	514,942	1,026,325	922,179	2,644,018
Germany	237,785	521,231	1,058,406	1,076,891	2,894,312
United Kingdom	280,335	583,826	1,278,097	1,195,895	3,338,153
United States	1,111,805	21,34,457	2,858,664	3,338,422	9,443,348
Grand Total	3,266,374	6,530,344	9,791,060	9,770,900	29,358,678

It is possible to add a third dimension (and so on) and, as in geometry, the structure will be a cube. A cube is basically a structure in which all the aggregations of measures by dimensions are stored.

Some dimensions can have one or many hierarchies for its members. For example:

- Geography dimension might have a hierarchy: country, region (such as east, central, mountain, west), state (such as Texas, Florida, California), county, city, and postal code.

- Time might have a hierarchy: year, half-year (or semester), quarter, and month.

An example of a hierarchy is demonstrated in Figure 15.1.

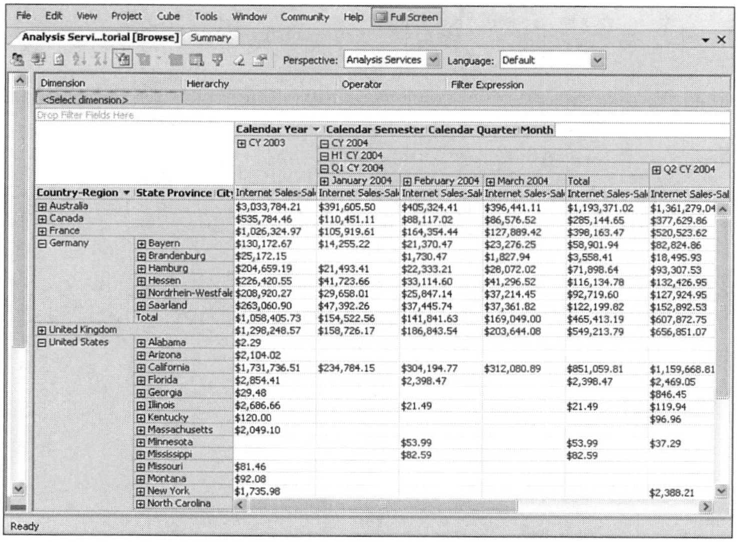

FIGURE 15.1 Multidimensional data with hierarchies.

The following walk-through should help you achieve a better understanding of OLAP and its subsequent use by Reporting Services.

1. Start Business Intelligence Development Studio and create a new Analysis Services project. Give it a name Analysis Services Sample.
2. In Solution Explorer, right-click Data Sources, and select New Data Source from the shortcut menu. The Data Source Wizard begins. You can think of Data Source as a connection to the database. Click Next on the Welcome screen.
3. On the Select How to Define the Connection screen, click the New button. Enter the requested information. To connect to SQL Server database, select Native OLE DB\SQL Native Client as the Provider.
4. Enter the server name (for the local server, you can use either server name, `localhost` or `"."` dot). Select the authentication (Windows authentication is preferred). Select or enter AdventureWorksDW as the database.
5. Click Next. On the Impersonation Information screen, enter impersonation information. Selecting Use the Service Account should work in most of the cases. Leave the default name for the data source: Data Source Adventure Works DW.

Now that you have created a data source, the next set of steps is to create a Data Source view:

1. In Solution Explorer, right-click Data Source Views and then select New Data Source View from the shortcut menu. Click Next and select Adventure Works DW as the data source. Click Next.
2. The wizard examines the data source and brings up a dialog box in which tables or views from the data source can be selected. Select `FactInternetSales`, `DimCustomer`, `DimGeography`, and `DimTime`. Click Next. In the Completing the Wizard screen, enter Adventure Works DW Source View. Click Finish to complete the wizard.
3. BI/Visual Studio brings up the design diagram. The next step is to create friendly names. Right-click FactInternetSales, and then select Properties from the shortcut menu. Remove the prefix "Fact" in the `Friendly Name` property. For all other tables in the diagram, remove the prefix "Dim" in the `Friendly Name` property. After completion of this step, BI Studio looks similar to Figure 15.2. Figure 15.2 basically shows an essence of the Unified Data Model. You can connect to various data sources, create calculated fields, and establish relationships—all without any changes to the original data. Unlike in previous versions, flattening and denormalizing of analysis data are no longer required.

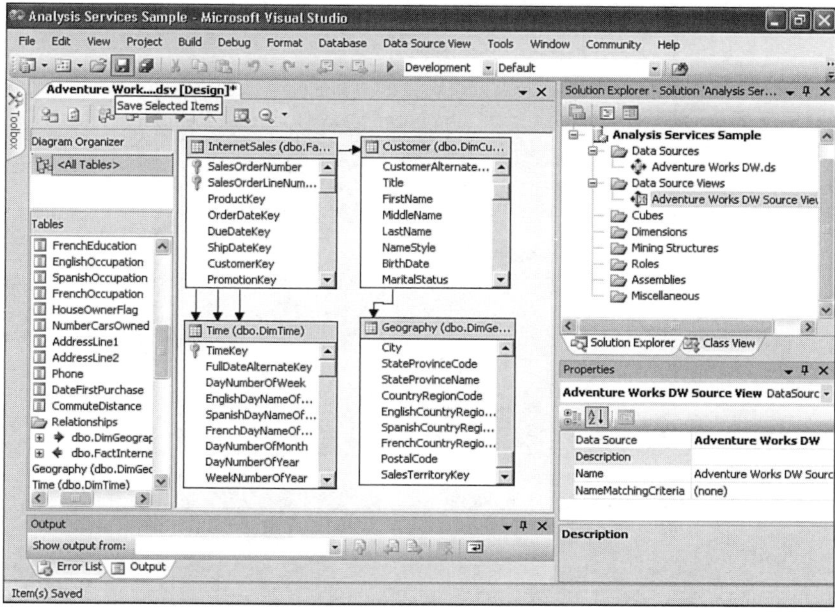

FIGURE 15.2 Unified Data Model.

In the next set of steps, you will create a new Analysis Services cube:

1. In Solution Explorer, right-click Cubes, and then select New Cube from the shortcut menu. After reading the information, click Next on the Welcome screen. Accept the defaults on the Select Build Method screen: Build the Cube Using Data Source, Auto Build, and Create Attributes and Hierarchies. On the Select Data Source View screen, accept the default: Adventure Works DW Source View. Click Next. After processing completes, click Next on the Detecting Fact and Dimension Tables screen.

2. On the Identify Fact and Dimension Tables screen, select Time as the Time dimension table. It should look similar to Figure 15.3. The Cube Wizard looks at the data model that you have designed in Data Source view and determines the correct fact and dimension tables.

3. In the Select Time Periods dialog box, map the time table columns as follows:

   - Year—`CalendarYear`
   - HalfYear—`CalendarSemester`
   - Quarter—`CalendarQuarter`
   - Month—`EnglishMonthName`
   - Date—`FullDateAlternateKey`

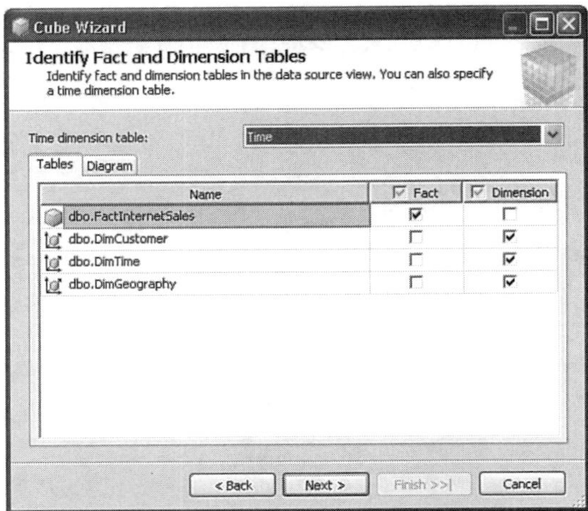

FIGURE 15.3 Fact and dimension tables.

4. Click Next and on the Select Measures screen, deselect everything, except Sales Amount, Tax Amt, Freight, and Internet Sales Count. Note that the wizard automatically selects Internet Sales when one of the measures (for example, Freight) is selected. Only numeric values are shown for the selection on this `dialog` box. The Internet Sales table contains other nonnumeric columns, such as Order Number. Because it is nonnumeric, it cannot be selected as a measure. Note that the Customer Key is not included on this selection. This is because the wizard knows that it is a relationship, based on the Data Source view and does not include it in aggregations. Also note several columns with the word "Key" in their names. These are relationship columns. The wizard displays these as measures because the columns are numeric and you did not include tables that those columns reference in the `Data Source` view. Hence, the wizard made an assumption that the column must be a measure. Lastly, note that Internet Sales Count is not a column in the Internet Sales table, it is automatically generated by Analysis Services. Internet Sales Count represents the number of line items sold on any given level.

5. Click Next. The wizard detects hierarchies. Click Next. Note that there are only two dimensions in the Review New Dimensions window: Customer and Time. If you expand Customer, you would notice that Geography is a hierarchy under the Customer dimension. Geography is not an independent dimension because there is no direct relationship between Internet Sales and Geography, only through Customer. See Figure 15.4. You can also expand the Attributes folders to see Customer's attributes, such as First Name and Last Name.

6. Click Next and name the cube Adventure Works DW Cube. Click Finish to complete the wizard. You should see a screen similar to Figure 15.5.

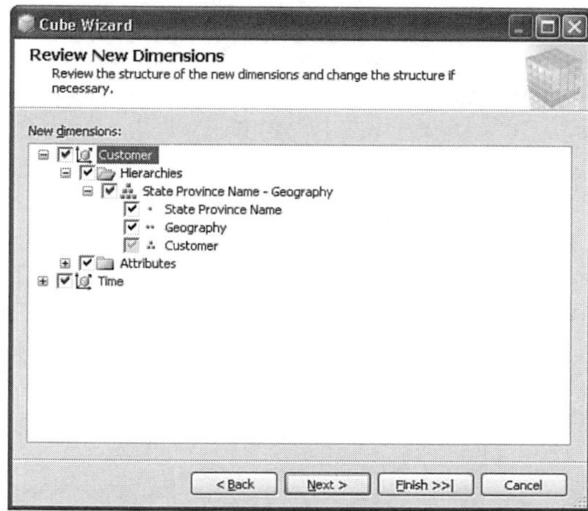

FIGURE 15.4 Reviewing new dimensions.

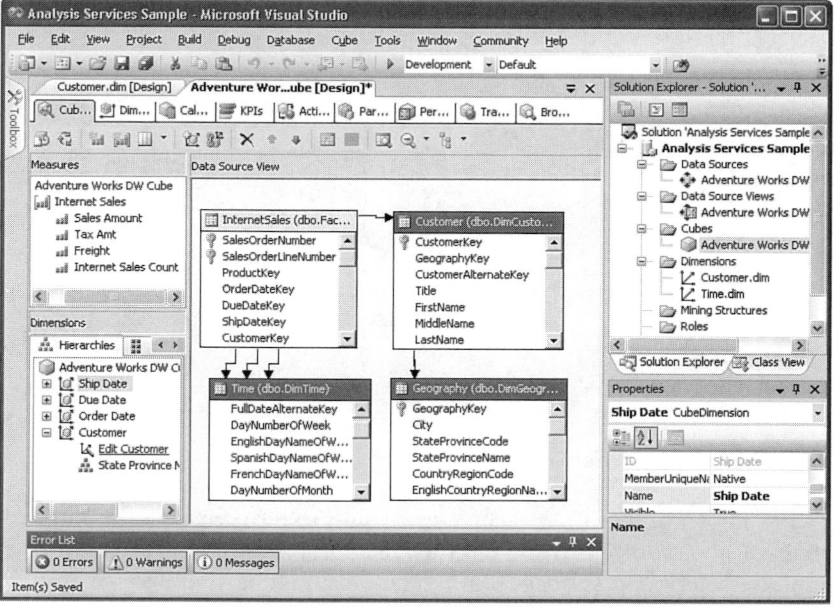

FIGURE 15.5 Cube design screen.

Now let's modify the Customer dimension to create a more logical Geography hierarchy than the wizard detected for us:

1. Under the Dimension folder in Solution Explorer, double-click the Customer dimension. From the Attributes panel, drag the English Country Region Name attribute to

the position right above the State Province Name level in the Geography Hierarchy. From the Attributes panel, drag the City attribute to the position right below the State Province Name level. When thinking about a hierarchy and what level to place a particular attribute, consider what "contains" or "has" what. For example, country has many states and, thus, should be on the higher level compared to state. Correspondingly, on the diagram, Country should receive less schematic "dots" than state.

2. Right-click the Geography level from the State Province Name-Geography hierarchy and select Delete from the context menu. Geography level is a geography key that does not carry useful information for our business analysis. Customer has many attributes, which might not be useful for the high-level analysis that we are trying to do. You should see a screen similar to Figure 15.6 after this step is completed.

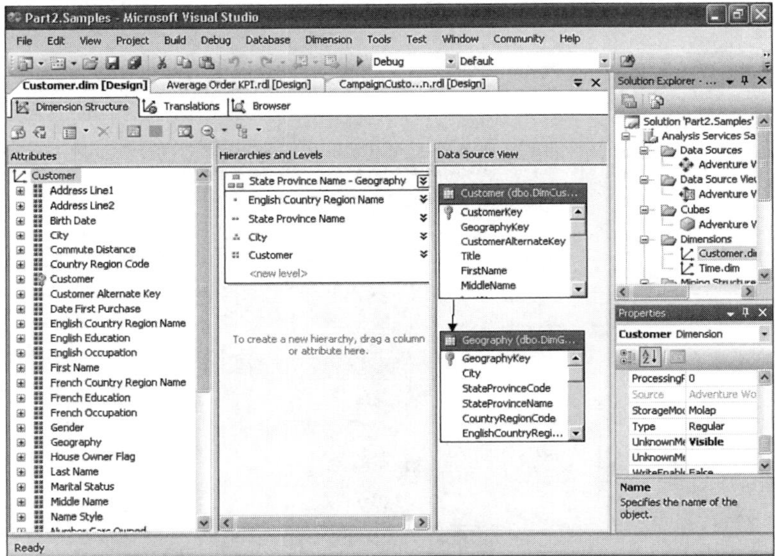

FIGURE 15.6 Dimension design screen.

The following steps will modify the Time dimension to properly order months of the year. Alphabetically, months are ordered such as: April, August, and so on. After ordering by key in place, you obtain correct ordering: January, February, and so on. You need this ordering when working with Key Performance Indicators later in this chapter.

1. Double-click the Time dimension in Solution Explorer. In the Hierarchies and Levels, modify the name of the hierarchy from CalendarYear—CalendarSemester—CalendarQuarter—EnglishMonthName—FullDateAlternateKey to Date by right-clicking the hierarchy and selecting Rename from the shortcut menu. This is done to simplify queries that you will write in the future.

2. In the Attributes pane, click on the EnglishMonthName attribute of a Time dimension. In the Properties window (normally docked in the lower-right corner), click the KeyColumns property and click the ellipses (...). This brings up the DataItem Collection Editor dialog box.

3. Click the Remove button to delete the existing member DimTime. EnglishMonthName. Click the Add button to add a new member. In the DataItem Collection Editor under the Misc pane, click Source and then click the ellipses (...) next to Source. The Object Binding dialog box opens.

4. In the Object Binding dialog box, select ColumnBinding as the Binding type and MonthNumberOfYear as the Source column. Click OK to complete the Object Binding dialog box.

5. Make sure that the OrderBy property has the value Key.

Now you are ready to deploy your solution:

1. On the main menu, select Build, Deploy Solution. After deployment completes, double-click the Adventure Works DW Cube in Solution Explorer, and then click the Browser tab, which is the last tab in the Adventure Works Cube [Design] window.

2. Use the Reconnect button to refresh the Browser tab. Keep in mind that after the cube structure is modified and changes are deployed, you should use the Reconnect button to browse the most recent updates. BI Studio should show something similar to Figure 15.7.

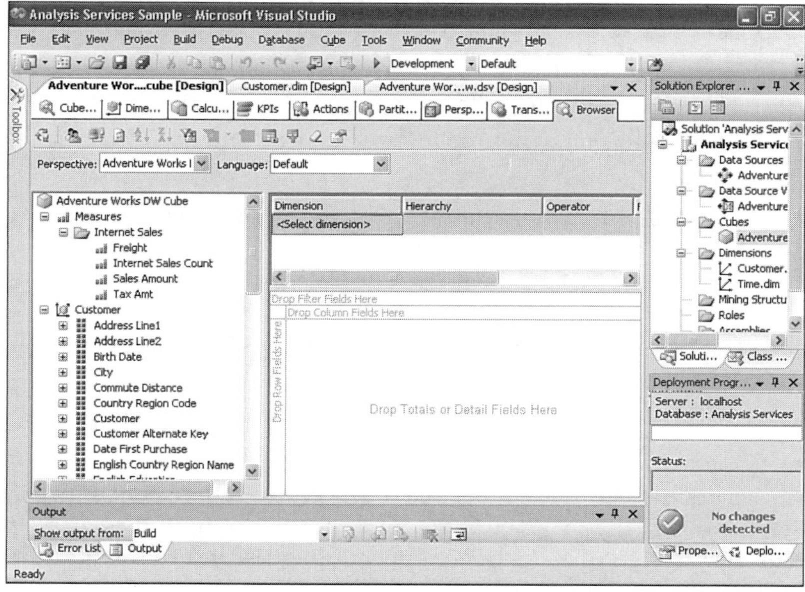

FIGURE 15.7 Cube browser.

To see the results of your work, drag and drop the Sales Amount from the Internet Sales measure to the center of the pivot table control, where it says "Drop Totals or Details Fields Here." Drag and drop English Country Region Name from the Customer dimension on the row part of the pivot table control, where it says "Drop Row Fields Here." The pivot table should display information similar to Table 15.1. You have now completed and verified the cube. This is a very basic cube that will help you to understand how to use Reporting Services with Analysis Services. More details about cubes and advanced features of Analysis Services can be found in the SQL Server Books Online.

One of the new features added in Analysis Services 2005 that has high potential for use in Reporting Services is Key Performance Indicators (KPIs). Key Performance Indicators are designed to evaluate performance criteria that a business, usually, considers strategic in nature. Performance is evaluated against a specified goal and has to be quantifiable. Some of the KPI examples are: stock performance, cost of operations, customer satisfaction, and so on.

Let's add a KPI to the just-completed cube:

1. In Solution Explorer, double-click the Adventure Works DW Cube. Click the KPIs tab. Right-click the surface of the KPI Organizer pane, and select New KPI from the shortcut menu. Name this KPI Average Item Price. This KPI is useful, for example, if Adventure Works' management had determined that Internet sales have the minimum order-processing costs when an average price per item sold is $100 or more. In turn, maximum order-processing cost is when the average price per item sold is less than $10.

2. For the Value Expression, enter the following MDX query:

   ```
   [Measures].[Sales Amount]/[Measures].[Internet Sales Count]
   ```

3. For the Goal Expression, enter 100.

4. For the Status Expression, enter the following query:

```
Case
    When [Measures].[Sales Amount]/[Measures].[Internet Sales Count] < 10
         Then -1
    When [Measures].[Sales Amount]/[Measures].[Internet Sales Count] <= 50
        Then 0
    When [Measures].[Sales Amount]/[Measures].[Internet Sales Count] >= 100
         Then 1
End
```

5. In the Trend Expression, enter the following MDX query. This query compares current values of the average order size to the previous time period (depending on the level of detail, this could be a year, month, and so on). If the current period exceeds the previous one, the trend is good; otherwise, it needs improvement.

```
Case
When
    ([Order Date].[Date],
    [Measures].[Sales Amount])
    /
    ([Order Date].[Date],
    [Measures].[Internet Sales Count])
    >=
    ([Order Date].[Date].PrevMember,
    [Measures].[Sales Amount])
    /
     ([Order Date].[Date].PrevMember,
     [Measures].[Internet Sales Count])
Then 1
Else -1
End
```

6. Click the Browser View button on the KPI toolbar. Click the Process button on the KPI toolbar, and then click Run in the dialog box. Analysis Services processes KPI. After the process has completed, close the Process Progress and Process Cube dialog box. In the browser view, you should see KPI indicators, similar to Figure 15.8.

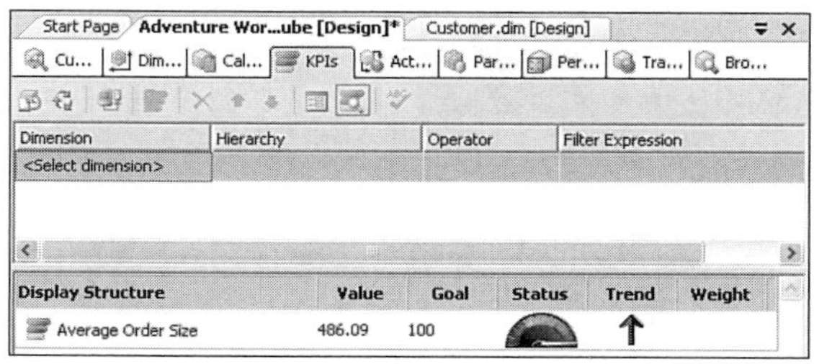

FIGURE 15.8 KPIs (Key Performance Indicators).

Now let's create a mining structure. Adventure Works' management wants to create a targeting advertisement on the website to promote bicycle sales. Adventure Works had collected data from existing customers and can target those already, based on the existing data, but what about new customers making purchases? When should Adventure Works display links to bicycles to be the most effective and nonobtrusive in the advertising campaign? Similarly, what kind of customer should be targeted for a targeted mail campaign?

1. In Solution Explorer, double-click Adventure Works DW Source View. Right-click in the diagram area and select Add/Remove Tables from the shortcut menu. Add the vTargetMail view. This is the view based on the data in Adventure Works DW tables, which adds a BikeBuyer field to the DimCustomer table. This field is derived from the Internet Sales table, where the product purchased was a bicycle.

2. In Solution Explorer, right-click Mining Structures, and then select New Mining Structure from the shortcut menu. Click Next on the Welcome screen. Accept the default (From Existing Relational Database or Data Warehouse) by clicking Next. Accept the default mining algorithm (Microsoft Decision Trees) on the Select the Data Mining Technique screen. Click Next. Accept the default Adventure Works DW Source View for the Data Source view. Click Next. Select vTargetMail as the Case table, and then click Next. Remember from earlier in this chapter that Case table is a table that is being analyzed to determine patterns in the data.

3. Leave CustomerKey as the key, and then select Bike Buyer as Predictable. Note that the Suggest button has become available. Click it and note that based on the data sample, Age is the best input for the model.

4. Because the table that you have for tests does not have an Age column and to simplify further efforts, let's use Birth Date instead of Age. It is possible to use the `DATEDIFF()` function to calculate an age of a customer, but because Birth Date provides essentially the same (time-frame) information as Age, you can leverage Birth Date. You should see a screen similar to Figure 15.9. Click Next.

5. On the Specify Columns' Content and Data Type screen, click Detect. The wizard samples data. Note that the Bike Buyer's Content Type changed from Continuous to Discrete. The wizard queried the data and determined that the data is discrete, based on the fact that the Bike Buyer contains an integer value with just a few actual values: 1 and 0. Click Next.

6. In the Mining Structure name, enter Bike Buyer Structure and in the Mining Model name, enter Bike Buyer Model. Select Allow Drill Through. Click Finish. Note Customer Sales Structure appears under Mining Structures in Solution Explorer.

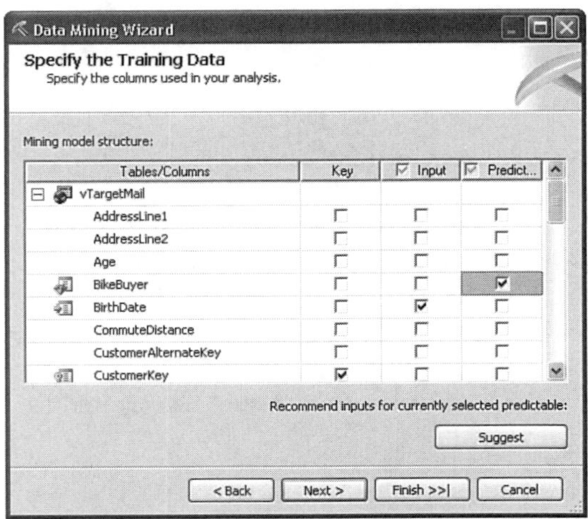

FIGURE 15.9 Data Mining Wizard.

Now you are ready to deploy your Data Mining Model. Click the Build, Deploy Solution menu. After deployment completes, click the Mining Model Viewer tab. Note the decision tree that was built; based on the data, it should look similar to Figure 15.10.

The decision tree indicates that customers born in 1969 are almost three times as likely to purchase a bike as other customers and customers born before 9/22/1931 are least likely to purchase a bike.

As an exercise to better understand data mining, click through other tabs, such as Mining Accuracy Chart. Click the Lift Chart tab under the Mining Accuracy Chart tab and note that the model provides at least 1.4 times better prediction than random guesses.

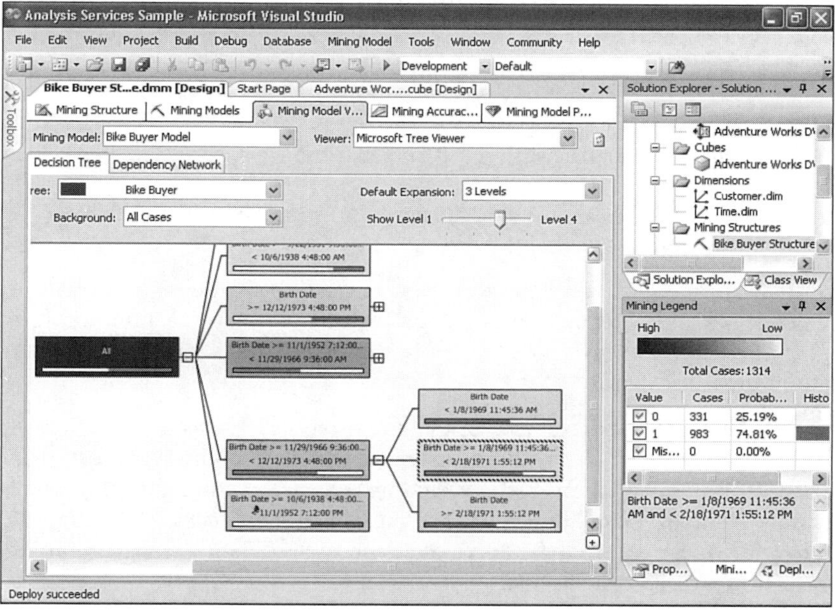

FIGURE 15.10 Decision tree.

Click the Mining Model Prediction tab. Click Select Case Table on the diagram and choose vTargetMail. Drag and drop the BikeBuyer field from the Input Table on the grid located below the diagram on the screen. Drag and drop the Bike Buyer field from the mining model on the grid. On the third row of the source column, click and select Prediction Function from the drop-down menu. In the same row, select PredictProbability and drag and drop `Bike Buyer` from the `Bike Buyer` model to the Criteria/Argument column of the third row. Click the drop-down next to the Switch to Query Result View (looks like a grid) button on the toolbar and select Query. The following query is displayed. This is a DMX query comparing actual in vTargetMail table and value predicted by a model.

```
SELECT
  [Bike Buyer Model].[Bike Buyer],
  PredictProbability([Bike Buyer Model].[Bike Buyer]),
  t.[BikeBuyer]
From
  [Bike Buyer Model]
PREDICTION JOIN
  OPENQUERY([Adventure Works DW],
    'SELECT
      [BikeBuyer],
      [BirthDate]
    FROM
      [dbo].[vTargetMail]
    ') AS t
ON
  [Bike Buyer Model].[Birth Date] = t.[BirthDate] AND
  [Bike Buyer Model].[ Bike Buyer] = t.[Bike Buyer]
```

Now, you are ready to query OLAP data and data-mining structures from Reporting Services. The following are the steps:

1. On the main menu, select File, Add, New Project. Select Report Server Project from the list of installed Business Intelligence Projects templates. Name the new project AnalysisServicesSamples. Click OK. Note that this is the same procedure as for creating any report project.

2. Right-click on the Reports folder under the AnalysisServicesSamples project, and select Add New Report from the shortcut menu. The Report Wizard starts. Click the Next button to advance from the Welcome screen. On the Select the Data Source screen, select New Data Source, use the name AnalysisServicesData, and select Microsoft SQL Server Analysis Services as the type of data source. Use an appropriate connection string, for example:

   ```
   Data Source=localhost;Initial Catalog="Analysis Services Sample"
   ```

   Select Make This a Shared Data Source. The Report Wizard should look similar to Figure 15.11.

3. Click Next. Note that the Design the Query screen does not allow you to paste in a query. This is by design to avoid potential issues with complex MDX or DMX queries. Click the Query Builder button.

4. In the Metadata pane, expand Measures/Internet Sales/Internet Sales and Customer hierarchies. Drag and drop Sales Amount from Measures on the area marked "Drag Levels or Measures Here to Add to the Query" (we will abbreviate this as "design area" from now on). Drag and drop English_Country_Region_Name on the design area. So far, the process is not very different from working with pivot tables. However, in this case, Query Builder only allows you to design queries that produce table-like output. The Query Builder should look similar to Figure 15.12.

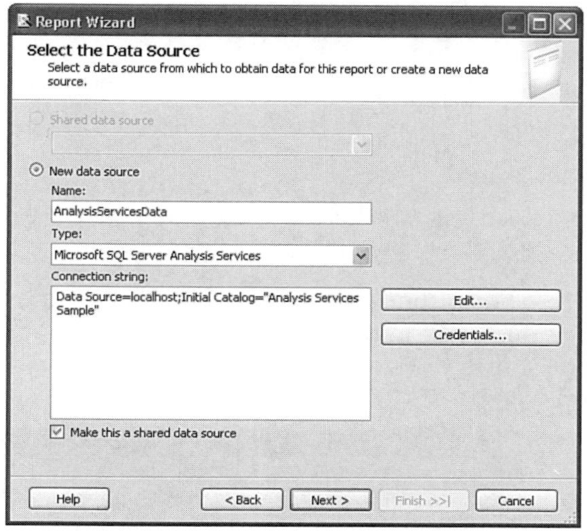

FIGURE 15.11 Analysis Services data source.

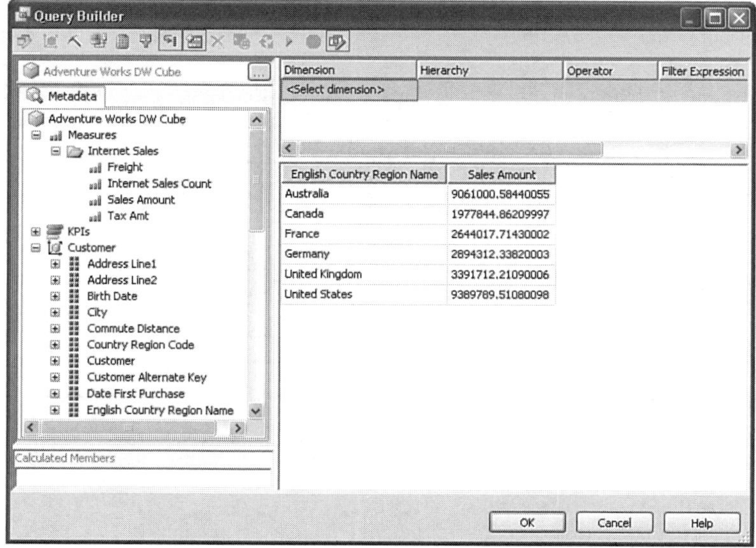

FIGURE 15.12 Multidimensional query designer.

5. Click OK and note the MDX query created by the Query Builder:

```
SELECT NON EMPTY { [Measures].[Sales Amount] } ON COLUMNS,
    NON EMPTY {([Customer].[English Country Region Name].
        ➥[English Country Region Name].ALLMEMBERS)}
```

```
    DIMENSION PROPERTIES MEMBER_CAPTION,
    MEMBER_UNIQUE_NAME ON ROWS
FROM [Adventure Works DW Cube] CELL PROPERTIES VALUE, BACK_COLOR, FORE_COLOR,
    FORMATTED_VALUE, FORMAT_STRING, FONT_NAME, FONT_SIZE, FONT_FLAGS
```

6. On the Select the Report Type screen, accept the default: Tabular. Click Next. On the Design the Table screen, click the Details button to add the available fields to Displayed Fields. Click Next.

7. Select Bold on the Choose the Table Style screen. Click Next. Name this report SalesReport. Click the Finish button. Click the Preview tab. You should see a screen similar to the one shown in Figure 15.13.

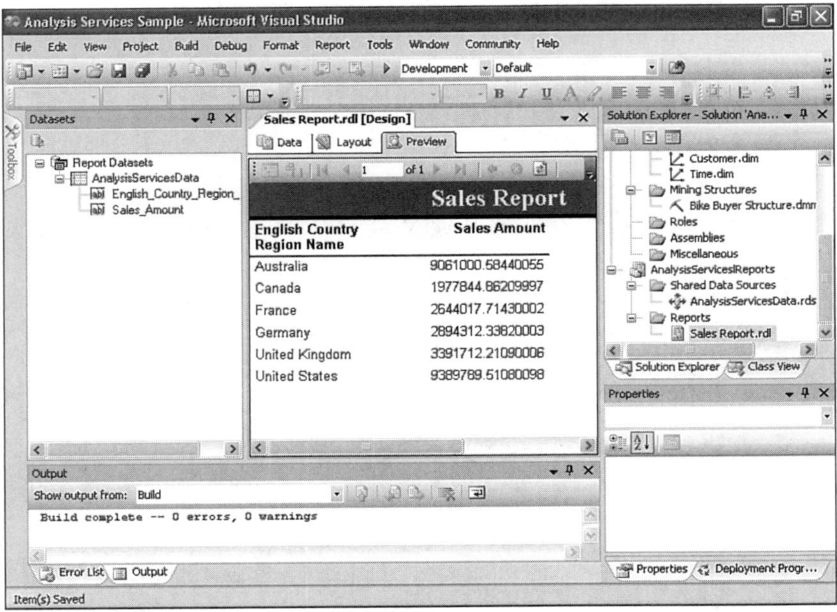

FIGURE 15.13 Result of a multidimensional report.

You have just pulled data from the OLAP cube.

NOTE

There is a bug in the RTM release of SSRS 2005 that affects OLAP reports built using the Report Wizard. If you use the Data tab, the MDX query will be lost.

The fix to this bug should be provided in the next service pack.

There are a couple of workarounds:

1. **You can repeat step 5 to redesign a query, using the designer provided under the Data tab.**
2. **Immediately after running Report Wizard, right-click on the report and select View Code from the context menu, edit the XML, and remove everything between the** `<rd:MdxQuery>` **tag and the** `<QueryDefinition>` **tag. The final code should look like this:** `<rd:MdxQuery><QueryDefinition ...` **Save the file.**

Let's make this report a bit more complicated and add a second dimension: Time. You will use the SalesReport that you have developed as a base for the following steps:

1. In Solution Explorer, right-click on SalesReport and select Copy from the shortcut menu. Right-click the report project and select Paste from the shortcut menu. Rename Copy of SalesReport to TimedSalesReport.
2. Double-click TimedSalesReport and click the Data tab in Report Designer.
3. Expand the Order Date dimension. Drag and drop Calendar Year on the design area. Once again, Query Builder flattens the OLAP output. Toggle the design mode and note that the MDX query now has a second dimension.

```
SELECT
NON EMPTY
    {[Measures].[Sales Amount] } ON COLUMNS,
NON EMPTY
    {([Customer].[English Country Region Name].[English Country Region
Name].ALLMEMBERS *
    [Order Date].[CalendarYear].[CalendarYear].ALLMEMBERS ) }
    DIMENSION PROPERTIES MEMBER_CAPTION, MEMBER_UNIQUE_NAME ON ROWS
FROM [Adventure Works DW Cube]
CELL PROPERTIES VALUE, BACK_COLOR, FORE_COLOR, FORMATTED_VALUE,
FORMAT_STRING, FONT_NAME, FONT_SIZE, FONT_FLAGS
```

4. Click the Layout tab and delete the table control from SalesReport. Place a matrix control in place of the table control. From the Datasets window, drag and drop Sales_Amount on the data region of the matrix control, drag and drop CalendarYear on the column area, and drag and drop English_Country_Region_Name on the Rows area of the matrix control. Now, you should see a screen similar to Figure 15.14.

FIGURE 15.14 Result of a multidimensional report with Time dimensions.

Now let's create a report that leverages Key Performance Indicators (KPIs). Once again, you will use the SalesReport that you have developed as a base for the following steps:

1. In Solution Explorer, right-click on SalesReport and select Copy from the shortcut menu. Right-click the report project and select Paste from the shortcut menu. Rename Copy of SalesReport to ItemPriceKPI.

2. Double-click ItemPriceKPI and click on the Data tab in Report Designer. Right-click in the design area and select Clear Grid from the shortcut menu. In the metadata, expand KPIs. Drag and drop the Average Item Price KPI on the design area. The design area now shows a grid with a single row with four columns corresponding to the details of KPI: Average Item Price Value, Average Item Price Goal, Average Item Price Status, and Average Item Price Trend.

3. From the Customer dimension, drag and drop State_Province_Name. Click on Layout view and if it has a table or matrix control, delete it. Add a new table control. Add two more column to the table. Drag and drop English_Country_Region_Name, State_Province_Name, Average_Item Price_Value, Average_Item_Price_Goal, and Average_Item_Price_Status fields from the AnalysisServiceData data set to the Detail region of the table. Click the Preview tab. You should see a screen similar to Figure 15.15.

You can validate the status works well and displays 1 when Average Order Size > 100, 0, and when it is <= 50, and display -1 when the Average Order Size is < 10.

FIGURE 15.15 Result of a multidimensional report with KPIs.

Note that all the KPI data is numeric. This version of Reporting Services does not include KPI controls, but KPI controls are easy to emulate. The following several steps show how to do it. You can create your own KPI graphics or leverage KPI controls from Visual Studio (by default located at `C:\Program Files\Microsoft Visual Studio 8\Common7\IDE\PrivateAssemblies\DataWarehouseDesigner\KPIsBrowserPage\Images`).

Let's embed three images—`Gauge_Asc0.gif`, `Gauge_Asc2.gif`, and `Gauge_Asc4.gif`—corresponding to three distinct states of the gage's status: empty, half, and full. The steps to emulate KPI controls are as follows:

1. From the Toolbox, drag and drop an image control on the Detail area of the grid inside of the column Status. The Image Wizard begins. On the Welcome screen click Next, select Embedded Image on the Select the Image Source screen, and then click Next. If there are no embedded images, click Add New Image and add images. After you are done, click Finish.

2. Click the image and in the Properties window, change the `Value` property from `gauge_asc4` to the following expression:

```
=IIF (Fields!Average_Order_Size_Status_.Value=-1, "gauge_asc0",
        IIF(Fields!Average_Order_Size_Status_.Value=0,"gauge_asc2",
        "gauge_asc4")
                 )
```

As you can tell by now, this expression directs Reporting Services to display an appropriate image. Note that image names are displayed as constants in the Expression Editor. Do not forget to include image names in double quotes, such as `"gauge_asc0"`. You should see a screen similar to Figure 15.16.

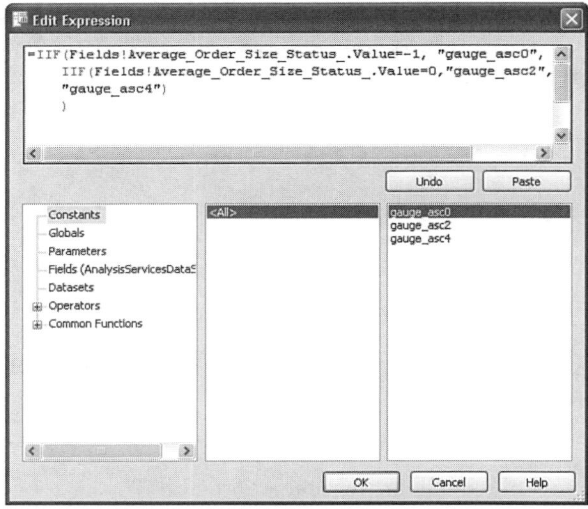

FIGURE 15.16 Adding graphical KPIs.

3. Click OK to close the Expression Editor.
4. If desired, you can modify formatting, such as the column headers to improve the report's look. Click the Preview tab. You should see a screen similar to Figure 15.17. This approach to adding images would just as easily work with reports from relational data.

You might have noticed that in the KPI example Brunswick in Canada, for example, does not have sales data (that is, nothing was sold there). In the real-life report, you should have excluded output of empty (or irrelevant data). Such filtering should be done, ideally, in a query. Report Server could be leveraged as well, for example, using the `Visibility` property of a report item.

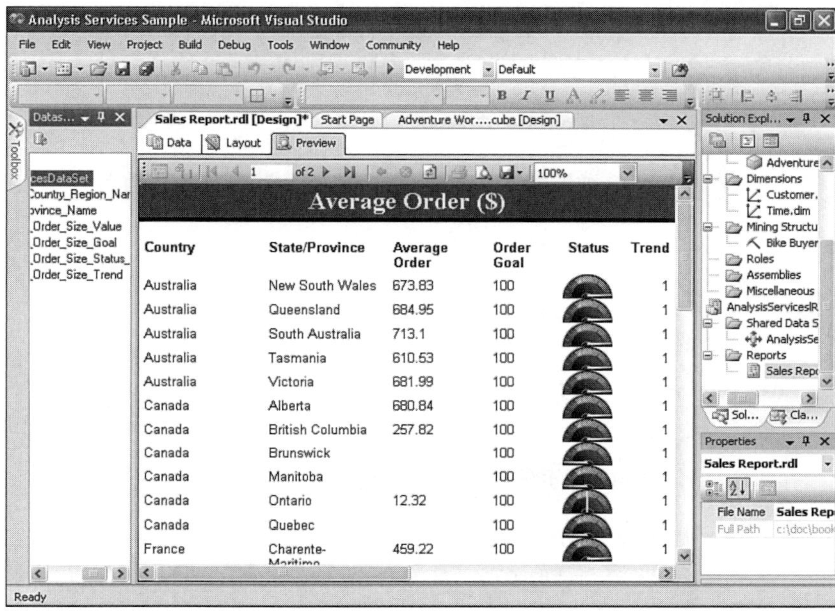

FIGURE 15.17 Resulting report after adding graphical KPIs.

Creating Data-Mining Reports

As a last exercise in this chapter, let's create a report that will leverage Data Mining capabilities of SQL Server:

1. In Solution Explorer, right-click the Reports folder and select Create New Report from the shortcut menu. Use the AnalysisServicesData shared data source that was created earlier in this chapter. Click Next.

2. On the Design the Query window, click the Query Builder button. By default, Query Builder starts in MDX Query Design mode. To switch to DMX Query Design mode, click the third button on the Query Builder's toolbar, which is called Command Type DMX (this button depicts a mining pickax). This button switches between MDX and DMX designer to correspondingly query OLAP cubes and data mining models. Click OK on the warning dialog box.

3. On the Mining Model window, click the Select Model button. Expand the tree and select the Bike Buyer Model. On the Select Input Table(s) window, click Select Case Table (see Figure 15.18).

4. Change the data source to Adventure Works DW, select ProspectiveBuyer (see Figure 15.19), and then click OK.

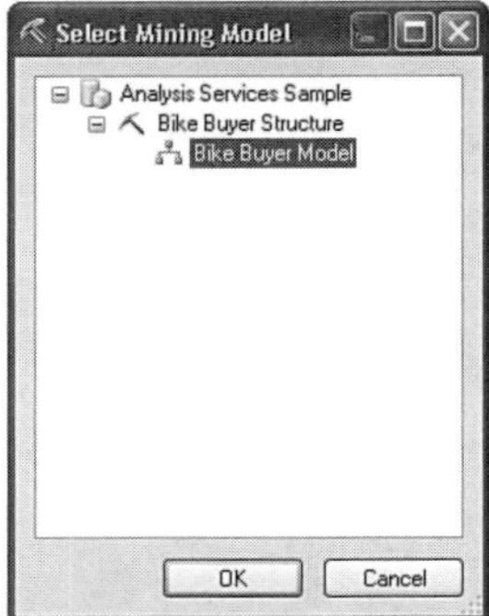

FIGURE 15.18 Select Mining Model window.

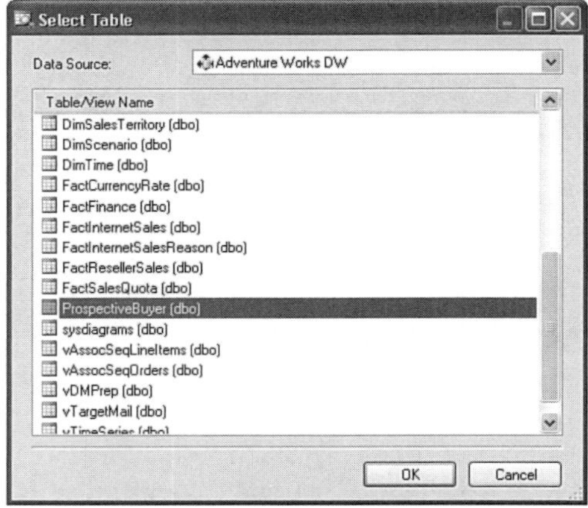

FIGURE 15.19 Selecting a table for analysis.

5. Drag and drop `Bike Buyer` from the `Bike Buyer` model to the grid below; in the source column of the second row of the grid, select Prediction Function in the drop-down menu within a cell. In the Field column, select the PredictProbability function; and drag and drop the Bike Buyer field from the model to the Criteria/Argument field column. Enter Probability as an alias for this expression.

6. From the ProspectiveBuyer table (located in Select Input Table window), drag the following fields: FirstName, LastName, and EmailAddress. This allows you to have a report that can be used for a personalized email campaign promoting Adventure Works' bikes. You should see a screen similar to Figure 15.20.

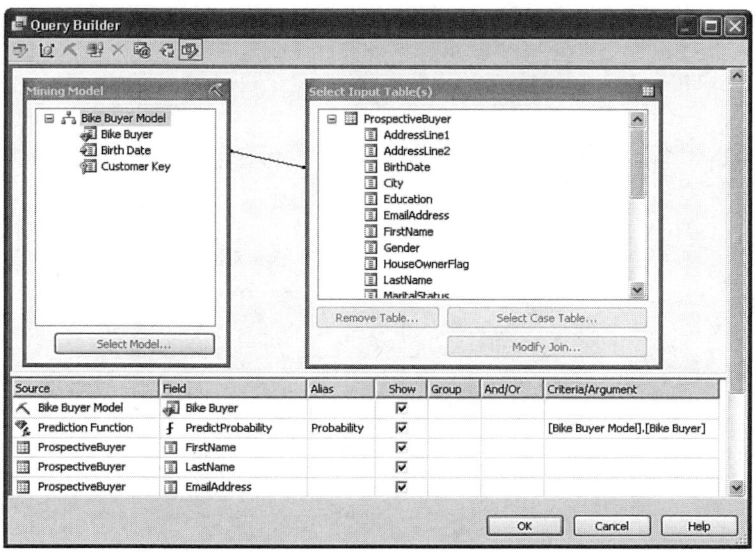

FIGURE 15.20 DMX Query Builder.

7. Click OK to complete Query Builder. The following is the query:

```
SELECT
  [Bike Buyer Model].[Bike Buyer],
  (PredictProbability([Bike Buyer Model].[Bike Buyer])) as [Probability],
  t.[FirstName],
  t.[LastName],
  t.[EmailAddress]
From
  [Bike Buyer Model]
PREDICTION JOIN
  OPENQUERY([Adventure Works DW],
    'SELECT
      [FirstName],
      [LastName],
      [EmailAddress],
      [BirthDate]
    FROM
      [dbo].[ProspectiveBuyer]
    ') AS t
ON
  [Bike Buyer Model].[Birth Date] = t.[BirthDate]
```

8. On the Select Report Type screen, accept the default Tabular by clicking Next, and add all the fields to Details in the Displayed Fields section. Click Next, and accept

the default style by clicking Next. Name the report CampaignCustomerEvaluation. Format the fields to improve layout and click Preview. The screen should look similar to Figure 15.21.

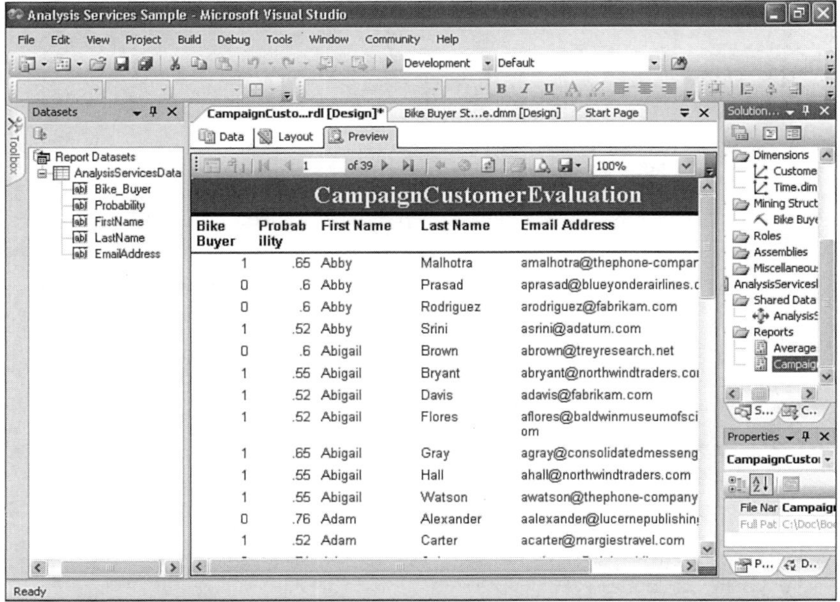

FIGURE 15.21 Data-mining report.

Summary

Analysis Services consists of two components: Online Analytical Processing (OLAP) and Data Mining (DM). OLAP is designed to summarize data and DM is designed to look for patterns and trends in data.

Microsoft has added new Analysis Services and Data Mining capabilities to SSRS 2005. Some of the key capabilities that can be leveraged by SSRS are as follows:

- Unified Data Model (UDM)—Is designed to simplify access to data and combines the best of relational and analytical models.
- Key Performance Indicators (KPIs)—Are designed to evaluate performance criteria that a business, usually, considers strategic in nature. Performance is evaluated against a specified goal and has to be quantifiable. Some of the KPI examples are stock performance, cost of operations, customer satisfaction, and so on.
- Graphical Query Builders for Online Analytical Processing (OLAP) and Data Mining—Are designed to simplify development of multidimensional and data-mining queries by providing a very intuitive graphical user interface.

Ad Hoc Reporting *NEW in 2005*

CHAPTER 16

IN THIS CHAPTER

- Issues Facing Ad Hoc Reporting
- Client-Side Reporting with SSRS
- Report Models and the Model Designer

This chapter begins with a few words about needs and challenges for ad hoc reports and some definitions.

A lot of things have changed for business in the post dot-com era, but one thing that remains is the need for accurate and timely data. Most businesses want to analyze and report on up-to-the-minute data. Moreover, a lot of analysts want to analyze the data kept in their organization's data warehouse(s) to test their theories or to spot trends. This kind of analytical reporting does not preclude the nicely printed and formatted reports for C-level executives, but rather serves as the foundation for new reports.

Issues Facing Ad Hoc Reporting

The challenge in doing this kind of analysis has often been with the technology. Technologists such as report developers are usually keen on SQL and their reporting tools. They know the ins and outs of relational databases, the different kinds of joins, and the concepts behind OLAP. They might or might not be so keen on the business and repercussions of certain trends.

The opposite is most likely true for business analysts. The typical analyst knows what he wants to see or at least has a theory that he wants to collect data for to prove or disprove. Analysts might not know or care that to get a typical sales order, he must join six or seven tables together. Analysts are not technologists.

What the analyst needs is a flexible, yet powerful tool to build his own reports and do his own analysis without overbearing technical terms.

Client-side Reporting with SSRS

SSRS attempts to address these issues with two main tools, Report Builder and Model Designer.

Before a user can create a client-side report, an analyst or technologist must create a report model. The report model is built with the aid of Visual Studio, and contains metadata about the underlying database.

The purpose of the metadata is to describe the relationships between the various tables in the RDBMS in terms of entities, attributes, and relationships (roles), which can then be used by Report Builder users to help them build ad hoc reports.

This helps to abstract the DBMS into business objects that the nontechnologist should recognize.

The second part of the equation is the actual Report Builder. The Report Builder is the tool used to create ad hoc reports.

It is a Windows forms-based .NET application that can be accessed through a URL (using the http://<localhost>/reportserver/reportbuilder/reportbuilder.application URL, where `<localhost>` is the name of the computer that is running Report Server) or from Report Manager (using the http://<webservername>/reports URL and then clicking Report Builder).

Report Builder uses the report model to present the end user with the abstracted view of business objects. Although Report Builder is a powerful report-development application, Visual Studio provides many more features for report developers and is required to build models for Report Builder's consumption.

Report Models and the Model Designer

As previously mentioned, the first step in creating end-user reports is the creation of the report model. The model is written in a declarative language called Semantic Definition Model Language (SDML). The Semantic Definition Model Language is based on the Unified Modeling Language (UML), and it contains many of the same paradigms. It is similar to the RDL in that it is an XML-based communications language. The report model abstracts the RDBMS into business objects the end user would recognize.

To be effective for the end user, the model author must include some key pieces of information about the database. This type of information includes the following:

- A map of table names and column names into business objects
- Information about the relationships between tables that would otherwise be stored in primary keys or foreign keys
- Hierarchical information or logical groupings about your objects
- Permissions for users to see objects

From Report Builder, the model aids the user in selecting what information she wants to see, and, consequently, building the query for the data source of the resulting report.

To build these models, model developers must use a tool called Model Designer. Like Report Designer, it is built in to Visual Studio/Business Intelligence Development Studio. The template project type is called "Report Model Project." Models can be generated against SQL Server or Analysis Services.

NOTE

Model Designer and, subsequently, Report Builder can only build reports against SQL Server or Analysis Services. To build reports for other data sources, such as Oracle, you can employ linked servers or the unified data model (UDM). Both provide a thin abstraction layer.

Developers can generate models in two ways. The first way to generate models is based on a set of preexisting rules. This is the way the wizard and the autogenerate functionality work. The other way is to connect using a data source, and start designing the model by hand.

You will take a look at both methods later in this chapter.

Report Model Projects

As previously mentioned, report model projects are what the Model Designer uses to generate models. There are three kinds of files that it uses to generate models. These files correlate to the major steps in models generation. The first kind of file is the Data Source (.ds).

The second type of file is the Data Source view. The Data Source view provides the model information about the underlying data store. It is kind of like an entity relationship diagram, in that it provides information about the database schema, but is written in XML. The model uses the Data Source view to query the database, making the Data Source view the bridge between the model and the data source. The final type of file is the actual model file (.sdml). The model can only reference one data source, and one Data Source view.

Model File Content

A report model contains three main sections:

- **Semantic models**—A collection of business objects in terms familiar to a business analyst.

  The semantic model also contains the relationships of these business objects to one another.

- **Physical model**—The outline of the database schema. This contains information about the tables and views in the data source.

- **Bindings**—The map between the physical model and the semantic model.

The data source and Data Source view are used to make up the physical model. The semantic model is a combination of the physical model along with semantic objects and bindings.

Entities

The first of these objects is called an entity. The entity is really the crux of the semantic model because it maps tables and views.

An entity can map to multiple tables or views, and itself has a collection of objects called attributes, expressions, folders, and source fields. Entities should have names that are recognizable to a business analyst. For example, instead of the obscure table name `tbl_sls_ordr`, the entity would be named `Sales Order`.

As you add relational items to the Data Source view, you can map these items into entities. The binding property of the entity tells Report Builder the table(s) or view(s) to which the entity refers.

Roles

In a way, roles take us back to Database Design 101. Roles store information about the relationship between entities. The relationship information is basically the cardinality between the objects. This can be one to one, one to many, or many to many. As an example, a store entity can have only one address, whereas a customer can have many orders. Roles also contain information about which attributes in each entity are the defining ones in terms of the cardinality relationship. So, if the `AddressID` field on the store entity is what you need to obtain the proper address data from the address entity, then the role that contains information about the relationship storing that `AddressID` is the field to use to correlate the two entities.

End users see the relationships play out when browsing entities in Report Builder. Roles are also what enable the infinite drill-down feature in Report Builder.

Source Fields and Expressions

If roles contain information about the primary and foreign fields, source fields contain information about the columns. A source field is an attribute that maps to a table column and gives the column a friendly name. Source fields can only be added after the parent entity's binding property has been set. For example, `LastName` on the `Person` table could be a source field on the person entity.

Expressions should have a familiar ring to them. Expressions in a report model take one or more source fields, and manipulate them with functions, operators, and/or constants to derive a calculated value. These expressions are just like expressions in Report Designer. They are based on VB.NET, and automatically provide access to `System.Math` and `System.Convert`. Functions from the `Microsoft.VisualBasic` namespace and references to other assemblies or custom code can be used as well.

A good example of what could be an expression is the combination of `FirstName` and `LastName` to create a new field called `Name`.

Folders

Folders allow you to group collections of entities. Folders can also contain other folders and perspectives. Folders allow you to add hierarchical information to the model. Folders can also be used to group items together regardless of hierarchical relationships. For example, because Report Builder users can navigate folders in a manner similar to Windows Explorer, you can move infrequently used items into a folder to hide them from the users.

Perspectives

Perspectives help to give us a narrower view or a view of a subset of the model. Perspectives can help limit users to see only information to which they have access. For example, a company might have a model that contains information about all the financial data items for that company. One of the things perspectives can help us do is to limit what budgetary information users can see to only information about their department's budgets.

Perspectives are contained in the model, and the model designers and wizards don't create them for you. They have to be manually created and model items must be placed in them. Perspectives can contain other model objects, such as entities folders, roles, source fields, and expressions. Just by placing items into a perspective does not exclude them from the rest of the models. Items can still be placed in other folders and perspectives.

Creating a Model Project

To create a model, you need to complete a few steps. The first is to create a report model project. Then, you give the project a data source and a Data Source view. Finally, you can create the models. In the following steps, you create a model based on the `AdventureWorks` catalog:

1. Create a new project. Open Visual Studio or Business Intelligence Development Studio. Click File and then New Project.
2. In the dialog box that opens, if not selected by default, select Business Intelligence Projects under Project Types.
3. Under Templates in the right pane in the active dialog box, select Report Model Project.
4. Call the project "First Model" and change the location to C:\rs2005. Make sure Create Directory for Solution is checked. See Figure 16.1.

Creating a Data Source

Now that you have an empty project, the next thing to do is connect it to a data source. Remember the data source has to be SQL Server (or abstracted through linked servers or UDM).

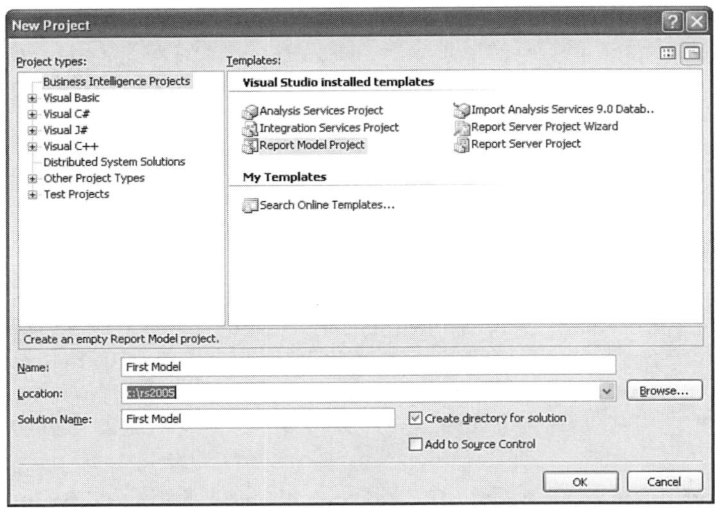

FIGURE 16.1 Creating new business intelligence projects.

Unlike Report Designer, no other data sources are accepted directly:

1. Open Solution Explorer and right-click on the Data Sources folder. Click Add New Data Source. This launches the New Data Source Wizard.
2. Skip the welcome page by clicking Next.
3. On the next page, select Create a Data Source Based on an Existing or New Connection, and then click New.
4. Enter "localhost" as the name of the server to connect to.
5. Select Windows Authentication.
6. In the Select or Enter a Database Name list, select "Adventure Works."
7. Click Test Connection; if you get an OK dialog box, click OK. If not, try to resolve the error using the debug information given, and then try again.
8. Click OK. At this point, you should have a screen that looks similar to Figure 16.2.
9. Click Next.
10. At this point, you could change the name of the data source. If it is not already, call the new data source Adventure Works.
11. Click Finish.

A new data source called Adventure Works should appear in the Data Sources folder in Solution Explorer.

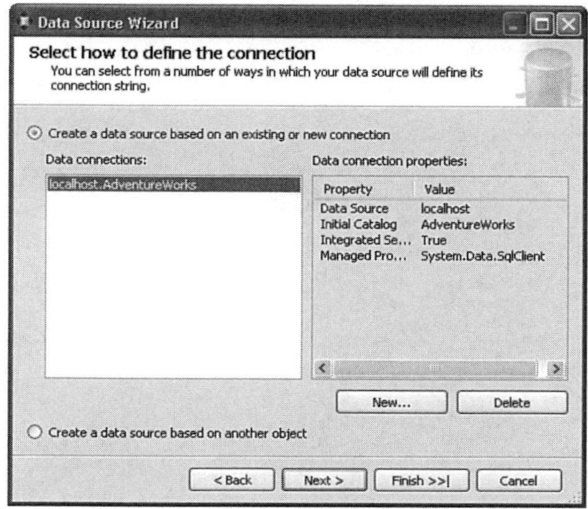

FIGURE 16.2 Defining the connection.

Creating a Data Source View

The next step in the creation of a model is the creation of the Data Source view. Recall, from earlier, that the Data Source view contains information about the physical layout of the database. To create a Data Source view, complete the following steps:

1. Open Solution Explorer and right-click on the Data Source Views folder. Click Add New Data Source View. This launches the New Data Source View Wizard.
2. Select the Adventure Works data source and click Next.
3. The next screen asks you to select the tables and views that are going to be included in the semantic model. Click the >> button to move all the objects from the Available Objects list box to the Included Objects list box. See Figure 16.3.
4. Click Next.
5. Name the Data Source view "Adventure Works DSV."
6. Click Finish.

A new Data Source view called "Adventure Works DSV" should appear in the Data Source Views folder in Solution Explorer.

The wizard is smart enough to detect if the underlying data source has no foreign key constraints. In this case, the wizard gives you an extra screen before selecting which tables to include in the Data Source view. The screen gives you three types of matching logic so it can infer relationships in the data store. If your DBMS does not follow any of these conventions, you will have to add the data source relationships yourself. Figure 16.4 shows you a copy of the screen.

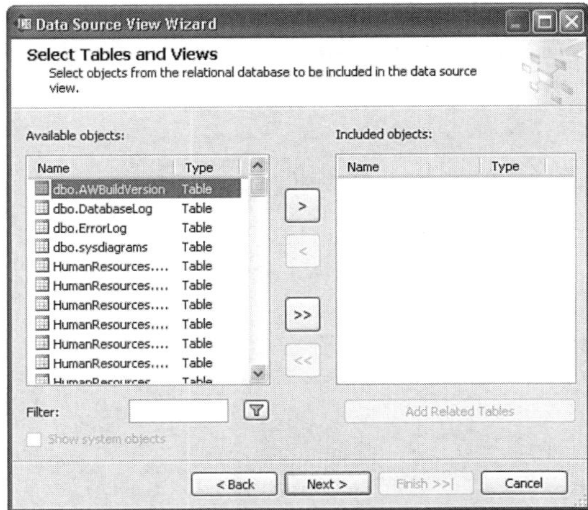

FIGURE 16.3 Selecting the tables and views.

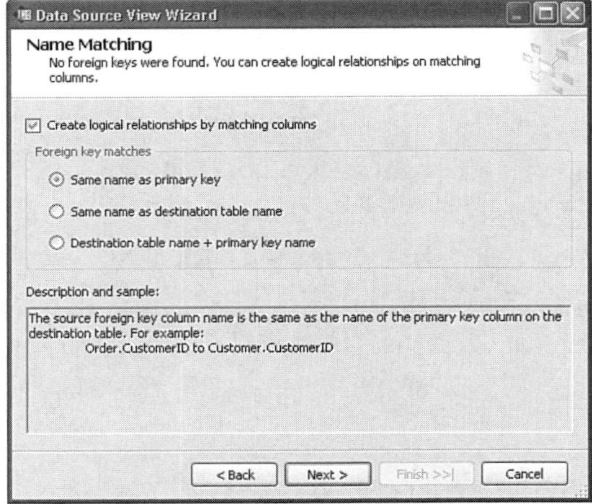

FIGURE 16.4 Name Matching screen of the Data Source View Wizard.

After the wizard is complete, double-click on the Adventure Works DSV file in Solution Explorer. This opens a document showing you the relationships that the wizard has just inferred. See Figure 16.5.

To get the document to fit on one page, you might have to click the View menu, point to Zoom, and then click To Fit.

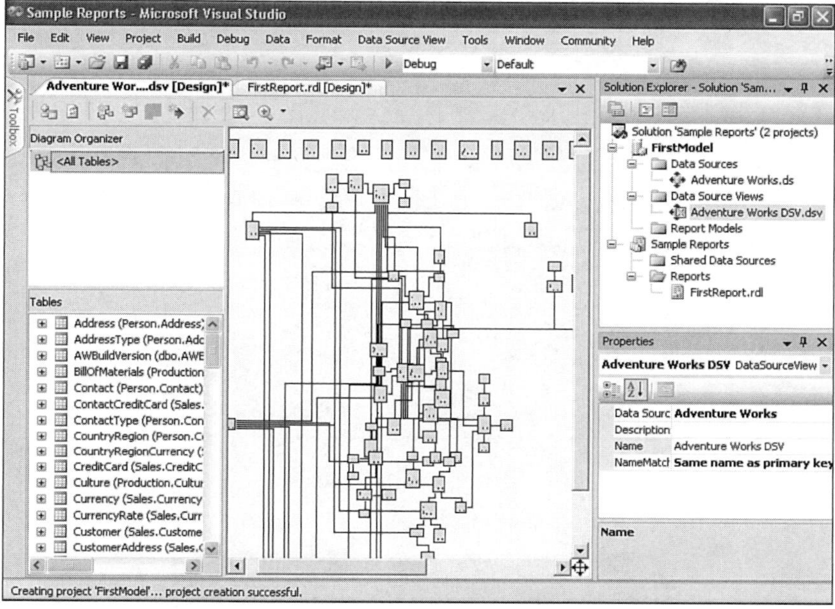

FIGURE 16.5 Data Source view.

Creating a Report Model

Finally, you can create the actual model. To create the model, complete the following steps:

1. Open Solution Explorer and right-click on the Report Models folder. Click Add New Report Model. This launches the New Report Model Wizard.

2. Click Next on the welcome screen.

3. The next screen is the screen to select Data Source views. At this point, only the "Adventure Works DSV" should show up. Select this and then select Next.

4. The next screen is the Model Generation Rules screen, which is shown in Figure 16.6. This allows you to select from a predefined set of rules to ease the model generation process. For our purposes, the defaults are fine. Click Next.

5. The next screen asks you to create statistics. Because Report Builder uses database statistics to aid it in the model generation process, it is important to make sure your statistics are up to date. Otherwise, it might miscalculate some factors, such as drill down and aggregates. It is recommended to update statistics whenever the data source or Data Source views have changed. Click Update Statistics Before Generating, if necessary.

   Click Next. See Figure 16.7.

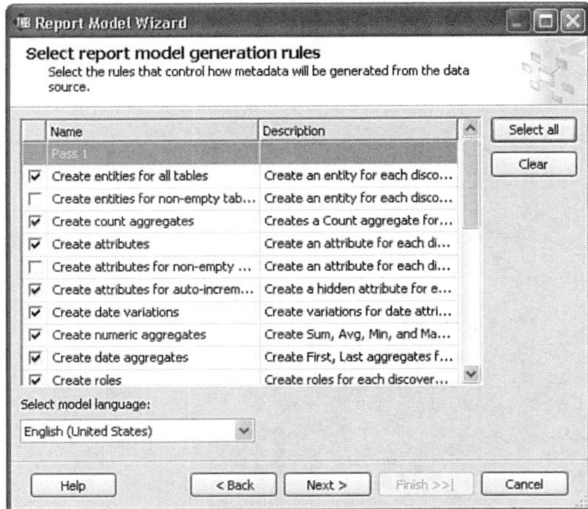

FIGURE 16.6 Selecting report model generation rules.

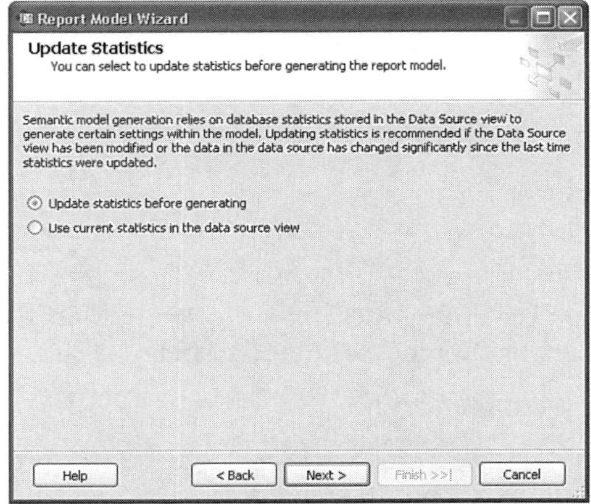

FIGURE 16.7 Update Statistics screen of the Report Model Wizard.

6. Name the model "Adventure Works model," and then click Run. Figure 16.8 shows the resulting screen.

7. Click Finish. Figure 16.9 shows the completed model.

Modifying Items in the Model

The way entities show up in the Model Designer reflects how they will show up in Report Builder. To make things more meaningful for the end user, many of the properties or entities can be customized. Working with the model involves some of the same basic concepts as working with Report Designer. The properties of any object can be modified from the properties window.

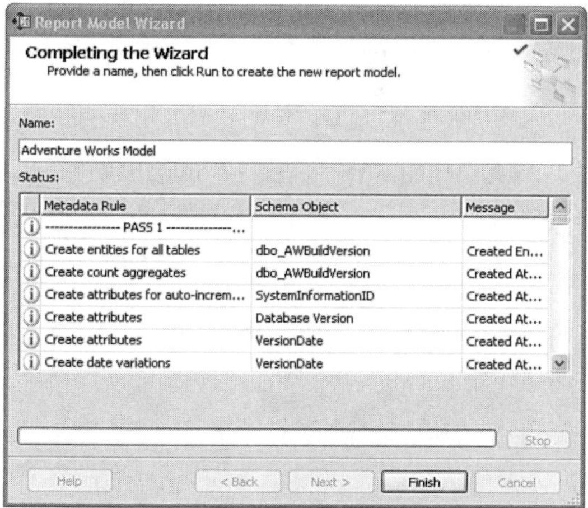

FIGURE 16.8 Completing the Wizard screen of the Report Model Wizard.

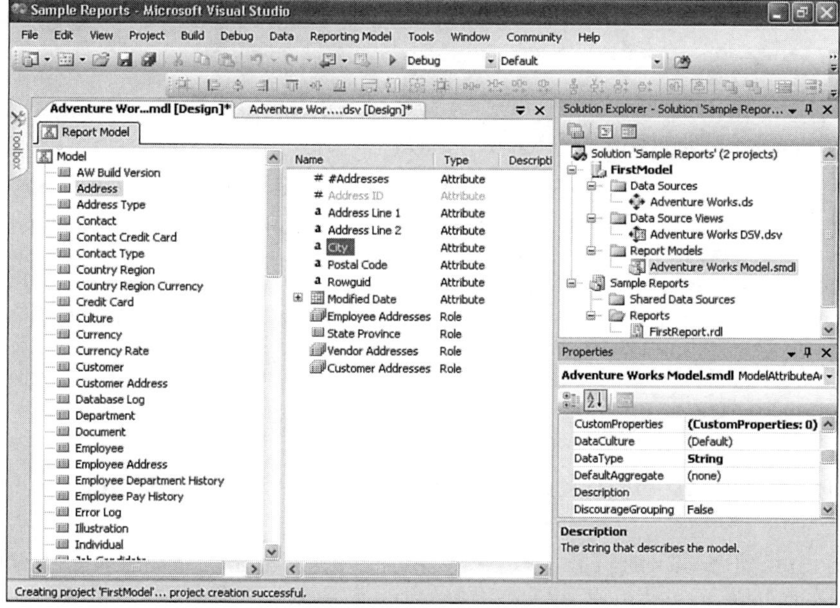

FIGURE 16.9 Completed database model.

Some of the things you can customize include sorting, instance selection, and inheritance. What this means is that attributes can be set to come from other entities or that users can see a filtered list of instances of an entity. Entities can also predefine formatting of their attributes. For example, attributes that reflect currency can be formatted as currency depending on the user's localized settings. The order in which things appear in the entity browser can also be customized. By default, entities appear sorted in alphabetical order, but you can move certain entities to the top if users are going to report off them frequently.

To modify items in the model, it is simply a matter of right-clicking in the treeview or listview. The Report Model menu in the Model Designer also gives the same menu options. To delete any item, simply navigate to the item, right-click it, and choose Delete from the shortcut menu.

To add an entity, folder, or perspective, do the following:

1. Navigate to the top of the treeview.
2. From the Report Model menu, select New Entity, New Perspective, or New Folder.

From this point, each of these items has their own caveats.

If you choose to add a new entity, the name given to the entity is simply `NewEntity`. You must navigate to `NewEntity`, right–click it, select Rename from the shortcut menu, and rename it to what you want. To be effective, the binding information has to be set as well. When adding folders, a similar process has to be followed. You must navigate to the entity or to the top entity in the tree, right–click it, and select New Folder. A new folder called New Folder is created. The location of the new folder is dependent on where you were when you right-clicked to add the new folder. You must right-click on it, and select Rename from the shortcut menu to rename it.

To add a new role, attribute, or source field, click on any detail item, and then select the option you need from the Report Model menu. When you add a new role, a pop-up appears with a list of entities. Select an entity, and then assign the bindings in the properties window. Role bindings are nothing more than a list of relations defined in the Data Source view. When adding or modifying an expression, the Expression Editor is shown. From here, you can design the expression and name it. When adding a source field, select New Source Field from the Report Model menu. After adding the source field, you must rename it and set the bindings from the properties window. Source field bindings refer to a list of columns from the Data Source view.

When adding or modifying perspectives, a specialized dialog box opens that allows you to add/remove items from the perspective.

When adding and removing perspectives, you might notice that adding one object seems to add others, and removing it removes other objects as well. This is because of the hierarchical nature of the items. When a parent item, such as a folder or attribute, with variations get added or removed, all of its children get added and removed as well. The same thing applies for roles and identifying attributes. When a role is selected, the corresponding role is selected along with the entity it leads to. The reverse is also true. When an identifying attribute is deselected, any other entities that use that identifying attribute get deselected as well. To reselect those entities, the identifying attribute must get reselected.

Publishing the Model

When you are done creating or updating the model, you can publish the model just as you would a report. In a published model, the data source and the SMDL file (semantic model file) are placed in the Report Server. Because the information in the Data Source view is incorporated into the semantic model, the Data Source view does not get published. If the information in the Data Source view, or for that matter, anything in the semantic model, needs to be updated, simply publish an updated model.

After the model is published, it can be secured using Reporting Services' role-based security. To use the model in Report Builder, a user must have access to it.

After you are ready to deploy the semantic model, the deployment steps closely resemble the deployment steps in Report Designer.

1. Right-click on the project file in Solution Explorer, and select Properties.
2. Review the target folder's properties. There is one target folder for the data sources, and there is another target folder for the semantic models.
3. Verify the Overwrite Data Sources option is on the intended setting. This option is similar in name and function to the one in Report Designer.
4. Click OK.

To deploy the model and data source, right-click on the project file in Solution Explorer, and select Deploy from the shortcut menu. To deploy just the model file, right-click on the semantic model and click Deploy.

Creating Models from Report Designer

A second way to create a model is from Report Manager. Report Manager has the ability to take any SQL Server or Analysis Services data source and generate a model from it. You can complete the following steps to generate a model from Report Manager:

1. Go to the Report Manager web page. By default, it is located at http://localhost/Reports.
2. Click the New Data Source button.
3. Enter a name for this data source. Call this "AdventureWorks DS". You can also enter a brief description.
4. Enter a connection type of "Microsoft SQL Server".
5. Make sure that the Enable This Data Source check box is checked.
6. Enter "Data Source=localhost;Initial Catalog=AdventureWorks" in the Connection string text box.
7. Select Windows Integrated Security.
8. Click OK. You should return to the Folder view screen. Click on the data source you just created ("AdventureWorks DS").

9. Click the Generate Model button.
10. Enter a name for this model. Call it "Adventure Works DS Model." If you want to, you can change where the model is located and give it a description. For now, just leave these fields blank.
11. Click OK.

Features of Report Builder

Report Builder is the second part of the two-part solution for end-user reporting. As previously mentioned, Report Builder is a click-once, client-side .NET application that can be launched from the Report Manager website. Report Builder uses Microsoft Office paradigms, so it should be easy for end users who use Microsoft Office to start using it, yet it still creates reports using standard RDL. Figure 16.10 shows how to access Report Builder.

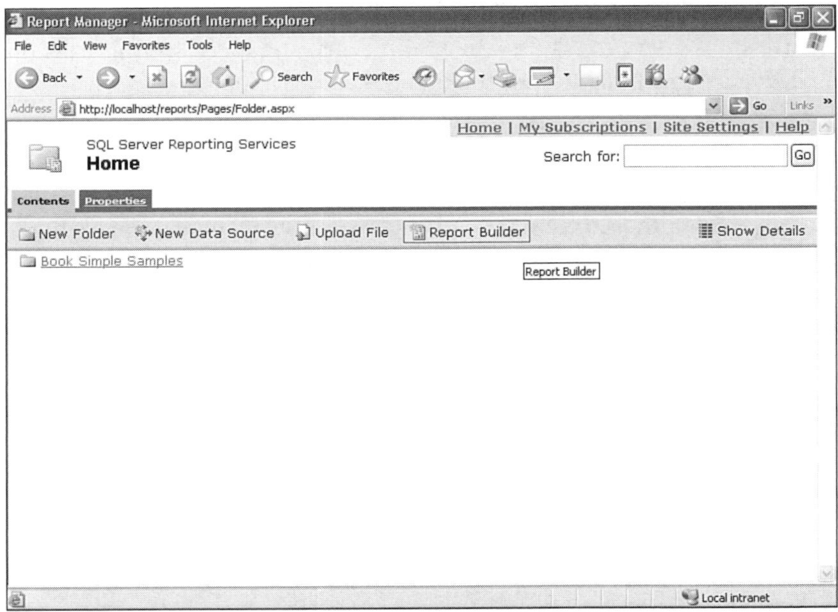

FIGURE 16.10 Starting Report Builder from the Report Manager web interface.

Report Builder uses the models stored on the Report Server. Report Builder calls these models data sources, not to be confused with the data source that is part of the model. Through Report Builder, the end user knows nothing of the actual data source used by the model. End users will most likely be referring to the model as the data source, as shown in Figure 16.11. Keep in mind that because the models are secured by the Report Server, users will not be able to access models to use as data sources for their report if the appropriate permissions have not been set.

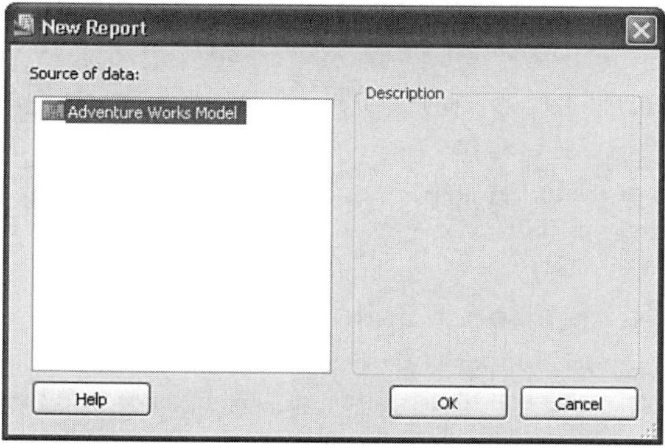

FIGURE 16.11 Selecting a model to use with Report Builder.

Report Builder has predefined templates available for matrix, table, and chart report layouts. Note that lists and rectangles are not supported. To use a template, the user simply has to click on a template in the left pane. The Report Builder interface is presented in Figure 16.12.

After selecting a template, the end user simply has to drag and drop fields from the Report Data Explorer onto the data region provided. Report Data Explorer is nothing more than the entity explorer. Attributes and expressions make up the fields that are usable from within the entity explorer.

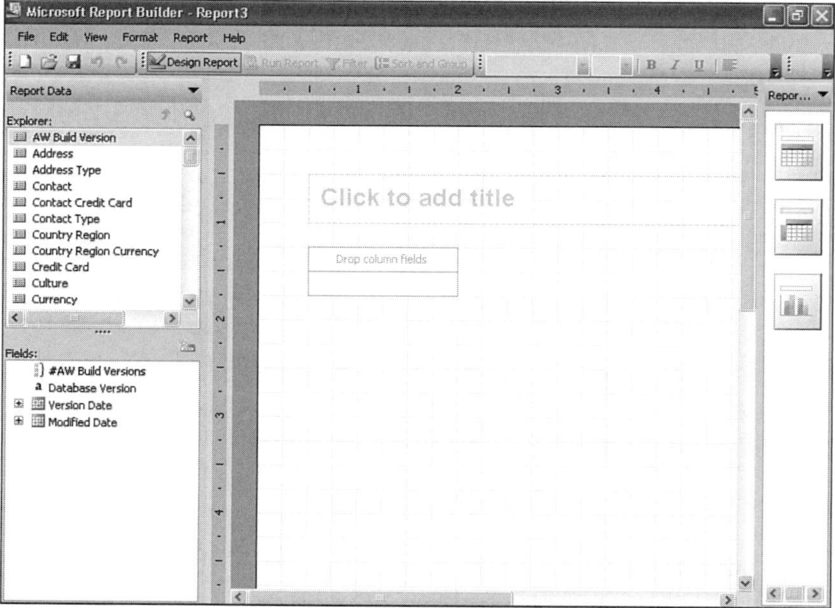

FIGURE 16.12 Report Builder after the model selection.

Some basic features are also available through Report Builder. Formatting can be done to any text box on the report layout. Data can be filtered, sorted, and grouped. A full range of export formats, such as PDF, TIFF, Excel, HTML, XML, CSV, and TIFF are also available to end users.

Report Builder saves reports to the Report Server. After being published, the reports can be managed like any other reports.

Building Reports with Report Builder

Building reports with Report Builder is fairly simplistic compared to Report Designer. The complexities of connecting to the data source and SQL Server are taken care of by the model. All that needs to be selected are attributes and expressions from the entity explorer.

First, launch Report Builder. After launching Report Builder, a list of models appears that are available for you to use as your data source. Refer to Figures 16.11 and 16.12 for reference. After selecting the data source, Report Builder opens up to the report layout section. Figure 16.12 shows what the screen should look like in the default table view.

On the left side is the entity explorer. Below the entity explorer is the list of attributes and fields. On the right side is the list of style templates—`Table`, `Matrix`, or `Chart`. By clicking on one of these templates, you can create a new report with that layout.

Now, let's try to build a simple report with Report Builder.

The requirements for this sample report are as follows: The marketing department wants to see the breakdown of subtotals for sales orders by quarter and by year. They are not sure what mechanism would be best to display the data, so they request it in tabular format and in a pivot table.

Tabular Report

Complete the following steps to produce the report:

1. Select Table Report from the Report Layout menu on the right side.
2. Select Sales Territory from the entity explorer.
3. Under the Explorer pane, though still on the left side, is the list of fields and attributes. Select a name and drag it over to the layout view where it says "Drag and drop column fields."
4. After dragging the name over to the layout view, the entity explorer should have switched to entities that have a role relating to sales territory. From this list, select Sales Order Headers.
5. From the Attribute Fields menu, drag Order Year, which is located under Order Date, over next to the Sales Territory name. The mouse pointer should turn blue to signify that the table is ready to add a column.

NOTE

The Model Builder automatically creates expressions based on dates. These expressions are usually date parts.

Certain entities and attributes also might have a '#of <Entity>' expression. The rules chosen during the wizard are the driving factor behind these. The Model Builder also chose whether to include a distinct count of values based on database statistics.

6. Drag Order Quarter (also located under Order Date) over next to Order Year.
7. Drag Total Sub Total over next to Order Quarter. After doing this, notice three total lines that appeared. One of the nice features of Report Builder is that it automatically groups and sums data for you.
8. Enter Total Product Sales by Quarter by Territory in the text box above the table where it says "Click to add Title."

Figure 16.13 should show you what your report should like.

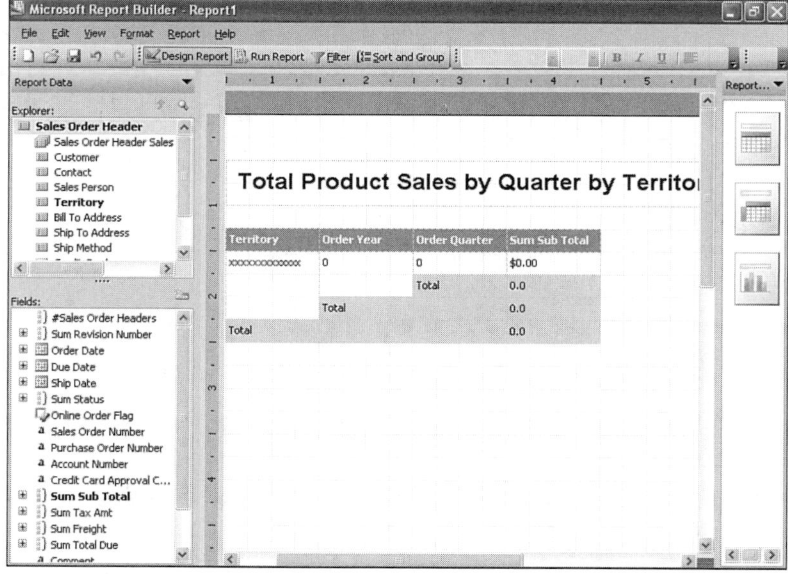

FIGURE 16.13 View of a report in Report Builder.

The report can be previewed by clicking on the Run Report button from the toolbar.

Click-Through Reports

When the report is in Preview mode, the end user can hover over the Sum of Sales Totals number and notice that it is actually a link to another report. This type of report is called a click-through report and is automatically generated by Report Builder.

Click-through reports are based on roles. After a user has selected to display a certain type of aggregate attribute, if the attribute has roles linking over to another entity, Report Builder automatically generates a report listing the contents of that aggregate. You could potentially drill down to the lowest level, and at each stage Report Builder would generate a report based on that entity. This feature is called infinite drilldown. It is one of the benefits of putting work into generating models that contain information about all the relationships in the DBMS.

Saving/Publishing Reports

Now that you have completed this basic report, let's try to save it. Unlike in Visual Studio, the RDL file that has been generated by Report Builder cannot be saved on the user's hard drive. To save client-side reports, users must have access to publish reports in at least one folder on the Report Server. An easy way to enable this access is to enable the My Reports option on the Report Server.

This gives users permissions to their own My Report folder.

After enabling My Reports, saving a report is a simple matter. The menu options inside Report Builder are similar to the same commands in Microsoft Office. The only difference is that you are saving to the Report Server and not a file server. To save the existing report to the Report Server and call it "Sales by Territory—Table," follow these steps:

1. Click the File menu, and then click Save As.
2. In the root folder of the Report Server, enter the filename "Sales by Territory—Table," and click OK.

Matrix/Pivot Table Report

Now, let's continue on to make the same report using a pivot table or matrix. The concepts are the same; just the data region is different.

1. If you have already closed Report Builder, reopen it.
2. Select the Matrix Report style from the Report Layout section on the right pane.
3. From the entity explorer, select Sales Territory, and drag the name attribute over to the matrix where it says "Drag and drop row groups."
4. From the entity explorer, select Sales Order Headers, and drag the Order Year under Order Date to the matrix layout where it says "Drag and drop column groups."
5. Similarly, select Order Quarter and drag it over to the matrix columns groups. Place it under Order Year. The mouse pointer should turn blue when it is ready to add a column group.
6. Select Sum Sub Total and drag it to the detail section of the matrix where it says "Drag and drop totals."

7. Add a title to the report; call it Sales by Territory.
8. To make things easier to see, let's use some basic formatting to separate the quarters from the years. Right-click the inner 0, and select Format from the shortcut menu.
9. Go to the Fill tab and select Gold as the color. Then go to the Alignment tab and choose Center for the horizontal alignment. Do the same for the Adjoining Total text box. This should make all quarters-related information headers gold.
10. Do the same thing to the upper 0 and the adjoining total, except select Green as the color. Select Center for the horizontal alignment. On the Border tab, click the Outline button to put an outline border around the year.
11. Right-click the Sum Sub Total text box, select Format from the shortcut menu, go to the Number tab, and select the currency format.

When everything is complete, your report design should look similar to Figure 16.14.

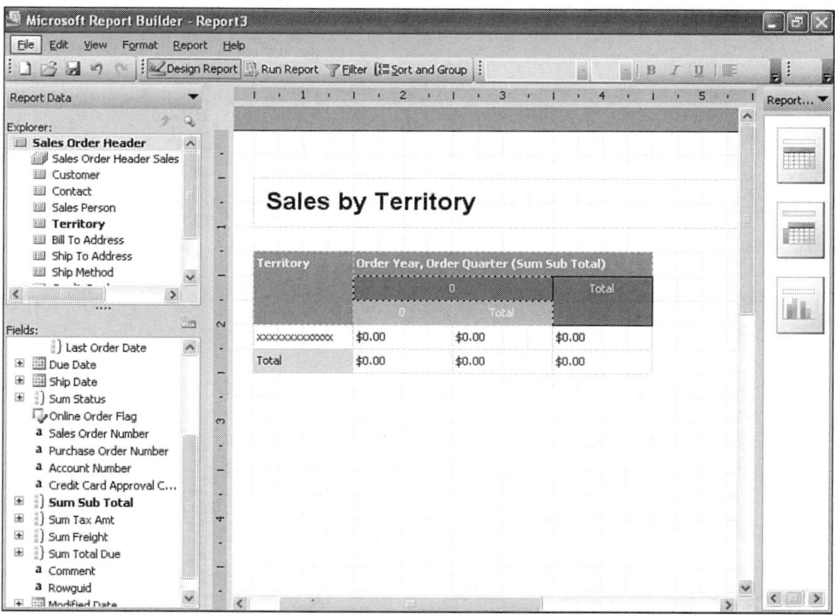

FIGURE 16.14 Finalized report design.

When the report is previewed, it looks similar to Figure 16.15.

Save this report on the Report Server as "Sales by Territory—Matrix."

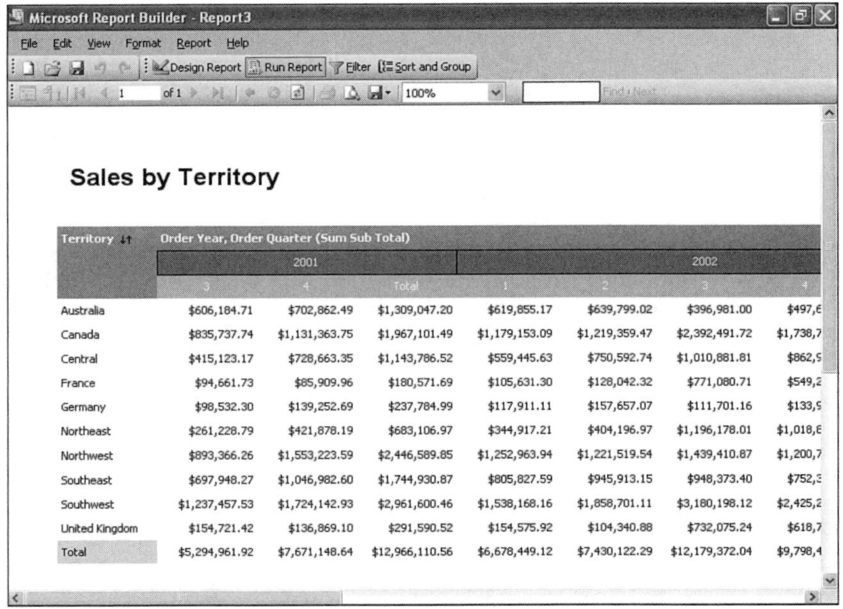

Sales by Territory

Territory	Order Year, Order Quarter (Sum Sub Total)						
	2001			2002			
	3	4	Total	1	2	3	4
Australia	$606,184.71	$702,862.49	$1,309,047.20	$619,855.17	$639,799.02	$396,981.00	$497,
Canada	$835,737.74	$1,131,363.75	$1,967,101.49	$1,179,153.09	$1,219,359.47	$2,392,491.72	$1,738,7
Central	$415,123.17	$728,663.35	$1,143,786.52	$559,445.63	$750,592.74	$1,010,881.81	$862,
France	$94,661.73	$85,909.96	$180,571.69	$105,631.30	$128,042.32	$771,080.71	$549,
Germany	$98,532.30	$139,252.69	$237,784.99	$117,911.11	$157,657.07	$111,701.16	$133,
Northeast	$261,228.79	$421,878.19	$683,106.97	$344,917.21	$404,196.97	$1,196,178.01	$1,018,
Northwest	$893,366.26	$1,553,223.59	$2,446,589.85	$1,252,963.94	$1,221,519.54	$1,439,410.87	$1,200,7
Southeast	$697,948.27	$1,046,982.60	$1,744,930.87	$805,827.59	$945,913.15	$948,373.40	$752,
Southwest	$1,237,457.53	$1,724,142.93	$2,961,600.46	$1,538,168.16	$1,858,701.11	$3,180,198.12	$2,425,
United Kingdom	$154,721.42	$136,869.10	$291,590.52	$154,575.92	$104,340.88	$732,075.24	$618,7
Total	$5,294,961.92	$7,671,148.64	$12,966,110.56	$6,678,449.12	$7,430,122.29	$12,179,372.04	$9,798,4

FIGURE 16.15 Preview of the report in Report Designer.

Summary

End-user reporting provides some fairly significant challenges. SQL Report Services answers this challenge with a combination of tools: the Model Designer and Report Builder.

The Model Designer is used by someone familiar with the data source to create a model that represents the database objects in terms of business objects.

The idea is to present the end user with collections of objects that they would recognize.

Report Builder is a Windows forms-based application that can be launched from the Report Manager website. It uses the report models as a data source, and, in combination with user input, it generates standard RDL documents as reports. Report Builder uses Microsoft Office paradigms so end users who use Microsoft Office should take to the product easily. The reports can then be saved onto the Report Server for later use.

PART III

Reporting Services Administration and Operations

IN THIS PART

Managing Reports, Data Sources, and Models

CHAPTER 17

IN THIS CHAPTER

- Deployment Options in Visual Studio
- Deployment Through Report Manager
- Deploying Reports Through SQL Server Management Studio
- Changing Report Properties
- Setting Report History and Snapshots
- My Reports

Managing Report Server content on SSRS is fairly straightforward. After developing reports, the first thing you need to do is to learn how to deploy them. After reports are deployed, a number of options and properties can be set on the Report Server. These options range from the fairly mundane, such as moving reports from one folder to another, to more complex options, such as managing report histories and snapshots.

Deployment Options in Visual Studio

Because Visual Studio is the primary report development tool, it should come as no surprise that it has the capability to deploy reports. You can actually set it up to deploy reports every time you build your projects. In addition, you can use Visual Studio to overwrite existing data sources on the server, hence setting the proper location for use in production.

ServerName

First, you need to set the server name for deployment of your project. You can do this by setting the project properties through the IDE. This is actually much simpler than it sounds. If you have closed the AdventureWorksReports Samples reports project, open it again.

1. Open Solution Explorer (View, Solution Explorer).

2. Right-click on the project and select Properties.
3. You should have a screen that looks similar to Figure 17.1.

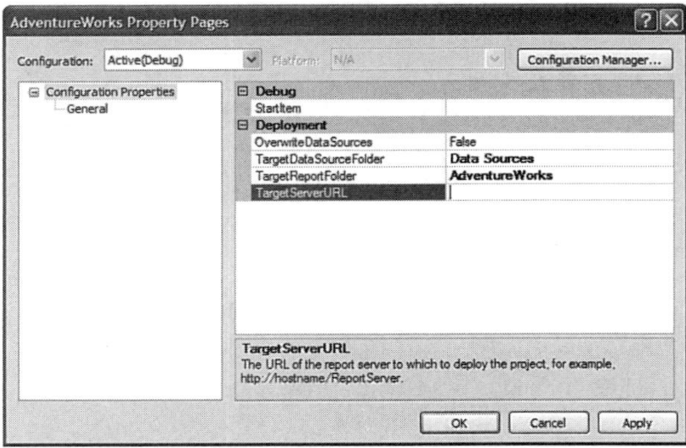

FIGURE 17.1 Deployment properties for the AdventureWorks project.

Now all you have to do is set the server name. The server name and virtual directory have to be placed in the TargetServerURL property. The format is `http://{ServerName}/{VirtualDirectory}`. By default, if you have installed the server locally, its property is filled in as `http://localhost/ReportServer`.

Report Folder Location

TargetReportFolder is another major property.

By default, it sets itself to the project name. The folder name is the name of the folder created on the Report Server to house your reports. You can leave it blank and reports will deploy on the root folder.

Overwriting Data Sources

One of the most important properties is OverwriteDataSource as it will change the location of the data source on the Report Server.

By default, when Visual Studio deploys, it creates the data source for your reports. The key here is it creates the data source, but never updates it even if you have updated the data source in your project. The exception to this is when the report has an embedded data source in its data sets.

The purpose of this switch is to force the upgrade of shared data sources. If you need to overwrite the data sources, set this to true, and you will be on your way.

Target Folder for Data Source *NEW in 1005*

This property (TargetDataSourceFolder) is similar to the folder for reports. This is actually new in SSRS 2005. The previous version had no such option. Remember this only applies to shared data sources.

Building and Deploying Reports

When you set all the properties, you should have a screen that looks similar to Figure 17.2.

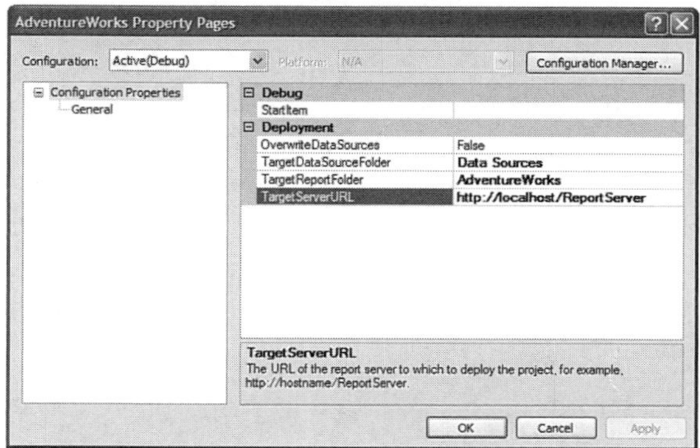

FIGURE 17.2 Completed deployment properties for the AdventureWorks project.

When you are ready to deploy the reports and data sources, complete the following steps:

1. From Solution Explorer, right-click on the project.
2. Select Deploy.

After a quick permissions check with the chosen Report Server, Visual Studio should allow you to deploy the project. At this point, you should see the folders created in Report Manager. See Figure 17.3.

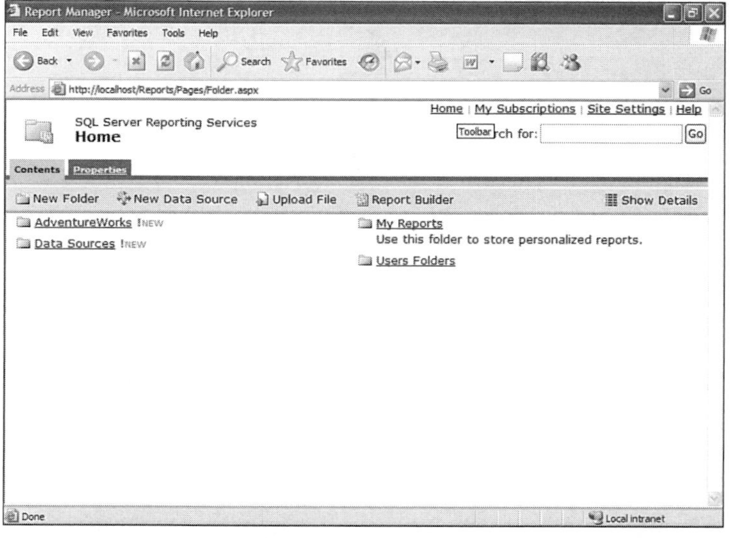

FIGURE 17.3 Deployed AdventureWorks project.

Deployment Through Report Manager

As covered in Chapter 1, "Introduction to SQL Server Reporting Services (SSRS)," the Report Manager web application is the main user interface. All administrative functions can be called from here. It also serves as the main user interface into the Report Server. Essentially, it checks user permissions, and if you have permission to do a task, it presents you with the interface to do it. By default, administrators on the machine on which the Report Server is installed have full permissions to all functions.

Creating a New Folder

First, you need to set up a folder into which you will deploy the reports. If you want, you can deploy it onto the root of the Report Server; however, it can get difficult to manage with a large number of reports.

In the Report Manager user interface, a row of buttons displays across the top. See Figure 17.4.

To get acquainted with Report Manager, let's use it to publish some reports manually. The first thing to do is to create a new folder by clicking on the New Folder button. You should see a screen similar to Figure 17.4.

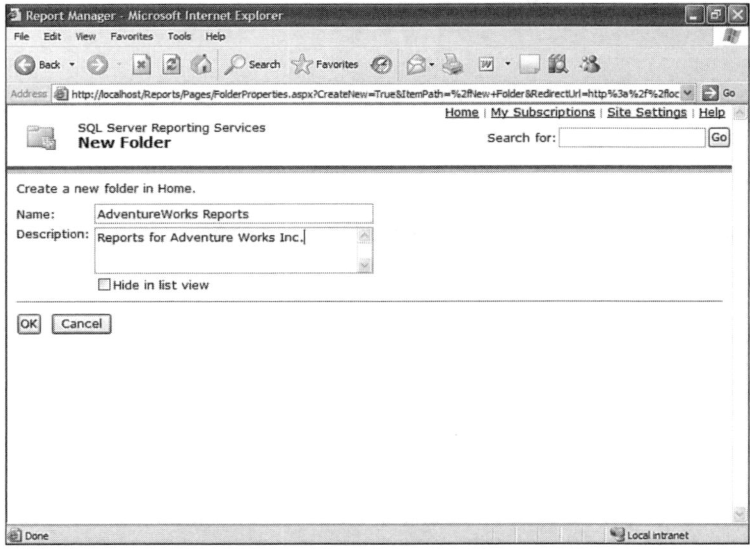

FIGURE 17.4 Creating a new folder.

Complete the following steps to finish adding the new folder:

1. Change the Name field to AdventureWorks Reports.
2. Change the Description field to Reports for Adventure Works Inc.
3. Click OK.

This should return you to the main screen, and you should see your folder present. If you click on the folder, the user interface shows you its contents; however, it will be empty because it was just created and you haven't published anything yet.

Setting Up a Data Source

It is time to set up a shared data source for the report that you will be publishing. The shared data source is beneficial because you have many reports that use the same database catalog for information. To set up a shared data source, perform the following steps:

1. If you haven't done so already, click the AdventureWorks Reports folder.
2. Click the New Data Source button on the toolbar. The contents of the browser window should look similar to Figure 17.5.

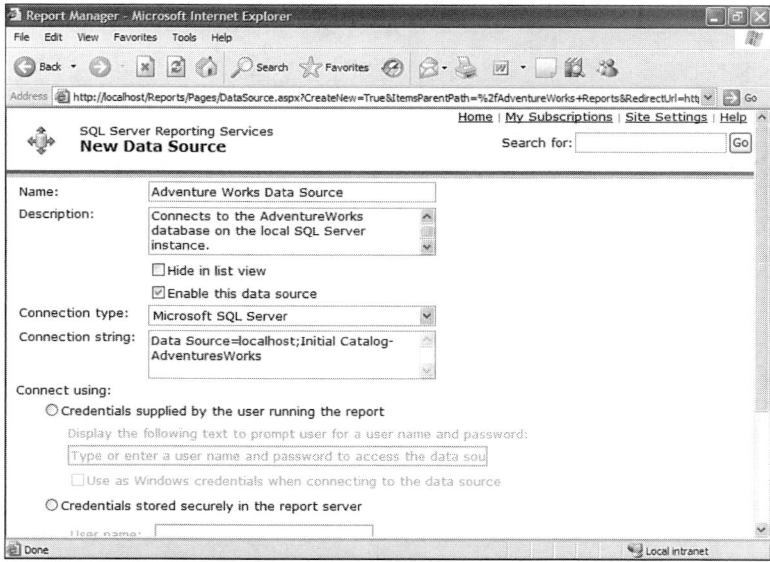

FIGURE 17.5 Creating a new data source.

3. In the Name text box, enter Adventure Works Data Source.
4. In the Description field, enter "Connects to the AdventureWorks database on the local SQL Server instance."
5. Select Microsoft SQL Server for the connection type.
6. Enter the following connection string: `Data Source=localhost;Initial Catalog=AdventureWorks`.
7. Select Windows Integrated Security.
8. Click OK.

Clicking the OK button should return you to the folder contents and your data source should be displayed.

Uploading a Report

Now it is finally time to upload your reports. This is a pretty straightforward process, but you need to know the location of the RDL files on your hard drive. If you do not remember, go back to the Visual Studio solution, click on the report inside Solution Explorer and look at the properties for the report list. Take note of the `Full Path` property. This is the location of the RDL file on your PC.

Let's continue on and use the Report Manager to upload our reports. To upload reports, perform the following steps:

1. Click the Upload File button on the toolbar.
2. Click Browse and browse to the location of the RDL file.
3. Change the `Name` property. See Figure 17.6.

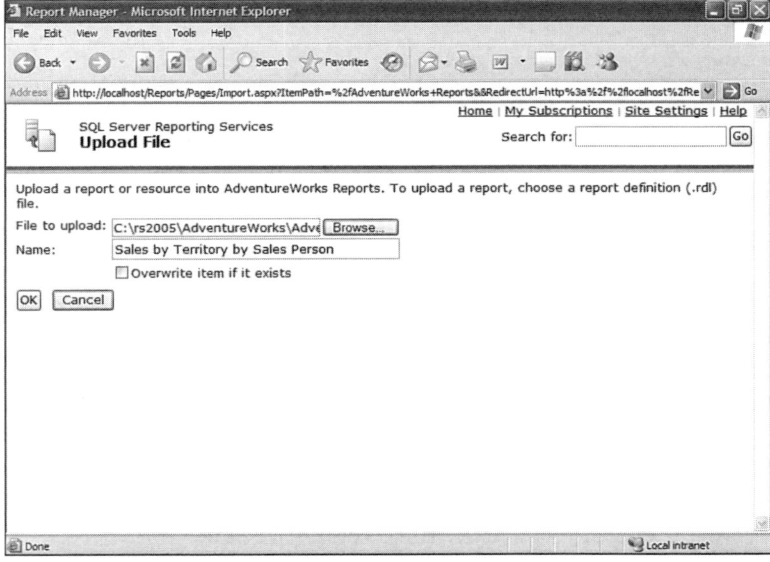

FIGURE 17.6 Uploading a file from the AdventureWorks project.

4. If you want to update an existing copy of the report, check the Overwrite Item if It Exists check box.
5. Click OK.

Report Manager should now display the folder contents with the report and data source in it.

Changing the Data Source

Because you are using a shared data source, it makes sense to change the report to use the shared data source. Changing the report to use the shared data source entails the following steps:

1. Click on the report.
2. Click the Properties tab.
3. Go to Data Sources on the left menu.
4. Select the A Shared Data Source option.
5. Click Browse.
6. Drill down into the folder list until you see AdventureWorks DataSource and select it. You should now see a screen similar to Figure 17.7.

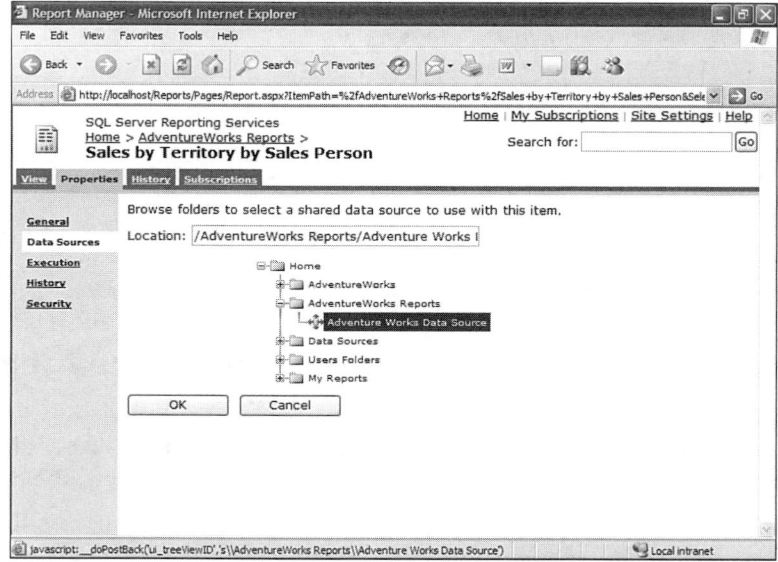

FIGURE 17.7 Setting the data source for a report through Report Manager.

7. Click OK.
8. You should now be on the data source property window. Click Apply.

If you do not want to use the shared data source, you can choose to use a custom one.

Simply select Custom Data Source on the data source properties window and fill in the values for the data source properties just as you would have if it had been a shared data source. An example of this is shown in Figure 17.8. In place of using Windows security, it shows how to connect with a SQL Server logon and password. For simplicity's sake, the logon is "sa"; however, in a production environment, you should use more granular permissions.

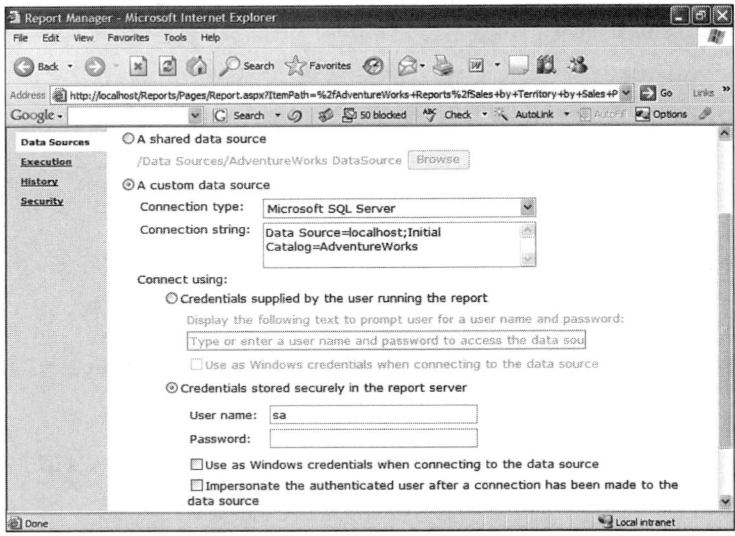

FIGURE 17.8 Defining a custom data source for a report through Report Manager.

Now if you click on the report, it should render inside the window.

Deploying Reports Through SQL Server Management Studio

Deploying reports through SQL Server Management Studio is not incredibly different from using Report Manager. The concepts are the same (as are the steps); the only difference is that you use a smart client tool instead of a web browser.

Creating a New Folder

Complete the following steps to create a new folder using SQL Server Management Studio:

1. Open SQL Server Management Studio.
2. Change the server type to Reporting Services. See Figure 17.9.
3. Click the Connect button.
4. In Object Explorer, navigate to the Home folder, as shown in Figure 17.10.

5. Right-click on the Home folder and select New Folder.
6. Change the Name field to AdventureWorks Reports.
7. Change the Description field to "Reports for Adventure Works Inc." See Figure 17.11.
8. Click OK.

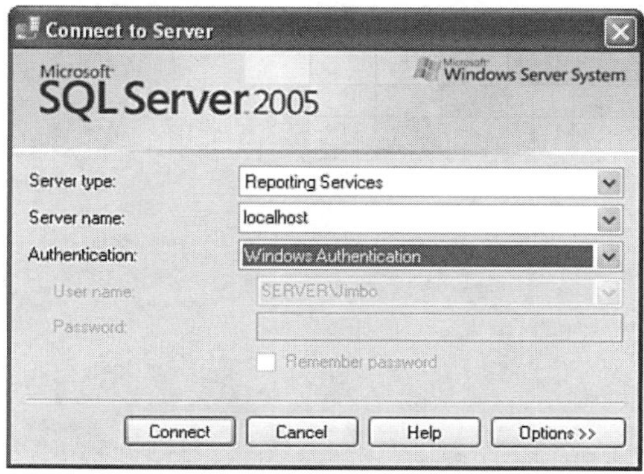

FIGURE 17.9 Using SQL Server Management Studio to connect to SSRS.

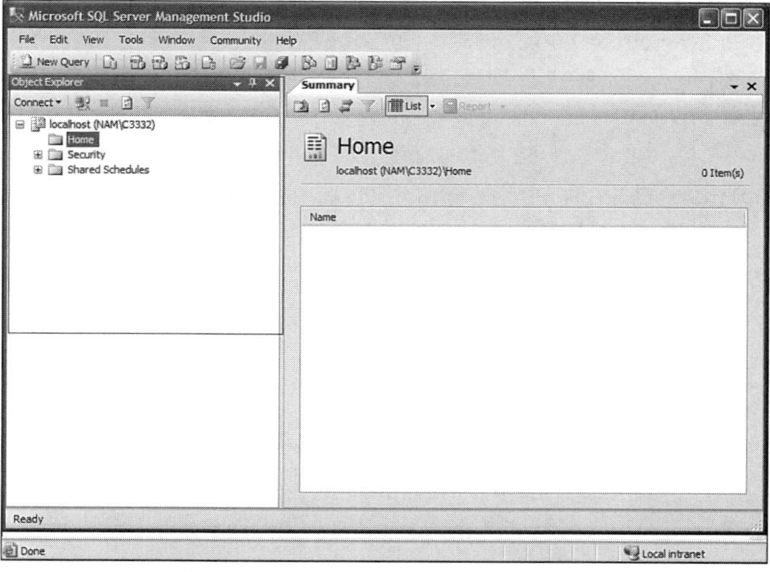

FIGURE 17.10 SQL Server Management Studio's Object Explorer.

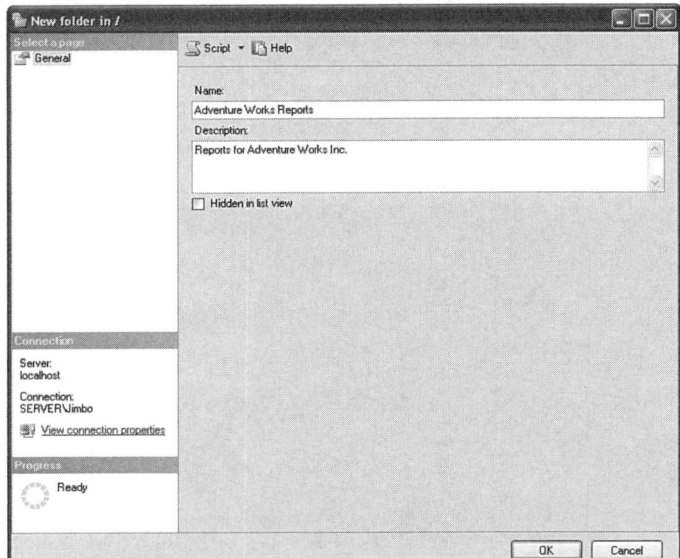

FIGURE 17.11 Adding a new folder in SQL Server Management Studio.

Setting Up a Data Source

SQL Server Management Studio can be used to create data sources, just like Report Manager. To set up a data source using SQL Server Management Studio, complete the following steps:

1. Right-click on the new folder and select New Data Source.
2. In the Name text box, enter AdventureWorks DataSource.
3. In the Description field, enter "Connects to the AdventureWorks database on the local SQL Server instance."
4. On the Connection tab, select Microsoft SQL Server for the Data Source Type.
5. Enter the following connection string: `Data Source=localhost;Initial Catalog=AdventureWorks`.
6. Select Windows Integrated Security.
7. Your screen should look similar to Figure 17.12. Click OK.

Uploading a Report File

After creating the folder and adding a data source, you are now ready to upload the RDL files to the Report Server. Just like everything else so far, SQL Server Management Studio does not differ all that much in concept. Complete the following steps to upload a report:

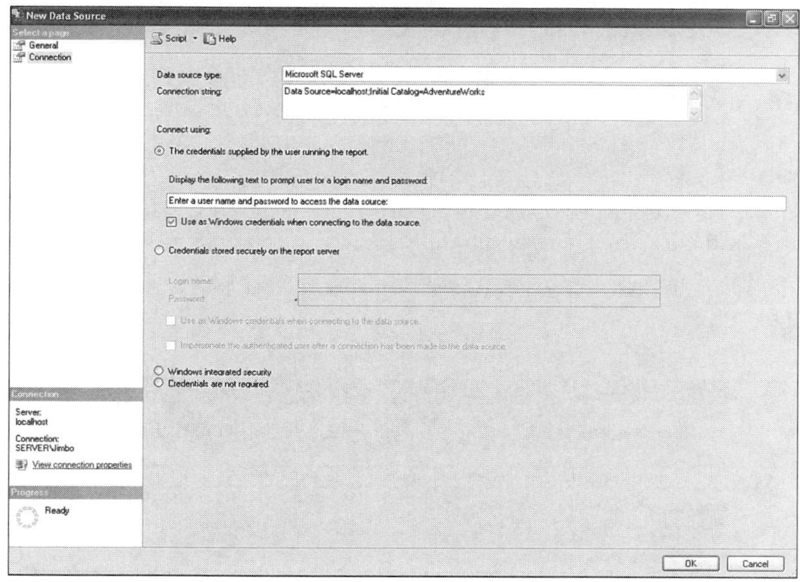

FIGURE 17.12 Adding a new data source through SQL Server Management Studio.

1. Right-click on the Adventure Works folder, and select Import File.
2. Select the file to upload.
3. Your screen should look similar to Figure 17.13. Click OK.

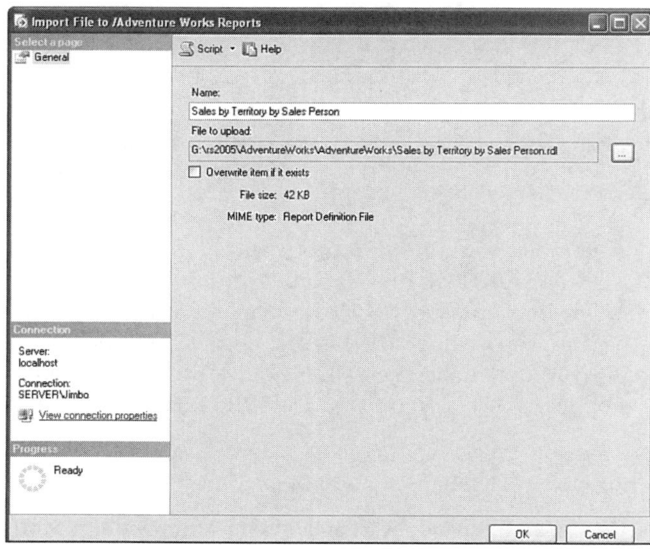

FIGURE 17.13 Uploading a file through SQL Server Management Studio.

Changing Report Properties

Now that you have published the Adventure Works sample reports, let's change some properties. Most report properties can be changed.

Basic Properties

To start modifiying properties, open any report by clicking on it. Then select the Properties tab and click the General tab (left side). See Figure 17.14.

You can modify the name or description of any report. Just enter the new name/description and click Apply.

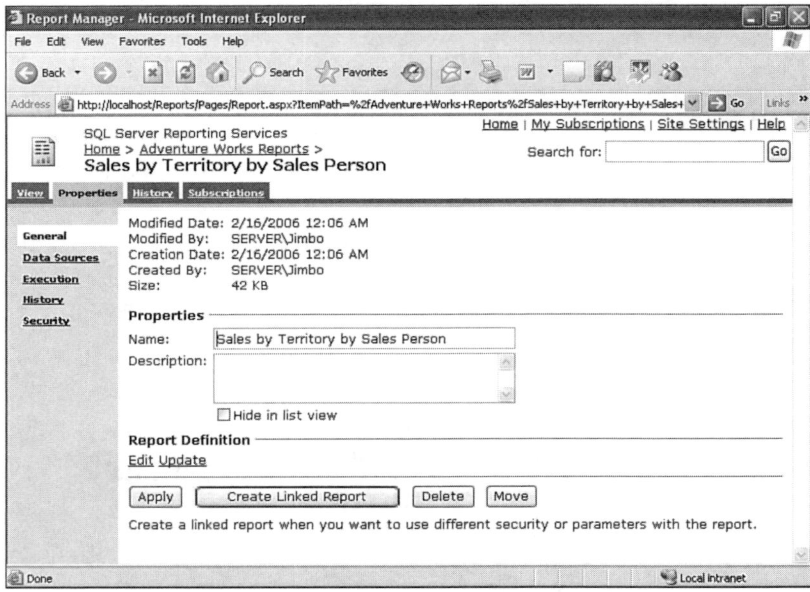

FIGURE 17.14 Report properties.

Some other options include the ability to retrieve and update the RDL definition of a report. Ideally, you should store RDL files in some form of Source Control, such as Visual Source Safe or CVS. This helps not only with storage, but also with version control and history. However, because the RDL is stored in the ReportServer database, you can also choose to download it. To download the RDL file, click the Edit button and a File Download dialog box opens. If you want to update the RDL for any report, click the Update button.

Another obvious function is Delete, which deletes a report.

Many of the functions have equivalents in SQL Server Management Studio. They are all accessible through Object Explorer. First connect to the Report Server using SQL Server Management Studio. Then through Object Explorer, navigate to the reports. Most basic functions are available by right-clicking on the report, and they have similar names to that in Report Manager. Right-click on a report and select Edit to save the RDL. Right-click on a report and select Replace Report to update the RDL saved on the Report Server. Right-click a report and select Properties to change the name.

Moving Reports

The Move button allows you to move a report. To move a report, complete the following steps:

1. Click on the report to be moved and select the Properties tab.
2. Under General in the left menu, click the Move button.
3. Choose the new location from the treelist.
4. Click OK.

To move reports from the SQL Server Management Studio, do the following:

1. Open SQL Server Management Studio and connect to the Report Server.
2. In Object Explorer, select the report to be moved.
3. Right-click the report and select Move.
4. Click the "..." button.
5. Select the new location from the treelist.
6. Click OK.

Linked Reports

A linked report is a "copy" of a report with a different set of parameter values or other properties. Linked reports share the same RDL definition with the source report, and, as such, when the parent reports' RDL gets updated, the linked reports get updated as well. A single, nonlinked report can be the parent of any number of linked reports, but a linked report cannot be the parent of another linked report.

Linked reports may share the same RDL and data sources, but just about every other property can be modified. These include the following:

- **Name and Description**—Linked reports can have a completely different name and description. To the end user, it can look like a completely separate report.
- **Location**—Linked reports can exist anywhere in the catalog.
- **Parameters**—Linked reports can be used with a completely different set of parameter values from the originating report. This helps in presenting the linked report as a completely separate entity. This can also be the primary motivation for creating the linked report.

- **Security**—Different role assignments can be assigned to the linked report.
- **Report Execution and Report History**—The report execution and report history properties can vary from a linked report to the original.
- **Subscriptions**—Subscriptions to linked reports are completely separate than those of the parent.

After the linked report has been created, it can be treated like another item in the catalog. Linked reports can be deleted at will with no further repercussions. However, if the parent report of the linked report is deleted, all subsequent linked reports become invalid. At this point, either the linked report must be deleted or it must be pointed to a different report definition.

Creating a linked report is fairly straightforward, and it can be done through either Report Manager or SQL Server Management Studio. Complete the following steps to create a linked report through Report Manager:

1. Open the report and click the Properties tab.
2. Click the Create Linked Report button.
3. Enter a name and description. Just like any other report, the description is optional.
4. If you want to place the linked report in another folder, click the Change Location button and choose the new location.
5. When all the steps are complete, your screen should look similar to Figure 17.15. Click OK.

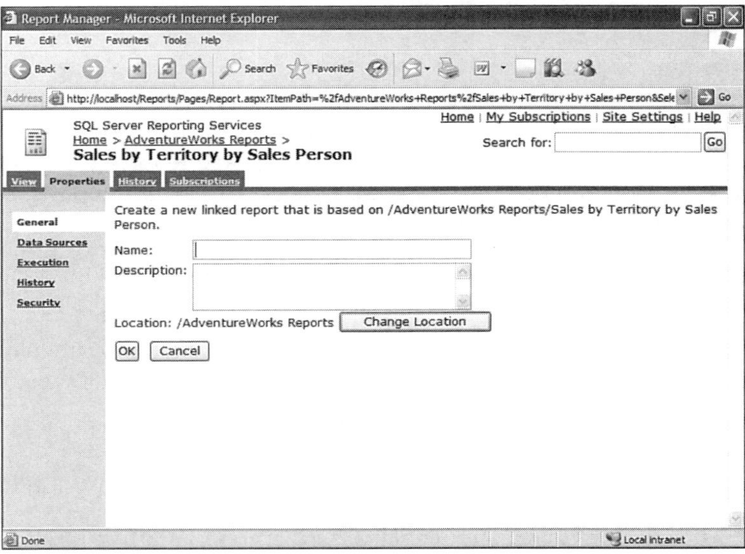

FIGURE 17.15 Creating a new linked report.

Creating a linked report through SQL Server Management Studio is essentially the same process. Here are the steps:

1. Open SQL Server Management Studio, and connect to the Report Server.
2. From Object Explorer, navigate to the report for which you want to create the linked report.
3. Right-click on it and select New Linked Report.
4. Enter a name for the new report, and, optionally, enter a description.
5. If you want to place the linked report in another folder, click the "..." button next to the Create Linked Report in This Folder option, and choose the new location.
6. Figure 17.16 show the completed screen. Click OK.

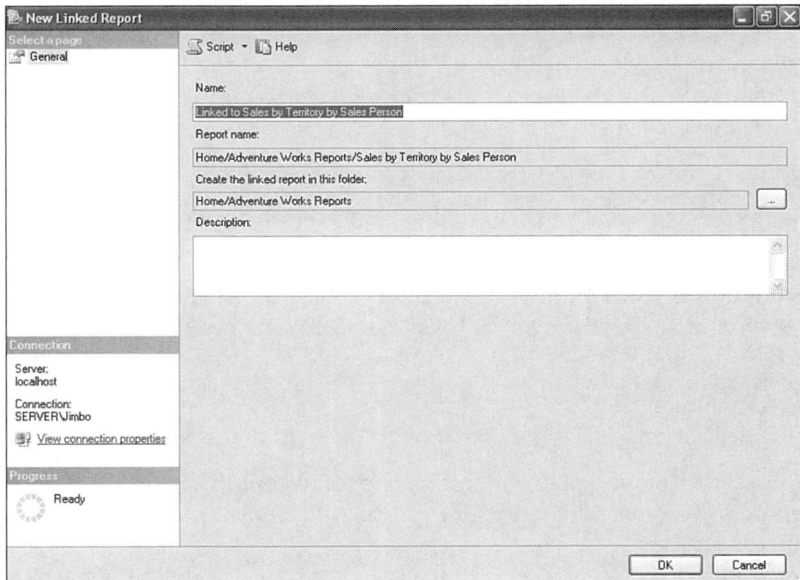

FIGURE 17.16 Creating a new linked report through SQL Server Management Studio.

Setting Report History and Snapshots

Most of the reports, including many of the samples, don't really tax modern hardware. However, in some cases, there might be a report in production that could be hundreds of pages, or could tax the database server with expensive queries. In these cases, it would be helpful to be able to cache reports, so that the report-rendering engine and the database server don't waste resources.

SSRS attains the preceding goals by retaining something called report history. The history is a collection of previously run reports called snapshots. A snapshot is a copy of the report at a point in time. If the report layout or data changes, the snapshot remains the same and does not reflect the update.

Report Server Settings to Affect Report History

There are two levels of settings when setting report history. The first level is Report Server–wide, and is accessible through the Site Settings link or by clicking on the server itself in Object Explorer through SQL Server Management Studio. The other settings are at the report level, and can override the sitewide settings.

The only global parameter for the Report Server as a whole is how many snapshots to keep in history. By default, the sitewide settings are set to keep an unlimited number of snapshots in history; however, most reports are set to run on the fly, and not set to render from a snapshot. If an administrator decided to change this value, the old snapshots would be deleted as the maximum number of snapshots is reached.

The rest of the settings for snapshots are set at the report level, and can be set either through the Report Server or through SQL Server Management Studio. To access the setting through the Report Manager, click the report, select the Properties tab, and select History. From SQL Server Management Studio, right-click on the report and select Properties and then select History.

The first option is Allow Report History to Be Created Manually.

This allows the New Snapshot button to appear on the History page in Report Manager. Using this button, users can then select to create a snapshot themselves.

The second option is Store All Report Execution Snapshots in History. This stores a copy of each snapshot in the report history. Users can then look back over time and see how the report has changed.

Another option allows users/administrators to generate report snapshots on a custom or shared schedule. The snapshots generated over time will help to form the history.

The last option defines how many snapshots are to be kept in history. This allows us to use the Report Server's default setting or override it by allowing a limited number or infinite number of copies.

From a security perspective, users must have the Manage Report History task inside their roles to generate snapshots. The end users must also have the View Reports role to view the report history. Report snapshots are not meant for, and not recommended to be used on, a report that contains secure or confidential data. If a report uses a data source that prompts the user for a password, or one that requires integrated security, the snapshot cannot be created.

Creating Snapshots

Snapshots contain the following data:

- A copy of the resultset(s) brought back by the data sources of the report.
- The report definition at the time when the snapshot was created. Keep in mind that this will not take into account any recent changes.

- Parameter values that were used while processing the reports and/or query.
- Any embedded resources for a report. If the report relies on an outside resource, that resource is not saved on the RS database.

To add a snapshot using Report Manager, follow these steps:

1. Open the report for which you want to create a snapshot, and click the History tab.
2. Click the New Snapshot button, as shown in Figure 17.17.

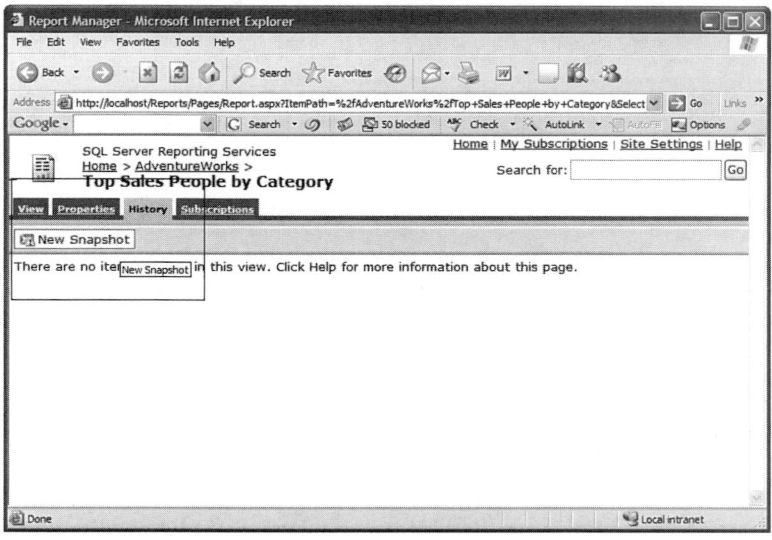

FIGURE 17.17 Creating a snapshot.

3. A new snapshot should appear, with the date it was created and the size.

To create a snapshot using SQL Server Management Studio, complete the following steps:

1. Using Object Explorer, navigate to the History folder under the report for which you want to create a snapshot.
2. Right-click the History folder, and select New Snapshot. See Figure 17.18.
3. Right-click on the History folder again and select Refresh to make sure the snapshot appears.

Deleting Snapshots

After snapshots have been created, they can only be deleted—not modified. There are two ways to delete a snapshot.

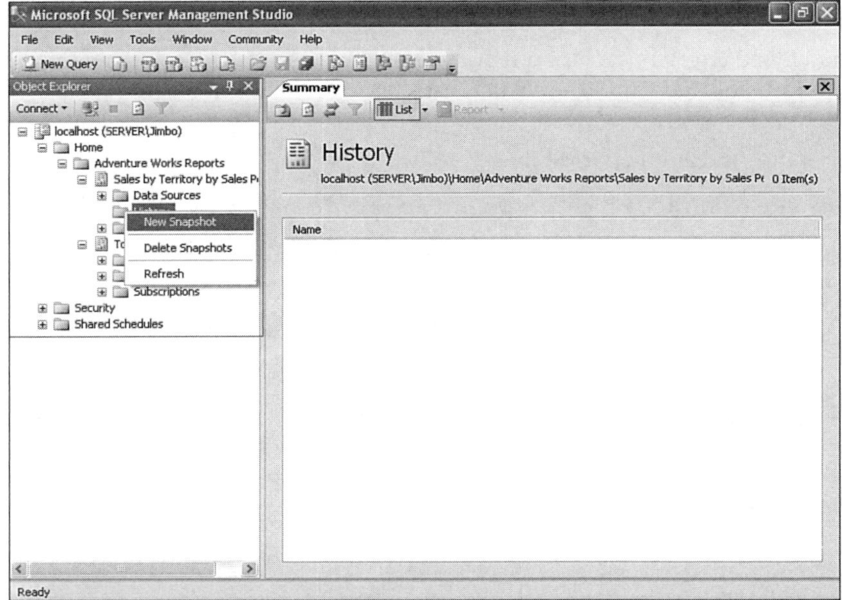

FIGURE 17.18 Creating a snapshot through SQL Server Management Studio.

The first way involves using either SQL Server Management Studio or Report Manager to delete individual snapshots in the report history. From Report Manager, navigate to the report and click the History tab. Then select the check boxes next to the individual snapshots and click the Delete button. From SQL Server Management Studio, use Object Explorer to navigate to the History folder under the report, right-click it, and select History.

Right-clicking on the History folder gives the user an option to Delete All Snapshots. Otherwise, right-click on an individual snapshot and select Delete.

The second way to delete snapshots is to simply lower the number of snapshots the Report Server should keep. This forces the older snapshots to be deleted as needed.

My Reports

The My Reports folder creates an individual workspace for each user in the Report Server. The individual users can use it for any number of things as they see fit. These might include storage space for reports in progress, or as a holding area for reports not yet ready to be published. There is no way for an administrator to control the size or amount of content end users choose to place in their My Reports folder.

The structure of the My Reports folder is somewhat analogous to the My Documents folder in Windows. Just like My Documents is a pointer to `C:\Documents and Settings\...`, My Reports actually points to a folder called `/User Folders/<username>/My Reports`. This folder doesn't actually get created in the Report Server catalog until a user actually uses the My Reports feature.

Enabling My Reports

The My Reports feature is disabled by default in a new installation of SSRS. After being enabled, it is effective for the entire user base, meaning it cannot be enabled for some users but not others. A number of considerations must be considered before enabling it.

First, you need to consider server resources. My Reports is a powerful feature. It is effectively like giving end users access to a file share with unlimited space. In SSRS 2000, end users only had Visual Studio to create reports—a not-so-appealing option for many end users. Now with Report Builder, end users can easily create new reports to suit their needs and store them on the Report Server.

Second, you need to consider security. With the My Reports feature turned on, end users can create new security policies and publish reports for other users from the My Reports folder. This might at first seem helpful for administrators, but the propagation of security policies could prove difficult to manage later.

If an administrator chooses to enable the My Reports feature, it is a fairly straightforward process. Here are the steps to enable My Reports:

1. Using Report Manager, click the Site Settings option.
2. Check the Enable My Reports to Support User-Owned Folders for Publishing and Running Personalized Reports check box.
3. Select a default role to apply to each user's My Reports folder. The default is a role called My Reports. See Figure 17.19.
4. Click Apply.

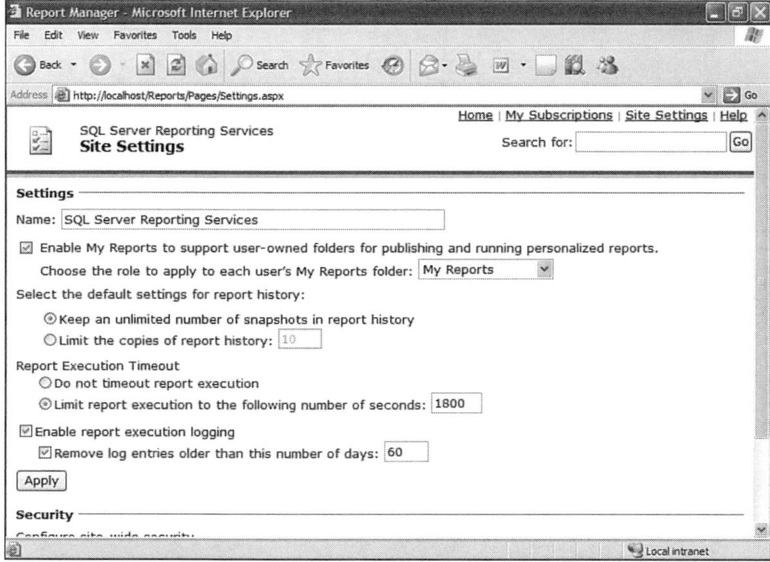

FIGURE 17.19 Enabling My Reports.

From this point forward, a user will see the My Reports folder pop up under the root folder in the catalog. In addition, administrators will see the User Folders folder, along with their My Reports folder. Of course, a user cannot create a folder called My Reports at the root folder level. The name My Reports has been reserved.

Disabling My Reports

Should My Reports have to be disabled, simply deselect the check box under Site Settings. From this point forward, users can create a folder called My Reports; however, no special redirection occurs. Any actual folder that has been created under the User Folders folder will remain.

Summary

In this chapter, you have seen how to deploy reports through both Report Manager and Visual Studio. Report Manager allows end users the ability to set basic report properties and modify a report's data source.

Report Manager also allows end users to link reports, move reports, and create report snapshots.

If administrators allow it, end users also can have their personal report repositories in their My Reports folders.

Securing Report Server Items

CHAPTER 18

IN THIS CHAPTER

- Reporting Services Security Model
- Defining Custom Roles

Because SSRS is a .NET application, many of the existing .NET security paradigms come into play when securing access to the Report Server. From the end user's viewpoint, SSRS uses role-based authorization built on top of Windows authentication. If using a custom authentication mechanism, the underlying principals are the same. It is simply up to the authorization mechanism to define valid users and roles (called principals).

Reporting Services Security Model

Role-based authorization is not a new concept. It is a proven mechanism that is implemented in a variety of ways. One of the most common, everyday items that uses role-based authorization is the file system. If your PC's file system is based on NTFS, you have the ability to place access control lists (ACLs) on certain folders. ACLs specify users or groups of users (generically called principals), permissions to read, write, or execute items within a folder, or the folder itself. If a folder does not have ACLs placed on it, the folder then simply inherits its permissions from the parent folder. The administrator of the computer can, of course, change access to certain folders, but is not allowed to place himself in the access pool.

Drawing from the file system's paradigm, the SSRS security models it very similarly. Within SSRS, there are a fixed number of predefined roles, which can be assigned to users. These roles are used to give permissions to execute certain tasks on folders or other report items. Examples of some of the built-in roles include Browser, Content Manager, and System Administrator.

When SSRS installs, it sets up the local administrator pool with the System Administrator and Content Manager roles.

This is the absolute minimum security that can be applied. SSRS requires that at least one principal, a valid user or group, be assigned to the System Administrator role, and likewise to the Content Manager role. This ensures that the Report Server cannot be locked out from the outside.

There are no users added. Users cannot interact with the Report Server until someone in the local Administrators group assigns them to either one of the predefined roles, or a custom role.

When the time comes to start adding users, administrators have the choice to add users to a certain role, or to many roles. Users can even have different permissions on different report items. For example, a user might be a Content Manager, which allows the user to publish reports, in one folder, yet only be a Browser (read only) in another folder.

As mentioned in the chapter introduction, SSRS uses Windows authentication by default. The list of valid users and groups rests in the hand of the authentication services. When a user or group (referred to as a principal from this point forward) is added to a role, the principal is validated against the authenticating authority.

On a Report Server, authentication through the Windows security extension (default method) is performed by IIS. The user and group accounts that you specify in role assignments are created and managed through Active Directory.

If a customer security extension is used, it is up to the extension to validate the principal.

What Can Be Secured?

Although it might not be the most efficient approach, the reality is that just about every report item can be secured individually. Some things that don't follow this rule are subscriptions and schedules because they are used in conjunction with a report and not as an independent part of it. Table 18.1 describes how report items and their security work.

TABLE 18.1 Report Items and Effects of Security

Report Item	How Security Applies
Folder	Securing a folder usually ends up securing all the items within that folder. When SSRS is installed, only local administrators are Content Managers on the root folder. This ensures that no user can browse the catalog, unless given explicit rights to do so. The exception to this is the My Reports folder. My Reports, if it's enabled, creates a pseudofolder within the catalog in which users are given permissions to publish their own reports.

TABLE 18.1 Continued

Report Item	How Security Applies
Report	Reports and linked reports can be secured to control levels of access. For example, the View Reports task allows users to view a report as well as report history, whereas Manage Reports allows them to change report properties. Manage Report History allows users to generate snapshots.
Model	Primarily used to secure access to the model, it can also be used to secure reports for which the model acts as a data source. Models can also be secured internally by securing model items with perspectives, specifying role assignments on all or part of a model, and securing items such as the root node, folders, entities, and relationships within the model.
Resources	Resources are items in the Report Server that provide content to user. An example of a resource can be an HTML file or Word document. Securing a resource limits access to the resource and its properties. The View Resources permissions are needed to access the resources.
Shared data sources	Securing shared data sources limits access to the data source and its corresponding properties. To view the data source properties, users need the View Data Sources permission; likewise Manage Data Sources gives permissions to modify them.

How Role Assignments Work

To continue with the file system analogy, one has to ask what are we actually putting limits on? The answer is who can read, write, and execute on objects within the file system. A cursory glance at Table 18.1 gives a similar perspective. By securing a report item, you are actually putting limits on what actions can be taken using that item. The actions are called tasks in SSRS.

SSRS comes with 25 different tasks. Tasks cannot be added to or taken away from. Table 18.1 has already mentioned the names of a few tasks, such as View Reports and Manage Reports.

Tasks themselves actually encompass a set of underlying permissions. For example, the Manage Folders task actually gives the end user the ability to create, delete, update, and modify a folder and its properties. If a user visits the Report Manager without the permissions to Manage Folders, none of the buttons or UI elements will be enabled.

The underlying permissions are nice to know about, but not very practical, as task is the lowest level of assignment. To get assigned permissions to complete an operation, the permissions have to be implemented into a task. The task or tasks have to then be placed in a role to be performed. Hence, if the View Models task is not included in a role, or the role is not included in a role assignment, users cannot view report models.

Tasks themselves come in two different categories, as follows:

- **Item-level tasks**—Tasks that act on an item in the Report Server catalog, such as folders, models, reports, and resources
- **System-level tasks**—Tasks that can be performed on objects that are not in the catalog but are global in scope, such as site settings and shared schedules

As you might have already guessed, the role is the central tenet of role-based security. Roles are collections of tasks. SSRS comes with a few predefined roles, but administrators can also create roles to suit their needs. A single role can only contain one of the two task types, that is, either item-level tasks or system-level tasks. Because of this, there are item-level roles and system-level roles. A role is only active when it is assigned to a user.

When a user tries to perform an action, the Report Server checks what permissions are required to perform that action. The required permissions are expressed in the roles required for access. It then checks to make sure that the user requesting the action has sufficient privileges to perform that action. Again, the easiest way is to check if the user is either a member of the specified role, or if the roles contain the required tasks and, hence, permissions.

Relationships Between Roles, Tasks, and Users

The relationship between items that need to be secured, roles, and users is called a policy. The policy is what is responsible for mapping out the minimum set of permissions required for securing a report item. An individual policy is a mapping of users or groups (principals) with a required role needed for access. Each item in the catalog can have multiple policies defined; however, no single item can have two policies that apply to the same principal.

For example, suppose you have a user named George and you need to grant George access to view reports in the Adventure Works folder. To do so, you specified that George can have the Browser role. After doing this, you created a policy. The policy can be modified by granting more roles to George, hence increasing George's permissions to, for example, Content Manager; however, you cannot create a second policy with George. What you can do is create a group, for example "Adventure Works Content Managers," and place George in that group. You can then give the group the role of Content Manager.

So, in the end, what are George's permissions? Well, because roles are really nothing more then a collection of tasks, George can perform all the tasks that Content Managers and Browsers can perform. This is why the policies are called additive.

By this point, you are probably thinking that security is a lot of trouble. If every item can have a policy, and polices are additive, granting permissions can quickly get out of hand. The thing to remember here is that just because you can do something doesn't mean that you should.

When you apply a policy to a folder, or some other items, you are, by default, applying the same policy to children of that folder/item. This makes it easy to change and apply policies. The recommended best practice is to secure folders within the Report Server catalog. By securing the folder, administrators are securing everything within that folder. This is the same model used in NTFS. Every child item of a folder automatically inherits the parent folder's permissions. Whenever an item's permissions need to change, just break the inheritance and SSRS starts a new policy with that item.

Overview of Built-In Roles

For most organizations, the built-in roles should suffice. If they do not, keep in mind that the Report Server administrators can create custom role definitions. If you need to create a custom role definition, it might be helpful to stage that role definition in a development environment.

Tables 18.2 and 18.3 describe the predefined roles and their corresponding tasks. Keep in mind that when a task is called "Manage …" that it implies the ability to create, modify, and delete.

TABLE 18.2 Item-Level Roles

Role Name	Description
Browser	Allows users to browse through the folder hierarchy, view report properties, view resources and their properties, view models and use them as a data source, and, finally, execute reports, but not manage reports. It is important to note that this role gives Report Viewer the ability to subscribe to reports using their own subscriptions.
Content Manager	Allows users to manage folders, models, data sources, report history, and resources regardless of who owns them. This role also allows users to execute reports, create folder items, view and set properties of items, and set security for report items.
Report Builder	Allows users to build and edit reports using Report Builder and manage individual subscriptions.
My Reports	Allows users to build reports and store the reports in their own personal folder. They can also change the permissions of their own My Reports folder.
Publisher	Allows users to publish content to the Report Server, but not to view it. This role is helpful for people who are allowed to develop reports against a development or test data source, but are not allowed to view reports against the production data source.

TABLE 18.3 Tasks Assigned to Item-Level Roles

	Browser	Content Manager	My Reports	Publisher	Report Builder
Consume reports		X			X
Created linked reports		X	X	X	

TABLE 18.3 Continued

	Browser	Content Manager	My Reports	Publisher	Report Builder
Manage all subscriptions		X			
Manage data sources		X	X	X	
Manage folders		X	X	X	
Manage individual subscriptions	X	X	X		X
Manage models		X		X	
Manage report history		X	X		
Manage reports		X	X	X	
Manage resources		X	X	X	
Set security for individual items		X			
View data sources		X	X		
View folders	X	X	X		X
View models	X	X			X
View reports	X	X	X		X
View resources	X	X	X		X

There are two built-in, system-level roles. These roles follow the same pattern as the item-level roles in that one role allows view access to systems settings, and the other allows them to be modified. Keep in mind that you can also create new system-level roles. Tables 18.4 and 18.5 break down the system-level roles and tasks.

TABLE 18.4 System-Level Roles

Role Name	Role Description
System Administrator	Allows members to create and assign roles, set systemwide settings (Report Server properties and Report Server security), share schedules, and manage jobs
System User	Allows members to view system properties and shared schedules

TABLE 18.5 Tasks Assigned to System-Level Roles

	System Administrator	System User
Execute report definitions	X	X
Generate events		
Manage jobs	X	
Manage Report Server properties	X	
Manage Report Server security	X	
Manage roles	X	
Manage shared schedules	X	
View Report Server properties	X	X
View shared schedules	X	X

After the Report Server is installed, the local Administrators group is assigned two roles. The first role is the Content Manager, and the second is the System Administrator role. Individually, the roles limit access to certain areas. The Content Manager role can manage everything within the Report Server catalog.

System Administrators can manage the Report Server. With the combination of these two roles, local administrators are able to do anything to the Report Server.

Assigning Built-In Roles

First, to use any method of authorization, you need to create some principals. As an example, you will use some Windows Groups: AdventureWorksSalesManagers and AdventureWorksSalesPeople. Go ahead and create these Windows groups on your Report Server, and place some users in them. The examples assume that the Adventure Works sample reports have been published to the Report Server and that there are two folders. There might be three folders if you have published the sample report model.

You can assign roles to an object either through the Report Manager website or through SQL Server Management Studio. The following sections cover steps to assign roles through the Report Manager.

Assigning Roles Through Report Manager

Role assignments can be done through either Report Manager or SQL Server Management Studio. Complete the following steps to assign roles through management studio:

1. Navigate to the Adventure Works Sample Reports folder.
2. Click the Properties tab. Then select Security from the left menu. The screen should resemble Figure 18.1.

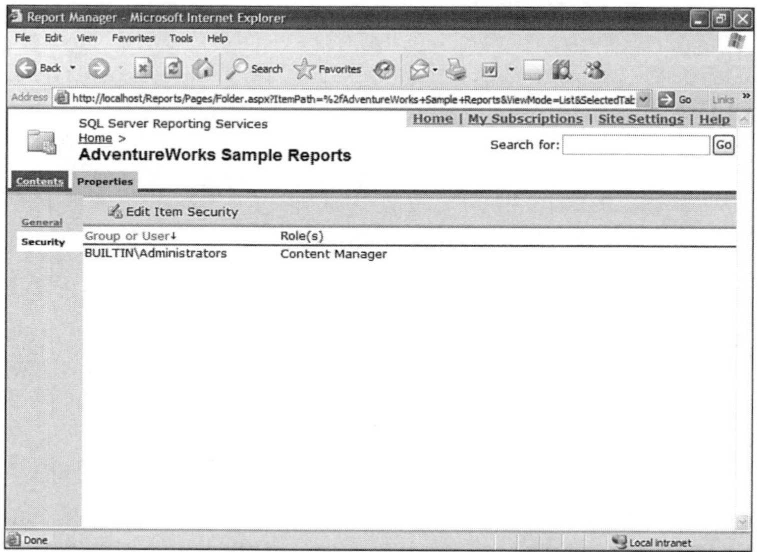

FIGURE 18.1 Item security on the Properties tab.

3. Click the Edit Item Security button. A dialog box opens that looks similar to Figure 18.2. Click OK in this dialog box.

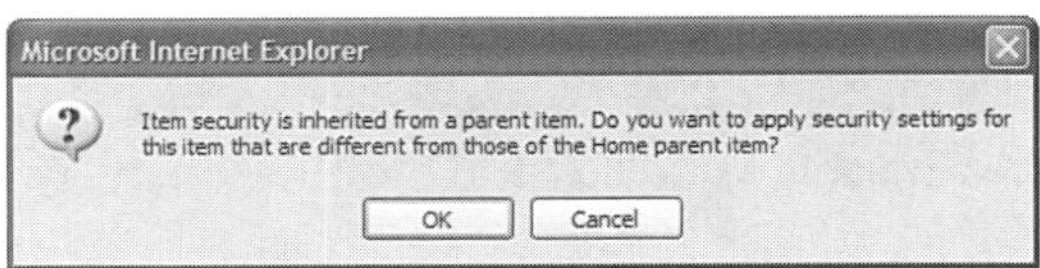

FIGURE 18.2 Confirmation dialog box to break security inheritance.

4. Click the New Role Assignment button, as shown in Figure 18.3.

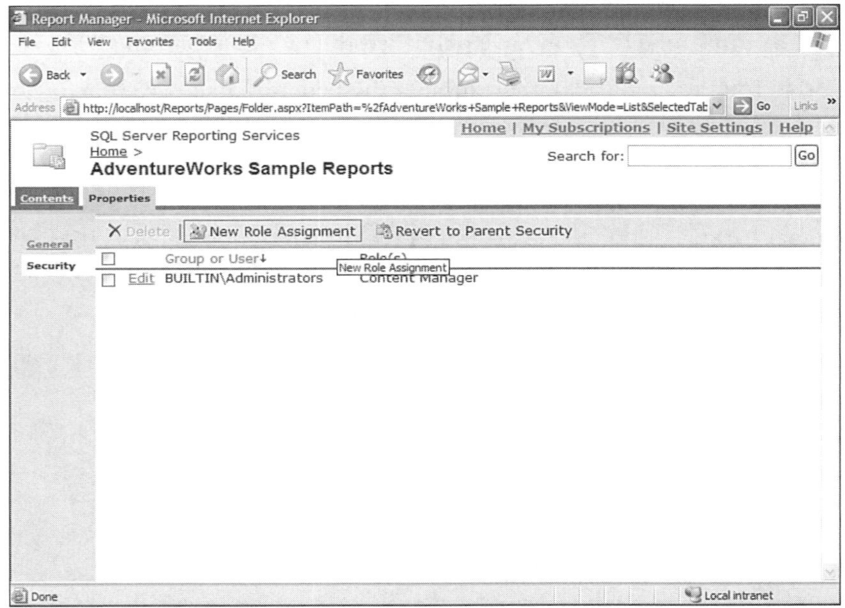

FIGURE 18.3 New Role Assignment button.

5. Enter AdventureWorksSalesManagers in the Group or User Name text box, and select the Content Manager role, as shown in Figure 18.4.

6. Click OK.

To revert back to the parent security, click the Revert to Parent Security button, as shown in Figure 18.5.

To modify an item's security, select a user or group by clicking the Edit check box next to the assigned principal under Security (on the left). This returns you to the role assignment screen, where roles can be added or removed.

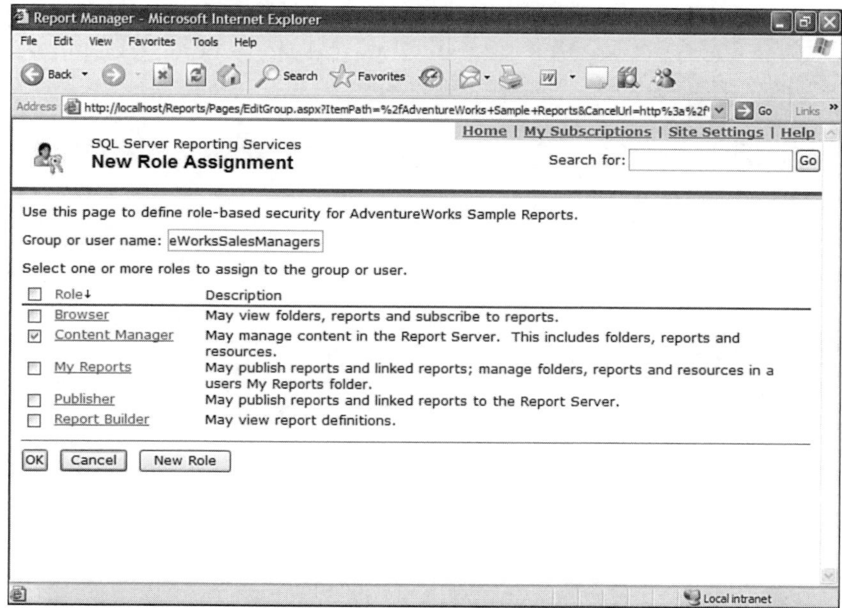

FIGURE 18.4 Granting AdventureWorksSalesManagers Content Manager roles.

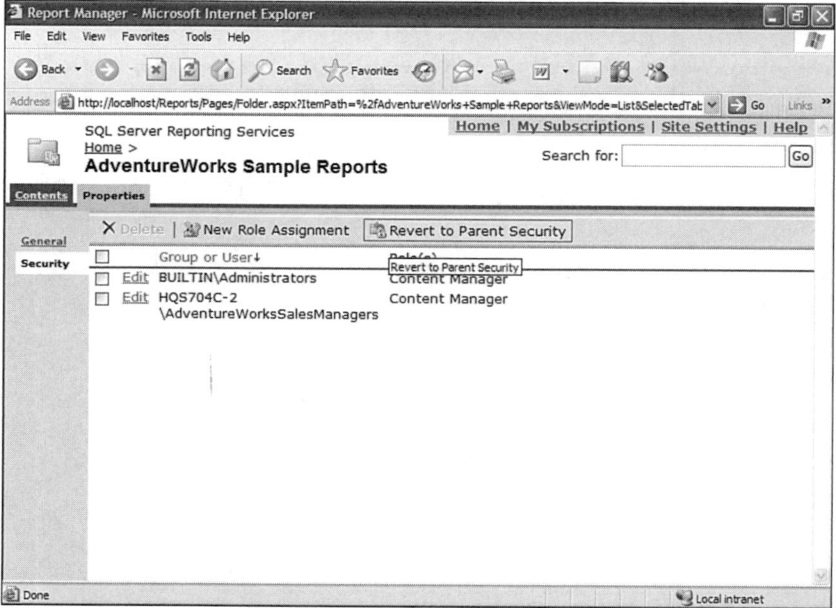

FIGURE 18.5 Revert to Parent Security button.

To delete a role assignment, select the check boxes next to the principals to delete, and select the Delete button. Figure 18.6 illustrates how this can be done. A confirmation box appears asking users to confirm deletion of the item(s). Click OK.

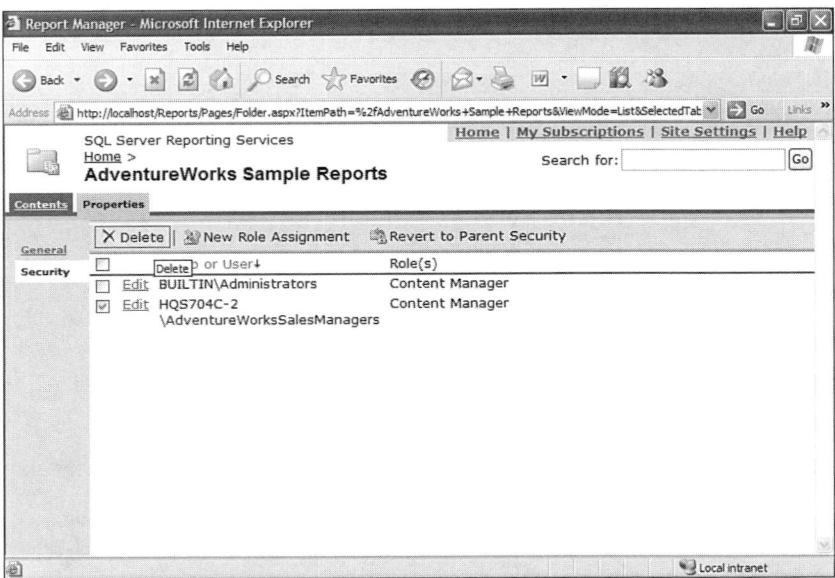

FIGURE 18.6 How to delete a role assignment.

To give Adventure Works' sales managers some visibility into the inner workings of the Report Server, let's outline the steps required to give the group the System Users role.

1. Click Site Settings.
2. Under Security, select Configure Site-wide Security. Figure 18.7 shows the resulting screen.
3. From here, it is very similar to setting item-level security. Select the New Role Assignment button.
4. Enter AdventureWorksSalesManagers in the Group or User Name text box, and select the System User role, as shown in Figure 18.8.
5. Click OK.

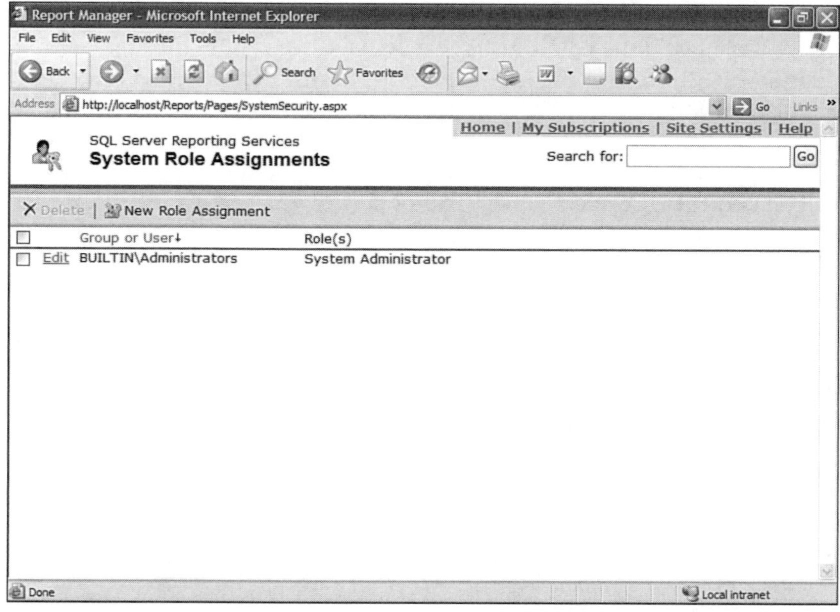

FIGURE 18.7 System Role Assignments screen.

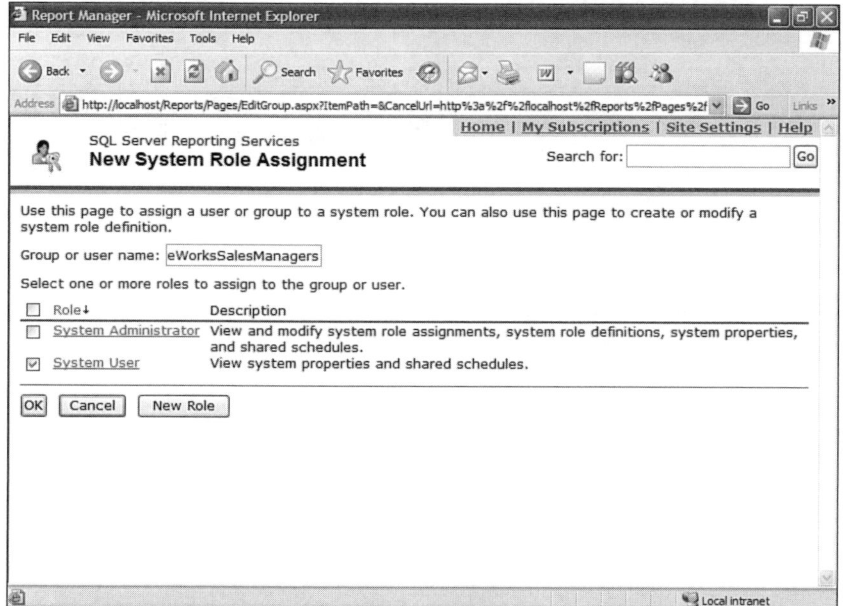

FIGURE 18.8 Adventure Works Sales Managers as System Users.

Assigning Roles Through SQL Server Management Studio

Everything we have just done could just as easily have been done through SQL Server Management Studio. Complete the following steps to add item-level security through SQL Server Management Studio:

1. Open SQL Server Management Studio.
2. Click File and then Connect Object Explorer.
3. Change the server type to Reporting Services.
4. Click the Connect button.
5. In Object Explorer, right-click on the Adventure Works Sample Reports folder under Home, and select Properties.
6. Select the Permissions page.
7. Click the Add Group or User button.
8. Enter the name of the group in the text field, and click OK.
9. Select the Content Manager role for the AdventureWorksSalesManagers group. The screen should look similar to Figure 18.9.
10. Click OK.

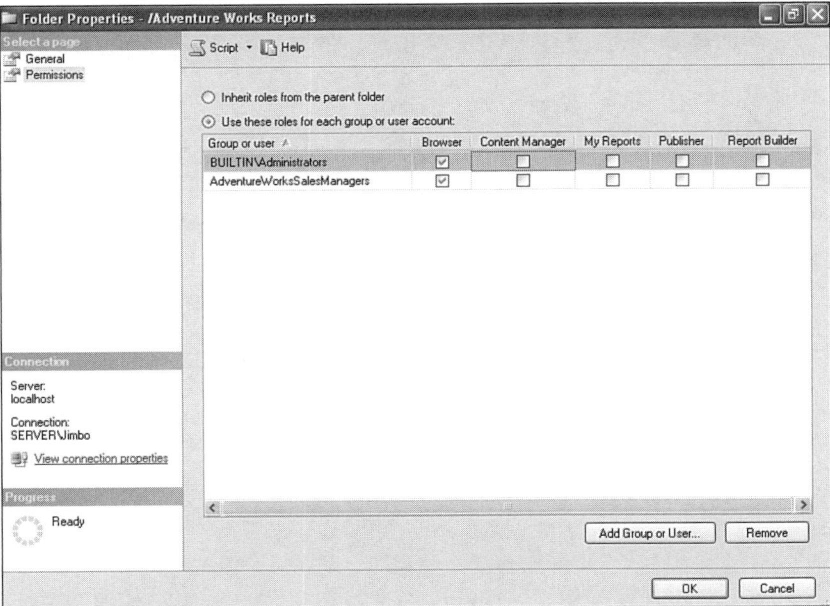

FIGURE 18.9 Assigning permissions through SQL Server Management Studio.

System-level roles can also be assigned with SQL Server Management Studio. The following steps grant the System User role to the AdventureWorksSalesManagers group:

1. Open SQL Server Management Studio.
2. Click File and then Connect Object Explorer.
3. Change the server type to Reporting Services.
4. Click the Connect button.
5. In Object Explorer, right-click on the server name and select Properties.
6. Select the Permissions page.
7. Click the Add Group or User button.
8. Enter the name of the group in the text field, and click OK.
9. Select the System User role for the AdventureWorksSalesManagers group.
10. Click OK.

To modify a role assignment, follow the steps to get to the appropriate property window. From the property window, select Permissions and update the lists of tasks. To delete a role assignment, select the role from the property window, and click the Remove button.

Defining Custom Roles

SSRS allows administrators to create custom-defined roles to suit individual needs. This can be a very helpful feature for organizations that desire a finer degree of granularity, or if the built-in roles simply do not suffice. Administrators can also modify any existing role.

Before jumping into creating new roles, a quick word of caution: It is very easy to get carried away with creating custom roles. There might only be 25 tasks altogether (16 item level and 9 system level), but there are many different combinations you could create. At this point, the Manager role might be just as cumbersome as managing individual tasks.

Creating/Modifying a Custom Role

One of the role SSRS lacks is a true "view only" type of role. The following steps outline how you could use Report Manager to create such a role. Later, you will use SQL Server Management Studio to do the same thing.

1. Open Report Manager, and select Site Settings from the upper-right side.
2. The process for creating an item-level role versus a system-level role is identical, so simply select Configure Item-Level Role Definitions or Configure System-Level Role Definitions. For this example, select Configure Item-Level Role Definitions.
3. Click the New Role button.
4. Enter View Only Role in the Name text box and "May View reports but not subscribe to them" in the Description field, as shown in Figure 18.10.

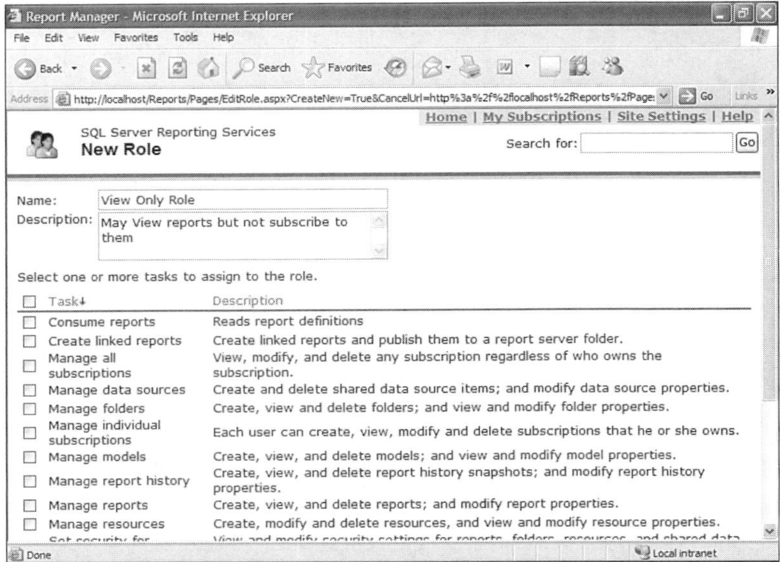

FIGURE 18.10 New View Only role.

5. Select View Folders, View Models, View Reports, and View Resources from the tasks, as shown in Figure 18.11.
6. Click OK.

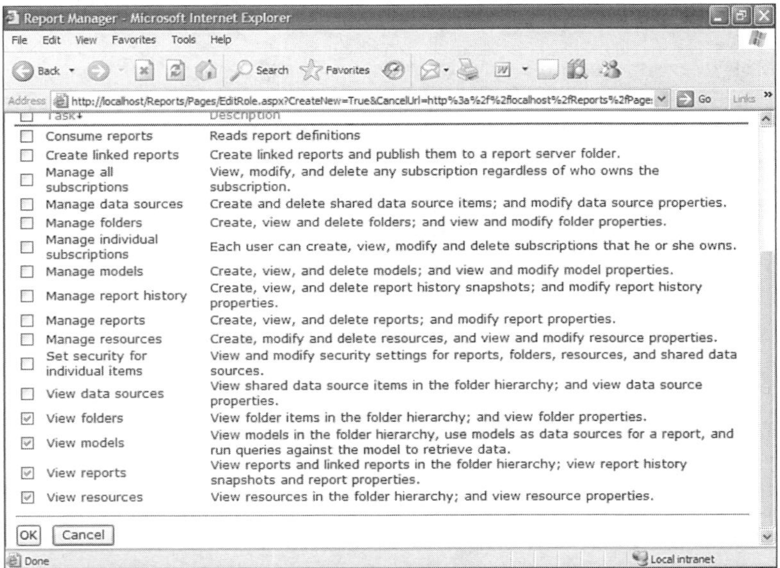

FIGURE 18.11 Tasks to assign the View Only role.

Figure 18.12 shows how the new role functions just like any of the predefined roles.

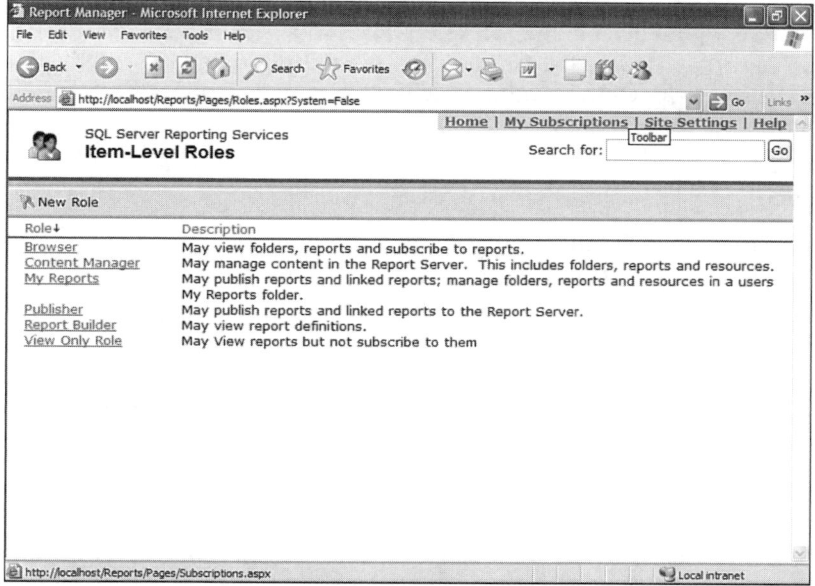

FIGURE 18.12 New View Only role functions just as the built-in roles.

To modify a role, simply click on the role name after selecting Configure Item-Level Role Definitions or Configure System-Level Role Definitions. Update the list of tasks, and then click OK.

To delete a role, follow the same processes as modifying the role, except click the Delete button at the bottom of the screen. Click OK when it asks you to confirm.

Managing Roles with SQL Server Management Studio

The following steps create a new View Only Role using SQL Server Management Studio:

1. Open SQL Server Management Studio.
2. Click File and then Connect Object Explorer.
3. Change the server type to Reporting Services.
4. Click the Connect button.
5. In Object Explorer, open the Security folder. At this point, if you want to create a system-level role, open the System Roles folder; otherwise, open the Roles folder.
6. Right-click the Roles folder and select New Role from the context menu.
7. Enter View Only Role in the Name text box and "May View reports but not subscribe to them" in the Description field.

8. Select View Folders, View Reports, View Models, and View Resources from the tasks.

9. Click OK.

To modify a role, right-click on any role and select Properties. The same screen appears as for adding a new role. Update the task list and/or description and select OK. To delete a role, select the role from Object Explorer, right-click the role, and select Delete from the context menu.

Summary

SSRS uses role-based security in a similar fashion as Windows itself. Roles are groups of tasks. SSRS contains two different types of tasks—system-level tasks and item-level tasks. Item-level tasks are actions that affect the catalog, such as View or Browse. System-level tasks are actions that can be taken on items outside the catalog, but are global in Report Server scope such as shared schedules.

The combination of principal, item, and role is called a policy. Every item in the catalog can either have a policy defined for it explicitly or will inherit the parent item's policy.

If the built-in roles do not suffice, the administrator is free to make his own.

Subscribing to Reports

CHAPTER 19

IN THIS CHAPTER

- Overview of Subscriptions
- Overview of Delivery Extensions
- Creating a Simple Subscription
- Creating a Data-Driven Subscription
- Managing Subscriptions

One of the most convenient things about SSRS is its capability to deliver reports right to the end user without ever having to navigate to the Report Server through subscriptions.

If you have the Enterprise Edition of SSRS, the reports can even be customized based on data from queries. Another nice thing is that the end user, if they have the appropriate permissions, can set subscriptions up for themselves. This chapter explores the ins and outs of subscribing to reports and managing subscriptions to reports.

Overview of Subscriptions

A subscription is akin to setting up a job on the Report Server to deliver a report to a user at a specified point in time. This provides a nice alternative to actively going to the Report Server and running the report.

Parts of Subscriptions

Subscriptions all have some common components/requirements. In addition to the following, you must also have access to view the report, and have a role assignment that includes the task "Manage individual subscriptions" before you can subscribe to it. Common components/requirements of report subscriptions include the following:

- The report has to be able to run independently, that is, the data sources must use either stored credentials or no credentials.

- The report must have a configured delivery method. The built-in ones include email and file sharing.
- You must specify a rendering extension for the subscribed report.
- Some trigger or event is required to run the subscription. Usually, this is a scheduled event, based on either a custom or shared schedule.
- The parameter values for any parameter in a report must be specified or defaulted.

Uses of Subscriptions

Subscriptions have a number of possible uses that can be used to meet a number of requirements:

- Deliver reports to end users (the most common use of subscriptions).
- Save reports for offline viewing. This is usually done using PDF or web archive formats.
- Send long-running reports or large reports directly to disk.
- Preload the Report Server's cache.

Standard Versus Data-Driven Subscriptions

SSRS has two different kinds of subscription options. The first kind is called the standard subscriptions. Users can create and manage standard subscriptions for themselves. All the information for the subscription is static, which means that the information has to be specified when the subscription is created, and cannot be modified at runtime.

Data-driven subscriptions are similar to the standard subscription with one important difference. The data used for the subscription must come from a query. This makes data-driven subscriptions incredibly powerful. The list of recipients is derived via a query, which makes it ideal for recipient lists that can change frequently. Users can use data-driven subscriptions to create customized reports for recipients based on preferences of that recipient or that recipient's role within the organization. Even the delivery style and location can be customized. Data-driven subscriptions are usually kept in the domain of report administrators, and are typically not administered by end users.

NOTE

Data-driven subscriptions are only available in SQL Server 2005 Enterprise and Developer Editions.

Delivery Options

Reports are delivered using delivery extensions. Two delivery extensions come preloaded into SSRS and can be used by end users, although they cannot be configured. These are an email delivery extension and a file share delivery extension. Like many other parts of SSRS, end users can create their own delivery extensions if the existing ones are not sufficient. One kind of delivery extension an administrator can use that an end user cannot use is called the null delivery extension. As the name implies, it doesn't actually deliver a report anywhere. Instead, it is typically used to preload the Report Server cache or generate snapshots.

Subscription Processing

If you are familiar with SQL Server Notification Services, you might find the model that SSRS uses to process subscriptions familiar. SSRS responds to events. As events occur, SSRS matches these events to subscriptions that should be triggered by one or more of these events. When a subscription is triggered, the Report Server uses the information stored along with the subscription to process the report. When the report is done processing, the Report Server passes it along with the delivery information stored with the subscription to the appropriate delivery extension.

When processing a standard subscription, the Report Server's job is relatively simple. Because standard subscriptions contain only one report that does not vary by user, it simply processes the report and sends it on its merry way.

The processing of a data-driven subscription is considerably more complex. For a data-driven subscription, the number of reports, deliveries, and even parameters to pass to those reports depends on the data passed in. The Report Server must generate a report and deliver it based on every record returned from the data set generated by the query.

Overview of Delivery Extensions

SSRS comes bundled with two main delivery extensions: email and file share. Although skilled developers can implement their only delivery extensions, the prepackaged ones should suffice for most people.

Email

Email can be used to deliver reports, or it can be used to deliver a hyperlink to the generated report; the contents of the message are based on the data included with the subscription.

The Subject line contains, by default, the Report Name (`@ReportName`) and the time it was run (`@ExecutionTime`). Of course, the user can modify this to suit her needs.

The body text can contain an embedded report or the report can come as an attachment. This depends on the rendering extension used. The HTML and MHTML extensions embed the report in the email body. All other extensions generate an attachment to the message.

The email extension is not available if the Report Server has not been set up for email. To set up email, use the Reporting Services Configuration Tool.

From the RS Configuration Manager, select Email Settings and then enter the sender address and name of the SMTP server.

The size limitations of email apply to subscribed reports as well. If the report is delivered as an attachment and the size of the attachment is too large, the report might not get delivered. Second, the Report Server does not validate the email addresses entered when creating the subscription or during runtime in the case of data-driven subscriptions.

Delivering to a File Share

The file share delivery extension drops rendered reports to a specified file share. The extension does not create a folder; however, it does drop files into any standard UNC share. As with any file share, the account that the Report Server service is running under must have access to the share to write to it successfully. The naming format for a UNC share is as follows:

```
\\<servername>\<sharename>
```

Remember not to include a trailing backslash.

After the report is rendered, a file is created using the specified delivery extension. For example, if the delivery extension specified is PDF, a PDF file is created on the file share.

Because a file is fairly static, an interactive feature in the rendered reports is made static. Hence, things like matrixes and charts will retain the default views.

Creating a Simple Subscription

Report Manager and SQL Server Management Studio can both be used to create a standard subscription, which use both email and file share delivery. Complete the following steps to make an email-based subscription using Report Manager:

1. From Report Manager, open the report to be subscribed to, and select the Subscriptions tab.
2. On the Subscriptions tab, click New Subscription.
3. If necessary, select Report Server Email in the Delivered By drop-down list.
4. Enter the recipient list in the To text box. If you have multiple recipients in the list, the entries need to be separated by semicolons (;).
5. If the user has permissions to manage all subscriptions, the Cc and the Bcc text boxes as well as the Reply to text box appear. The same rules apply to these as to the To text box in regard to the formatting of email addresses.
6. Modify the Subject line as required.
7. To embed a copy or to attach a copy of the report, check the Include Report check box. Depending on the rendering format, the server will decide if it can embed the report or include it as an attachment.
8. To send a link to the only version of the report, check the Include Link check box.
9. Pick the rendering format from the Render Format drop-down list. Remember that WebArchive embeds results in the report; everything else is an attachment.

10. Modify the priority and add a comment if desired.
11. If dealing with a parameterized report, set the parameters for the report.
12. Select a time to process the subscription. To set a new schedule, select the When the Scheduled Report Run Is Complete option and click the Select Schedule check box. If the report is executed from a scheduled snapshot, the subscription fires after the snapshot has been executed by clicking on the When the Report Content Is Refreshed option.

After you have completed entering the necessary information, the window should look similar to Figure 19.1.

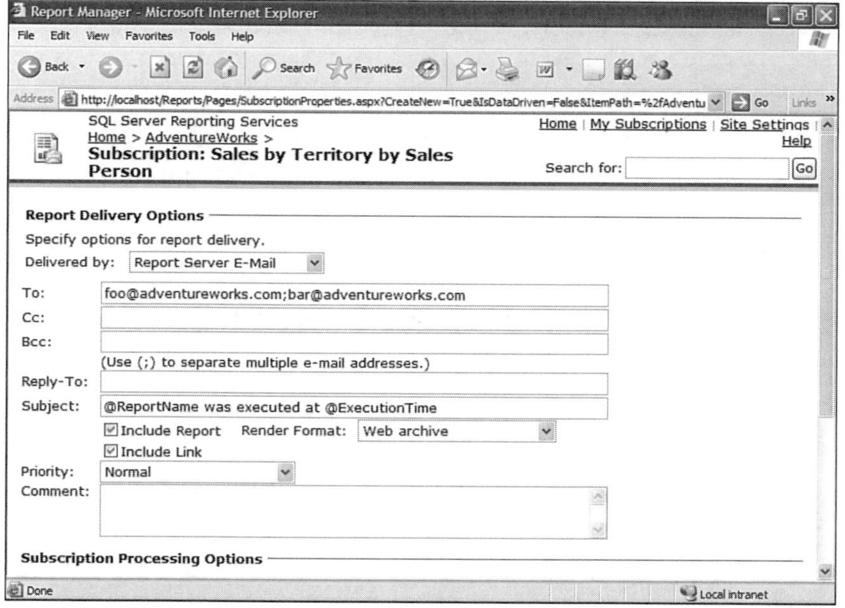

FIGURE 19.1 Email delivery subscription.

File Share Delivery

As previously mentioned, another way to deliver reports is directly to a file share. This can also be done through both SQL Server Management Studio and Report Manager. Complete the following steps to complete the task through Report Manager:

1. From Report Manager, open the report to be subscribed to, and select the Subscriptions tab.
2. On the Subscriptions tab, click New Subscription.
3. Select Report Server File Share in the Delivered By drop-down list.

4. Enter the desired filename in the File Name text box. The Add a File Extension when the File Is Created check box tells the server to add the extension when the file gets created. As long as it is checked, the end user should not add the extension to the file.
5. Enter the path to drop the report in the Path text box.
6. Select a render format from the Render Format drop-down list. Because the files are static, it is not recommended to pick a format that can be used interactively or might include multiple files. In other words, stay away from HTML.
7. Enter the credentials for a user with permission to access the share in the Username and Password text box. Use the <domain>\<username> format.
8. Specify file overwriting options. Choosing the Do Not Overwrite the File if a Previous Version Exists option keeps delivery from occurring if a similarly named file exists. It is recommended to use one of the other two to keep such issues from becoming problematic.
9. If dealing with a parameterized report, set the parameters for the report.
10. Set the schedule as you did earlier when setting up Email Delivery.

When complete, the screen should look similar to Figure 19.2.

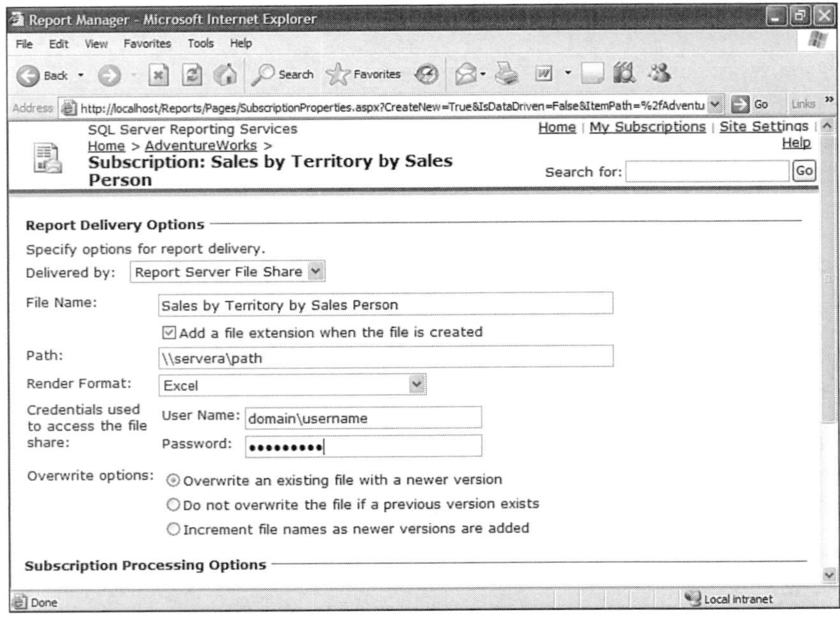

FIGURE 19.2 File share delivery subscription.

Recall from earlier, SQL Server Management Studio can be used to create subscriptions to reports. To demonstrate how to use SQL Server Management Studio to produce subscriptions, we will rebuild the subscriptions you just created using Report Manager.

To start, let's rebuild the subscription using email delivery using SQL Server Management Studio:

1. Navigate to the Subscriptions folder under the report to which you want to subscribe.
2. Right-click and select New Subscription. The Report Subscriptions properties page should open.
3. From here, the options are the same as in Report Manager.
4. Select Report Server Email in the Notify By text box.
5. Fill in the To field and, if visible, the CC and BCC fields.
6. Choose Delivery Options and a Render format.
7. Optionally, modify the priority and add a comment.
8. If the report has parameters, fill in the parameter values.
9. Click the Scheduling tab and enter information regarding when to process the subscription. The screen should look similar to Figure 19.3.
10. Click OK.

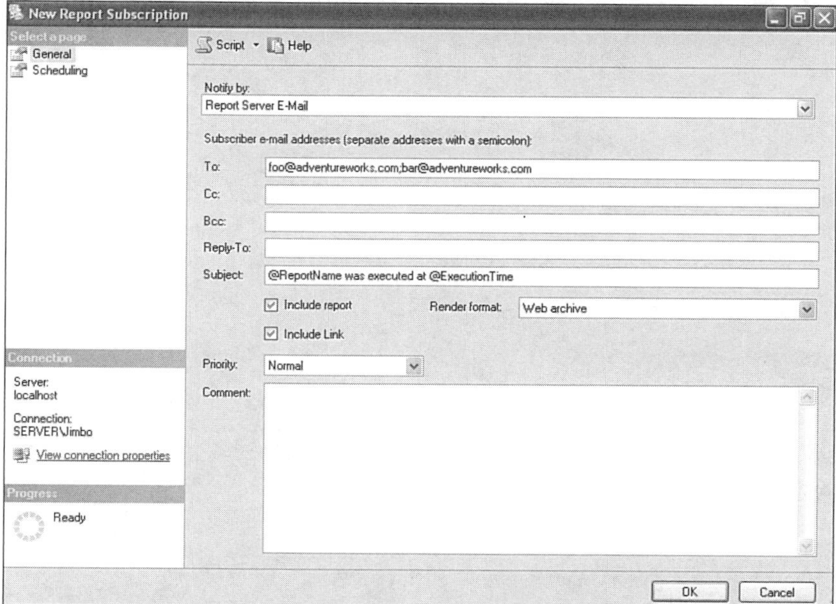

FIGURE 19.3 Email delivery subscription through SQL Server Management Studio.

Now let's rebuild the file share subscription using SQL Server Management Studio:

1. Navigate to the Subscriptions folder under the report to which you want to subscribe.
2. Right-click and select New Subscription. The Report Subscriptions properties page should open.
3. From here, the options are the same as in Report Manager.
4. Select Report Server File Share in the Notify By text box.
5. Enter a filename, and if the Add File Extension when File Gets Created check box is not checked, you have to enter a file extension.
6. Choose a path.
7. Choose a render format.
8. Enter a username and password with access to the file share directory.
9. Choose one of the overwrite options.
10. If the report has parameters, fill in the parameter values.
11. Click the Scheduling tab and enter information regarding when to process the subscription. The screen should look similar to Figure 19.4.
12. Click OK.

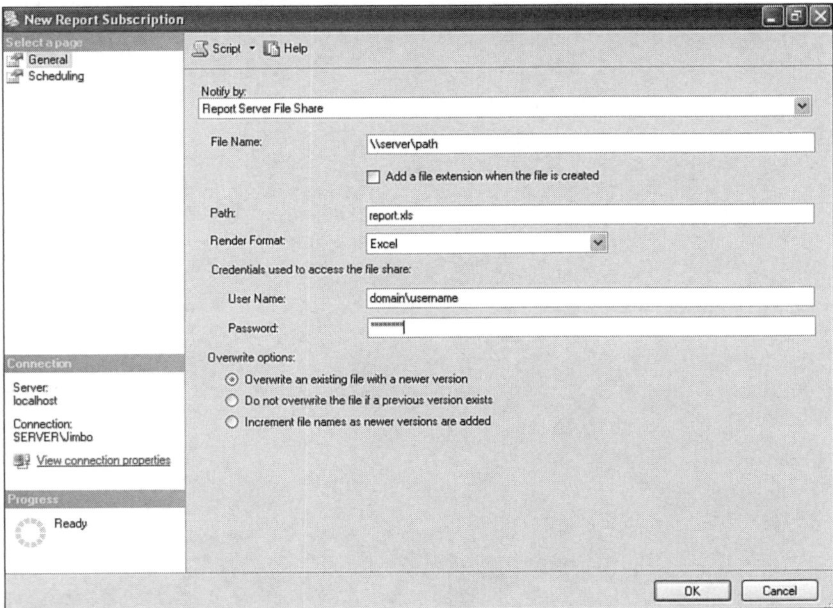

FIGURE 19.4 File share delivery through SQL Server Management Studio.

Creating a Data-Driven Subscription

The steps to create a new data-driven subscription are not too terribly different than the steps needed to create a standard subscription. The large difference in the data-driven subscription model is that the parameters for the recipient list and the rendering extension ET are all derived from a query. To aid end users in creating a data-driven subscription, both SQL Server Management Studio and Report Manager have wizards to set up all the information. Remember that to use a subscription, the report's data sources must have stored credentials or no credentials.

Creating a Subscriptions Database

Before creating a data-driven subscription, the end user must create a data set that can be used to hold the information for the subscription. To create a Subscriptions database, open the SQL Management Studio and run the following script:

```
use master
go
if exists(select name from master.dbo.sysdatabases where name = 'Subscriptions')
begin
    drop database [Subscriptions]
end
    create database [Subscriptions]
go
use [Subscriptions]
go
create table [SubcriptionInfo]
    ([To] nvarchar(50),
     [Format] nvarchar(50),
     [EmailAddress] nvarchar(50),
     [EmployeeId] nvarchar(50),
     [Linked] nvarchar(50),
     [IncludeReport] nvarchar(50))
go
insert into [SubcriptionInfo] (
[To],[Format],[EmailAddress],[EmployeeId],[Linked],[IncludeReport])
select FirstName + ' ' + LastName [To],
    Format = case (EmployeeId%2) when 0 then 'MHTML' else 'PDF' end,
    EmailAddress,
    b.EmployeeId,
    Linked =  case (EmployeeId%2) when 0 then 'True' else 'False' end,
    IncludeReport =  case (EmployeeId%2) when 0 then 'True' else 'False' end
from AdventureWorks.Sales.SalesPerson a, AdventureWorks.HumanResources.Employee b,
    AdventureWorks.Person.Contact c
where a.SalesPersonId = b.EmployeeId
    and c.ContactId = b.ContactID
```

The preceding script creates a new database called Subscriptions. When setting up the data-driven subscription, a custom data source is created to connect to the table and pull the subscription information. It also pulls in the salespeople information from the AdventureWorks catalog, and sets some preferences.

Report Manager

Like everything else thus far, you can use both SQL Server Management Studio and Report Manager to create data-driven subscriptions. As always, we start with Report Manager, and later show you how to create data-driven subscriptions with SQL Server Management Studio. The following steps show how to create a data-driven subscription using Report Manager:

1. Navigate to the Employee Sales Summary report from the Sample Reports included with SSRS, click the Subscriptions tab, and select New Data Driven Subscription.
2. Enter a description, and choose Report Server Email for the delivery method. Select Specify for This Subscription Only under the prompt for the data source for the recipient information.
3. Enter the information needed to log in to the Subscriptions database.
4. Enter the following query to select information for the recipient list:

```
select *, datepart(m,getdate()) [month],
    datepart(yyyy,dateadd(yyyy,-1,getdate())) [year]
from [SubcriptionInfo]
```

5. You can click the Validate button to execute the query on the Report Server and check to see if it is valid.
6. Change the following values on the delivery settings from the defaults:
    - `To` gets its value from `EmailAddress`.
    - `IncludeReport` gets its value from the `Include Report` field.
    - `Renderformat` gets its value from `Format`.
    - `IncludeLink` gets its value from `Linked`.
7. Next enter the parameters from the database query:
    - `Month` comes from the `Month` field.
    - `Year` comes from the `Year` field.
    - `Employee` comes from the `EmployeeId` field.
8. Finally, create a custom schedule for the subscription or choose if it should be run on a shared schedule or after a new snapshot has been created. More information on creating shared schedules is in Chapter 20, “Report Execution and Processing.”

SQL Server Management Studio

As previously mentioned, data-driven subscriptions can be created using SQL Server Management Studio as well as Report Manager. The following steps show how to re-create the data-driven subscription created earlier through Report Manager using SQL Server Management Studio:

1. Using Object Explorer, navigate to the Subscriptions folder under the Employee Sales Summary report, right-click on the Subscriptions folder, and select New Data Driven Subscription. This should start the Data Driven Subscription Wizard.
2. Click Next on the Welcome screen of the wizard. Enter a description, and choose Report Server Email for the delivery method.
3. Select Custom Data Source and enter the information needed to log in to the Subscriptions database.
4. Enter the query from step 4 in the preceding set of steps, and click Validate to confirm the data source and query run.
5. Change the following values on the delivery settings from the defaults:
   - `To` gets its value from `EmailAddress`.
   - `IncludeReport` gets its value from `IncludeReport`.
   - `Renderformat` gets its value from `Format`.
   - `IncludeLink` gets its value from `Linked`.
6. Next enter the parameters from the database query:
   - `Month` comes from the `Month` field.
   - `Year` comes from the `Year` field.
   - `Employee` comes from the `EmployeeId` field.
7. Finally, create a custom schedule for the subscription or choose if it should be run on a shared schedule or after a new snapshot has been created.

Managing Subscriptions

Like most things in SSRS, subscriptions can be managed with either Report Manager or SQL Server Management Studio. Report subscriptions are managed just like any other property of a report.

To view, modify, or delete subscriptions from Report Manager, navigate to the report, open it, and select the Subscriptions tab. From here, the Report Manager shows all the subscriptions for a particular report, including the description, how it is triggered, what the current status is, and when it was last run. Users can sort on any one of these fields to help find the subscription they are looking for. If a subscription does not exist, it gives you the option to create one. To modify any particular subscription, click the Edit button on the data grid. To delete a subscription, check the check box on that row of the data grid and click the Delete button. Click OK on the confirmation prompt.

All of these actions can be accomplished through SQL Server Management Studio as well. The concept is the same as usual. Using the SQL Server Management Studio's Object Browser, navigate to the report. Underneath the report is a Subscriptions folder. From here, the rest of the steps are pretty much the same as for Report Manager. Right-click on the Subscriptions folder to create a new subscription. Right-click on a subscription to modify or delete it.

My Subscriptions

One feature that is unique in Report Manager is the My Subscriptions link next to the Site Settings. This link consolidates all the subscriptions a user has created across the entire catalog.

This provided end users and administrators a single place to manage all of their subscriptions. The My Subscription page allows users to sort by Report, Description, Folder, Trigger, Last Run, and Status. Just like the subscriptions page for any other report, the Edit button allows users to modify the subscription. To delete the subscription, check the check boxes on the rows corresponding to the subscription to be deleted and click the Delete button. Click OK on the confirmation prompt. Unlike the subscriptions page for any report, you cannot create a subscription. The My Subscriptions page is shown in Figure 19.5.

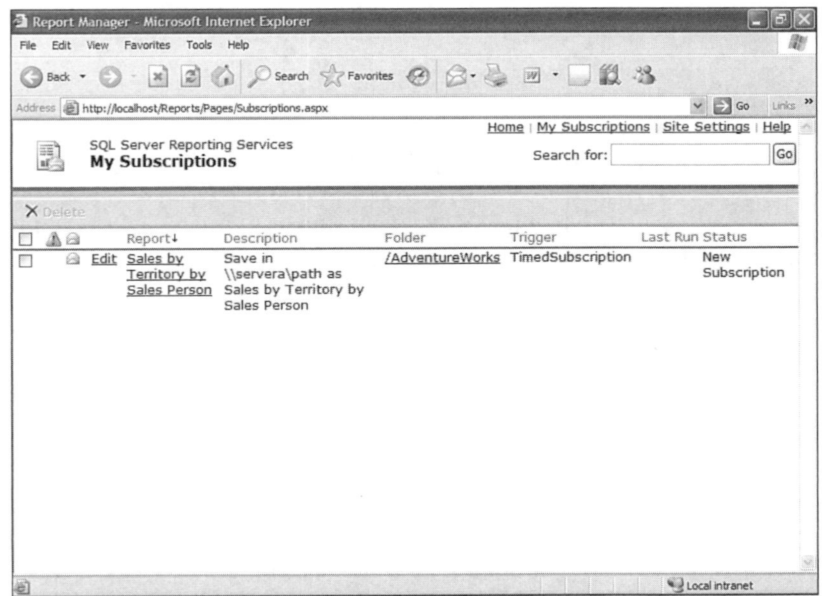

FIGURE 19.5 My Subscriptions page.

Monitoring Subscriptions

As mentioned previously, the individual subscription pages for a report, as well as the My Subscriptions page, have a Status column on them.

The Status column is crucial for monitoring the execution of a subscription in case the subscription runs into a processing error. If the Report Server detected a delivery error, the error is reported in the server's trace log. One case in which an exception might not be logged is if the trigger fails to occur, such as when a snapshot fails, or a scheduled event does not run.

The Report Server service logs (located in `C:\Program Files\Microsoft SQL Server\MSSQL.3\Reporting Services\LogFiles`) include any information about delivery statuses. For example, if the delivery extension is email, these logs should include records from processing and delivery. The log does not tell you if the email was opened.

Deleting/Inactivating Subscriptions

When a subscription fails to process, it is referred to as "inactive." These subscriptions should be taken care of or fixed immediately. The following are some common causes of inactive subscriptions:

- Changing the data source a report uses from having stored credentials or having no credentials to using integrated security or prompting the user for a username or password
- The removal or disabling of a delivery extension
- Changing the name or type of a report parameter after the subscription has already been created
- Changing how a report runs from being on demand, to executing a cached copy

When an event occurs that causes a subscription to later be inactive, the effect might not be immediately known. For example, if a scheduled subscription were to run on Sunday night, and the data source was changed to the next Friday, it would not be until the following Sunday that the subscription would become inactive. When the subscription does become inactive, a message is attached to the subscription to explain why and possibly what steps can be taken to resolve the issue.

Summary

Subscriptions are a powerful way to deliver reports directly to end users. There are two types of subscriptions—standard and data driven. The standard subscription uses static, hard-coded information to process the reports. The data-driven subscription retrieves all of the information for processing the subscription—recipient list, report parameters, and so on—from a database query.

End users can manage their subscriptions from the My Subscriptions page. Administrators can monitor the status of the subscription processing through the Report Server log.

Report Execution and Processing

CHAPTER 20

IN THIS CHAPTER

- Managing Schedules
- Report Execution and Processing
- Report Execution History

In this chapter, you explore some of the information that can be captured at runtime, and learn how to set up shared schedules that can be used to coordinate actions within the Report Server.

Managing Schedules

Schedules are used within SSRS to trigger executions of subscriptions and snapshots, generally classified as events. Schedules can trigger a one-time event, or cause events to run continuously at specified intervals—monthly, daily, or hourly.

Schedules create events on the Report Server. Actions within the Report Server, such as expiring a snapshot or processing a subscription, are triggered by the event. What SSRS actually does is create a scheduled job on the database server that hosts the SSRS database. The SQL Agent then runs the jobs, which usually contain nothing more than the command to execute a stored procedure to trigger an event. The other half of the Scheduling and Delivery Processor within SSRS is the Report Server Windows service referred to as SQL Server Reporting Services under services in Control Panel.

This service is responsible for querying the database server for events and running the processes that those events trigger. Both sides of the Scheduling and Delivery Processor must be enabled for it to work. If the SQL Agent on the database server is turned off, the jobs do not run, hence the events do not fire and the corresponding actions are not taken. If the Report Server service is down, the jobs show that they ran successfully, but no processing actually occurs.

Types of Schedules

There are two types of schedules used in SSRS: a shared schedule and a report-specific schedule. The relationship is analogous to the relationship between a shared data source and a custom data source. The shared schedule can be used to trigger a number of events throughout the Report Server. A report-specific schedule is used for one and only one specific event. A second event might occur at exactly the same time, but as far as SSRS is concerned, it is a different schedule. Because they are so similar the question often brought up is, "When should you use a report-specific schedule over a shared schedule?" In general, create a report-specific schedule if a shared schedule does not provide the frequency or recurrence pattern that you need.

Table 20.1 details the difference between shared schedules and report-specific schedules.

TABLE 20.1 Shared Versus Report-Specific Schedules

	Shared Schedule	Report-Specific Schedule
Permissions needed to create/modify	Needs system-level permissions	Can be created by individual users
Can be temporarily disabled?	Can temporarily pause and then resume shared schedules	Have to be modified to change the time
Manageability	Are managed centrally from the Site Settings tab in the Report Manager or Object Browser	Have to be managed from the individual items
Customizable	Cannot be customized for a specific item	Can be easily modified without any other down-stream implications

Creating/Modifying Schedules

The process for creating or modifying schedules is generally the same whether it is a shared or report-specific schedule. The only difference is the scope. For the shared schedule, it is created once and can be referenced in a subscription or property page when you need to specify schedule information.

From Report Manager or Object Explorer, administrators can specify which items use the shared schedule. Report-specific schedules are created and referenced by only that one report, subscription, or report execution operation to determine cache expiration or snapshot updates.

To create a shared schedule using SQL Server Management Studio, follow these steps:

1. From Object Explorer, navigate to the Shared Schedules folder, right-click on Shared Schedules, and select New Schedule.
2. Enter a name for the schedule.

3. Select how often you want the schedule to recur or select Once for a one-time event.
4. Click OK.

Alternatively, you can create a shared schedule from Report Manager by completing the following steps (see Figure 20.1):

1. Navigate to Site Settings.
2. Click Manage Shared Schedules under the Other section toward the bottom of the screen.
3. Click New Schedule.
4. Enter a name and how often the schedule should recur, and then click OK.

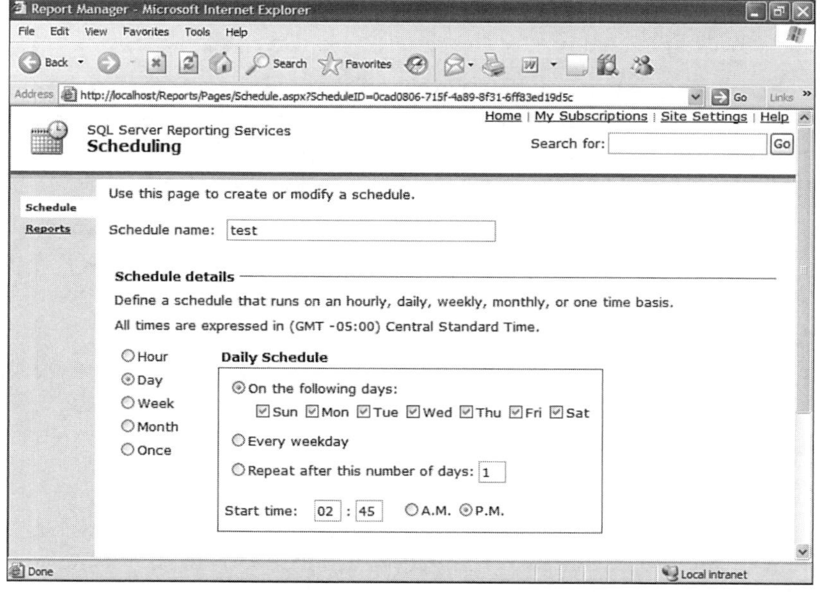

FIGURE 20.1 Creating a new shared schedule in SSRS.

After being created, a schedule can be modified at any time. Modifying the schedule of a running process (subscription, snapshot, and so on) does not cause that process to stop. If the process that a schedule triggered is already running, modifying the schedule serves only to start the process again at the new time.

Deleting a schedule does not guarantee that the events that it triggers will stop firing. Deleting a shared schedule only serves to create report-specific schedules for any items that reference it. A better way to stop a schedule is to expire it, by putting an end date on it. Expired schedules are indicated as such by the status field. Schedules that have been expired can be restarted by extending the end date.

Another alternative is to pause a shared schedule. A paused schedule can be resumed at a later date and time. Report-specific schedules cannot be paused. Pausing a schedule is similar to modifying it. Pausing the schedule of a process that is already running or of one that is in queue only stops the subsequent runs. It has no effect on the currently executing process.

NOTE

Administrators can pause schedules from Report Manager.

To pause a shared schedule, select it from the list of the Report Manager schedules, and click the Pause button. The same process is used to delete a shared schedule.

Report Execution and Processing

SSRS's Report Processor generally executes reports in a three-stage process:

- **Data gathering**—Involves the process used to get the report definition from the Report Server database, initializes parameters and variables that are in expressions, and performs other preliminary processing that prepares the report for data. The data-processing extension then connects to the data source and retrieves the data.
- **Layout processing**—Combines the report data with the report layout from the report definition. Data is processed by row for each section. Sections include the report header and footer, group headers and footers, and detail. Aggregate functions and expressions are also processed at this time.
- **Rendering**—Takes the intermediate format and the rendering extension paginates the report and processes expressions that cannot be processed during the execution stage. The report is then rendered in the appropriate device-specific format (MHTML, Excel, PDF, and so on).

Depending on the method of access, the server determines if it needs to execute all three processes or if it can skip one or two. The trick is in the report history. If the administrator specifies that the report should be rendered from a snapshot or cache, the report is rendered from the intermediate format stored in the database. Otherwise, the Report Server starts its processing from the data gathering stage. Report processing for drill-through reports is similar, except that reports can be auto generated from models rather than report definitions. Data processing is initiated through the model to retrieve data of interest.

Report Execution Timeouts

The time it takes to process a report can vary tremendously. While reports process, they take up time on the Report Server and possibly the report data source. As a matter of practice, most long-running reports take a long time to process due to a long-running query.

SSRS uses timeouts to set an upper limit on how much time individual reports can take to process. Two kinds of timeouts are used by SSRS. The first kind is the query timeout. The second kind is the report execution timeout.

Query timeouts specify how long an individual query can take to come back from the data source. This value is specified inside the reports, by specifying the timeout property while creating a data set. Query timeouts can also apply to data-driven subscriptions.

The report execution timeout is the amount of time a report can take to process. This value is specified at a system level, and can be overridden for individual reports. To set this setting, click the Site Settings tab and modify the Report Execution Timeout property. The default value is 1800 seconds.

SSRS evaluates the execution timeout for running jobs every 60 seconds. What this means is that every minute, SSRS enumerates through every running job and compares how long it has been running against how long it is supposed to run. The downside of this is that reports actually have a bit more time than the specified timeout value in which to run. If the timeout for a report is set to 30 seconds, SSRS does not check to see if it exceeded the timeout until 60 seconds, so the report actually gets an additional 30 seconds of runtime.

Running Processes

A process in the Report Server is also called a job. The two kinds of jobs are user jobs and system jobs. User jobs are those jobs that are started by individual users or by a user's subscription.

Some examples of user jobs include the following:

- Running an on-demand report
- Rendering a report from a snapshot
- Generating a new snapshot
- Processing a subscription

System jobs are those jobs that are started by the Report Server, including the following:

- Processing a data-driven subscription
- Scheduling a generation of a snapshot
- Scheduling report execution

As mentioned in the previous section, SSRS comes by every 60 seconds and checks on the status of any in-progress jobs. These jobs could be querying their data source, rendering into intermediate format, or rendering into final format. It drops the status of these jobs into the Report Server database. This generally means that a job has to be running for at least 60 seconds for it to be canceled or viewed. To cancel or view running jobs, click the Manage Jobs link under Site Settings. From here, administrators can view user and system jobs and cancel any running job.

NOTE

Canceling a running job does not guarantee that a query has stopped processing on the remote data server. To avoid long-running queries, specify a timeout for the query during the report development phase.

Large Reports

Most of the reports shown so far in the samples are fairly small and easy to run. However, in the real world, you might run into a report that, when rendered, equals hundreds of pages. For these reports, you need to take into account some special considerations.

First, the amount of time a report takes to process is almost directly proportional to the amount of rows returned from the database query, and how long it takes to get those rows back. It is a good idea to check with the DBA before running long-running queries against a database. Also, check the execution plan of the query before running it. Perhaps further indexing can be done. Lastly, don't bring back any more rows than needed. Modern RDBMs are very good at sorting and grouping data. Let the RDBMS group and sort the data where it can; this saves CPU cycles on the Report Server as well as the network traffic.

Second, take into account the rendering format. You should note that different rendering extensions have different effects on the Report Server. The fastest extensions and those that use the least amount of RAM are those whose output is essentially text—MHTML, CSV, and XML. Excel and PDF are very resource intensive, whereas TIFF and JPEG fall in between the two extremes.

Third, take into account the delivery method of the report. If a report uses pagination, it can be rendered like any other report. The default rendering format is HTML, which includes a soft page break. The page break is included intentionally and, in effect, produces a sort of poor man's paging. If a report is extremely large, this helps to deliver it via browser. If the report is delivered via subscriptions, it makes sense to deploy it to a file share and let the user's desktop be responsible for opening it. This takes the load off the Report Server and is the recommended course of action if using PDF or Excel.

The following list includes some general tips to help handle large reports:

- Make sure the report supports pagination.
- Run the report as a scheduled snapshot, and do not let it be run on demand.
- Set the report to use a shared data source. Shared data sources can be disabled, ensuring the report cannot be run on demand.
- Limit access to the report to ensure that only those who need to run it can run it.

Report Execution History

In these days of endless audits, SOX (Sarbanes-Oxley), and now PCI (Payment Card Industry), it is becoming essential to know when someone within an organization accesses data. It is also helpful to know this information from an organizational and planning perspective. As more and more reports get published, how often reports get looked at and by whom could be essential information.

What Is the Execution Log?

To address these issues, SSRS keeps an execution log of reports that it has run. Because the database is what stores the data, the log is still good, even in a scale-out environment. The log has a myriad of useful information, such as what reports are run, who has run them, and how long they took to process. Some of the other information it has includes the following:

- Name of the physical machine that ran the report (Report Server—not database server)
- Unique ID of the report
- Unique ID of the user running the report
- Whether the request came from a user or system process
- What rendering format was used
- Values of the report parameters
- When the report process started and when it finished
- Amount of time the server took to process the report in milliseconds
- Type of data used for execution (live, cached, snapshot, history)
- Final status code of the report processing (success or first error code)
- Final size of the rendered report in bytes
- Number of rows returned in the data sets of the rendered reports

How to Report Off the Execution Log

The downside of the execution log is that it is not in a human-readable format. To remedy this, Microsoft has distributed a SQL Server Integration Services Package that can be used to port the data from the Report Server's internal execution log table to another database to be used for querying and reporting against the log. There are even some sample reports against the resulting execution log table. If you are still using SQL Server 2000, an equivalent DTS package does the same thing.

Three files are central to the extraction and reporting of the execution log. All three files should be located in the `<Program Files\Microsoft Sql Server\90\Samples\Reporting Services\Report Samples\Server Management Sample Reports\Execution Log Sample Reports>` directory. The first file is `Createtables.sql`, which is the script used to create the tables for the RSExecutionLog database. The second two files, `RSExecutionLog_Update.dtsConfig` and `RSExecutionLog_Update.dtsx`, form the integration package that pushes the data from the Report Server catalog into the RSExecutionLog database.

Creating the RSExecutionLog Database

You can create the RSExecutionLog database by completing the following steps (see Figure 20.2):

1. Open SQL Server Management Studio, connect to the database engine, and select Master as the default database.
2. Run the following query:

```
create database RSExecutionLog
go
use RSExecutionLog
go
```

3. Open the `createtable.sql` file and execute it in the RSExecutionLog database. The results of the script should be as follows:

```
Dropping tables...
Creating ReportTypes...
Creating Reports...
Creating Users...
Creating Machines...
Creating RequestTypes...
Creating SourceTypes...
Creating FormatTypes...
Creating StatusCodes...
Creating ExecutionLogs...
Creating ExecutionParameters...
Creating RunLogs...
Script completed.
```

4. Double-click on the dtsx file and click Execute to execute the package.

To keep data in the RSExecutionLog database current, periodically run the integration package. The package is designed to import new data, without overwriting or removing existing data. To remove old data in the RSExecutionLog database, run the `Cleanup.sql` script.

Overview of the Sample Reports

Three reports come included with the sample reports packages.

The first report (`Execution Status Codes.rdl`) includes a summary of reports run by the status they received. This shows the failure rate of reports on the server as well as why the processes failed.

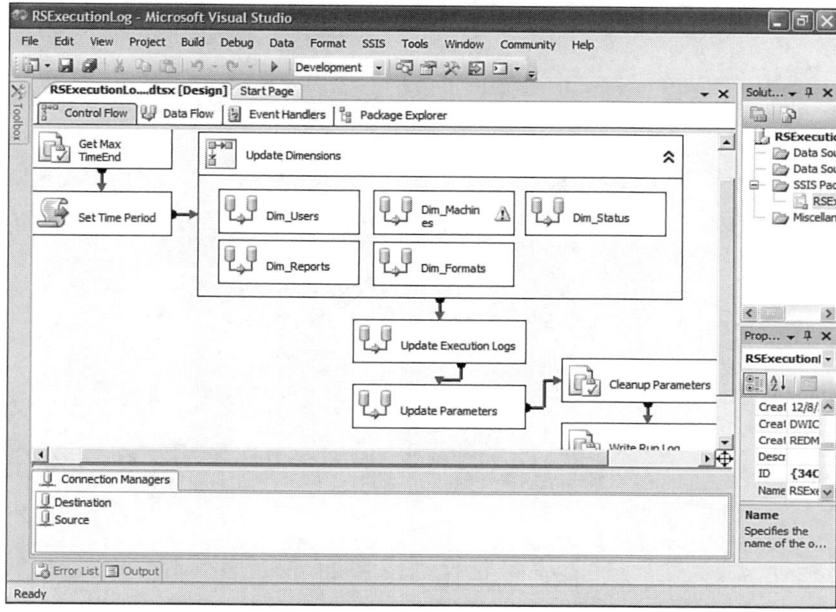

FIGURE 20.2 RSExecutionLog SSIS package.

The second report (`Execution Summary.rdl`) gives an overview of report executions. It includes some key metrics, such as the number of report processed per day, the top ten most requested reports, and the longest-running reports. This report is shown in Figure 20.3.

The last report (`Report Summary.rdl`) is similar to the execution summary, but gives the execution overview of a specific report.

The sample reports can actually be published to the Report Server and accessed like any other report (they get logged like any other report as well). The only caveat with these reports is having to set the end date to one day ahead of the current date to include the current day's execution. The reason for this is that the date parameters have no way to accept time, and, hence, time default to 12:00 a.m. (start of the day). This might come up as an issue when you develop your own reports as well.

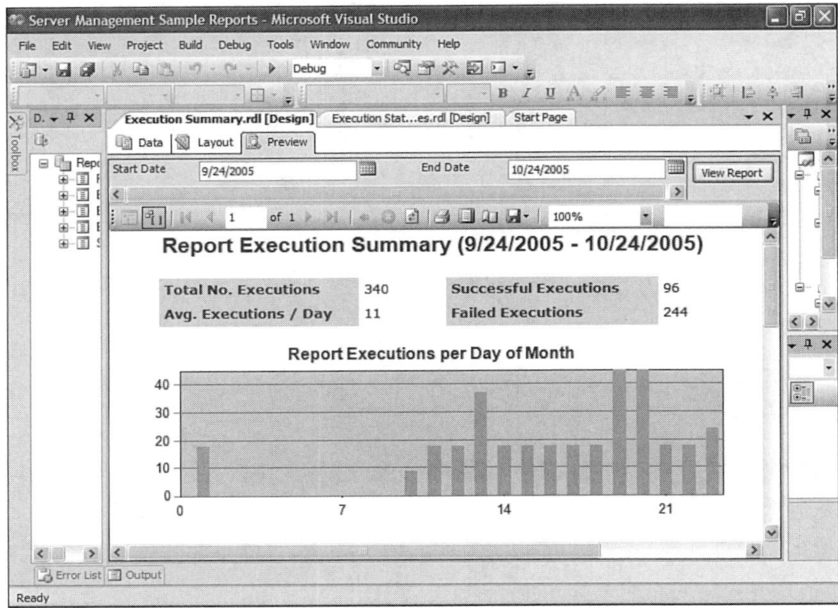

FIGURE 20.3 Report Execution Summary report.

Summary

Report schedules allow the coordination of activities within the Report Server. There are two types of schedules—report-specific schedules and shared schedules. The relationship between the two is analogous to the relationship between a custom-defined data source and a shared data source.

A job is any process running on the Report Server. SSRS comes by every 60 seconds to poll what processes are running on the Report Server. Report execution history gives the end users the ability to retrieve from SSRS who accessed what report, when, and using what parameters. Using a SQL Server Integration Services package, you can collect this information into a database for auditing purposes. SSRS comes with three sample reports to query this information from the catalog.

Deploying and Configuring SSRS

CHAPTER 21

IN THIS CHAPTER

- Overview of Deployment Scenarios
- Requirements for a Standard Deployment
- Requirements for a Scale-Out Deployment
- Configuring SSRS
- Key Management

SSRS can be deployed in a number of ways from a single-server deployment to a scale-out deployment in a web farm. This, in many ways, makes SSRS an ideal solution for companies that want to start out small, but be able to grow into a much larger solution.

Just like anything else, there are limits to what you can do with what edition (see Chapter 4 "Reporting Services Deployment Scenarios," specifically the section "Key Features of SSRS by SQL Server 2005 Editions"), but it is not a technical issue—rather it is a matter of licensing and the related cost. This chapter covers the various deployment scenarios, and explains how to configure individual settings on the Report Server.

Overview of Deployment Scenarios

SSRS has two main deployment scenarios. The first is possibly the simplest—the single-server deployment. In this scenario, a single machine is responsible for hosting both major components of SSRS—the database and the Report Server.

The second major scenario is the scale-out deployment, in which the database is on one machine, possibly a clustered virtual machine, and the Report Server is on another machine or on a web farm.

Advantages/Disadvantages of the Standard Model

The standard model, or single-server deployment model, might sound simple and easy to do at first, and it is certainly the way to do it for a development workstation, or a simple trial or proof of concept. However, you should consider a couple of things when debating whether to use this model in a production environment.

Performance Impact of the Standard Model

The primary consideration for most administrators after cost is performance. Having both the database and the Report Server on the same machine might sound tempting on the financial front because SSRS is included with the SQL Server Relational Engine; however, both the relational engine and Report Server love RAM and CPU cycles. SSRS is going to use all the RAM it can get or whatever it needs (the lower of the two numbers) to render a report. Rendering reports, and especially rendering large reports, also chews up lots of CPU cycles. Adding this overhead to an older machine that is already struggling with the database server is not advisable.

Disk Space Requirements for SSRS

Anyone who has known a DBA, or who has been one, knows there is one thing all DBAs love—storage. They just can't seem to get enough of it, even in today's environments with large Storage Area Networks (SANs) and hundreds of spindles—the DBA always wants more. This is for good reason.

SSRS, like most databases, installs with a very small footprint. It's almost, and possibly is, negligible. However, depending on how SSRS is used, the disk space requirements can grow pretty large.To understand how space is used inside the SSRS database, an overview of the different types of objects and how they are stored is required.

By now, it should be understood that the SSRS database holds the RDL files, data sources, models, and all metadata, such as folders and access control lists (ACLs). This might seem like a lot to store, but, in reality, this is rather small, and only in the most extreme cases should this cause issues. Session state information for SSRS is stored in the Report Server temporary database. Because only one row is generated per user session, this should not get very large, and grows at a predictable rate.

Other things stored in the database can, however, grow to be very large. Resources for reports are stored in the catalog as a binary large object (BLOB). It's a sure bet that your friendly neighborhood DBA hates BLOBs. When a BLOB is stored initially with the report RDL, it might not be such a big deal; however, if a resource is stored as part of a report in an archive solution, this can get very large very quickly. Cached reports or temporary snapshots are stored in the Report Server temporary database as a BLOB in intermediate format. Because cached reports include raw query results, the BLOB can get pretty large. Another disk space consideration when using cached reports with parameterized reports is that a separate copy of the cached report is generated for each combination of report parameters. The bottom line is that if you are using temporary snapshots, prepare to use disk space. On the same token as temporary snapshots are report history snapshots. The only difference between them is that report history is saved inside the Report Server database and not the Report Server temporary database.

Availability Impact of Standalone Deployment

If the performance impact of the single-server deployment can be shrugged off, the availability impact of it can't be. Having one machine be the central data store and Report Server creates a single point of failure in an enterprise environment. This makes having a backup essential to save the system from some unforeseen calamity. Not much more can be said about it. It is up to the administrator to decide how critical the functionality SSRS provides is. If it can be down for as much time as needed to restore from tape, or if SSRS is not yet important enough to be deployed in a redundant manner, then a standalone deployment should suffice.

Advantages/Disadvantages of the Scale-Out Model

The scale-out model of deployment has two main advantages over the standalone model—performance and availability. However, it has one major downside—cost. Because in the scale-out model, the database server is separate from the web server, the performance penalty of combining the database engine with the Report Server's rendering engine gets nullified. In addition, the database can be clustered in a virtual server to provide a highly availability.

With modern SAN technologies, the database can even be replicated to a remote site. SSRS's application server lives on a separate server. The server is simply the first node in what could become a network load balanced (NLB) cluster. The cluster gives the ability to scale out for performance/availability or both. Scaling out also helps with dispersing the workload generated by scheduled subscriptions because each machine on the cluster looks for events that trigger a subscription to process. The cluster also allows one node to be removed for upgrades/maintenance and then be placed back online when the maintenance is complete.

NOTE

NLB clusters are not a function of SSRS; rather, they are a function of the OS or hardware. SSRS is just an application that can be placed on an existing NLB cluster.

All of this flexibility comes at a price—literally. The only editions to support a scale-out deployment are Developer and Enterprise Editions. Microsoft does not offer support for Developer Edition, and does not license it for use in a production environment. Second, every machine in a scale-out deployment has to be licensed separately for Enterprise Edition. More than anything, the cost of a scale out is what keeps most shops from adopting it.

Requirements for a Standard Deployment

In a standard deployment, the web server/application server and the database server are installed on the same machine. For this reason, it is important that the minimum hardware requirements be met or exceeded. It is also helpful to have the NETBIOS name or IP address of the Simple Mail Transfer Protocol (SMTP) server handy as well as the service account used to execute the reports in unattended mode and the credentials with which to log in to the database.

After collecting all the necessary information, you just need to run setup and configure the Report Server. Sounds easy, doesn't it? While running, the installation program offers two main options. The first option is the default installation. This is the option used for running the standard deployment. This option sets up the database server and the Report Server on the same machine. The second option is called the Files Only option. This option is used primarily in scale-out deployments. For the brave or simply curious, this option can be used to set up SSRS locally; however, the administrator must run the Report Services Configuration Tool after the install completes and configure the options herself.

Requirements for a Scale-Out Deployment

As you have seen earlier in this chapter, SSRS can be deployed in a scale-out fashion on a web farm. Each machine in the web farm runs both the correct web server or website to host the report server and the SQL Server Reporting Services. As anyone who has managed a web farm knows, in theory any machine on the farm should be easily replaceable with another in the same configuration, and state cannot be stored on any box on the farm. SSRS accomplishes this task by using data source configuration information and reports inside the Report Server database. The application servers just need to register themselves with the database server. This might sound simple, but it is not trivial. Luckily, SSRS 2005 has given administrators much better tools to aid in this configuration process.

Overview of Report Server Initialization

Because SSRS uses potentially sensitive information, it is important to secure it appropriately. This is compounded by the fact that in a scale-out situation multiple Report Servers need to encrypt and unencrypt the data stored in the database. To understand how SSRS accomplishes this, you need a bit of knowledge about encryption and encryption techniques.

In general, there are two kinds of encryption—symmetric and asymmetric. Symmetric is very fast because it uses only one possible key to encrypt and unencrypt the data. However, this form of encryption has its drawbacks. How can you share information that has been encrypted with the symmetric key without compromising the key? The answer is to use asymmetric encryption. Asymmetric encryption uses a combination of keys, one public and one private. The public key can be shared with another host and can be used to decrypt messages encrypted with the private key. The same can be said for the private key. Asymmetric encryption is relatively very slow, so it should not be used to encrypt/unencrypt frequently.

SSRS uses both types of encryption in a simple, yet intelligent way. For every Report Server database, SSRS generates a unique symmetric key that can then be used to encrypt the data. At this point, every Report Server that needs access to the data must publish its public asymmetric key along with its unique installation ID and client ID to the Report Server database. The Report Server database then uses the public asymmetric key to encrypt the internal symmetric key and share it with the client. After being encrypted with the client's public asymmetric key, the symmetric key cannot be decrypted by anyone else without the private key. Administrators can actually watch this process unfold by watching the changes in the Keys table during the activation process. The process of exchanging public keys and symmetric keys is called *activation*.

Activation is a two-phase process. The first phase is the Announce Self phase, and the second phase is the Activated phase. The Announce Self phase covers the reading of the keys from the Keys tables and, if needed, the writing of the client's public key to the Keys table. The Activated phase is the time the Report Server gets the symmetric key in encrypted form.

NOTE

Because the private keys are stored under the user's profile in SSRS, changing the user the service runs under could force a reactivation.

The process of adding and removing machines in the scale-out deployment model is simply the process of running activation over again. The same is true for taking an SSRS installation and pointing it to a different database.

Steps to Set Up SSRS in a Scale-Out Configuration

SSRS requires an existing NLB or server cluster. It does not create or set one up for you. The basic steps to set up a scale-out configuration include installing SSRS on the node, configuring the node, and finishing the configuration by editing the configuration files.

The following steps start the install of SSRS on a node of a new server cluster:

1. Run SSRS setup on the node that will become part of the cluster. The critical step here is to do a file only installation. When using the SQL Server Installation Wizard, this option is labeled Install But Do Not Configure the Server.
2. Run the SQL Server Surface Area Configuration Tool to configure the Report Server. The Report Server service must be up and running for this to work because it is what registers the installation with the Report Server database.
3. Open the Reporting Services Configuration Manager.
4. Configure the virtual directories for use by the Report Server and Report Manager. In most scale-out deployments, this should be identical on all machines.
5. Continue to the Database Setup page and enter or select the name of the SQL Server database instance to connect to. Click Connect to connect to the instance and retrieve the list of running databases. To create a new database, click New. The new database is created with the ID of whoever is running the configuration tool.
6. Enter the credentials for SSRS to use to log in to the database.

7. Click Apply for SSRS to connect to the database and complete the activation process.
8. Click the Encryption Keys tab and make a backup of the SymMetric key.
9. Click the Initialization tab, and make sure the Initialized check box is checked. If it is not, click the Initialize button.
10. Continue to enter the email settings and unattended execution account. At this point, you can verify that the Report Server is operational by requesting a page from the Report Server virtual directory (`/ReportServer`). Repeat steps 1-10 for every server in a web farm.
11. Open the `rsreportsserver.config` file and change the `<UrlRoot>` tag to use the cluster name instead of the machine's physical name.
12. Open the `rswebapplication.config` file and change the `<ReportServerUrl>` tag to use the cluster name instead of the machine's physical name.

To add nodes to an existing cluster, follow these steps:

1. Run SSRS setup on the node that will become part of the cluster. The critical step here is to do a file only installation. When using the SQL Server Installation Wizard, this option is labeled Install But Do Not Configure the Server.
2. Run the SQL Server Surface Area Configuration Tool to configure the Report Server. The Report Server service must be up and running for this to work because it is what registers the installation with the Report Server database.
3. Open the Reporting Services Configuration Manager.
4. Configure the virtual directories for use by the Report Server and Report Manager. In most scale-out deployments, this should be identical on all machines.
5. Continue to the Database Setup page and enter the name of the SQL Server database instance to connect to. Click Connect to connect to the instance and retrieve the list of running databases. To connect to an existing database, click Upgrade. All nodes on the same scale-out deployment must point to the same database.
6. Enter the credentials for SSRS to use to log in to the database.
7. On the Initialization tab, the entry for the new node should exist, but the Initialized check box should not be checked.
8. Launch the Report Server Configuration Tool on a machine that has already been initialized.
9. On the Initialization tab, select the machine that is to be added to the scale-out configuration and select Join. At this point, the Initialized check box should appear for both machines in the configuration.

10. Open the `rswebapplication.config` and the `rsreportserver.config` files and change the `<ReportServerUrl>` and the `<UrlRoot>` tags, respectively, to state the cluster name instead of the network name.

NOTE

To use ASP.NET with a web farm, the `validationKey` and `decryptionKey` should be the same on every machine in the web farm. Details of how to accomplish this can be found in the following Microsoft Knowledge Base Article: http://support.microsoft.com/default.aspx?scid=kb;en-us;Q312906.

To remove a server, simply uninitialize it by opening the Reporting Services Configuration Tool from any node on the cluster, selecting the node to be removed, and clicking the Remove button. To move a node, remove the node from its existing setup and follow the steps to add it to the new cluster.

Configuring SSRS

It is rare that administrators ever have to install something without having to change it later. Luckily, SSRS 2005 comes with a slick, new configuration tool to help you do just that.

As you have already seen, the Reporting Services Configuration Manager puts a pretty face on most of the options you would want to configure. To be sure, there are still other options out there; however, they require manual editing of the configuration files.

Configurable Components

Each tab in the Reporting Services Configuration Manager shown in Figure 21.1 is for a different component of SSRS. Modifying the component's different options is very straightforward, and the built-in Help does an excellent job of walking you through the configuration.

Table 21.1 lists some of the configurable components.

TABLE 21.1 Configurable SSRS Components

Component Name	Description	Default Value (If Applicable)
Server Status	The status of SQL Server Reporting Services. Allows you to stop and start the server.	No default value
Report Server Virtual Directory	The virtual directory used for the Report Server.	ReportServer
Report Manager Virtual Directory	The virtual directory for the Report Manager.	Reports

TABLE 21.1 Continued

Component Name	Description	Default Value (If Applicable)
Windows Service Identity	The identity used to run SSRS's Windows service account.	LocalSystem
Web Service Identity	The identity under which the application pool that runs the web service runs.	NetworkService
Database Setup	The database and credential used to access the Report Server's catalog.	No default value
Email Settings	The SMTP settings for sending out email.	No default value
Execution Account	The account used to perform unattended operations.	No default value
Initialization	The component used to configure the initialization of a Report Server in a scale-out deployment.	No default value
Encryption Keys	The Backup/Restore/Change/Delete symmetric encryption key.	No default value

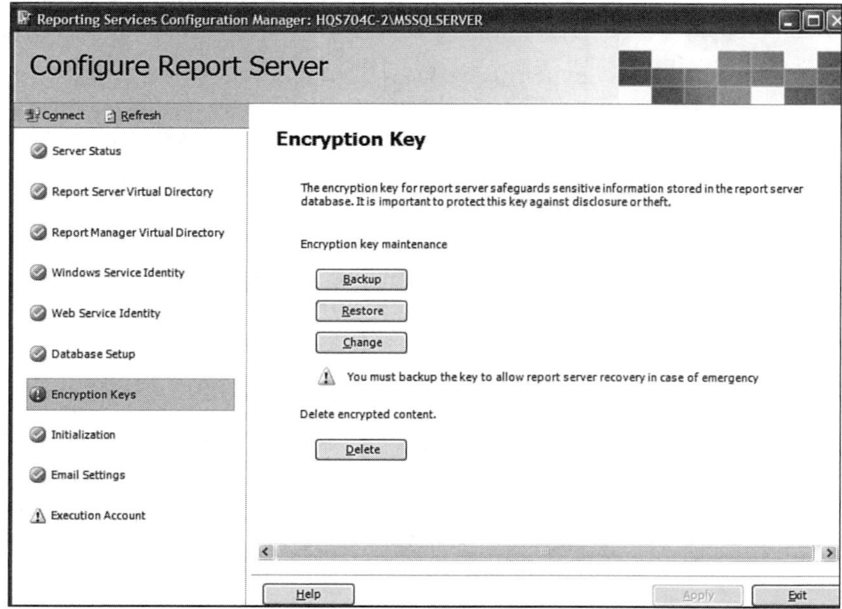

FIGURE 21.1 Reporting Services Configuration Manager.

For most shops, the defaults should more than suffice. If any component's options need to change, the value should come from the administrator in charge of the environment.

Configuration Files

All configuration options for SSRS are stored in XML-based configuration files. Although the sensitive data, such as database connection strings, is encrypted, most of the options can be configured with a simple text editor such as Notepad. If a value is encrypted, it must be edited via a tool such as `rsconfig.exe` utility, which is a command-line tool to edit the encrypted database information or `rskeymgmt.exe`, which is an encryption key management tool.

As with editing any text-based configuration file, there is some inherent risk. Because the files are XML, all of the configurable elements are going to be in either an element or an attribute. A number of things can happen when editing one or more of these files. If the file is changed successfully, the configuration change is applied with little to no effect on end users.

Things do get interesting if a mistake happens. Should the XML become malformed, the server ignores the bad file until the server is restarted. At that point, the server fails to start. If the configuration is a valid XML document and the configuration value is simply invalid, the server uses the default value if one exists. Otherwise, the server fails to start.

Table 21.2 summarizes the configuration files.

TABLE 21.2 Summary of the Configuration Files

Filename	Description	Path
`RSReportServer.config`	Configuration file for the Report Server web service and Report Server Windows service. It contains information about required database connections, deployment configurations, session information, cache management configuration, and so on.	`\Reporting Services\ReportServer`
`RSWebApplication.config`	Configuration file for Report Manager. Includes information for report distribution.	`\Reporting Services\ReportManager`
`ReportingServicesService.exe.config`	Configuration file of the Report Server NT service for which it specifies the Trace setting.	`\Reporting Services\Report Server\Bin`
`RSReportDesigner.config`	Configuration file that stores information about rendering and data extensions for Report Designer.	`\Microsoft SQL Server\90\Tools\Binn\VSShell\Common7\IDE`

Key Management

By now, you have seen what it takes to activate the Report Server(s). It is not trivial, and it does not take long for very important encrypted data to start filling the Report Server's catalog.

This poses the question of what to do about the encryption keys. The symmetric key is never exposed in an unencrypted fashion, and the public keys are tied to the account running the Report Server Windows service and web service. The database knows nothing. Should a hardware failure happen, it is relatively easy to restore the database and hook a new Report Server to it. However, the new machine will not be able to decrypt the data stored in the catalog. What's one to do?

Thankfully, the developers who wrote SSRS gave you a tool called `rskeymgmt.exe`. The Reporting Services Configuration Manager (shown in Figure 21.2) also contains similar functionality. Both tools allow you to back up and restore the symmetric key. Effectively, these two tools allow end users to perform the following tasks:

- Perform a backup of the symmetric key. This provides safeguards against disaster recovery, and provides a helpful tool to perform a server migration.
- Restore a symmetric key from another Report Server instance over to the current installation.
- Change the symmetric key and reencrypt all data in a Report Server database. This is helpful should the key ever get compromised, a key individual leave the organization, or as a proactive practice to safeguard the data.

FIGURE 21.2 Encryption tab in the Reporting Services Configuration Manager.

Backing Up the Symmetric Key

Taking a backup of the symmetric key should be performed immediately after installing SSRS. Because there is only one symmetric key for every Report Server database, the backup only needs to be performed once unless the key is changed or the backup is lost. Always have a backup of the symmetric key handy. The following list describes some situations in which the backup will become useful:

- Changing the service account under which the Report Server Windows service runs, or changing its password
- Renaming the machine or changing the instance name of the SQL Server relational engine that hosts the Report Server database
- Migrating or changing the Report Server database of an existing installation
- Restoring the Report Server installation due to hardware failure

To back up the symmetric key, you must have a password to give to the utility. The password is used as an encryption key to encrypt the symmetric key before saving it. This ensures that the symmetric key is never seen unencrypted. Don't forget the password or let it be compromised.

You can complete the following steps to back up the symmetric key with the Reporting Service Configuration Manager:

1. Open the Reporting Services Configuration Manager and click on the Encryption Keys tab.
2. Click Backup.
3. Enter a strong password, and enter the location in which to store the resulting file.
4. Click OK.

In a similar fashion, this can be done from the command line with the `rskeymgmt.exe` utility:

```
rskeymgmt -e -f rsdbkey.snk -p<password>
```

Restoring the Symmetric Key

Should disaster ever strike, and the key needs to be restored, you must have both the files with the key and the password for that file. Should the restored backup not contain a valid symmetric key for the Report Server database, the Report Server will not be able to unencrypt the data. In the absolute worst case, an administrator might have to delete all the encrypted data, and then reenter it.

To restore the symmetric key with the Reporting Service Configuration Manager:

1. Open the Reporting Services Configuration Manager and click on the Encryption Keys tab.
2. Click Restore.

3. Select the location of the file (in most cases this is the `*.snk` file), which contains the symmetric key. Type the password that unlocks the file.

4. Click OK.

To do the same thing from the command line, run the following command:

```
rskeymgmt -a -f rsdbkey.snk -p<password>
```

Changing the Symmetric Key

Changing the symmetric key involves generating a new key, and reencrypting all encrypted data that was stored using the old key. It is certainly not something that needs to happen every day, although it is a good idea to do it from time to time as a best practice. Think of it as changing the administrator or sa password. The processes should also be done when the key has been compromised.

To change the symmetric key, the web service for the SSRS needs to be disabled. In a scale-out situation, all machines running the web service must be disabled. When the key has been successfully changed, the administrator can reenable the web service on the Report Server(s). To disable the web access to SSRS, use the SQL Server Surface Area Configuration Tool:

1. Open the Surface Area Configuration Tool and select Surface Area Configuration for Features.

2. Select Reporting Services from the navigation menu on the left.

3. Select Web Service and HTTP Access.

4. Uncheck the Enable Web Service and HTTP Access check box.

5. Click Apply.

Remember to do this for every machine in a scale-out situation. After the web service has been disabled, changing the symmetric encryption keys is fairly straightforward.To change the symmetric key with the Reporting Service Configuration Manager, complete the following steps:

1. Open the Reporting Services Configuration Manager and click the Encryption Keys tab.

2. Click Change.

3. Click OK to acknowledge the computer(s), instance number, and installation ID.

The command to do this via the command line is also fairly simple:

```
rskeymgmt -s
```

Before changing the encryption key for a Report Server installation via the command line, you need to stop the web service and HTTP access. After the change is complete, you need to restart the windows service and reenable the web service. For a scale-out deployment, this needs to be done on all of the Report Servers. After the key has been updated, the administrator can reenable web access.

Deleting the Symmetric Key

By deleting the symmetric key, you give up any hope of ever retrieving the encrypted data. All of it will have to be reentered from the ground up. In a scale-out situation, all of the Report Servers deployed will have to be reinitialized. Proceed with extreme caution. After the keys have been deleted, the following items will definitely be affected:

- Data source connection strings
- Credentials stored in the catalog
- Reports that are based on Report Builder models (the models use shared data sources)
- Subscriptions

To delete the symmetric key with the Reporting Service Configuration Manager, complete the following steps:

1. Open the Reporting Services Configuration Manager and click the Encryption Keys tab.
2. Click Delete.
3. Click OK.

The command to do this via the command line is also deceptively simple:

```
rskeymgmt -d
```

After deleting the encryption keys, you need to restart the Report Server Windows service. For a scale-out deployment, you need to restart the Report Server Windows service on all Report Server instances.

Summary

Deploying SSRS in its simplest form is very straightforward. A single server, although simple, cheap, and easy to maintain, does have its penalty when it comes to performance and reliability. A scale-out deployment that might make more sense from a reliability and performance perspective will cost in terms of licensing. It is up to the administrator to decide at what point the buck stops and what is more important.

Either way, after installing, various configuration options are possible. The Report Server Configuration Manager is the Swiss army knife for configuring SSRS. Its graphical interface makes it a cinch to change configuration options in SSRS.

After SSRS is up and running, back up the symmetric key and keep it in a safe place. From time to time, it might be wise to rotate it. Should you lose it, the only option is to delete the keys and reenter all encrypted data.

PART IV

Developing for Reporting Services

IN THIS PART

Implementing Custom Embedded Functions

CHAPTER 22

IN THIS CHAPTER

- Adding Embedded Code
- Debugging Embedded Code

The simplest form of custom code available in SSRS is expressions, which were discussed in Chapter 8, "Expressions." The next level of coding complexity is a custom embedded code in a report.

Adding Embedded Code

To get a better understanding of how embedded custom code is used in a report, report developers can assume all of the code placed in the code window gets compiled into a make-believe class called `Code`. You can add properties and methods to the make-believe `Code` class, and call class members from expressions in the report, which has the class defined.

Embedded code is compiled into a report's intermediate format and gets executed as needed when the report is rendered. Report Designer provides a simple text area to allow editing of the embedded code. To access the code editor, complete the following steps:

- Use the Report, Report Properties menu (if the Report menu is not available, click within the report design area). Alternatively, right-click on the area surrounding the report's body and select the Properties menu.
- Click the Code tab in the Report Properties dialog box.

You should see a window similar to Figure 22.1 and can type the code in the Custom code area.

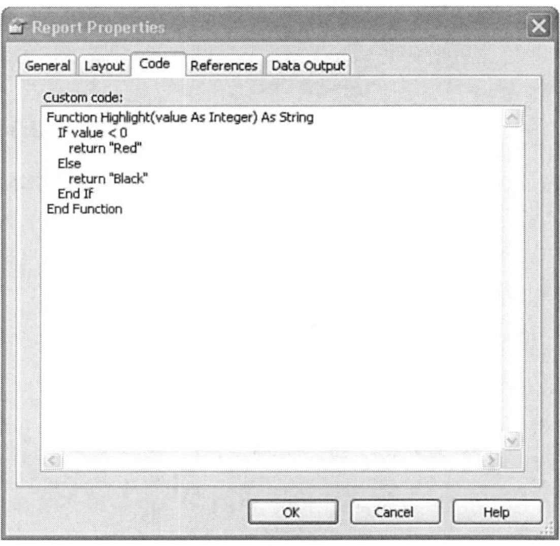

FIGURE 22.1 Code editor.

The code editor is basically a multiline text box, and it does not provide any productivity assistance, such as Intellisense or debugging. You have to be extremely careful while using this code editor. For example, only one level of "undo" action is allowed, as compared to Visual Studio's infinite undo.

For all of its difficulties, embedded code provides several key benefits for a developer, including the following:

- A more elegant approach (as compared to expressions) to medium-complexity coding scenarios
- A single repository for functions and methods that can be reused by multiple items within a single report, as opposed to complex copy-and-paste expressions
- Direct access to the exception handling functionality of VB.NET

Every developer knows function reuse is beneficial over copy-and-paste programming. Take the following fictitious example. Suppose two developers were assigned the parallel development of a single report. One developer used embedded code, whereas the other one used simple expressions. One of the initial goals was to highlight negative values in red. Later, this goal changed to a more complex requirement, such as color-coding numeric ranges. The developer who used embedded code could adapt to the change in requirements quickly, and would make his manager happy, probably getting a bonus in the process.

Embedded functions must be written in VB.NET. If you prefer C#, you would have to develop a custom assembly. This topic is covered in Chapter 23, "How to Create and Call a Custom Assembly from a Report."

The following steps add the function used in the preceding narrative:

1. Open the report properties by either clicking the Report, Report Properties menu, or right-clicking on the area surrounding the report's body and selecting Properties.
2. In the Report Properties dialog box, click the Code tab and enter the following function:

   ```
   Function Highlight(value As Integer) As String
      If value < 0
         return "Red"
      Else
         return "Black"
      End If
   End Function
   ```

3. Drag a `Textbox` from the Toolbox to the report and place the following code in the `Background Color` property:

   ```
   =Code.Highlight(me.value)
   ```

4. Place -1 (minus one) in the `Value` property.
5. Open the report in Preview mode to see the text box with a red background.

Debugging Embedded Code

SSRS does not provide any facilities to step through the embedded code, and, thus, you have two options: You can either debug code in Visual Studio .NET or use some pre–Visual Basic tricks for debugging. The first trick is to label code lines. This is beneficial to locate both compile-time and runtime errors. The following code fragment shows how to label code lines. It also has errors that have been intentionally placed for demonstration purposes.

```
Function Add(n As Integer)
1: i = i + n
2: return i
End Function
```

When you build a report with the code snippet or try to preview the report that calls this code, SSRS reports two issues (one warning and one error):

- **Warning**—There is an error on line 0 of the custom code: `[BC42021] Function without an 'As' clause; return type of Object assumed.` Warnings are only displayed if at least one error is found.

- **Error**—There is an error on line 1 of the custom code: `[BC30451] Name 'i' is not declared`. Only the first error is displayed.

With a small code fragment such as the preceding example, finding errors might not be an issue. For a code fragment that has a significant number of lines, locating the one with an error can be a burden.

NOTE

Keep in mind that labels can only be present inside of functions or subroutines and can repeat inside of different functions.

TIP

To properly determine line numbers, deliberately add an error and preview the report. The SSRS error indicates the line number.

TIP

To avoid laborious efforts of numbering and renumbering of lines, you should only label key expressions or the first line of functions. Alternatively, you can use labeling to narrow down a line with an error.

The second trick is to locate a line that causes runtime errors by using a `TRY-CATCH` block:

```
Function DivByZero()
     Dim x As Integer
     Try   ' Set up structured error handling.
3:         x = x/ 0
      Catch ex As Exception
          Return ex.ToString() & vbCrLf & "Exception at Line: " & CStr(Erl)
      End Try
End Function
```

The result of the call to the function `DivByZero()` is

```
System.OverflowException: Arithmetic operation resulted in an overflow.
at ReportExprHostImpl.CustomCodeProxy.DivByZero()
Exception at Line: 3
```

Note that function `DivByZero()` uses the undocumented function `Erl` to return a line number for the line of code that produced the error. `Erl` really returns a label number (in the preceding code, it is 3).

When you do not implement error handling, and then make a call to a function within the `Value` property of a report item, the report item shows "`#Error`" as a result.

Depending on the precision of a return value provided from a function, other potential results are "`Infinity`" or "`NaN`" (Not a Number).

TIP

Always check the Error List window after a Build operation has completed, and make sure that there are no warnings. Best practice suggests eliminating all warnings in production code.

Exceptions within other properties can be caught during the Build operation.

Summary

Custom embedded code can provide a more elegant approach to medium-complexity custom code than expressions through function reuse, centralized code repository, and additional error-handling options.

Custom embedded code is a VB.NET code embedded in a report. A code is embedded as a part of a report definition (RDL) file and compiled together with the container report. Many errors are caught by the compiler when a reporting solution is built.

Although embedded code allows a developer to use full object-oriented functionality of VB.NET, embedded code is mostly used for simple logic. It is possible to develop complex embedded code, but this is not usually done due to limited debugging facilities and limited functionality of the embedded code editor. The embedded code editor is a simple text box that does not have advanced features, such as code completion, available in Visual Studio.

When functions are too complicated for embedded code to handle efficiently or you have a preference to use C# instead of Visual Basic, you can develop and call a custom assembly from a report. The next chapter explains how to leverage a custom assembly within a report.

How to Create and Call a Custom Assembly from a Report

CHAPTER 23

IN THIS CHAPTER

- Strong-Named Custom Assemblies
- .NET Security Primer for a SSRS Administrator
- Assemblies That Require Other Than Execute Permissions
- Debugging Custom Assemblies

SSRS comes with a comprehensive set of functions that can be used within reports. However, you might need to add custom functionality that is not covered by the set of common functions or is too complicated for embedded code to handle efficiently. Second, if you, as a developer, are hard set on C# as a language of choice, a custom assembly is the way to go. A couple of examples of functionality that are better handled by a custom assembly are encryption and trend analysis.

NOTE

Trend plotting functionality is available in the full version of the Dundas' chart. However, the chart does not provide trend calculation information to a report. In some cases, trend information might be needed to trigger some action, such as formatting on a report, and this is where trend analysis assembly might be useful.

Let's start with a simple example and develop a function `GetLibraryInfo()`, which returns a single string with a library version information.

Start Visual Studio 2005 and create a new Class Library Project. Let's call the project RSCustomLibrary; see Figure 23.1.

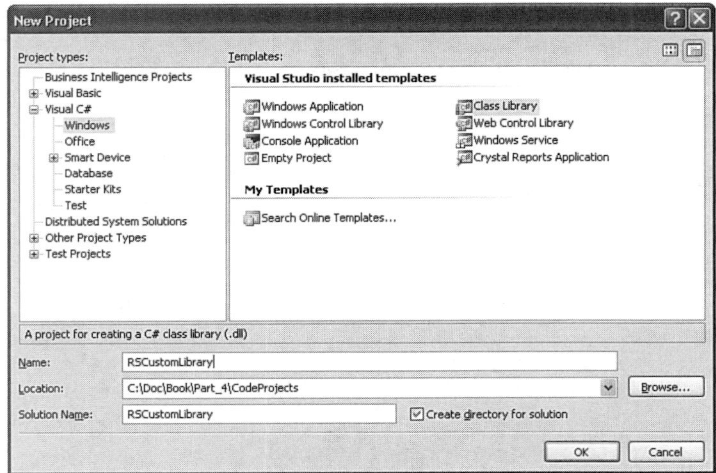

FIGURE 23.1 New library project.

Visual Studio creates a project with a single class `Class1`. Let's rename the file `Class1.cs` in Solution Explorer to `MainClass.cs`. Note how Visual Studio changed the name of the class in the code.

Substitute code in the class module with the following code:

```
using System;
using System.Reflection; //Need to have this so we can get the Assembly information
namespace RSCustomLibrary
{
    public class MainClass
    {
        //Method GetLibraryInfo() returns this custom Assembly information
        //RSCustomLibrary, Version=1.0.0.0, Culture=neutral, PublicKeyToken=null
        public static string GetLibraryInfo()
        {
            return Assembly.GetExecutingAssembly().GetName().ToString();
        }
    }
}
```

TIP

To simplify a custom assembly test, developers can use a simple Windows application to call assembly's methods. This allows testing assembly's functionality prior to tests with SSRS.

The compiled assembly must be located in directories in which it is accessible by

- Report Designer (the default directory is `C:\Program Files\Microsoft Visual Studio 8\Common7\IDE\PrivateAssemblies`). This allows calling an assembly from reports in preview mode.
- Report Server (the default directory is `C:\Program Files\Microsoft SQL Server\MSSQL.3\Reporting Services\ReportServer\bin`). This allows calling assembly from reports deployed on Report Server.

NOTE

Report Designer and/or Report Server reports an error if it can't find the library:
`[rsErrorLoadingCodeModule] Error while loading code module: 'RSCustomLibrary, Version=1.0.0.0, Culture=neutral, PublicKeyToken=null'. Details: Could not load file or assembly 'RSCustomLibrary, Version=1.0.0.0, Culture=neutral, PublicKeyToken=null' or one of its dependencies. The system cannot find the file specified.`

Let's now use our custom assembly in a report. You first have to reference the assembly:

1. Open the report properties using the Report, Report Properties menu.
2. In the properties dialog box, click the References tab.
3. Click "..." and navigate to the library. See Figure 23.2 for details.

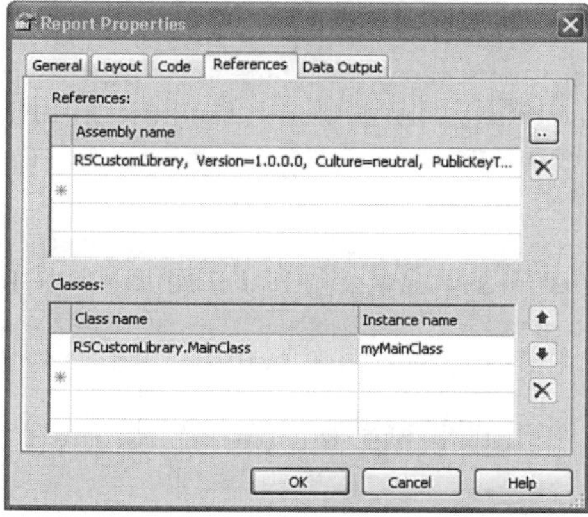

FIGURE 23.2 Reference custom assembly.

Developers can navigate to any location where the library is present, such as the bin directory of the library project. This operation only records the reference to the assembly and not a specific location of this assembly. Report Designer adds the following RDL to reference an assembly:

```
<CodeModules>
    <CodeModule>RSCustomLibrary, Version=1.0.0.0,
        Culture=neutral, PublicKeyToken=null
    </CodeModule>
</CodeModules>
```

4. Enter a Class Name and an Instance Name. Filling in a Class Name and an Instance Name is optional for static methods. When you specify a Class Name and an Instance Name, Report Designer creates an instance of the specified class and, subsequently, you can access the class inside of a report using the class' instance name. Report Designer adds the following RDL:

```
<Classes>
  <Class>
    <ClassName>RsCustomLibrary.MainClass</ClassName>
    <InstanceName>myMainClass</InstanceName>
  </Class>
</Classes>
```

   When specifying a Class Name, you need to prefix the name of the class with its assembly, such as `RSCustomLibrary.MainClass`. Otherwise, the SSRS compiler returns an error: `[rsCompilerErrorInClassInstanceDeclaration] Error in class instance declaration for class MainClass: [BC30002] Type 'MainClass' is not defined.`

5. Call the assembly from one of the report's expressions. A static method can be called as `=<AssemblyName>.<ClassName>.<StaticMethodName>`; in this case, `=RSCustomLibrary.MainClass.GetLibraryInfo()`. An instance method can be called as `=<Code>.<InstanceName>.<PublicMethodName>`; in this case, `=Code.myMainClass.GetLibraryInfo()`. A static method does not require an instance, but can still be accessed through the instance if so desired.

Now that you have referenced a custom assembly in a report and copied binaries to the Report Designer's directory, the assembly can be called from the report in preview mode of the Report Designer. However, calling the assembly will not work if you try to debug or deploy this assembly to a Report Server if no additional steps are taken.

This chapter explains the additional steps needed to make a deployed assembly available to reports.

NOTE

The procedures that you have seen thus far allow referencing a custom assembly, but because you have not yet set security for the assembly, the assembly can only be called in preview mode.

Sometimes, you might need to pass initialization parameters to a class in a custom assembly. This is done by overriding the `OnInit()` method of the `Code` object of a report. This can be done by editing the RDL directly or using the code editor. To open code editor, use the Report, Report Properties menu and click the Code tab in the Report Properties dialog box.

See Figure 23.3 for details.

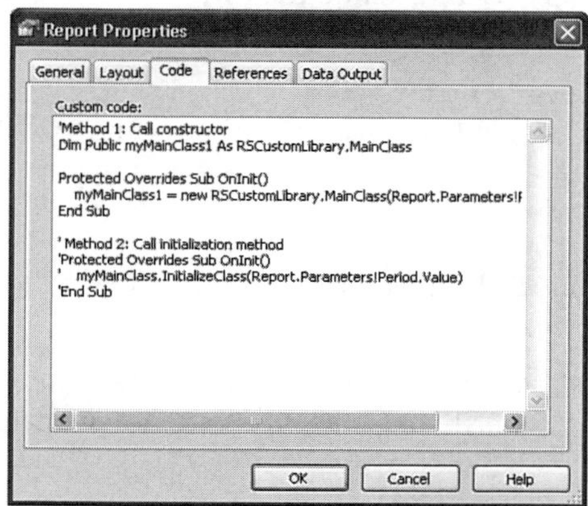

FIGURE 23.3 Using the code editor to override `OnInit()` method.

To initialize a class, you can either create a new instance of the class inside of `OnInit` and pass parameters to a class constructor or write a public initialization method for a class and call this method from `OnInit`.

When you create a new instance of the class, make sure that the instance name used in the `OnInit` method does not conflict with the instance name you have created when you referenced an assembly.

```
<Code>
    Dim Public myMainClass1 As RSCustomLibrary.MainClass
    Protected Overrides Sub OnInit()
       myMainClass1 = new RSCustomLibrary.MainClass(Report.Parameters!Period.Value)
    End Sub
</Code>
```

To invoke this initialization method, from a report you can use the following expression: `=Code.myMainClass1.GetLibraryInfo()`.

NOTE

If there is a conflict between the instance created in a report's reference and any of the instances generated in the code, SSRS generates an error:

`[rsCompilerErrorInClassInstanceDeclaration] Error in class instance declaration`

```
for class RsCustomLibrary.MainClass: [BC30260] 'myMainClass' is already
declared as 'Private Dim myMainClass As <unrecognized type>' in this class.
```

When you call a public initialization function, create an instance of the class using the Report, Report Properties menu and then click the References tab.

Then call the initialization function from `OnInit`. Make sure that the instance name used in `OnInit` corresponds to the instance name used when you referenced an assembly.

```
<Code>
    Protected Overrides Sub OnInit()
        myMainClass.InitializeClass(Report.Parameters!Period.Value)
    End Sub
</Code>
```

To invoke this initialization method, you can use the following expression: `=Code.myMainClass.GetLibraryInfo()`.

Within the `OnInit` method, you can use items from the Globals, Parameters, and User collections. The Fields and ReportItems collections are not available when the `OnInit` method is invoked.

NOTE

Do not forget to prefix the collection name with `Report` **(such as** `Report.Parameters`**); otherwise, you will receive an error:** `[rsCompilerErrorInExpression] The Value expression for the textbox 'textbox2' contains an error: [BC42024] Access of shared member, constant member, enum member or nested type through an instance; qualifying expression will not be evaluated.`

To take advantage of initialization, you need to add a constructor to the assembly. The updated assembly may have the following code:

```
using System;
using System.Reflection; //Need to have this so we can get the Assembly information
namespace RSCustomLibrary
{
    public class MainClass
    {
        static int mPeriod = -1;
        public MainClass()
        {}
        public MainClass(int Period)
        {
            mPeriod = Period;
        }
```

```
        public void InitializeClass(int Period)
        {
            mPeriod = Period;
        }
        //Method GetLibraryInfo() returns this custom Assembly information
        //RSCustomLibrary, Version=1.0.0.0, Culture=neutral, PublicKeyToken=null
        //AND initialization status:
        //
        public static string GetLibraryInfo()
        {
            return Assembly.GetExecutingAssembly().GetName().ToString()
                + (
                    (mPeriod != -1) ?
                        " Initialized with value=" + mPeriod.ToString()
                        : " Not initialized"
                  );
        }
    }
}
```

Note the operator `"?"` (question mark) usage in the code. If you are not familiar with this operator, it is similar to the `IIF` function or the `IF-THEN-ELSE` statement.

> **NOTE**
>
> **If you choose to use a constructor to initialize the class, an explicit default constructor (constructor with no parameters) is required. If no default constructor is defined, SSRS returns an error:** `[rsCompilerErrorInClassInstanceDeclaration] Error in class instance declaration for class RsCustomLibrary.MainClass: [BC30455] Argument not specified for parameter 'Period' of 'Public Sub New(Period As Integer)'.`

It is very likely that the first deployed version of an assembly will not be perfect and one day you will need to update an assembly. You can update an assembly using one of four ways:

1. Maintain the same assembly attributes (such as Version and Culture) and replace an assembly in Report Designer and SSRS directories. Maintaining assembly attributes is a key for this method because the report's RDL contains this information in the `<CodeModule>` descriptor. If an assembly's attributes change, the reports can no longer call it. This method is the best for frequent assembly updates, while maintaining classes and method signatures. This method of updates is especially relevant during debugging and testing.

2. Update the assembly attributes and update all the references (using Report Designer or directly editing the `<CodeModule>` tags) to reference the new version of the assembly.

3. Create a strong-named assembly (see the next section, "Strong-named Custom Assemblies," for more details) and store it in the Global Assembly Cache (GAC). The GAC allows multiple versions of an assembly. Reports can call any of the versions stored in the GAC. Thus, you can keep both versions of the assembly and refer to either one.

4. As in the previous method, create a strong-named assembly, store a version of an assembly in the GAC, and force SSRS to redirect all the calls to the new assembly. In this case, an administrator would need to modify the `Web.config` and `ReportService.exe` configuration files to add the following entry:

```
<configuration>
   <runtime>
      <assemblyBinding xmlns="urn:schemas-microsoft-com:asm.v1">
         <dependentAssembly>
            <assemblyIdentity name="RSCustomLibrary"
                              publicKeyToken="..."
                              culture="..." />
            <bindingRedirect oldVersion="1.0.0.0"
                             newVersion="2.0.0.0"/>
         </dependentAssembly>
      </assemblyBinding>
   </runtime>
</configuration>
```

Strong-Named Custom Assemblies

The .NET Framework allows sharing of assemblies through the GAC. The GAC is a `%systemroot%\assembly` directory on a computer on which .NET Framework is installed. GAC can be managed through `%systemroot% \Microsoft.NET\Framework\`*`version`* `GACUTIL.exe` or the Assembly Cache Viewer extension of Windows Explorer; see Figure 23.4. Additional details of using this tool can be found at: http://msdn2.microsoft.com/library/34149zk3.aspx.

Assemblies must have a strong name to be stored in GAC, so the .NET runtime can uniquely identify each assembly, even assemblies with the same name. A strong name is the combination of the assembly's name, the four-part version number, the culture (if provided), a public key, and a digital signature stored in the assembly's manifest.

Visual Studio 2005 made it very simple to sign an assembly through the Signing tab of the Project Designer. To access the Signing tab, select a project node in Solution Explorer, and then on the Project menu, click Properties. When the Project Designer appears, click the Signing tab.

By default, Reporting Services does not allow calls to strong-named custom assemblies directly from reports. This is probably a good thing because enabling SSRS to call strong-named assembly poses security risks.

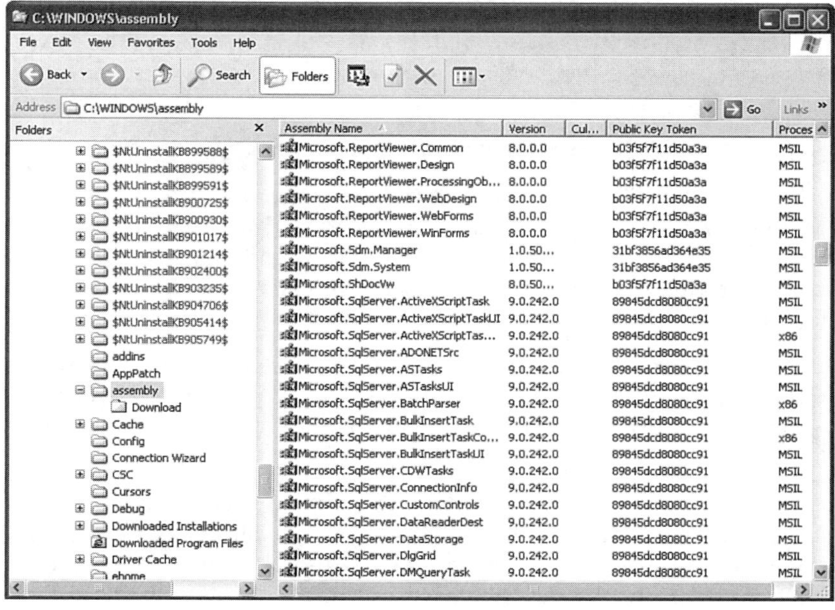

FIGURE 23.4 Assembly Cache Viewer.

To enable calls to strong-named custom assembly in Reporting Services, you can use one of the methods described in Table 23.1. Both methods described in Table 23.1 have security risks associated with them.

TABLE 23.1 Methods of Enabling a Strong-Named Assembly

Method	Accomplished By	Security Risk
Allow a strong-named assembly to be called by partially trusted code using the assembly attribute AllowPartiallyTrustedCallersAttribute	In the assembly attribute file, add the following assembly-level attribute assembly:[AllowPartiallyTrustedCallers] (<assembly:AllowPartiallyTrustedCallers> for VB projects)	Makes assembly callable from any other assembly (partially or fully trusted)
Grant FullTrust security permission to report expressions in Reporting Services **Caution! High security risk. Never use this method in the production environment.**	Find Report_Expressions_Default_Permissions code group in rspreviewpolicy.config and/or rssrvpolicy.config and modify PermissionSetName to state PermissionSetName="Full Access"	Grants FullTrust to all custom assemblies that are called in report expressions

Security risks are especially relevant to the strong-named custom assemblies that require more than `Execute` permissions (discussed in the later section, "Assemblies That Require Other Than Execute Permissions").

.NET Security Primer for a SSRS Administrator

Although the details of .NET security are outside the scope of this book, a brief security overview will help you to better understand the security of SSRS assemblies. You can find more security-related topics in the Microsoft .NET Framework documentation (http://msdn.microsoft.com/library/default.asp?url=/library/en-us/dnnetsec/html/netframesecover.asp).

By default, custom assemblies are granted `Execute` permission in Reporting Services. The `Execute` permission set enables code to run, but not to use protected resources. For example `Execute` permission allows string manipulations, but not access to the file system.

The worst outcome of a malicious call to the assembly with `Execute` permission is a potential denial of service attack in which a malicious assembly causes excessive CPU and memory use, thereby impacting performance of other software components running on the computer on which such an assembly is installed.

NOTE

When a developer calls a .NET namespace, it might not be immediately clear if the `Execute` permission is sufficient. For example, the `GetExecutingAssembly()` method requires `FileIOPermission`. However, it might be logically concluded that the `Execute` permission is sufficient because the method retrieves information about the assembly it is called from and the assembly should be loaded in the memory. It so happens that the call to this method does `PathDiscovery` to check the assembly's path and thus requires `FileIOPermission`.

After an assembly is enabled for additional permissions, the impact of a malicious call could be more dramatic, such as data loss.

.NET common language runtime (CLR) employs code access security, which allows an administrator to assign permissions to an assembly. When an assembly makes a call to a protected resource (for example, file IO), the runtime checks if an assembly has appropriate permissions to do so. During the call, CLR evaluates all the assemblies in the call stack for permissions. This prevents an `AssemblyA` with restricted permissions (such as `Execute`) to call an `AssemblyB` with less restrictions to perform an operation on a protected resource.

An administrator sets the security policy by editing XML configuration files. SSRS has three configuration files: `rssrvpolicy.config`, `rsmgrpolicy.config`, and `rspreviewpolicy.config` (outlined in Table 23.2). Depending on the end goal, one or more files should be edited.

TIP

An administrator should always create a backup of SSRS configuration files prior to any modifications.

TABLE 23.2 SSRS Configuration Files

Filename	Location (Default Installation)	Description
`rssrvpolicy.config`	`C:\Program Files\Microsoft SQL Server\MSSQL.3\Reporting Services\ReportServer`	The Report Server policy configuration file. This file contains security policies for the Report Server and affects execution of the following: 1. Custom expressions and assemblies deployed to a Report Server 2. Custom data, delivery, rendering, and security extensions deployed to the Report Server
`rsmgrpolicy.config`	`C:\Program Files\Microsoft SQL Server\MSSQL.3\Reporting Services\ReportManager`	The Report Manager policy configuration file. These security policies affect all assemblies that extend Report Manager; for example, subscription user-interface extensions for custom delivery.
`rspreviewpolicy.config`	`C:\Program Files\Microsoft Visual Studio 8\Common7\IDE\PrivateAssemblies\RSPreviewPolicy.config`	The Report Designer stand alone preview policy configuration file. This file contains security policies for Report Designer and affects the following: 1. Execution of custom expressions and assemblies in reports during preview in Report Designer 2. Execution of custom extensions, such as data-processing extensions, that are deployed to Report Designer

TIP

Use Microsoft Knowledge Base Article KB842419 (http://support.microsoft.com/?kbid=842419) for the step-by-step process of working with security permission settings in SSRS.

Administrators can edit configuration files manually, using any text editor (possible, but not recommended method) or employ the help of the .NET Framework Configuration Utility (`mscorcfg.mcs`).

TIP

Use the .NET Framework Configuration Utility (`mscorcfg.mcs`) to simplify permission creation and minimize a chance of malformed XML.

The easiest way to start this utility is from Control Panel, Administrative Tools, .NET Framework 2.0 Configuration. This tool is shown in Figure 23.5.

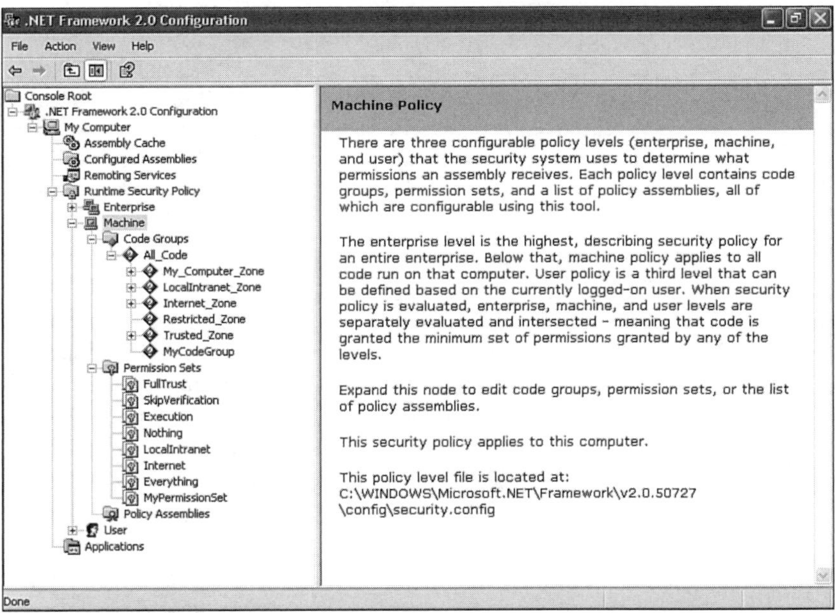

FIGURE 23.5 .NET Framework Configuration Utility.

The .NET Framework Configuration Utility edits the computer's security policy file stored located at (make sure to adjust path for the proper version of.NET) `C:\WINDOWS\Microsoft.NET\Framework\v2.0.50727\config\security.config`.

Instead of editing SSRS configuration files manually, an administrator can use the .NET Framework Configuration Utility and then copy the `<PermissionSet>` and `<CodeGroup>` from the `security.config` file to an appropriate SSRS configuration file.

TIP

To simplify finding `<PermissionSet>` and `<CodeGroup>` elements that need to be copied to the SSRS configuration file, an administrator can choose to create a permission set and a code group with easily distinguishable names, which could be as simple as `PermissionSet` and `MyCodeGroup`. Then, an administrator can use a text editor to search and copy the appropriate permissions.

There are three levels of security policies:

- Enterprise level is the highest and applies to the entire enterprise.
- Machine policy applies to all code run on that computer.
- User policy applies the currently logged-in user.

A lower level can place further restrictions on the policy settings from the highest level, but cannot expand the permissions. As a result, code is granted the minimum set of permissions granted by any of the levels.

To set permissions for an assembly, follow these steps:

1. Create a permission set or use one of the predefined sets, such as `Execution` (each assembly in SSRS gets this set by default). Additional permission sets are `FullTrust`, `Internet`, `None`, and more.
2. Create a code group that maps a permission set to an assembly or, more specifically uses `Membership Condition` to perform this mapping.

Figure 23.6 shows security permission configuration objects (configured as an XML in `.config` files) for an assembly.

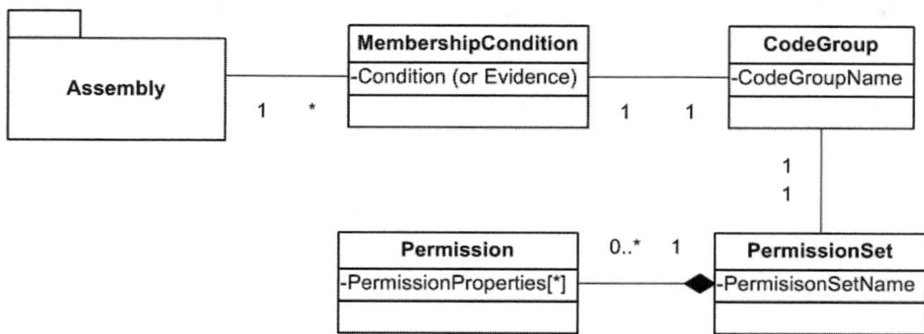

FIGURE 23.6 Assembly security permission objects.

Each permission set contains zero or more permissions. A permission is a logical subdivision of system functionality (or access control to a protected resource). Examples of permissions are `Registry` (controls access to the computer's registry, as a whole or by an individual key), `File IO` (controls access to a single file or a whole file system), `Printing` (controls access to printing resources), `SQL Client` (controls access to SQL Servers), and more.

Each permission supports one or more properties that provide more details for a permission. For example, the `File IO` permission allows specifying an individual file that can be accessed for either one or all of the following: `Read`, `Write`, `Append`, and `Path Discovery`. `Security` is somewhat an obscure permission because its attributes are presented as security permissions.

Some of the permissions that `Security` allows to specify are `Enable Assembly Execution` (`Execute` permission) and `Assert Any Permission That Has Been Granted`. `Assert Any Permission That Has Been Granted` in turn enables an assembly to do exactly what the permission implies, that is, to assert security permissions, such as `File IO`.

A code group uses `membership condition` to associate an assembly with a permission set. The most commonly used membership conditions are of `URL` and `Strong Name` type. `URL` membership uses a path to an assembly and `Strong Name` uses exactly what it implies, the strong name of an assembly.

NOTE

Some literature uses the term "evidence" to refer to the `membership condition` **type.**

When SSRS calls an assembly, the assembly, in turn, tries to access a protected resource the .NET CLR checks if administrators have set up the appropriate permissions. The CLR then checks the call stack to evaluate permissions for each assembly and makes sure that the minimum combined permission is applied. This prevents a malicious assembly with `Execute` permission to do anything bad by calling another assembly with `FullTrust` permission.

Assemblies That Require Other Than Execute Permissions

A developer who wants to grant custom assemblies privileges beyond `Execute` permission needs to edit one or both configuration files: `C:\Program Files\Microsoft SQL Server\MSSQL.3\Reporting Services\ReportServer\`**`rssrvpolicy.config`** and/or `C:\Program Files\Microsoft Visual Studio 8\Common7\IDE\PrivateAssemblies\`**`RSPreviewPolicy.config`**.

NOTE

Reporting Services 2000 used different configuration files (`RSReportServer.config` **and** `RSReportDesigner.config`**). SSRS 2005 uses** `rssrvpolicy.config` **and** `RSPreviewPolicy.config` **for permission-related configuration.**

To have access to system resources, such as `File IO`, from the assemblies, you need to add the following to one or both `rssrvpolicy.config` and `RSPreviewPolicy.config` configuration files (refer to Table 23.2).

Correspondingly, this configuration setting ensures successful execution of the assembly deployed to the Reporting Services and assembly used by Report Designer.

```
<PermissionSet
   class="NamedPermissionSet"
   version="1"
   Name="MyPermissionSet"
   Description="A custom permission set to grant read access to a configuration
➥file.">
   <IPermission
      class="FileIOPermission"
      version="1"
      Read="C:\configuration.xml"
      Write="C:\configuration.xml"
   />
   <IPermission class="SecurityPermission"
      version="1"
      Flags="Execution, Assertion"
   />
</PermissionSet>
```

The preceding configuration section is a definition of a `NamedPermissionSet` with the name `MyPermissionSet`, which is located under the `<NamedPermissionSets>` tag in the configuration file (`rssrvpolicy.config` and/or `RSPreviewPolicy.config`). `MyPermissionSet` grants the assembly two security permissions:

- `Execute`—Allows executing code in the assembly. This permission was discussed earlier in this section.
- `Assert`—Allows asserting other defined permissions in the code. In this case, it allows asserting a `FileIOPermission`.

`MyPermissionSet` also grants the assembly a `FileIOPermission` permission to read and write configuration files. The named permission set is optional and used to create a fine granularity of permissions that are not already defined by built-in permissions.

In addition, the following `<CodeGroup>` configuration needs to be added to the configuration file (`rssrvpolicy.config` in this particular case).

```
<CodeGroup class="UnionCodeGroup"
   version="1"
   PermissionSetName="MyPermissionSet"
   Name="MyCodeGroup"
   Description="A special code group for my custom assembly.">
```

```
   <IMembershipCondition class="UrlMembershipCondition"
      version="1"
      Url="C:\Program Files\Microsoft SQL Server\MSSQL.3\Reporting Services\
ReportServer\bin\RSCustomLibrary.dll"/>
</CodeGroup>
```

Note that CodeGroup refers back to MyPermissionSet. Alternatively, CodeGroup could have used a predefined set, such as FullTrust: PermissionSetName="FullTrust".

Note how the Url property of the UrlMembershipCondition condition points to the library that was deployed for use by SSRS. You might have spotted this because the rssrvpolicy.config configuration was edited and the library was deployed to SSRS' binary directory (C:\Program Files\Microsoft SQL Server\MSSQL.3\Reporting Services\ReportServer\bin\).

For Report Designer, the configuration file would have changed to RSPreviewPolicy.config and the deployment directory (and, thus, the value of the Url property) would be C:\Program Files\Microsoft Visual Studio 8\Common7\IDE\PrivateAssemblies\RSCustomLibrary.dll.

The position of CodeGroup is extremely important. It has to be positioned like the following code fragment:

```
...
            </CodeGroup>

          <CodeGroup class="UnionCodeGroup"
           version="1"
           PermissionSetName="FullTrust"
           Name="MyNewCodeGroup">
            <IMembershipCondition class="UrlMembershipCondition"
               version="1"
               Url="C:\Program Files\Microsoft Visual Studio PrivateAssemblies
                     ➥\RSCustomLibrary.dll"/>
          </CodeGroup>
        </CodeGroup>
    </CodeGroup>
</PolicyLevel>
...
```

This code fragment gives the RSCustomLibrary.dll FullTrust or unrestricted permission. As mentioned previously, because FullTrust is a predefined PermissionSet, it does not require you to specify anything in the <NamedPermissionSets> section of the configuration file.

For a code to acquire the appropriate permission, it **must** first assert the permission:

```
FileIOPermission permission = new FileIOPermission(FileIOPermissionAccess.Read |
FileIOPermissionAccess.Write, @"C:\configuration.xml");
try
{
   permission.Assert();
   XmlDocument doc = new XmlDocument();
   doc.Load(@"C:\configuration.xml");
   ...
}
```

Alternatively, a method's attribute can carry an assertion:

```
[FileIOPermissionAttribute(SecurityAction.Assert, ViewAndModify=
                                                  @"C:\ configuration.xml")]
```

The details of what happens during `Assert` are outside the scope of this book. You can find a very good explanation of `Assert` at http://blogs.msdn.com/shawnfa/archive/2004/08/23/219155.aspx.

What happens if you properly set all configurations, but did not do an `Assert`? In this case, .NET throws a `SecurityException`, such as the following:

```
Request for the permission of type
'System.Security.Permissions.FileIOPermission, mscorlib, Version=2.0.0.0,
Culture=neutral, PublicKeyToken=b77a5c561934e089' failed.
```

Debugging Custom Assemblies

The best debugging tool for debugging custom assemblies, no surprise, is Visual Studio. There are two debugging options:

- Debug with a single instance of Visual Studio. This is done by creating a single solution that contains both a Reporting Services project and a custom assembly project. You would set breakpoints in a custom assembly and run the report in `DebugLocal` mode. The easiest way to start `DebugLocal` is to right-click on the report that needs to be tested and select Run from the shortcut menu.
- Debug with two instances of Visual Studio: one has a report project and another custom assembly. Set breakpoints in the custom assembly, click debug, and from the list of processes select `devenv.exe` that corresponds to the report project. After you run a report that calls the assembly in preview mode, the debugging session will break at defined breakpoints.

Debugging with a single instance of Visual Studio (`DebugLocal` method) requires several setup steps:

1. Include both the report project and a custom assembly project in a single solution.
2. Set breakpoints in a custom assembly.
3. Set up the report project as a startup project by right-clicking the project in Solution Explorer and selecting `Set as StartUp Project` from the shortcut menu.
4. Set up a report as a start item. Right-click the project in Solution Explorer and select Properties from the shortcut menu, then from the Start Item drop-down, select a report that you want to debug, as shown in Figure 23.7.
5. Start debugging from the Debug, Start Debugging menu or by pressing F5. Use F11 to step through the report.

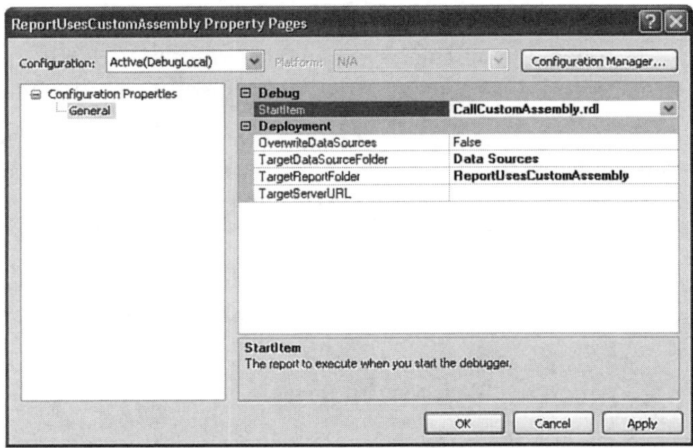

FIGURE 23.7 Project Configuration dialog box.

Running the `GetLibraryInfo()` example that was developed earlier in the chapter did not create any issues when you ran it in preview mode (Report Preview tab). This is because preview mode does not enforce security permissions. Let's try to run `GetLibraryInfo()` in `DebugLocal` mode. Visual Studio breaks on the `GetExecutingAssembly()` call and shows an exception:

```
System.Security.SecurityException was unhandled by user code Message="Request
for the permission of type 'System.Security.Permissions.FileIOPermission,
mscorlib, Version=2.0.0.0, Culture=neutral, PublicKeyToken=b77a5c561934e089'
failed."
```

So, what happened with your code and why didn't it work?

First, you have to check if the configuration was properly set. Reading of the configuration file was discussed earlier, but `GetLibraryInfo()` does not really read a configuration file. All it does is call the `GetExecutingAssembly()` function.

```
public static string GetLibraryInfo()
{
    return Assembly.GetExecutingAssembly().GetName().ToString()
        + (
            (mPeriod != -1) ?
                " Initialized with value=" + mPeriod.ToString()
                : " Not initialized"
          );
}
```

The clue here is the fact that the assembly is trying to retrieve information about itself. So, it must mean that you need some kind of permission to that assembly file.

Earlier in this chapter, you learned that the `GetExecutingAssembly()` requires the `PathDiscovery` permission. To configure Report Designer for debugging of this library, copy the library to `C:\Program Files\Microsoft Visual Studio 8\Common7\IDE\PrivateAssemblies\` or, better yet, set an output path for the library in Visual Studio. In Solution Explorer, right-click the library project, select Properties, click the Build tab, and enter `C:\Program Files\Microsoft Visual Studio 8\Common7\IDE\PrivateAssemblies\` for the Output Path, as shown in Figure 23.8.

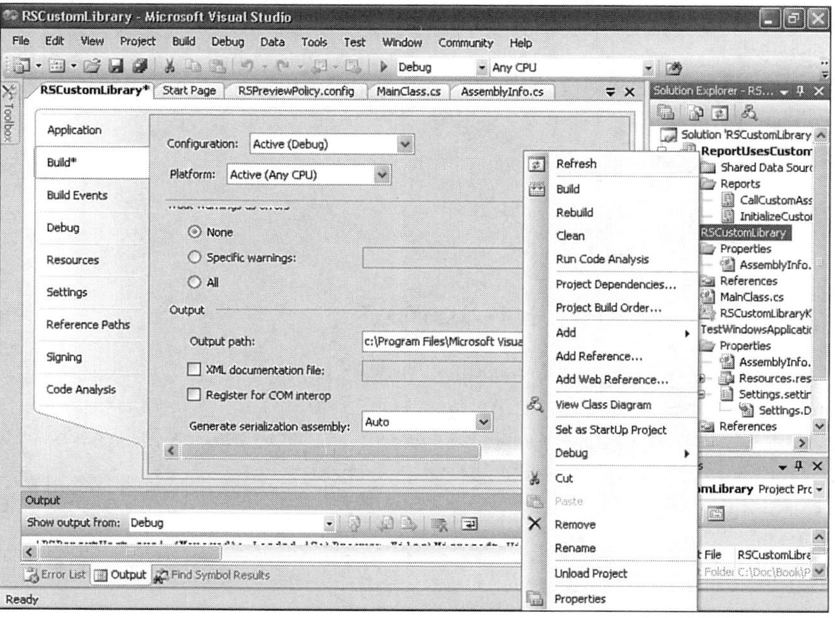

FIGURE 23.8 Library Properties interface.

The benefit of setting an output path is that Visual Studio realizes that it was using this library (through Report Designer) and, thus, is able to replace it. If Visual Studio compiles the library to an alternative location and a developer is trying to copy to the `C:\Program Files\Microsoft Visual Studio 8\Common7\IDE\PrivateAssemblies\` directory, afterward he might not be able to do that. This is because Visual Studio will be "holding" this library during and after debugging. Visual Studio will require restart so it can release the "hold" and so the library can be replaced.

The next step is to create a `<PermissionSet>` with `PathDiscovery` permission in `C:\Program Files\Microsoft Visual Studio 8\Common7\IDE\PrivateAssemblies\RSPreviewPolicy.config`:

```
<PermissionSet
   class="NamedPermissionSet"
   version="1"
   Name="GetLibraryInfoPermissions"
   Description="A custom permission set to grant read access to a configuration
➥file.">
   <IPermission
      class="FileIOPermission"
      version="1"
      PathDiscovery="C:\Program Files\Microsoft Visual Studio
➥8\Common7\IDE\PrivateAssemblies"
   />
   <IPermission class="SecurityPermission"
      version="1"
      Flags="Execution, Assertion"
   />
</PermissionSet>
```

And in the same file, add the following:

```
<CodeGroup class="UnionCodeGroup"
 version="1"
 PermissionSetName="GetLibraryInfoPermissions"
 Name="MyNewCodeGroup">
  <IMembershipCondition class="UrlMembershipCondition"
     version="1"
     Url="C:\Program Files\Microsoft Visual Studio 8 Visual Studio 8\
➥Common 7\IDE\PrivateAssemblies\RSCustomLibrary.dll
</CodeGroup>
```

to this location:

```
...
   ADD HERE (before the second CodeGroup above the PolicyLevel)
        </CodeGroup>
    </CodeGroup>
</PolicyLevel>
...
```

The final step is to Assert the permission in the code, as follows:

```
public static string GetLibraryInfo()
{
    try
    {
        FileIOPermission permission = new Perrmission
                       (FileIOPermissionAccess.PathDiscovery,
                       @"C:\Program Files\Microsoft Visual Studio 8\Common7\
                       ➥\IDE\PrivateAssemblies\RSCustomLibrary.dll");
        permission.Assert();
    }
    catch (SecurityException ex)
    {
        return ex.Message;
    }
    return Assembly.GetExecutingAssembly().GetName().ToString()
              + ((mPeriod != -1)?
              " Initialized with value=" + mPeriod.ToString()
              : " Not initialized");
}
```

Summary

Custom assemblies greatly expand functionality (as compared to expressions and embedded code) that can be accessed from a report. A custom assembly can be written in any .NET language. Custom assemblies can leverage a full set of productivity enhancements available in Visual Studio .NET, such as Intellisense, source code management, full debugging capabilities, and much more.

Custom assemblies can be used for complex code, where usage of expressions and embedded code is no longer elegant. If a custom assembly requires more than default Execute permission, you need to have a good understanding of .NET security and SSRS configuration, modify configuration files to set assembly's permissions, and assert the permissions in the assembly's code.

How to Use URL Access

CHAPTER 24

IN THIS CHAPTER

- How to Integrate URL Access in an Application

URL Access is one of the easiest methods available to developers to incorporate SSRS functionality into custom applications. URL Access is designed to provide the highest level of performance when used to view and navigate reports. URL Access achieves this performance by bypassing the web service interface and communicating directly with the Report Server. On the other hand, because URL Access does not access the web service, URL Access' functionality is limited to viewing and navigating reports.

NOTE

SSRS programmers who have implemented custom security extensions (Chapter 26, "Writing Custom Reporting Services Extensions," discusses some details of custom extensions) should know that SSRS still checks for permissions and a valid authorization cookie before allowing URL Access to a report. In a practical sense, this means that before reports can be accessed through the URL, a call must be made to the `LogonUser` method in the SSRS web service, and the resulting cookie must be relayed to the client's browser.

URL Access accepts various parameters that affect the report's rendering. For example, some parameters affect the framing of a report and specify whether the toolbar and document map are displayed. Other parameters specify a report's output format (HTML, IMAGE, EXCEL, CSV, PDF, XML). A set of commonly used parameters is discussed further in this chapter.

You can use URL Access to render a report in a browser by typing the URL Access command in the address bar or embed URL Access into applications that you develop.

Let's start from a simple example of a URL Access. One of the methods to discover what is possible through URL Access is to actually navigate through the Report Viewer (Report Server web UI) and see how it works. Let's start at `http://localhost/ReportServer` (generic syntax would be `http://<server>/ReportServer`, where `<server>` is a NetBIOS name, fully qualified domain name, or an IP address of a server on which Report Server is installed). When a developer uses Report Designer to deploy a report, the name of the project becomes the name of the folder on a Report Server.

NOTE

If you deploy a solution that contains a report, the report's path would be `/{Solution Name}/ {Project Name}/{Report Name}`. **If you deploy a project (right-click on the project and select Deploy from the shortcut menu), the report's path would be** `/{Project Name}/{Report Name}`.

For example, if you create a project with the name Generic, Report Designer creates a Generic folder. When you navigate to the Generic folder, the address changes to: http://localhost/ReportServer?/Generic&rs:Command=ListChildren. As it can be inferred from `Command=ListChildren`, this command renders a list of children, such as reports, data sources, or any other items located in the Generic folder.

You do not have to URL encode a URL Access string passed to a browser. Browsers should automatically encode it. The most common encoding is the space is replaced with "+" (plus sign) or an escape sequence "%20", "/" (slash) is replaced with an escape sequence"%2f", and ";" semicolon in any portion of the string is replaced with an escape sequence "%3A".

URL Access commands have corresponding calls in the Reporting Services web service. This case is no exception—the URL Access command `Command=ListChildren` corresponds to the `ListChildren()` method call of the SSRS web service. When a user clicks on one of the reports (let's use SimpleReport as a name of the report) in the SSRS web interface, you see the following URL address in a browser: http://localhost/ReportServer/Pages/ReportViewer.aspx?%2fGeneric%2fSimpleReport&rs:Command=Render.

`Render` perhaps is one of the most frequently used commands and also has a corresponding web method call in the SSRS web service called `Render()`. `Render` is called to generate a stream of data (this stream is a rendered report) in the format specified by a parameter. By default, a browser receives an HTML stream.

When appropriate for a particular rendering, URL Access uses implicit defaults. For example, by default a report is rendered with a toolbar. However, you do not see anything mentioning the toolbar in the URL address of the browser.

URL Access uses the following syntax `http[s]://<RSserver>/<RSpath>?/<Parameters>`.

<RSserver> is a NetBIOS name, fully qualified domain name (FQDN), or an IP address of a server on which Report Server is installed.

<RSpath> is a virtual directory path on which Report Server is installed (by default, it is installed to the ReportServer virtual directory).

<Parameters> can consists of a relative path of an item (report or other resource) in relation to the SSRS virtual directory followed by one or more parameters with the syntax &prefix:parameter=value. Valid prefix values are shown in Table 24.1 and valid parameters are shown in Table 24.2.

TABLE 24.1 Valid Parameter Prefixes

Prefix	Purpose	Example
No prefix	Treats this parameter as a report parameter. To pass a null value for a parameter, use ParameterName:isnull=true. Note: Report parameters are case sensitive.	&EmployeeID=123 &EmployeeID:isnull=true
rc	Denotes a report control parameter. Passes device information settings to rendering extensions. In the case of HTML (HTML Viewer), it is report framing information. Note: rc parameters are not case sensitive.	&rc:DocMap=True &rc:doCmaP=true &rc:Toolbar=True
rs	Denotes a Report Server parameter. Passes a parameter to SSRS. Note: rs parameters are not case sensitive and all have counterpart functions in the SSRS web service.	&rs:Command=Render
dsu	Specifies a username with which to access a data source.	&dsu:MyDataSource=MyUser
dsp	Specifies a password with which to access a data source. Subject to limitations and risks of security exposures. Basically, avoid using it whenever possible.	&dsp:MyDataSource=Password

Syntax requires each prefix to be followed by a parameter. Report parameters do not have prefixes and this is how URL Access determines that a particular parameter should be treated as a report parameter. If a URL Access command includes a report parameter that does not match any of the parameters defined in the report, SSRS reports an rsUnknownReportParameter error.

On the other hand, SSRS is very lenient with prefixed parameters and uses a default value when the value specified in URL Access is invalid. For example, rs:Command= Reindeer (note intentional misspell of Render) defaults to rs:Command=Render. This is a mixed blessing as it might not be immediately clear why a certain URL Access command does not work as you would have expected. However this handling minimizes errors.

Command is the most frequently used parameter and is used in almost all URL Access commands. Command's details and other available rs: parameters are shown in Table 24.2.

TABLE 24.2 rs:—Report Server Parameters

rs: parameter	Purpose
Command	Specifies the command to be executed. Valid commands include the following: GetDataSourceContents—Displays properties of a given shared data source as XML. Example: http://localhost/ReportServer?/Samples/Adventure+Works&rs:Command=GetDataSourceContents GetResourceContents—Renders a file in a browser. This is used to show images and other nonreport or data source file. Example: http://localhost/ReportServer?/Samples/flogo.jpg&rs:Command=GetResourceContents ListChildren—Lists items in a folder. Example: http://localhost/ReportServer?/Samples&rs:Command=ListChildren Render—Renders the specified report. Example: http://localhost/ReportServer/Pages/ReportViewer.aspx/Samples/SimpleReport&rs:Command=Render
Format	Specifies the format in which to render a report. Common values include HTML3.2, HTML4.0, HTMLOWC, MHTML, IMAGE, EXCEL, CSV, PDF, XML, and NULL.
ParameterLanguage	Provides a language for parameters passed in a URL. The default value is the browser language. The value can be a culture value, such as en-us or de-de. This is especially helpful for international deployments. For example, in Europe most of the countries reverse month and day position as compared with the United States.
Snapshot	Renders a report based on a report history snapshot.

Table 24.3 shows partial set of Report Control parameters. Report Control parameters target HTML Viewer to provide framing and the look and feel for a rendered report. More details on this topic are available in SQL Server Books Online.

TABLE 24.3 rc:—Report Control Parameters

rc: parameter	Target Rendering	Value
BookmarkID	HTML	Directs SSRS to position the report's viewing focus to the bookmark ID.
DocMap	HTML	Directs SSRS to show or hide the report document map. Valid values are true (default) or false.
DocMapID	HTML	Directs SSRS to position the report's viewing focus to the document map ID.

TABLE 24.3 Continued

rc: parameter	Target Rendering	Value
`DpiX`, `DpiY`	IMAGE	Specifies resolution of the output device in x|y-direction. 96 is the default.
`EndPage`, `StartPage`	IMAGE, PDF	Directs SSRS to render last|first page of the report. `StartPage=0` renders all pages. Defaults: `StartPage=1`, `EndPage=StartPage`.
`FieldDelimiter`	CSV	Specifies URL-encoded delimiter string. The default value is a comma (,).
`FindString`	HTML	Specifies the text to search for in the report. The default is an empty string.
`JavaScript`	HTML, MHTM	Indicates JavaScript supported in the rendered report.
`HTMLFragment`	HTML	Directs SSRS to return an HTML fragment instead of a full HTML document. An HTML fragment includes the report content in a TABLE element and omits the HTML and BODY elements. The default value is false. Images for a report must be retrieved separately.
`LinkTarget`	HTML	Specifies a target for hyperlinks in the report. LinkTarget=_blank opens a new target window. Other valid target names include a frame name, _self, _parent, and _top.
`MarginTop`, `MarginBottom`, `MarginLeft`, `MarginRight`	IMAGE, PDF	Specifies the margin value, in inches, for the report. It is an integer or decimal value followed by "in" (for example, 1in). Overrides the report's original settings.
`NoHeader`	CSV	Indicates whether the header row is excluded from the output. The default value is false.
`OmitDocumentMap`	EXCEL	Indicates whether to omit the document map for reports that support it. The default value is false.
`OmitFormulas`	EXCEL	Indicates whether to omit formulas from the rendered report. The default value is false.
`OmitSchema`	XML	Indicates whether to omit the schema name from the XML and to omit an XML schema. The default value is false.
`OutputFormat`	IMAGE	Specifies report's rendering graphical format: BMP, EMF, GIF, JPEG, PNG, or TIFF.

TABLE 24.3 Continued

rc: parameter	Target Rendering	Value
`PageHeight`, `PageWidth`	IMAGE, PDF	Specifies a report's page height/width in inches. You must include an integer or decimal value followed by "in". This value overrides the report's original settings.
`Parameters`	HTML	Shows or hides the parameters area of the toolbar. `Parameters=true` (default) shows, `Parameters=false` hides the parameters area. `Parameters=Collapsed` hides the parameters area, but allows the end user to toggle.
`Qualifier`	CSV	Specifies a string to put around results that contain strings equal to `FieldDelimiter` or `RecordDelimiter`. If the results contain the qualifier, the qualifier is repeated. The Qualifier setting must be different from the `FieldDelimiter` and `RecordDelimiter` settings. The default value is a quotation mark (").
`RecordDelimiter`	CSV	Specifies a record delimiter for the end of each record. The default value is `<cr><lf>`.
`RemoveSpace`	EXCEL	Directs an extension to eliminate small, empty cells from the result. A valid value is an integer or decimal value followed by "in". The default value is 0.125in.
`Schema`	XML	Indicates to SSRS to render the XML schema definition (XSD) versus actual XML data. A value of true indicates that an XML schema is rendered. The default value is false.
`Section`	HTML	Sets the report's viewing focus page. A value greater than the number of pages in the report displays the last page, negative values display page 1. The default value: 1.
`SimplePageHeaders`	EXCEL	Indicates whether the page header of the report is rendered to the Excel page header. A value of false indicates that the page header is rendered to the first row of the worksheet. The default value is false.
`SuppressLineBreaks`	CSV	Directs SSRS to suppress line breaks from the output. The default value is false. If the value is true, the `FieldDelimiter`, `RecordDelimiter`, and `Qualifier` settings cannot be a space character.

TABLE 24.3 Continued

rc: parameter	Target Rendering	Value
`Toolbar`	HTML	Shows or hides the toolbar. True is the default value. If the value of this parameter is false, all remaining framing options (except the document map) are ignored. The toolbar is not rendered through the SOAP API, but the Toolbar device information setting affects results of SOAP `Render` method.
`XSLT`	XML	Specifies the path of an XSLT to apply to the XML output, for example `/Transforms/myxslt`. The XSL file must be a published resource on the Report Server and you must access it through a Report Server item path. This transformation is applied after any XSLT that is specified in the report. When used, the `OmitSchema` setting is ignored.
`Zoom`	HTML	Sets the report zoom value as an integer percentage (`rc:Zoom=100` is the default) or in relation to the displayed page (`Page Width` (`rc:Zoom=Page%20Width`) or `Whole Page`). Supported by Microsoft Internet Explorer 5.0 and above.

How to Integrate URL Access in an Application

You can use URL Access to incorporate reports into Windows and web applications.

Several methods are available for web applications. The most common method is to use a URL Access command string as a source or IFRAME. In a simple case scenario, this could be an HTML file with the following code:

```
<IFRAME
    NAME="Frame1" SRC="http://localhost/ReportServer?/Samples/SimpleReport&
    ➥rc:Toolbar=false&rc:LinkTarget= Frame1", width = 50%, height = 50%>
</IFRAME>
```

The preceding code creates a frame on the page that is located in the upper-left corner and takes 50% of the page's "real estate." The frame changes size as the browser window changes size. The purpose of `&rc:LinkTarget= Frame1` is to make sure that all of the report's navigation happens inside of the frame called `Frame1`.

You can also add a link to a report in a web application or leverage the `rc:HTMLFragment` parameter.

You can also call SSRS web services to obtain needed information and then incorporate the returned stream into the application's HTML stream. More details on working with

SSRS web service can be found in Chapter 25, "How to Use Reporting Services Web Services."

URL Access methods for web applications described above, such as using URL Access command as a source for IFRAME, have a common downside. They all use the `HTTP GET` method, which is an equivalent to a form submission where `METHOD="GET"`.

There are a couple of potential issues with the `GET` method.

First, it might be easy to hack the URL string and make changes that would allow a malicious user to potentially get some proprietary information. A report's security restricts a user's access to a whole report, but does not prevent someone from experimenting with the parameters of a report.

By contrast, when you use URL Access with `METHOD="POST"`, you can use hidden fields to prevent users from changing parameters used in URL Access.

Second, the URL `GET` request's length is limited to the maximum allowed by the browser. Some browsers have this limit as low as 256 characters.

Internet Explorer's maximum URL request length is 2,083 characters, with 2,048 maximum path length. This limit applies to both `GET` and `POST` methods. POST, however, is not affected by this limitation for submitting name/value pairs, because they are transferred in the header and not the URL.

For more details, see the following Microsoft Knowledge Base Article: http://support.microsoft.com/default.aspx?scid=kb;en-us;208427.

NOTE

Limits on the length of `POST` requests can also be controlled by registry settings. For example in IIS 6.0, `HKEY_LOCAL_MACHINE\System\CurrentControlSet\Services\HTTP\Parameters` subkeys `MaxFieldLength` and `MaxRequestBytes` control the size of the header and subkeys `UrlSegmentMaxCount` and `UrlSegmentMaxCount` control segmentation. A segment is a part of a URL string separated by "/" (slashes). See http://support.microsoft.com/default.aspx?scid=kb;en-us;820129 for more details.

Changing the `GET` method to the `POST` method is fairly easy; for example, the following URL Access `GET` method

```
http://localhost/ReportServer?/Samples/SimpleReport&rs:Command=Render
    ➥&rc:LinkTarget=main&rs:Format=HTML4.0& EmployeeID=0947834
```

can be translated to the following `POST` method:

```
<FORM id="frmRender" action=" http://localhost/ReportServer?/Samples/SimpleReport"
   METHOD="POST" target="_self">
   <INPUT type="hidden" name="rs:Command" value="Render">
   <INPUT type="hidden" name="rc:LinkTarget" value="main">
```

```
    <INPUT type="hidden" name="rs:Format" value="HTML4.0">
    <INPUT type="hidden" name="EmployeeID" value="0947834">
    <INPUT type="submit" value="Button">
</FORM>
```

To integrate URL Access in a Windows application, you can embed a web browser control in a Windows form. An old-style COM component from the Internet Controls Library (shdocview.dll) can be used with Visual Studio versions prior to VS2005.

VS2005 is sporting a new .NET web browser control. Simply drag and drop this control from the Visual Studio 2005 Toolbox on your Windows form, and then set the URL property of a control to a URL Access string. It's that simple.

Summary

URL Access provides simple and efficient access to a report's rendering functionality. URL Access can be used through a simple HTML link, as a source of an IFRAME, through web browser control in Windows and web applications, and in SharePoint web parts.

URL Access is designed to provide the highest level of performance when used to view and navigate reports. URL Access achieves this performance by bypassing the web service interface and communicating directly with Report Server. On the other hand, because URL Access does not access the web service, URL Access' functionality is limited to viewing and navigating reports.

CHAPTER 25

How to Use Reporting Services Web Services

IN THIS CHAPTER

- Report Management Web Service *New in 2005* (ReportService2005.asmx)
- How to Script Reporting Services (Using the RS Utility)
- Working with Report Parameters
- Security When Calling a Web Service
- Some of the Commonly Used Methods with Short Code Snippets

In the previous chapter, you learned about URL Access functionality. URL Access provided high-performance access to SSRS for report viewing and navigation. However, URL Access does not provide sufficient access to SSRS' management functionality. SSRS' web services comes to the rescue and complements URL Access by providing full access to SSRS' management and rendering functionality.

An application that needs to incorporate both report viewing and report management functionality would typically use both URL Access and the SSRS web service. Combining the two is used for a couple of reasons: URL Access provides the best performance for the report viewing experience and handles framing of a report; in contrast, SSRS web service provides comprehensive access to SSRS functionality, including management functionality, which is not available in URL Access.

Because the web service employs Simple Object Access Protocol (SOAP) over HTTP, any SOAP-aware application or development tools can communicate with the SSRS web service. Technically, you can manually generate SOAP requests (which are basically XML text written to SOAP specifications) and pass those requests to the SSRS web service. Visual Studio generates a web proxy and makes using a web service as easy as using any .NET namespace.

Let's start with a simple example. This example walks through the use of the `Render()` function to access the SSRS web service, and then incorporates the resulting stream into a custom application. Much like parameter commands with the same name in URL Access, `Render()` and `ListChildren()` are the most frequently used functions in the SSRS web service.

As an example, let's create a simple function that retrieves a report from SSRS. Here are the steps:

1. Open Visual Studio 2005.
2. Create a C# project and call it `Embedded Report`.
3. Rename `Form1` that Visual Studio created to `MainForm`.
4. Add a reference to the Reporting Services web service by right-clicking on the project in Solution Explorer and selecting `Add Web Reference` from the shortcut menu, or by selecting `Add Web Reference` from the `Project` menu, as shown in Figure 25.1.

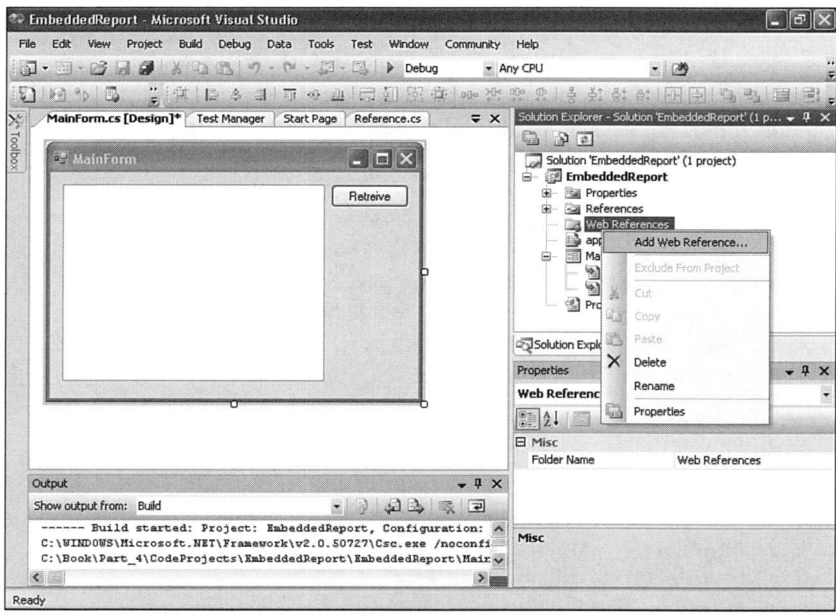

FIGURE 25.1 Adding web references in Visual Studio.

5. Select the most appropriate hyperlink or enter http://<server>/reportserver/ReportExecution2005?wsdl in the URL field of the Add Web Reference dialog box and click `GO`. Note <server> is the name of a server on which Report Server is installed. If development is performed on the same machine on which Report Server

is installed, select the `Web Services on the Local Machine` hyperlink. After Visual Studio completes this operation, it presents a selection such as the one shown in Figure 25.2.

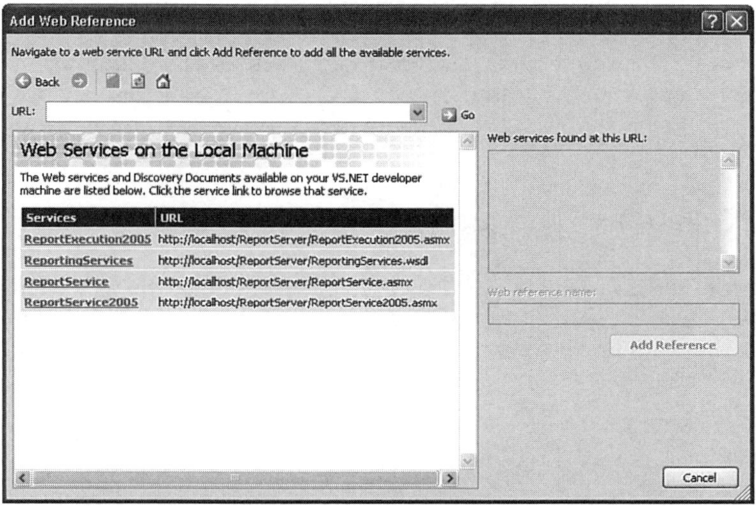

FIGURE 25.2 List of available web services.

Figure 25.2 is a typical list of web services for a computer that just has the Reporting Services web service. The list might be longer if there are any additional web services available on a computer. Four SSRS, which are outlined in Table 25.1, web services (or SSRS web service endpoints) are available in SSRS 2005.

TABLE 25.1 SSRS 2005 Web Services

Services	Typical Endpoint URL (SSRS Installed on `localhost`)	Functionality
ReportExecution2005 *New in 2005*	http://localhost/ReportServer/ReportExecution2005.asmx	Report execution endpoint contains functionality to control report processing and rendering. **Not compatible with SSRS 2000.**
ReportService	http://localhost/ReportServer/ReportService.asmx	SSRS 2000 backward compatibility interface.
ReportService2005 *New in 2005*	http://localhost/ReportServer/ReportService2005.asmx	Report and server management endpoint.

NOTE

To view a Web Service Description Language (WSDL) in a browser, add `?wsdl` after any of SSRS endpoint's URLs, such as http://localhost/ReportServer/ReportService2005.asmx?wsdl.

6. Select one of the web services (SSRS endpoints) after Visual Studio completes this operation (web reference is found).
7. Replace `Server Name` with `ReportExecution2005` in the Web Reference Name text box.
8. Click Add Reference.

Solution Explorer now displays `ReportExecution2005` as one of the web references. To permit the use of types in Reporting Services, you need to add a web proxy reference to each module that uses a web service. In a general case, the syntax of the reference looks like the following:

```
using <<NamespaseUsingWebProxy>>.<<Web Reference Name Given During Proxy
Creation>>;
```

In this specific example, you add:

```
using EmbeddedReport.ReportExecution2005;
using System.Web.Services.Protocols; //to handle SOAP xceptions
```

The second line is added to handle SOAP exceptions.

The following code generates XML output for a report. You can use other formats supported by rendering extensions, such as HTML.

```
static string GetReportXML2005(string ReportingServicesURL,
                               string ReportPath)
{
    //creates a new Web service (proxy) and set its credentials
    ReportExecutionService rs = new ReportExecutionService();
    //windows authentication
    rs.Credentials = System.Net.CredentialCache.DefaultCredentials;

    //Assign Web service url. This is optional operation. Default URL
    //is assigned during the creation of a proxy.
    //Typically http://<<server name>>/ReportServer/ReportExecution2005.asmx
    rs.Url = ReportingServicesURL;

    // Setup Render() call
    byte[] result = null;
    string encoding, mimeType, extension;
```

```
    Warning[] warnings = null;
    string[] streamIDs = null;

    try
    {
        //Should be called prior to Render() to set report's path
        rs.LoadReport(ReportPath, null);

        //Gets a byte stream with Comma Separated Value (XML) layout
        result = rs.Render("XML", null, out extension, out encoding,
                           out mimeType, out warnings, out streamIDs);
        return System.Text.Encoding.ASCII.GetString(result);
    }
    catch (SoapException e)
    {
        //Return exception message, if exception occured
        return e.Message;
    }
}
```

A call to `GetReportXML2005()` below demonstrates an assignment of the `/Samples/DemoList` report in the XML form to a text box `textBoxResult`:

```
textBoxResult.Text = GetReportXML2005(

                   "http://localhost/ReportServer/ReportExecution2005.asmx",

                   "/Samples/DemoList");
```

NOTE

If you want to incorporate the results of `Render()` in the web application, you can pass device information settings to retrieve an HTML fragment that does not contain a BODY element. The call would look similar to the following:

```
result = rs.Render("HTML",
"<DeviceInfo><HTMLFragment>True</HTMLFragment>
</DeviceInfo>", ...);
```

You might have noticed the following assignment in the code `rs.Url = ReportingServicesURL;` this is an optional operation because the web proxy already incorporates the URL of the server for which it was generated. This assignment is beneficial to make the code portable and enable it to access any specified SSRS web service.

Most parameters in the `Render()` function are optional and accept `null` values.

`Warning[] warnings;` contains an array of objects with information about errors and warnings for which SSRS did not generate exceptions. In production code, you need to make sure to incorporate handling for warnings.

The sample uses part of the information available in `SoapException`. `SoapException` has four properties:

- `Actor`—The code that caused exception.
- `Detail`—The XML describing application-specific error information. `Detail` is an `XMLNode` object and inner text from `Detail` can be accessed for the flow control, such as `if(ex.Detail["ErrorCode"].InnerXml == "rsItemNotFound") {/*handle the error*/}`.
- `HelpLink`—A link to a Help file associated with the error.
- `Messsage`—A message describing the error.

The Report Execution web service is very sensitive to the report's path, requires the path to start from "/" (slash), and does not accept URL-encoded strings. If the path is incorrect, web services returns an `ItemNotFoundException` exception. For example, for a report with the name `My DemoList` (note the space after the word My) located in the Samples directory, the URL-encoded path `/Samples/My%20DemoList` is not acceptable. It should cause an error with an exception similar to the following:

```
System.Web.Services.Protocols.SoapException: The item '/Samples/My%20DemoList'
 cannot be found.
---> Microsoft.ReportingServices.Diagnostics.Utilities.ItemNotFoundException:
 The item '/Samples/My%20DemoList' cannot be found.
```

SSRS web service can raise another exception for a missing or incorrect path:

```
System.Web.Services.Protocols.SoapException:
The path of the item "" is not valid.
he path must be less than 260 characters long and must start with slash.
```

The proper way to enter this path is `/Samples/My Demolist` (no URL encoding).

Actions in `GetReportXML2005()` should produce the same result as http://localhost/ReportServer/ReportExecution2005.asmx?/Samples/DemoList&rs:Command=Render&rs:Format=XML. The difference is that the web service call is not interactive, but the web service call allows an application to receive and process a report's XML internally.

The line `rs.Credentials = System.Net.CredentialCache.DefaultCredentials;` is very important. An application must supply credentials to the SSRS web service before it can access a report. `DefaultCredentials` is the Windows authentication for the user. Lack of proper credentials results in an exception:

```
An unhandled exception of type 'System.Net.WebException'
occurred in system.web.services.dll. Additional information:
he request failed with HTTP status 401: Unauthorized.
```

`System.Text.Encoding.ASCII.GetString` is used to convert a `byte[]` array that `Render()` returns to a string. Note that ASCII is an option suitable for text-based formats, such as XML and CSV. Other converters (such as Unicode) are available in the `System.Text.Encoding` namespace.

If you are using this book to assess SSRS 2000 web services, you need to keep in mind that `ReportingServices.asmx` and `ReportService.asmx` are the only available web services in that version. Web service call signatures in SSRS 2000 and SSRS are not always compatible. For example, the `Render()` method in SSRS 2000 has 12 parameters, whereas the same method in `ReportExecution2005.asmx` has 7 parameters. To make a SSRS 2000 style call to the `Render()` method, you have to select `ReportingServices.asmx` and add its reference in the code (here, the proxy name is `ReportingServices`) as follows:

```
using EmbeddedReport.ReportingServices;
```

Then, you replace the inside of a `try` block with the following:

```
ParameterValue[] reportHistoryParameters = null;
result = rs.Render(ReportPath, "XML",
    null, null, null, null, null,
    out encoding, out mimeType,
    out reportHistoryParameters, out warnings, out streamIDs);
return System.Text.Encoding.ASCII.GetString(result);
```

Report Management Web Service *New in 2005* (ReportService2005.asmx)

Previously in this chapter, you saw an example of the Report Execution web service (`ReportExecution2005.asmx`). Most of the report execution functionality is available using URL Access.

In contrast, only a few URL Access methods (such as `ListChildren()`) are available from the Report Management web service (`ReportService2005.asmx`). Thus, the Report Management web service is often used in combination with the Report Execution web service, and sometimes in combination with URL Access, to get the most comprehensive access to SSRS.

To access the Report Management web service, you can follow the same steps used earlier to access the Report Execution web service:

1. Add a web reference to the Report Management web service (`ReportService2005.asmx`).
2. Name the proxy `ReportService2005`.
3. Add a reference to the proxy in the code (using `EmbeddedReport.ReportExecution2005;`).
4. Call Report Management web service methods.

The following is an example of a console application returning items stored on SSRS starting from the root "/" folder.

```
static void Main(string[] args)
{
    //creates new Web service (proxy) and set its credentials
    ReportingService2005 rs = new ReportingService2005();
    rs.Credentials = System.Net.CredentialCache.DefaultCredentials;

    try
    {
        CatalogItem[] items = rs.ListChildren("/", true);

        Console.Write("Item Path, Item Name, Item Type, MimeType");
        foreach (CatalogItem ci in items)
        {
            Console.Write(ci.Path + "," + ci.Name + ","
                                   + ci.Type + "," + ype + "\n");
        }
        return;
    }
    catch (SoapException e)
    {
        Console.Write(e.Message);
    }
}
```

Valid items include `DataSources`, `Folders`, `LinkedReports`, `Reports`, `Resources`, and `Unknown` items.

How to Script Reporting Services (Using the RS Utility)

The RS utility is a scripting utility that enables access to Reporting Services functionality using Visual Basic .NET scripts. In scripts, you can define classes and use other object-oriented functionality of Visual Basic .NET.

By default, the RS utility is installed in the `C:\Program Files\Microsoft SQL Server\90\Tools\Binn` directory. SSRS comes with four sample scripts (located at `C:\Program Files\Microsoft SQL Server\90\Samples\Reporting Services\Script Samples`): deploy a report, cancel a job, set security on an item (report, folder, and so on), and change SSRS properties. You can dissect and modify those scripts to fit scenarios at hand. Scripting is a convenient way to automate repetitive administrative tasks or tasks that apply to a group of items.

Executing the "`rs /?`" command yields the following usage direction:

```
Microsoft (R) Reporting Services RS
Version 9.00.1399.00 x86
Executes script file contents against the specified Report Server.
RS -i inputfile -s serverURL [-u username] [-p password]
   [-l timeout] [-b] [-e endpoint] [-v var=value] [-t]

        -i  inputfile   Script file to execute
        -s  serverURL   URL (including server and vroot) to execute
                        script against.
        -u  username    User name used to log in to the server.
        -p  password    Password used to log in to the server.
        -e  endpoint    Web service endpoint to use with the script.
                        Options are:
                        Exec2005 - The ReportExecution2005 endpoint
                        Mgmt2005 - The ReportService2005 endpoint
                        Mgmt2000 - (Deprecated) The ReportService endpoint
        -l  timeout     Number of seconds before the connection to the
                        server times out. Default is 60 seconds and 0 is
                        infinite time out.
        -b              Run as a batch and rollback if commands fail
        -v  var=value   Variables and values to pass to the script
        -t  trace       Include trace information in error message
```

The following sample script gets a list of extensions registered with Reporting Services and, as a bonus, outputs the Report Server version and edition.

```
Public Sub Main()
    Dim Extensions As Extension() =
                                  rs.ListExtensions(ExtensionTypeEnum.All)

    Console.WriteLine("Report Server Version Number:" +

rs.ServerInfoHeaderValue.ReportServerVersionNumber)
    Console.WriteLine("Report Server Edition:" +
rs.ServerInfoHeaderValue.ReportServerEdition)
    Dim Ext As Extension
    Dim Type As String

    Console.WriteLine("Type      Name")

    For Each Ext In  Extensions
        Select Ext.ExtensionType
                        Case ExtensionTypeEnum.Delivery
                        Type = "Delivery"
                Case ExtensionTypeEnum.Render
                        Type = "Render  "
        Case ExtensionTypeEnum.Data
```

```
                Type = "Data     "
            Case Else
                Type = "Other    "
        End Select
        Console.WriteLine(Type + "   " + Ext.Name)
    Next
End Sub
```

`ReportServerVersionNumber` and `ReportServerEdition` are properties of Reporting Services. You need to call Reporting Services before the properties are set. If you place this call after you access Reporting Services properties, those properties will be empty. This is what you are doing in line `Extension()=rs.ListExtensions(ExtensionTypeEnum.All)`.

The scripting utility provides an internal reference to Reporting Services through the `rs` object, which is ready to be used in scripts without an explicit instance creation. The command to execute the script might look like the following:

```
rs -iRsUtilTest.rss -shttp://localhost/ReportServer
```

Working with Report Parameters

Report parameters are encapsulated by two classes: The `ParameterValue` class allows developers to set and retrieve report parameter values and the `ReportParameter` class is used to `Get` and `Set` properties of a parameter. Both `ParameterValue` and `ReportParameter` are necessary to get complete information about a parameter. However, the `ParameterValue` class is sufficient to set and retrieve values of a parameter. The following code snippet shows how to pass parameters to render a function. You can incorporate this code into the `GetReportXML2005()` function written earlier in this chapter by replacing the inside of the `try` block with the following code:

```
ParameterValue[] parameters = new ParameterValue[1];
parameters[0] = new ParameterValue();
parameters[0].Name = "SalesOrderNumber";
parameters[0].Value = "SO43659";
rs.SetExecutionParameters(parameters, "en-us");
result = rs.Render(format, devInfo, out extension,
                   out encoding, out mimeType,
                   out warnings, out streamIDs);
return System.Text.Encoding.ASCII.GetString(result);
```

In the previous example, you can see two out of three string properties of the `ParameterValue` class: `Name` and `Value`. The third property is a `Label` and is used as an alternate name for a parameter.

Note the usage of the `SetExecutionParameters()` function that assigns the parameter and parameter's language (because this is optional, you can pass `null`) to the current execution of a report.

`ReportParameter` is used in conjunction with `GetReportParameters()` and `SetReportParameters()`. `GetReportParameters()` retrieves a report's parameters properties (`ReportParameter` class) and can validate if an array of `ParameterValue` values passed to this function are acceptable for a report; `SetReportParameters()` sets properties of parameters. Commonly used public properties of the `ReportParameter` class are outlined in Table 25.2.

TABLE 25.2 Commonly Used Public Properties of the `ReportParameter` Class

Name	Description
AllowBlank	Indicates whether an empty string is a valid value for the parameter
DefaultValues	Gets or sets the default value of the parameter
DefaultValuesQueryBased	Indicates whether the default values of the parameter are based on a query
ErrorMessage	Indicates the error message returned when a parameter value has failed validation
MultiValue	Indicates whether the parameter is a multivalued parameter
Name	Gets or sets the name of a parameter
Nullable	Indicates whether the value of the parameter can be null
Prompt	Gets or sets the text that prompts the user for parameter values
PromptUser	Indicates whether the user is prompted for the value of the parameter
QueryParameter	Indicates whether the parameter is used in a query
ValidValues	Indicates the available ValidValues objects for the parameter
ValidValuesQueryBased	Indicates whether the parameter's valid values are based on a query

As you can probably tell, the `ReportParameter` class properties directly correspond to the report parameter properties that were set during the design phase. See Chapter 10, "Report Parameters."

Security When Calling a Web Service

Out of the box, SSRS supports Windows authentication and authorization. If you need to have custom authentication, SSRS provides this through custom authentication (or security) extensions. You have to develop a new security extension to handle custom authentication.

.NET Framework greatly simplifies Windows and Basic authentication handling through classes in the `System.Net` namespace.

Prior to deciding which authentication method to use, consider security implications of each form of authentication and SSRS virtual directory settings in IIS; see Figure 25.3.

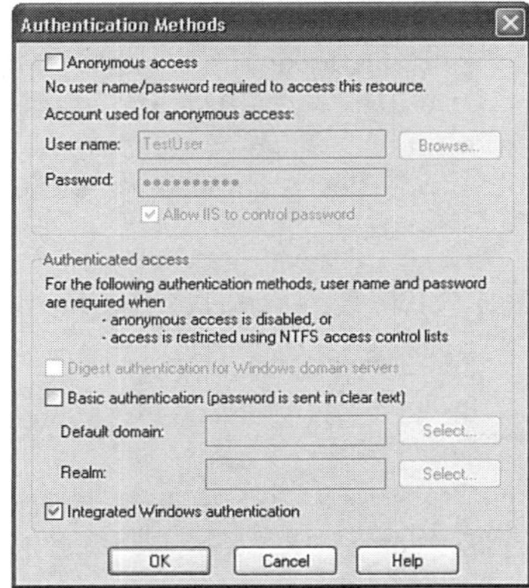

FIGURE 25.3 SSRS virtual directory settings in IIS.

As you might recall, we leveraged the .NET Framework to set Windows credentials in the `GetReportXML2005()` method earlier in this chapter:

```
rs.Credentials = System.Net.CredentialCache.DefaultCredentials;
```

To pass Basic authentication credentials, you can substitute the preceding code with the following code:

```
rs.Credentials = new System.Net.NetworkCredentials("user name", "password",
➥ "domain");
```

The credentials must be set prior to the use of any methods in SSRS web service. Calls to a web service method prior to setting credentials receive an error: `HTTP 401 Error: Access Denied`.

To increase security of web method calls, an administrator can configure IIS and SSRS to use SSL communications. SSRS uses `SecureConnectionLevel` (located in `RSReportServer.config`) to determine which web service methods require SSL connection. The default is `0` (noted in the configuration as `<Add Key="SecureConnectionLevel" Value="0" />`). `SecureConnectionLevel` has four levels that affect URL and SOAP interfaces that SSRS exposes:

- `0`—SSRS does not check for secure connections (SSL). Method calls can still be made over SSL (HTTPS) connections, if needed.
- `1`—SSRS checks for secure connections. If SSL is not available, the web service rejects the method (such as `CreateReport()` and `GetReportDefinition()`) calls that can pass sensitive information (such as user credentials). Because this setting is checked at the server, it is still possible to make a call that passes credentials before the web service handles the request. Method calls can still be made over SSL (HTTPS)

connections, if needed. Because `Render()` is not restricted by this setting, it might be possible for a hacker to intercept sensitive data from a report.

- 2—Most method calls, including `Render()`, are required to use SSL.
- 3—All method calls are required to use SSL. In this case, SSRS requires SSL/HTTPS for all web service method calls.

Some of the Commonly Used Methods with Short Code Snippets

All snippets require a proper SSRS endpoint reference as described earlier in the chapter, web and SOAP proxy references, and the following calls prior to calling any of the methods:

```
ReportingService2005 rs = new ReportingService2005();
rs.Credentials = System.Net.CredentialCache.DefaultCredentials;
```

- Find and cancel all jobs

```
Job[] jobs = null;
jobs = rs.ListJobs(); //Get a list of current jobs.
foreach (Job job in jobs)
{
   if (job.Status == JobStatusEnum.Running || job.Status ==
➥JobStatusEnum.New)
   {
      rs.CancelJob(job.JobID);
   }
}
```

- Create a folder item

```
rs.CreateFolder(strFolderName, strParentFolderName, null);
```

- Create a report item

```
FileStream stream = File.OpenRead("sample.rdl");
Byte[] rdl = new Byte[stream.Length];
stream.Read(rdl, 0, (int) stream.Length);
stream.Close();
rs.CreateReport(strReportName, strFolderName, false, rdl, null);
```

- Delete an item

```
rs.DeleteItem(strItemPath)
```

- Get an RDL of a report from SSRS

```
System.Xml.XmlDocument doc = new System.Xml.XmlDocument();
byte[] reportDefinition = rs.GetReportDefinition(strReportName);
MemoryStream stream = new MemoryStream(reportDefinition);
doc.Load(stream);
doc.Save(@"C:\sample.rdl");
```

Method calls can also be grouped together and executed as a single transaction, that is, commit and rollback as a whole. The following code snippet shows how this could be accomplished:

```
BatchHeader bh = new BatchHeader();
bh.BatchID = rs.CreateBatch();
rs.BatchHeaderValue = bh;
rs.<<MethodCall, like DeleteItem>>;
rs.<<MethodCall>>;
...
rs.ExecuteBatch();
```

Summary

SSRS web service complements URL Access with full access to SSRS management and configuration functionality. An application that incorporates both report viewing and report management functionality would typically use both URL Access and the SSRS web service. SSRS web service's function `Render()` allows you to retrieve a byte stream of a rendered report and use it for SSRS integration. SSRS comes with the `rs.exe` utility for scripting of the SSRS web service access using Visual Basic .NET scripts. The `rs.exe` utility is frequently used to automate high-volume management tasks: report deployment, security management, and so on.

Writing Custom Reporting Services Extensions

CHAPTER 26

IN THIS CHAPTER

- Common Considerations for Custom Reporting Services Extensions: Implementation, Deployment, and Security
- Delivery Extension
- Interactions Between User, SSRS, and a Delivery Extension

SSRS is designed for extensibility. In the previous chapters, you learned how to extend SSRS' reporting capabilities by writing a custom code that can be called from a report. Extensions, on another hand, are called by SSRS. Extensions are composed of four key categories: security, delivery, data processing, and rendering (see Chapter 3, "Reporting Services Architecture," Figure 3.1).

Typical extensions installed with SSRS are as follows:

- **Data processing**—Microsoft SQL Server, OLE DB (including OLEDBMD for Microsoft SQL Server Analysis Services), Oracle, ODBC, and XML. XML was one of the most frequent requests for data extensions in SSRS 2000. Many developers are happy to see XML data sources in SSRS 2005. Additional extensions that can be deployed in this category are SQL Server Integration Services (SSIS) and SAP data-processing extensions.
- **Delivery**—File share, eMail, NULL.
- **Render**—Excel, MHTML, HTML3.2, HTML4.0 (Microsoft Internet Explorer 5.0 or later), PDF, IMAGE (graphical image output, such as TIF, GIF, JPG), CSV, XML, NULL (used to place reports in cache and in conjunction with scheduled execution and delivery).

- **Other**—`SemanticQuery` and `ModelGeneration` to extend Report Builder's functionality. `EventProcessing` to act on the events generated by Report Server.

Security extensions are not typically installed. By default, SSRS uses Windows integrated authentication. A complete list of extensions installed on a particular instance of SSRS can be retrieved by calling `ReportingService2005.ListExtensions(ExtensionTypeEnum.All)` or by examining the `rsreportserver.config` file.

Rendering is, perhaps, the most developed category of extensions. With a wide range of rendering extensions and a multitude of applications (including Microsoft Office) that "understand" HTML, it is hard to think of a new rendering extension that would be immediately useful.

Some of the SSRS capabilities that customers are frequently looking for and that are currently not available "out of the box" are as follows:

- **Printer (fax) delivery**—The ability to print (fax) batches of reports without human interactions
- **.NET data set access**—An ability to access a data set that was created inside of an application
- **Custom authentication**—An ability to authenticate non-Windows clients

It is possible to work around the need to have certain functionality. For example, instead of delivery to a printer directly from SSRS, an administrator can configure delivery of a report to a file share and have a separate process monitoring and printing from such a file share by using the Windows `PRINT` command, such as `PRINT /D:\\<server URL>\<printer name> <files to print>`.

It is also possible to work around the scenario in which users cannot use Windows authentication. An administrator can create a Windows account for a user, configure IIS to accept Basic authentication (must enable SSL for better security), and ask the user to enter Windows credentials to access a report.

Although it is possible to work around some of the limitations, custom extensions can offer elegant solutions to supplement missing functionality.

A custom extension is a private or shared .NET assembly with a unique namespace (the exact name is not important, but it must be unique), and a class that implements the `IExtension` interface and one or more interfaces shown in Table 26.1. As with any .NET implementation, Visual Studio is the most frequently used development tool for development of assemblies and, therefore, extensions.

TABLE 26.1 Typical Set of Interfaces Used in Custom Extensions

Interface(s)	Applied to an Extension Category	Description
`IAuthenticationExtension`	Security	Implementation of this interface extends the authentication feature of SSRS. This interface is derived from `IExtension`.
`IAuthorizationExtension`	Security	Implementation of this interface extends the authorization feature of SSRS. This interface is not Common Language Specification (CLS)–compliant. This means that not all .NET languages can call or implement this interface; also C# and VB.NET can deal with this interface just fine. This interface is derived from `IExtension`.
`IDbConnection`, `[IDbConnectionExtension]`, `IDbTransaction`, `[IDbTransactionExtension]`, `IDbCommand`, `[IDbCommandAnalysis]`, `[IDbCommandRewriter]`, `IDataParameter`, `[IDataMultiValueParameter]`, `IDataParameterCollection`, `IDataReader`, `[IDataReaderExtension]`	Data processing	[Optional] and required interfaces of a class that implements a data-processing extension. Those interfaces are modeled after .NET data provider interfaces and defined in the `Microsoft.ReportingServices.DataProcessing` namespace.
`IDeliveryExtension`	Delivery	Implementation of this interface interacts with SSRS to share and validate an extension's settings and to execute delivery. This interface is derived from `IExtension`.
`IDeliveryReportServerInformation`	Delivery	Implementation of this interface is used in conjunction with `IDeliveryExtension`. SSRS supplies information about itself through this interface.
`IRenderStream`	Rendering	Implementation of this interface provides support for multiple streams rendering from a rendering extension.

TABLE 26.1 Continued

Interface(s)	Applied to an Extension Category	Description
`IRenderingExtension`	Rendering	Implementation of this interface is required for a rendering extension so the extension is recognized by SSRS. This interface is defined in the `Microsoft.ReportingServices.ReportingRendering` namespace.
`[ISubscriptionBaseUIUserControl]`	Delivery	Implementation of this interface provides a subscription UI for the Report Manager. This interface is what shows data-entry fields. For example, in the case of an email, it displays an interface to enter "TO:" email address, and so on. This interface extends `IExtension`. This interface is optional because a subscription can be created using SOAP API methods `CreateSubscription` and `CreateDataDrivenSubscription`. The class that inherits from this interface must also inherit from `System.Web.UI.WebControls.WebControl`.

Common Considerations for Custom Reporting Services Extensions: Implementation, Deployment, and Security

The reporting library provides three namespaces that supply interface definitions, classes, and value types that allow extensions to interact with SSRS:

- `Microsoft.ReportingServices.DataProcessing`—Used to extend the data-processing capability of SSRS.
- `Microsoft.ReportingServices.Interfaces`—Used to build delivery and security extensions.

  This namespace also allows you to maintain a cross-connection state. A class that implements the `IExtension` interface from this namespace is kept in memory for as long as SSRS is running.
- `Microsoft.ReportingServices.ReportRendering`—Used to extend the rendering capabilities of SSRS. This namespace is used in conjunction with the `Microsoft.ReportingServices.Interfaces` namespace.

Before you can successfully compile an extension, you must supply the reference to one or more `Microsoft.ReportingServices` namespaces as follows:

```
using Microsoft.ReportingServices.Interfaces;
```

A namespace can have optional interfaces, such as `IDbConnectionExtension` in `Microsoft.ReportingServices.DataProcessing`, and required interfaces, such as `IDbConnection` in the same extension's namespace. When an interface is required and a developer chooses not to implement a particular property or method of the interface, it is a best practice to throw a `NotSupportedException`. `NotSupportedException` is most appropriate for this purpose as it indicates methods (and properties) that did not provide implementation for methods described in the base classes (interfaces). The next best alternative is `NotImplementedException`. Note that optional interfaces do not require implementation at all.

Any Common Language Runtime (CLR) application interacts with the CLR security system. This book briefly covered the basics of .NET security in Chapter 23, "How to Create and Call a Custom Assembly from a Report," specifically in the section ".NET Security Primer for a SSRS Administrator." The same principles apply to extensions. Local security settings and SSRS configuration files define the code permissions that an extension's assembly receives. SSRS extensions must be a part of a code group that has the `FullTrust` permission set.

To deploy an assembly, a SSRS administrator must have appropriate permissions to write to the Report Server directory, Report Designer directory, and configuration files.

When a Report Server first loads an extension in memory, the Report Server accesses an assembly using service account credentials. Service account credentials are needed so an extension can read configuration files, access system resources, and load dependent assemblies (if needed). After an initial load, the Report Server runs an assembly using credentials of the user who is currently logged in.

An extension can be deployed for use by the Report Server, Report Manager, Report Designer, or all of the above. This is provided that the extension can be used by a tool. For example, Report Manager only uses delivery extensions.

The deployment procedure for an extension used by the Report Server, Report Manager, or Report Designer is basically the same, the only difference is the deployment directory and configuration files that need to be modified. To simplify further discussion, this book uses the following abbreviations:

- **`{AssmDir}`**—To abbreviate assembly deployment directories. The default Report Server binary directory is `C:\Program Files\Microsoft SQL Server\MSSQL.3\Reporting Services\ReportServer\bin`. The default Report Designer binary directory is `C:\Program Files\Microsoft Visual Studio 8\Common7\IDE\PrivateAssemblies`. The default Report Manager binary directory is `C:\Program Files\Microsoft SQL Server\MSSQL.3\Reporting Services\ReportManager\bin`.

- **{ConfigFile}**—To abbreviate configuration files (note the default file path). The default location for the Report Server configuration file is `C:\Program Files\Microsoft SQL Server\MSSQL.3\Reporting Services\ReportServer\`**`RSReportServer.config`**. The default location for the Report Designer configuration file is `C:\Program Files\Microsoft Visual Studio 8\Common7\IDE\PrivateAssemblies\`**`RSReportDesigner.config`**. The default location for the Report Manager configuration file is `C:\Program Files\Microsoft SQL Server\MSSQL.3\Reporting Services\ReportManager\`**`RSWebApplication.config`**.
- **{SecConfig}**—To abbreviate security configuration files. The default location for the Report Server security configuration file is `C:\Program Files\Microsoft SQL Server\MSSQL.3\Reporting Services\ReportServer\`**`RsSrvPolicy.config`**. The default location for the Report Designer security configuration file is `C:\Program Files\Microsoft Visual Studio 8\Common7\IDE\PrivateAssemblies\`**`RSPreviewPolicy.config`**. The default location for the Report Manager security configuration is `C:\Program Files\Microsoft SQL Server\MSSQL.3\Reporting Services\ReportServer\`**`RsMgrPolicy.config.`**

To deploy an extension, a report administrator can use the following steps:

1. Copy an extension assembly to the `{AssmDir}` directory. Remember to substitute `{AssmDir}` with any of the three directories this shortcut abbreviation. If an assembly with the same name exists in the `{AssmDir}` directory, stop the Report Server service, copy an assembly, and then restart the Report Server service.
2. Locate an entry in the `{ConfigFile}` under the `<Extensions>` tag tag ({ConfigFile} directories)> tag> that corresponds to a category (`{ExtCategory}`) of an extension: `<Delivery>`, `<Data>`, `<Render>`, `<Security>` (Authorization), `<Authentication>`, or `<DeliveryUI>`.
3. Add an entry for a newly created extension to a `{ConfigFile}`.

```
<Extensions>
   ...
   <(ExtCategory}>
      <Extension
          Name="{Unique extension name up to 255 characters}"
          Type="{Fully qualified name of the class implementing
➥ IExtension},
                {AssemblyName without .dll}"
          Visible="{false¦true; false indicates that extension is not
➥ visible in UI}"
      >
      {optional configuration data}
      </Extension>
   </(ExtCategory}>
   ...
</Extensions>
```

An example of `CustomFileShareProvider` for `rsreportserver.config` is as follows:

```
<Extensions>
   <Delivery>
       <Extension
         Name="Report Server Custom FileShare"
         Type="MyCorp.FileShareDeliveryProvider.CustomFileShareProviderClass,
         CustomFileShareProviderAssembly"
       >
       <MaxRetries>3</MaxRetries>
       <SecondsBeforeRetry>900</SecondsBeforeRetry>
       <Configuration>
          <StoreResultsAt>
            <FileShare>\\myserver1\result</FileShare>
            <FileShare>\\myserver2\result</FileShare>
          </StoreResultsAt>
        </Configuration>
      </Extension>
      ...
```

When an extension that implements the `IExtension` interface is invoked, SSRS calls two methods of the `IExtension` interface: `SetConfiguration` and `LocalizedName`. SSRS passes an XML fragment between `<Configuration>` and `</Configuration>` tags in the configuration file as a parameter to `SetConfiguration`, so the extension can take advantage of the flexibility that configuration offers. The `LocalizedName` property targets user interface implementations (such as Report Manager) and should return values for various languages. This way, an extension can be used around the world and does not have to be recompiled every time the extension is deployed in a new locale.

4. Finally, an administrator can grant `FullTrust` permission for an assembly by modifying the `{SecConfig}` file:

```
<CodeGroup class="UnionCodeGroup"
   version="1"
   PermissionSetName="FullTrust"
   Name="MyExtensionCodeGroup"
   >
      <IMembershipCondition class="UrlMembershipCondition"
         version="1"
         Url="C:\Program Files\Microsoft SQL Server\MSSQL\Reporting
Services\ReportServer\bin\MyExtensionAssembly.dll"
      />
</CodeGroup>
```

5. An administrator can verify deployment of an extension by using the `ListExtensions` method.

NOTE

Additional details about security are covered in Chapter 23, specifically in the section ".NET Security Primer for a SSRS Administrator."

To debug a deployed extension, complete the following steps:

1. Determine the processes that access the extension. For example, for a delivery extension that is accessed by Report Manager (because Report Manager runs in the content of IIS), the process is `aspnet_wp.exe` or `w3wp.exe`. Similarly, the subscription notification event is handled by SSRS, and SSRS (the process is `ReportingServicesService.exe`) invokes a delivery extension to execute a delivery. A data-processing extension can be accessed by Report Manager and from within an instance of Visual Studio (the process is `devenv.exe`).
2. Set breakpoints in the extension's code.
3. Attach Visual Studio to the calling process using, for example, the Debug, Attach to Process menu. The Attach to Process dialog box opens. You need to make sure that Show Processes from All Users check box is selected, after which you can select a process to attach to, and click Attach.
4. As the extension is invoked, Visual Studio breaks at set breakpoints, and you can step through the code.

Delivery Extension

The delivery extension sample is one of the three samples supplied by Microsoft and is installed by default in the directory `C:\Program Files\Microsoft SQL Server\90\Samples\Reporting Services\Extension Samples\PrinterDelivery Sample`.

Most of the delivery extensions require the Report Server Windows service to run under domain account credentials. Both email and printer delivery extensions, for example, require this condition to be satisfied. The first indicator that this condition is not satisfied is SSRS returning an error message: "`The Report Server has encountered a configuration error.`"

This error message is displayed in a `Status` column of Report Manager. More details of the error message are recorded to the SSRS log file (the default location is `C:\Program Files\Microsoft SQL Server\MSSQL.3\Reporting Services\LogFiles`):

```
ReportingServicesService!library!4!11/01/2005-17:21:40:: e ERROR:
Throwing Microsoft.ReportingServices.Diagnostics.Utilities.
➥ServerConfigurationErrorException: The report server has encountered
➥a configuration error. See the report server log files for more
➥ information., AuthzInitializeContextFromSid: Win32 error: 1355;
➥ Info: Microsoft.ReportingServices.Diagnostics.Utilities.
➥ ServerConfigurationErrorException: The report server has encountered
➥ a configuration error. See the report server log files for more information.
```

TIP

Error messages containing `AuthzInitializeContextFromSid` usually refer to incorrect configurations in access security to domain-level resources. One of the most frequent causes of this error is when the SSRS service is not configured to run under a domain account.

A delivery extension spends part of its "life" responding to subscription-related requests from SSRS and part responding to delivery-related requests from SSRS.

In addition to the `IExtension` interface, a delivery extension should also implement the `IDeliveryExtension` interface; see Table 26.2.

TABLE 26.2 Members of the IDeliveryExtension Interface

Property or Method	Name	Description
P	`ExtensionSettings`	Provides list of settings to SSRS. The settings are used by both subscription and delivery mechanisms. Report Manager uses this setting and an implementation of `ISubscriptionBaseUIUserControl` to present a UI to enter settings. For example, in the case of email delivery, this is "To:", "Subject:", "Priority", and so on. In the case of file share delivery, it is "Path:", "Render Format:", credentials to access the file share, and so on. So the settings are available during delivery, SSRS stores settings in a `Notification` object and passes `Notification` as a parameter to the `Deliver` method.
P	`IsPrivilegedUser`	Indicates whether the user is allowed access to all the functionality of the extension. This property is required so SSRS can manage the extension. SSRS sets this property to `false` (default) if the user accessing the extension does not have the `Manage All Subscriptions` permission as a part of her role.
P	`ReportServerInformation`	Contains the names of rendering extensions supported by a SSRS instance.
M	`Deliver`	Delivers the report to a user based on the contents of the notification. The notification contains information retrieved through the `ExtensionSettings` property, such as an email address for the email delivery.

TABLE 26.2 Continued

Property or Method	Name	Description
M	`ValidateUserData`	Determines whether a given set of delivery extension settings is valid. For example, this method can validate whether an email address provided as a setting is properly formatted.

Interactions Between User, SSRS, and a Delivery Extension

Figure 26.1 provides a partial class diagram for the printer delivery extension.

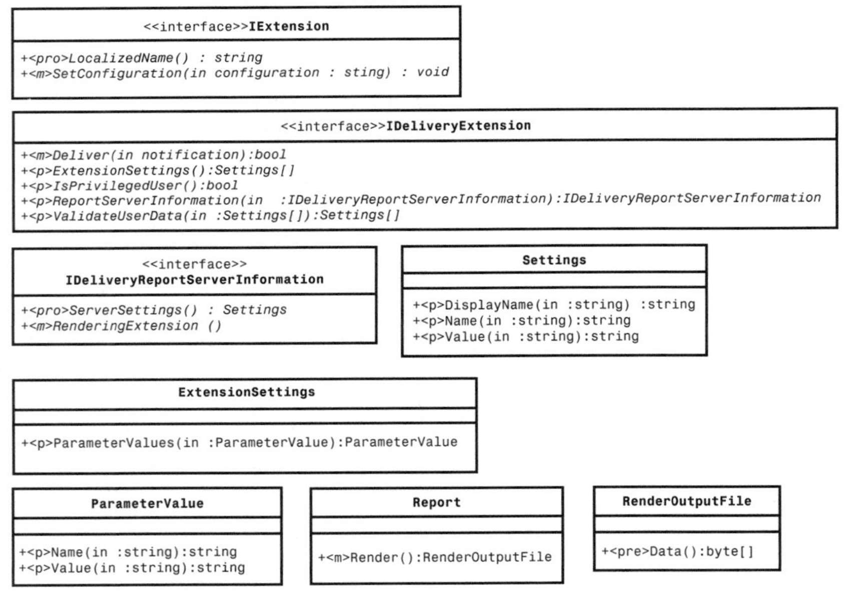

FIGURE 26.1 Partial class diagram for the printer delivery extension.

The user interacts with SSRS to create a subscription. The interaction could be done from a custom application using a SOAP API call to the SSRS web service's method `CreateSubscription()`. The interaction can also be performed through Report Manager, which performs the following:

- Interacts with `ISubscriptionBaseUIUserControl` implementation inside of a delivery extension to present a UI for data entry

- Collects data and passes data as `CreateSubscription()` parameters
- Interacts with SSRS to create a subscription, as presented in Figure 26.2

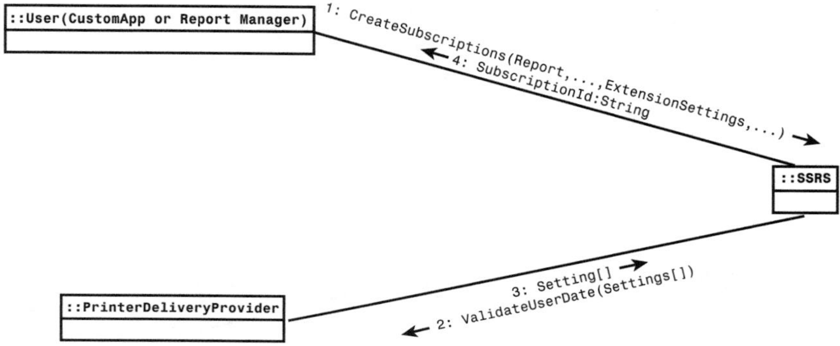

FIGURE 26.2 An application's interaction with SSRS to create a subscription.

Along with other parameters, `CreateSubscription()` accepts the full pathname of the report and the `ExtensionSettings` object, which, in turn, contain `ParameterValue` objects. `ParameterValue` objects contain name-value pairs with information that a delivery extension expects. For example, for email delivery, one of the parameter values is `"TO:"` information:

```
extensionParams(0) = New ParameterValue()
extensionParams(0).Name = "TO"
extensionParams(0).Value = "administrator@adventure-works.com"
```

SSRS then fills settings with information from `ParameterValue` and passes settings to a delivery extension for the validation (`ValidateUserData()` call). After being validated, SSRS stores settings with the subscription and returns a `SubscriptionID` string to a user.

When the time to "fire" a subscription comes, the SSRS scheduling engine sends a notification event to the Scheduling and Delivery Processor. See Figure 26.3 for the subscription delivery process.

The Schedule and Delivery Processor receives a notification event, matches it to the subscription, creates a `Notification` object, and calls the `Deliver` method in a delivery extension, passing `Notification` as a parameter of the call.

The delivery extension leverages SSRS's rendering extensions, using the `Notification.Report.Render` method. The `Notification.Report.Render` method returns the `RenderOutputFile` object. The `RenderOutputFile.Data` property contains a stream with a rendered report.

The delivery extension then "decides" what to do with the stream. In the case of the printer delivery extension, the stream is converted to a metafile and printed using functionality from the `System.Drawing.Printing` namespace.

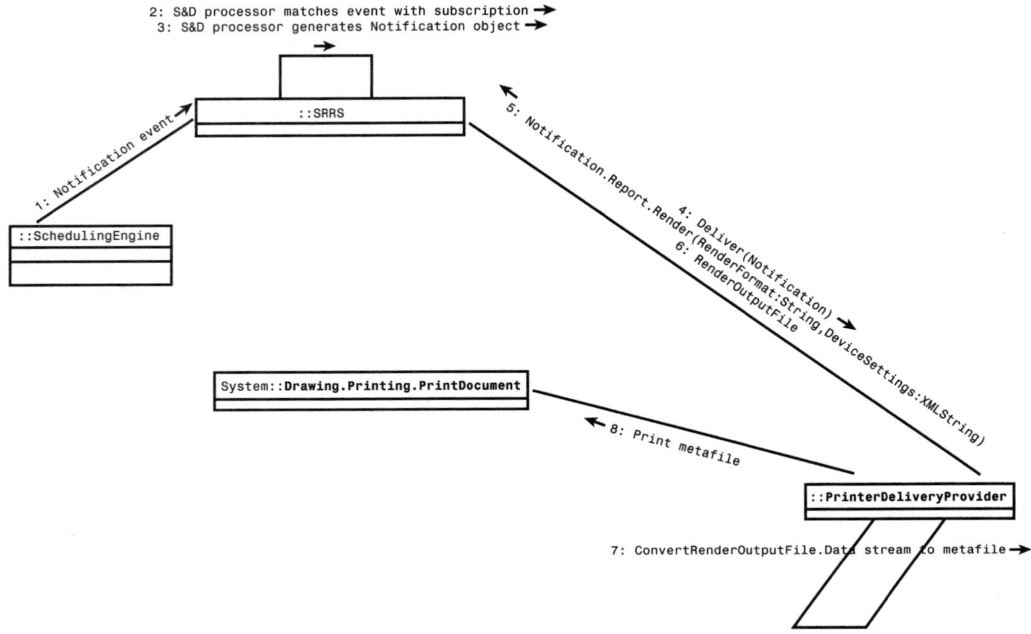

FIGURE 26.3 An application's interaction with SSRS to deliver a subscription to a printer.

Summary

SSRS supplies an infrastructure (interfaces, classes, value types, and customizable configurations) to allow developers to extend SSRS' capabilities. Developers can write extensions to extend security, delivery, data processing, and rendering functionality of SSRS.

Although extensions require more in-depth understanding of SSRS' inner workings and supporting infrastructure, the need to provide custom functionality sometimes takes a developer to the realm of extensions. The experience to see an extension coming to "life" is certainly very rewarding.

CHAPTER 27

Report Rendering Controls and SharePoint Services Web Parts

IN THIS CHAPTER

- Microsoft Visual Studio 2005 ReportViewer Web and Windows Controls *New in 2005*
- Microsoft SharePoint Web Parts

Microsoft Visual Studio 2005 ReportViewer Web and Windows Controls *New in 2005*

Visual Studio 2005 includes the freely distributable ReportViewer Windows and web forms controls.

ReportViewer greatly simplifies embedding of reports in an application.

The ReportViewer Windows control is shown in Figure 27.1.

ReportViewer can provide both standalone (local processing mode) and server-based (remote processing mode) rendering.

When ReportViewer is used in local processing mode:

- ReportViewer renders a report using built-in rendering capabilities of the control and then presents it to a user.
- SSRS is not used by ReportViewer to process a report in local processing mode.
- An application provides a client report definition (`.rdlc`) file, which has to be a part of the project and a data set for the control.

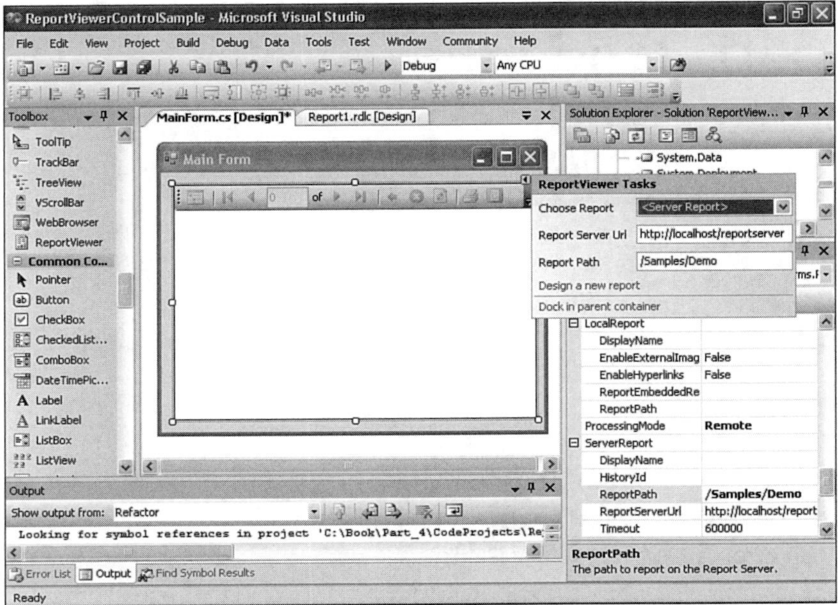

FIGURE 27.1 ReportViewer Windows control.

NOTE

Note that report definition file used for local processing has an extension of `.rdlc`. The extension denotes client RDL files. See http://msdn2.microsoft.com/ms252067.aspx for additional details.

The process to design client reports (`.rdlc` files) is different from designing server-based (`.rdl`) reports. `.rdlc` and `.rdl` files have a slightly different structure, but can be converted into each other.

Assume that you have already created a Windows or web form project. To display a report in ReportViewer, using the local processing mode, first you need to add a new data set using the following steps:

1. In Solution Explorer, right-click on the project (not the solution), point to Add, and select New Item. In the Add New Item dialog box, click DataSet. Enter a name for the data set (call it DSEmployeeEmail), and click Add. This adds a new XSD file named DSEmployeeEmail.xsd to the project and opens the DataSet Designer.
2. In DataSet Designer mode, open the Toolbox, and drag a TableAdapter onto the DataSet design surface. This launches the TableAdapter Configuration Wizard.
3. On the Choose Your Data Connection page, click New Connection. In the Data Source dialog box, select Microsoft SQL Server. Create connection to AdventureWorks database. Accept the default name AdventureWorksConnectionString. Click Next.

4. On the Choose the Command Type page, select Use SQL Statements.
5. On the Enter a SQL Statement page, enter the following T-SQL query (or use Query Builder), and then click Finish:

```
SELECT Person.Contact.FirstName, Person.Contact.LastName,
➥ Person.Contact.EmailAddress
FROM Person.Contact INNER JOIN HumanResources.Employee
ON Person.Contact.ContactID = HumanResources.Employee.ContactID
```

6. Click the Advanced Options button, deselect all check boxes in the Advanced Options dialog box, accept, and click Next.
7. On the Choose Methods to Generate page, accept the defaults Fill a DataTable with Method name Fill and Return a DataTable with Method name GetData. Click Next.
8. On the Wizard Results page, click Finish.

To create a client report that consumes the DSEmployeeEmail data set, complete the following steps:

1. In Solution Explorer, right-click Reports, point to Add, and click New Item.
2. In the Add New Item dialog box, click Report. In Name, type EmployeeEmails.rdlc and then click Add to open a graphical design surface. This is the Report Designer component of Visual Studio 2005.

NOTE

Note how Report Designer's interface for `.rdlc` reports is different from the one you have used to develop server-based reports for Report Server projects. For `.rdlc` reports, there is only a layout design interface. Data or Preview tabs are not available. In the case of `.rdlc` reports, DataSet Designer performs similar functions to the Data tab, and project execution/debugging performs functions of the Preview tab.

3. Finish designing the report layout, using techniques learned previously in the book. From the Toolbox window, drag and drop a Table report item on the report. In the Data Sources window, expand the DSEmployeeEmail data set and drag `FirstName`, `LastName`, and `EmailAddress` fields to the detail row of the table.

Complete the third and final set of steps to consume the client report in the ReportViewer control:

1. From the Toolbox window, drag and drop a ReportViewer control to Form1. (It was created automatically as a part of a project; you can rename it as needed.)

2.A. Click on the ReportViewer control and click on the tag to launch the ReportViewer Task panel. Click Choose Report from the drop-down and select a report that you want to display. Report names are shown in the form `<Project Name>.<Report Name>.rdlc`.

2.B. Alternatively, you can set ReportViewer's properties as follows:

- Set `PProcessingMode` to Local
- Expand LocalReport and set the `ReportEmbeddedResource` property to the name of the report form `<Project Name>.<Report Name>.rdlc`.

2.C. Alternatively, you can programmatically manipulate the ReportViewer control, as in the following code sample:

```
//To ensure that report is processed in the local processing mode
reportViewer.ProcessingMode = Microsoft.Reporting.WinForms.ProcessingMode.Local;

//Setup Report path
reportViewer.LocalReport.ReportEmbeddedResource=
                "ReportViewerControlSample_LocalProcessing.EmployeeEmails.rdlc";

//Render report
reportViewer.RefreshReport();
```

The `ReportViewerControlSample-LocalProcessing` project is included as a sample for this book and demonstrates ReportViewer in the local processing mode.

When used in the remote processing mode, ReportViewer performs the following tasks:

- First leverages SSRS to render a report
- Then retrieves a rendered report from SSRS and presents it to a user

To display a report in ReportViewer, using the remote processing mode, set ReportViewer's properties as follows:

- Set `ProcessingMode` to Remote
- Set `ReportServerUrl` to the URL of a Report Server, for example http://localhost/reportserver
- Set `ReportPath` to the path of the report on the server, for example `/Part2/RelationalDBReports/Sales Order`

Alternatively, you can programmatically set ReportViewer's properties and render a report as needed in your application using the following code snippet:

```
//To ensure that report is processed in the remote processing mode
reportViewer.ProcessingMode = Microsoft.Reporting.WinForms.ProcessingMode.Remote;
```

```
//Setup Report Server Url and Report path
reportViewer.ServerReport.ReportServerUrl = new Uri(txtReportServerUrl.Text);
reportViewer.ServerReport.ReportPath = txtPath.Text;

//Render report
reportViewer.RefreshReport();
```

The `ReportViewerControlSample-RemoteProcessing` project is included as a sample for this book and demonstrates ReportViewer in the remote processing mode.

Microsoft SharePoint Web Parts

SSRS 2000 Service Pack 2 included two SharePoint web parts: `SPExplorer` and `SPViewer`. The same web parts are included in SSRS 2005. Web parts can be used on a SharePoint site (Microsoft SharePoint Portal Server or Microsoft Windows SharePoint Services site). As the names imply, `SPExplorer` is designed to browse reports deployed on the Report Server and `SPViewer` is designed to view reports. `SPExplorer` and `SPViewer` can be used as standalone controls or can be integrated with each other. When used as a standalone control, the `SPExplorer` web part opens a new browser window to display a selected report. The standalone viewer is used to show a single report. The `Page Viewer` web part (part of the default SharePoint web parts library) can supply much of the functionality of either a standalone viewer using `URL Access` or standalone `SPExplorer` by accessing Report Manager's interface. `SPViewer` and `SPExplorer` web parts provide an additional SSRS-specific functionality that improves both the management and viewing experience. For example, `SPViewer` and `SPExplorer` can be connected with each other and as a user clicks through report links in `SPExplorer`, `SPViewer` displays the report. `SPExplorer` also provides a basic interface to create and manage subscriptions.

NOTE

SharePoint can be managed through administrative pages or the command-line administrative tool `stsadm.exe`. **More details can be found at http://www.microsoft.com/resources/documentation/wss/2/all/adminguide/en-us/stsf01.mspx ("Introducing the Administration Tools for Windows SharePoint Services"). The default location for** `stsadm.exe` **is** `C:\Program Files\Common Files\Microsoft Shared\web server extensions\60\BIN\`. **Local Administrators group permissions are required to execute** `stsadm.exe`.

SSRS and Windows SharePoint services can be installed in any order. For SSRS to properly function, a SharePoint administrator needs to perform the following steps:

1. Add Report Server and Report Manager virtual directories to the list of exclusions:

```
STSADM.EXE -o addpath -url http://localhost/ReportServer -type exclusion
STSADM.EXE -o addpath -url http://localhost/Reports -type exclusion
```

2. Make sure that the Report Server and Report Manager are using an application pool that is different from the one used by SharePoint services.

By default, SQL Server setup places SSRS web parts in the following location: C:\Program Files\Microsoft SQL Server\90\Tools\Reporting Services\SharePoint\RSWebParts.cab.

To deploy the web parts, a SharePoint administrator can use the following command:

```
STSADM.EXE -o addwppack -filename "C:\Program Files\Microsoft SQL
➥Server\90\Tools\Reporting Services\SharePoint\RSWebParts.cab"
```

Because we did not specify a virtual server in this example, the package should be installed on all Windows SharePoint Services-enabled virtual servers on the computer. To provide a specific virtual server for the package deployment, you can add an additional option: -url <Virtual Server URL>.

A site allows users to load only those web parts that are listed as safe in a Web.config file for a virtual server. The Stsadm.exe tool automatically adds the control to the <SafeControls> section for the virtual server specified on the command line.

After web parts are deployed, users (who have permissions to create websites and add content) can add SPExplorer and SPViewer web parts to a Web Part Page through the SharePoint window.

Summary

Visual Studio 2005 includes freely distributable ReportViewer Windows and web forms controls, which greatly simplify embedding of reports in Windows and web applications.

ReportViewer can be used in local and remote processing modes. When used in local processing mode, ReportViewer processes a report using internal rendering capabilities. When used in remote processing mode, ReportViewer retrieves rendered reports from the Report Server.

A special client report definition file with an extension of .rdlc is used by Report Viewer in local processing mode. Unlike .rdl reports, .rdlc does not embed data set information in the report, instead relying on data sets defined in a project.

Like SSRS 2000 Service Pack 2, SSRS 2005 includes two SharePoint web parts: SPExplorer and SPViewer. Web parts can be used on a SharePoint site (Microsoft SharePoint Portal Server or Microsoft Windows SharePoint Services site). As the names imply, SPExplorer is designed to browse reports deployed on the Report Server and SPViewer is designed to view reports. SPExplorer and SPViewer can be used as standalone controls or can be integrated with each other.

The next chapter discusses some ideas about programmatic modifications of a report's RDL files and custom report generators, which can leverage .NET XML capabilities.

Custom Report Definition Language (RDL) Generators and Customizing Report Definition

CHAPTER 28

Report Definition Language (RDL) is an XML-based language that contains data retrieval and layout information for a report.

Just like an XML, RDL can be easily read and edited in any text editor. RDL is designed to provide interchangeable editing capabilities for tools that "understand" RDL's schema. Ad hoc reporting capabilities and Report Builder has significantly reduced the need to programmatically generate RDL.

In some cases, however, a company might have a need to programmatically generate RDL. This is the case, for example, for a software development company in a business of writing development tools. In a limited number of cases, a company might also want to extend RDL to describe additional report items that are not available in SSRS. This could be a "fancy table" item, for example.

As an illustration, suppose that Adventure Works needs a quick (but not necessarily very "friendly") web-based mechanism to generate reports with limited functionality. You can expand the example further as needed.

To simplify XML processing, you can leverage members of the `System.Xml` namespace, such as classes `XmlDocument` and `XmlTextWriter`. SQL Server 2005 comes with a tutorial on how to create a custom RDL.

The tutorial, which can be found in SQL Server Books Online at the following location `SQL Server 2005 Tutorials/Reporting Services Tutorials/Generating RDL Using the .NET Framework` (or online at http://msdn2.microsoft.com/ms170667.aspx), starts with a blank report and creates a report's RDL piece by piece, using `XmlTextWriter`.

We use the term RDL template describes an XML that conforms to an RDL schema, but does not necessarily describe a functional report. This chapter demonstrates how to create and reuse the RDL template. For simplicity, the sample uses most of the RDL from the template and customizes just a few fields, such as `<Query>`, `<Fields>`, and `<ConnectString>`.

Suppose that the goal is to create a web application that will use an RDL template and will programmatically modify this template, based on user input.

The template is a report with a three-column table. The application allows customizing the template's query and the template's connection string. For simplicity, the application only uses the first three fields from a query and considers all of the fields being the `System.String` type.

To create a template, you can leverage Report Designer and start with a simple report that connects to the AdventureWorks database, selects three fields from any of the tables, and displays results in a table report item.

After the report is completed, you can convert it to an RDL template:

1. Right-click on the report in Solution Explorer and select View Code or view the report's RDL file in a text editor.

NOTE

The accompanying code contains changes to the `<CommandText>` **value to** `SELECT F1, F2, F3 FROM TBL`**; however, the value of this node is irrelevant because it gets completely replaced by the sample application. You can decide if complete replacement of** `<CommandText>` **is desirable for each individual template.**

2. Edit the RDL and replace every occurrence of the first query field name with some unique value, such as F1. Repeat the procedure for the rest of the fields (F2 and F3, respectively). When going through the replacement process, please keep in mind that Report Designer adds spaces between capitalizations (that is, `OrderId` gets changed to `Order Id`). This happens when Report Designer assigns values for the `<Header>` row report items.

The resulting RDL/XML should look similar to the following (only key points are shown) :

```
...
<ConnectString>
Data Source=localhost;Initial Catalog=AdventureWorks;Integrated Security=SSPI;
</ConnectString>
    ...
    <ReportItems>
      <Table Name="table1">
        <Details>
          <TableRows>
            <TableRow>
              <TableCells>
                <TableCell>
                  <ReportItems>
                    <Textbox Name="F1">
                      <rd:DefaultName>F1</rd:DefaultName>
                      <CanGrow>true</CanGrow>
                      <Value>=Fields!F1.Value</Value>
                    </Textbox>
                  </ReportItems>
                </TableCell>
        ...
        </Details>
        <Header>
          <TableRows>
            <TableRow>
              <TableCells>
                <TableCell>
                  <ReportItems>
                    <Textbox Name="textbox2">
                      <CanGrow>true</CanGrow>
                      <Value>F1</Value>
                    </Textbox>
                  </ReportItems>
                </TableCell>
        ...
        </Header>
     ...
     </Table>
  </ReportItems>
  ...
  <DataSets>
    <DataSet Name="DataSource">
      <Query>
        <CommandText>SELECT F1, F2, F3 FROM TBL </CommandText>
```

```
        <DataSourceName>DataSource</DataSourceName>
      </Query>
      <Fields>
        <Field Name="F1">
          <rd:TypeName>System.String</rd:TypeName>
          <DataField>F1</DataField>
        </Field>
        ...
    </DataSet>
  </DataSets>>
```

After changes are completed, you can deploy this RDL template. Because an RDL template conforms to RDL specifications, SSRS does not "complain" about such deployment despite the fact that this is not really a functional report.

To achieve the desired functionality, the sample uses the following namespaces:

- `System.IO` to access stream handling, particularly the `MemoryStream` class
- `ReportService2005` to interact with SSRS to retrieve a template and to store a report
- `System.Web.Services.Protocols` to handle SOAP exceptions
- `System.Xml` to access XML handling, particularly the `XmlDocument` class
- `System.Data.SqlClient` to validate a query and get field names

First, the sample loads a template and displays a connection string and the query (`CommandText`) from the template:

```
byte[] reportDefinition = rs.GetReportDefinition(templatePath);
MemoryStream stream = new MemoryStream(reportDefinition);
System.Xml.XmlDocument doc = new System.Xml.XmlDocument();
doc.Load(stream);
txtConnection.Text = doc.GetElementsByTagName("ConnectString")[0].InnerXml;
txtQuery.Text = doc.GetElementsByTagName("CommandText")[0].InnerXml;
```

As a next series of steps, the sample

1. Collects an updated string and a query from the UI and replaces the original values in the RDL template

   ```
   doc.GetElementsByTagName("ConnectString")[0].InnerXml = txtConnection.Text;
   doc.GetElementsByTagName("CommandText")[0].InnerXml = txtQuery.Text;
   ```

2. Executes a query to validate the query syntax

```
SqlConnection con = new SqlConnection(txtConnection.Text);
con.Open();
System.Data.SqlClient.SqlCommand cmd = new SqlCommand(txtQuery.Text, con);
SqlDataReader reader = cmd.ExecuteReader();
```

3. Gets the names of fields and replaces template strings with field names

```
reader.Read();
String strTmp = doc.InnerXml.Replace("F1", reader.GetName(0));
strTmp = strTmp.Replace("F2", reader.GetName(1));
strTmp = strTmp.Replace("F3", reader.GetName(2));
doc.InnerXml = strTmp;
```

4. Writes the result of changes as a report to a specified location

```
MemoryStream stream = new MemoryStream();
doc.Save(stream);
Byte[] definition = stream.ToArray();
stream.Close();
Warning[] warnings =
    rs.CreateReport(txtResultName.Text, txtResultPath.Text, false,
definition, null);
```

After the final report is deployed, it can be used just like any report. The purpose of the sample is to demonstrate the basic capabilities of an RDL generation. The sample provides rudimentary error handling and can use some performance improvements. For example, you can find better alternatives to validate a query and to retrieve fields than executing a `SqlDataReader`.

Summary

Report Definition Language (RDL) is an XML-based language used to describe reports. Because XML is designed to simplify data exchange between applications, so is an RDL. Although an addition of an ad hoc reporting tool (Report Builder) significantly reduced the need to write RDL generators, in a few cases in which the need exists, .NET XML handling functionality provides a productivity booster for an RDL generation.

PART V

Appendices

IN THIS PART

References and Additional Reading

APPENDIX **A**

Bertucci, Paul. *Microsoft SQL Server High Availability*. Sams Publishing, 2004, ISBN: 0672326256. http://www.samspublishing.com/title/0672326256.

Hirt, Allan with Cathan Cook, Kimberly L. Tripp, and Frank McBath. *Microsoft® SQL Server™ 2000 High Availability*. Microsoft Press, 2003, ISBN: 0-7356-1920-4. http://www.microsoft.com/MSPress/books/6515.asp.

Microsoft. *Course 2944: Updating Your Reporting Skills to Microsoft® SQL Server™ 2005 Reporting Services*. Microsoft Corporation, 2005. https://www.microsoftelearning.com/eLearning/offerDetail.aspx?offerPriceId=66793.

Microsoft. *SQL Server 2005 Books Online*. Microsoft Corporation, 2005. Download from http://www.microsoft.com/downloads/details.aspx?FamilyID=be6a2c5d-00df-4220-b133-29c1e0b6585f&displaylang=en or access online at http://msdn2.microsoft.com/en-us/library/ms203721(en-us,sql.90).aspx.

Misner, Stacia. *Microsoft® SQL Server™ 2000 Reporting Services Step by Step*. Microsoft Press, 2005, ISBN: 0-7356-2106-3. http://www.microsoft.com/MSPress/books/7304.asp.

Jackobson, Reed. *Microsoft SQL Server 2000 Analysis Services Step by Step*. Microsoft Press, 2000, ISBN: 0-7356-0904-7. http://www.microsoft.com/MSPress/books/4076.asp.

Platt, David S. *Introducing Microsoft® .NET, Third Edition*. Microsoft Press, 2003, ISBN: 0-7356-1918-2. http://www.microsoft.com/MSPress/books/6475.asp.

Scalability Experts, Inc. *Microsoft SQL Server 2005: Changing the Paradigm (SQL Server 2005 Public Beta Edition)*. Sams Publishing, 2005, ISBN: 0672327783. http://www.samspublishing.com/title/0672327783.

Seidman, Claude. *Data Mining with Microsoft® SQL Server™ 2000 Technical Reference*. Microsoft Press, 2001, ISBN: 0-7356-1271-4. http://www.microsoft.com/MSPress/books/4945.asp.

Glossary

APPENDIX B

action An end-user-initiated operation that, for example, can launch another report, open a URL, or transfer focus to a bookmark.

aggregate function A function that performs a summary calculation on a series of data and returns a single value. Each aggregate function uses the `Scope` parameter, which defines the scope (such as grouping, data set, or data region) in which the aggregate function is performed.

assembly A managed application module that contains class metadata and managed code.

authentication The process of validating that the user attempting to connect to Reporting Server is authorized to do so.

authorization The operation that verifies the permissions and access rights granted to a user to securable report items, such as folders, reports, (report) models, resources, and shared data sources.

collation A set of rules that determines how strings of character data are compared, ordered, and presented. Character data is sorted using collation information, including locale, sort order, and case sensitivity.

column In a table, the area in each row that stores the data value for some attribute of the object presented in the table. For example, in an `Employee` table a `FirstName` column would contain the first name of an employee.

common language runtime The engine that supplies managed code with services such as cross-language integration, code access security, object lifetime management, and debugging and profiling support.

configuration In SSRS, a name/value pair(s) that controls certain behaviors of SSRS, such as direct SSRS to load specified extensions or to use a specified encryption key.

connection An interprocess communication (IPC) linkage established between a SQL Server application and an instance of SQL Server.

connection string A string supplied to a data provider that provides information sufficient to connect to the data. An example of a connection string is: `Data Source=MyServer\MyInstance;initial catalog=AdventureWorksDW`.

constant A group of symbols that represents a specific data value. For example, 'abc' is a character string constant, '123' is an integer constant, 'April 19, 1999' is a date-time constant, and '0x02FA' is a binary constant.

cube A set of data that is organized and summarized into a multidimensional structure defined by a set of dimensions and measures.

data mart A subset of the contents of a data warehouse. A data mart tends to contain data focused at the department level, or on a specific business area.

data-processing extension A component in Reporting Services that provides query processing and data retrieval for a data source type that can be used in a report.

data set A set of data that is the result of executing T-SQL SELECT, Data Mining Expressions (DMX), or Multidimensional Expressions (MDX) statements.

data source An object containing information about the location of data. Data source leverages a connection string. *See* connection string

Data Source view An abstraction layer for a data source. Data Source view acts similarly to SQL Server view and allows joining multiple tables from a data source, creating calculated fields, and "renaming" fields from a data source. Data Source view describes this abstraction in XML and does not cause any modification to a data source.

data type An attribute that specifies what type of information can be stored in a column, parameter, or variable. There are two different data types: system-supplied and user-defined.

data warehouse A database designed for reporting and data analysis. A data warehouse typically contains data representing the business history of an organization.

database A collection of information, tables, and other objects organized and presented to serve a specific purpose, such as searching, sorting, and recombining data. Databases are stored in files.

decision support The systems designed to support the complex analytic analysis required to discover business trends for managerial decision making.

default A value (data value, option setting, collation, or name) assigned, or an action taken automatically by the system if a user does not specify the value or the action.

default database The database the user is connected to immediately after logging in to SQL Server.

default instance The copy of SQL Server that uses the computer name on which it is installed as its name.

Delete query A query (SQL statement) that removes rows from one or more tables.

delivery extension A component in Reporting Services that is used to distribute a report to specific devices or target locations, for example email delivery, shared folder delivery, or printer delivery.

dimension A structural attribute of a cube upon which the user wants to base an analysis, for example, geography dimension. Dimension describes data in a fact table.

dimension hierarchy One of the hierarchies of a dimension.

dimension table A table that contains the data from which dimensions are created.

drill through An action or a technique used to retrieve the detailed data by, for example, clicking a report item that contains summarized data.

enterprise The word "enterprise" is used in several different connotations throughout this book. When enterprise describes a business, it implies (according to Encarta dictionary) "organized business activities aimed specifically at growth and profit." According to the definition, an enterprise could be a company with a few employees or thousands of employees. However, typically, people think of an enterprise as a company that has a hierarchical management structure; division of responsibilities, such as operations, financial, sales, marketing, and so on; and more than a handful of employees.

Enterprise Edition An edition of a product that provides more powerful features than a product labeled as "standard." In addition to providing extended features, "enterprise" products are also designed to handle large user loads, scale up (use more memory and a large number of CPUs), scale out (have the capability of adding more servers to the installation), and have provisions for high availability.

expression In SSRS, a combination of variables, constants, functions, and operators that evaluate to a single data value. Simple expressions can be a constant, variable, column, or scalar function. Complex expressions are one or more simple expressions connected by operators.

fact A row in a fact table in a data warehouse. A fact contains values that define a data event such as a sales transaction.

fact table A central table in a data warehouse schema that contains numerical measures and keys relating facts to dimension tables. Fact tables contain data that describes specific events within a business, such as bank transactions or product sales.

field An area in a data set that stores a single data value.

foreign key (FK) The column or combination of columns whose values match the primary key (PK) or unique key in the same or another table.

function A piece of code that operates as a single logical unit. A function is called by name, accepts optional input parameters, and returns a status and optional output parameters. Many programming languages support functions, including C, Visual Basic, and Transact-SQL. Transact-SQL supplies built-in functions, which cannot be modified, and supports user-defined functions, which can be created and modified by users.

Hypertext Markup Language (HTML) A system of marking up a document so that it can be published on the World Wide Web. HTML provides formatting tags and can be viewed using a web browser (such as Microsoft Internet Explorer).

index In a relational database, a database object that provides fast access to data in the rows of a table, based on key values. The primary key of a table is automatically indexed.

inner join An operation that retrieves rows from multiple source tables where values from columns shared between the sources tables match to each other.

insert query A query that copies specific columns and rows from one table to another or to the same table.

instance A copy of SQL Server or SSRS running on a computer. A computer can run multiple instances of SQL Server 2005.

interface A defined set of properties, methods, and collections that form a logical grouping of behaviors and data. Classes are defined by the interfaces that they implement. An interface can be implemented by many different classes.

job A specified series of operations, called steps, performed sequentially by SQL Server Agent.

join A process or a result of combining the contents of two or more tables and producing a resultset that incorporates rows and columns from each table.

key A column or group of columns that uniquely identifies a row (PRIMARY KEY), defines the relationship between two tables (FOREIGN KEY), or is used to build an index.

key column A column referenced by a primary, foreign, or index key.

linked server A definition of an OLE DB data source used by SQL Server distributed queries. The data exposed by a linked server is then referenced as tables, called linked tables.

local server An instance of SQL Server running on the same computer as the application.

local variable A user-defined variable that is used within the statement batch or procedure in which it was declared.

locale A set of Windows operating system behaviors related to language, such as the code page, the order in which characters are sorted, the format used for dates and time, and the character used to separate decimals in numbers. SQL Server collations are similar to locales in that the collations define language-specific types of behaviors for instances of SQL Server.

measure A set of usually numeric values from a fact table that is aggregated in a cube across all dimensions.

Messaging Application Programming Interface (MAPI) An email API.

metadata The information describing the properties, such as the type of data in a column (numeric, text, and so on), the length of a column, the structure of database objects, such as tables, measures, dimensions, and cubes, and so on.

Multidimensional Expressions (MDX) A syntax used for defining multidimensional objects and querying and manipulating multidimensional data.

multiple instances Multiple copies of SQL Server or SSRS running on the same computer.

NULL An entry that has no explicitly assigned value. NULL is not the same as zero or blank.

numeric expression Any expression that evaluates to a number.

object In databases, one of the components of a database: a table, index, trigger, view, key, constraint, default, rule, user-defined data type, or stored procedure. In object-oriented programming, an instance of a class.

object variable A variable that contains a reference to an object.

OLE DB A COM-based API for accessing data. OLE DB supports accessing data stored in any format (databases, spreadsheets, text files, and so on) for which an OLE DB provider is available.

OLE DB consumer Any software that calls and uses the OLE DB API.

OLE DB for OLAP Formerly, the separate specification that addressed OLAP extensions to OLE DB. Beginning with OLE DB 2.0, OLAP extensions are incorporated into the OLE DB specification.

OLE DB provider A software component that exposes OLE DB interfaces. Each OLE DB provider exposes data from a particular type of data source, such as SQL Server databases, Microsoft Access databases, or Microsoft Excel spreadsheets.

online analytical processing (OLAP) A technology that uses multidimensional structures that aggregate data to provide rapid access to data for analysis. The source data for OLAP is commonly stored in data warehouses.

online transaction processing (OLTP) A data-processing system designed to record all of the business transactions of an organization as they occur. An OLTP system is characterized by many concurrent users actively adding and modifying data. Typically, OLTP systems perform large numbers of relatively small transactions.

Open Database Connectivity (ODBC) A data access application programming interface (API) that supports access to any data source for which an ODBC driver is available.

outer join A join that includes all the rows from the joined tables that have met the search conditions, even rows from one table for which there is no matching row in the other join table.

parameterization The act of using parameters or parameter markers instead of constant values.

parameterized report A published Reporting Services report that accepts input values through parameters.

path A locator information to access a file, such as `c:\myfile.txt`.

pivot The act of rotating rows to columns, and columns to rows.

pivot table A visual control that displays rows and columns in a crosstabular structure. Pivot tables are mostly used to display multidimensional data (cubes).

primary key (PK) A column or set of columns that uniquely identifies all the rows in a table.

property A named attribute of a control, field, or database object that defines one of the object's characteristics (such as size or color) or an aspect of its behavior (such as visible or hidden).

property pages A tabbed dialog box that allows specifying values for properties.

relational database A collection of information organized in tables.

relational database management system (RDBMS) A system that organizes data into related rows and columns. SQL Server is an RDBMS.

relationship A link between tables that references the primary key in one table to a foreign key in another table.

rendered report A fully processed report that contains both data and layout information, in a format suitable for viewing.

rendering extension A component in Reporting Services that is used to process the output format of a report. Rendering extensions included in Reporting Services are HTML, TIFF, XML, Excel, PDF, CSV, and Web archive.

report definition An `.rdl` file that contains information about the query and layout for a Reporting Services report.

report model A metadata description of business data used for creating ad hoc reports in Report Builder.

report processing extension A component in Reporting Services that is used to extend the report-processing logic beyond SSRS' "out-of-the-box" capabilities to process `List`, `Table`, `Matrix`, `Chart`, `Textbox`, `Line`, `Rectangle`, and `Image`. Developers can build or purchase a third-party report-processing extension to support custom data-bound controls embedded in reports.

Report Server administrator A user who is assigned to the `Content Manager` role, the `System Administrator` role, or both for a `Report Server`.

report snapshot A report that contains data captured at a specific point in time. A report snapshot is stored in an intermediate format containing retrieved data instead of a query and rendering definitions.

resultset The set of rows returned from a `SELECT` statement. The format of the rows in the resultset is defined by the column-list of the `SELECT` statement.

row A horizontal line in the table that contains all attributes of a single object modeled in the table.

script A collection of Transact-SQL statements used to perform an operation. Transact-SQL scripts are stored as files, usually with the `.sql` extension.

Secure Sockets Layer (SSL) A protocol that supplies secure data communication through data encryption and decryption.

security extension A component in Reporting Services that authenticates a user or group to a Report Server. The default security extension in Reporting Services is Windows authentication. Custom extensions can be created to support forms-based authentication or to integrate with third-party single sign-on technologies.

Security Identifier (SID) A unique value that identifies a user who is logged in to the security system. SIDs can identify either one user or a group of users.

SELECT The Transact-SQL or DMX statement used to return tabular data or the MDX statement that returns multidimensional data.

Select query A query that returns rows into a resultset from one or more tables.

server name A name that uniquely identifies a server computer on a network. SQL Server applications can connect to a default instance of SQL Server by specifying only the server name. SQL Server applications must specify both the server name and instance name when connecting to a named instance on a server.

shared dimension A dimension created within a database that can be used by any cube in the database.

sort order The set of rules in a collation that defines how characters are evaluated in comparison operations and the sequence in which they are sorted.

SQL collation A set of SQL Server collations whose characteristics match those of commonly used code page and sort order combinations from earlier versions of SQL Server. SQL collations are compatibility features that let sites choose collations that match the behavior of their earlier systems.

SQL expression Any combination of operators, constants, literal values, functions, and names of tables and fields that evaluates to a single value. For example, use expressions to define calculated fields in queries.

SQL query A SQL statement, such as `SELECT`, `INSERT`, `UPDATE`, `DELETE`, or `CREATE TABLE`.

SQL Server Authentication One of two mechanisms for validating attempts to connect to instances of SQL Server. Users must specify a SQL Server logon ID and password when they connect. The SQL Server instance ensures the logon ID and password combination are valid before allowing the connection to succeed.

SQL statement A SQL or Transact-SQL command, such as `SELECT` or `DELETE`, that performs some action with data.

stored procedure A precompiled collection of Transact-SQL statements stored under a name and processed as a unit.

string Contiguous character-based (letters, numbers, special characters) or binary (string of bytes) data value.

string functions The functions that perform operations on character or binary strings. Built-in string functions return values commonly needed for operations on character data.

Structured Query Language (SQL) The language understood by RDBMSs and used to create and manage database objects and perform data manipulations (insert, update, delete, and select queries). SQL Server 2005 uses a version of the SQL language called Transact-SQL.

subscription A request for a copy of a report to be delivered to a subscriber. The subscription defines what reports will be received, where, and when.

table A two-dimensional object, consisting of rows and columns, used to store data in a relational database. Each table stores information about one of the types of objects modeled by the database, such as information about sales orders.

time dimension A dimension that breaks time down into levels such as Year, Quarter, Month, and Day. In Analysis Services, a special type of dimension created from a date/time column.

tool A SQL Server application with a graphical user interface used to perform common tasks.

Transact-SQL The language understood by SQL Server and used to create and manage database objects and perform data manipulations (insert, update, delete, and select queries).

transaction A group of database operations combined into a logical unit of work that is either wholly committed or rolled back. A transaction is atomic, consistent, isolated, and durable.

transaction processing The data processing used to efficiently record business transactions, which are of interest to an organization (for example, sales, orders for supplies, or money transfers).

trigger A stored procedure that executes in response to a data manipulation language (DML) or data definition language (DDL) event.

underlying table A table referenced by a view, cursor, or stored procedure.

update The act of modifying one or more data values in an existing row or rows, typically by using the UPDATE statement. Sometimes, the term update refers to any data modification, including insert, update, and delete operations.

utility An application that can be executed from a command prompt to perform common tasks.

variable A read/write container for variable values.

WHERE clause The part of a SQL statement that specifies which records to retrieve.

wildcard characters The characters, including underscore (_), percent (%), and brackets ([ ]), used with the LIKE keyword for pattern matching.

Windows Management Instrumentation (WMI) An interface that provides information about objects in a managed environment, with extensions for SQL called WMI Query Language (WQL).

WMI Query Language (WQL) A subset of ANSI SQL with semantic changes adapted to Windows Management Instrumentation (WMI).

FAQ

APPENDIX C

The intention of this appendix is to share answers to some common questions about SSRS. The appendix is presented in the Q&A (question-and-answer) fashion.

Q Can I connect Report Builder to an Oracle database?

A A direct connection between Report Builder and Oracle is not supported; however, you can connect to an Oracle database by leveraging link servers or the Analysis Services Unified Data Model. Both provide a thin layer of abstraction and allow usage of any OLEDB- or ODBC-compliant data source, including Oracle.

Q Can I join two separate data sets in a report?

A Although it is not possible to join two data sets directly, it is possible to simulate this feature. Depending on what you are trying to accomplish, there might be options. For example, you can align two data regions, such as tables, and make sure that rows properly match. You can also synchronize two data sets by using the same query parameter as it was done in the `Sales Order` sample included with this book.

Q Can I use SSRS to update my sales data?

A Although it is possible to update a database using SSRS, developers should refrain from using SSRS in this fashion. For example, it is possible to create a report that passes parameters to a stored procedure (or a query), which, in turn, updates a database (and might return some data back to a report). Such a report produces an "unexpected behavior." Expected behavior of a report is to retrieve and display information.

Q I would like to embed Report Builder in my custom application. Is it possible?

A The current release of SSRS does not provide this functionality. It is possible to develop an RDL generator that will provide functionality similar to Report Builder.

Q I have noticed a new Printer icon on the Report Manager's Toolbar. Does this invoke the Printing Extension?

A No. This is the new ActiveX `RSPrintClient` control. This control provides client-side printing for reports viewed in HTML Viewer. The control presents the Print dialog box for a user to initiate a print job, preview a report, specify pages to print, and change the margins. Developers can use this control in the code to enable report-printing functionality.

Q Is there a 64-bit version of SSRS?

A Yes, SSRS 2005 is supported natively on both Itanium (IA64) and Extended Complex Instruction Set (x64; supported CPUs AMD64: Opteron and Athlon64; EM64T: Xeon). Business Intelligence Development Studio (BIDS) is not supported on IA64. Note that SSRS 2000 is not supported on a 64-bit platform.

Q How can I get the history of report executions?

A SSRS comes with a sample of packages and reports. Those samples provide administrators with a set of tools to view report execution history and performance characteristics. By default, those samples are installed at `C:\Program Files\Microsoft SQL Server\90\Samples\Reporting Services\Report Samples\Server Management Sample Reports\Execution Log Sample Reports`.

You can also look through SSRS execution log files in a text editor. By default, SSRS execution log files are written to the `C:\Program Files\Microsoft SQL Server\MSSQL.3\Reporting Services\LogFiles` directory.

Q What is WMI used for in SSRS?

A WMI is a set of management interfaces to retrieve and modify configuration information for SSRS. The root namespace can be found in `\root\Microsoft\SqlServer\ReportingServices\v9`.

Q What are the classes under the root namespace?

A There are two classes under the root WMI namespace for SSRS. The first is the `MSReportServer_ConfigurationSetting` class, which contains configuration information for the Report Server. The second is the `MSReportServerReportManager_ConfigurationSetting` class, which has similar information for Report Manager.

Q Do you have a code sample showing how to use WMI to get SSRS's properties?

A Please see the following short sample:

```
using System;
using System.Collections.Generic;
using System.Text;
using System.Management;
namespace SSRSWMI
{
    class Program
    {
        static void Main(string[] args)
        {
            const string WmiNamespace =
                @"\\localhost\root\Microsoft\SqlServer\ReportServer\v9\Admin";
            const string WmiRSClass =
                @"\\localhost\root\Microsoft\SqlServer\ReportServer\
                  v9\Admin:MSReportServer_ConfigurationSetting";
            ManagementClass serverClass;
            ManagementScope scope;
            scope = new ManagementScope(WmiNamespace);

            scope.Connect();// Connect to the Reporting Services namespace.
            // Create the server class.
            serverClass = new ManagementClass(WmiRSClass);
            // Connect to the management object.
            serverClass.Get();
            if (serverClass == null)
                throw new Exception("No class found");
            // Loop through the instances of the server class.
            ManagementObjectCollection instances = serverClass.GetInstances();
            foreach (ManagementObject instance in instances)
            {
                Console.Out.WriteLine("Instance Detected");
                PropertyDataCollection instProps = instance.Properties;
                foreach (PropertyData prop in instProps)
                {
                    string name = prop.Name;
                    object val = prop.Value;
                    Console.Out.Write("Property Name: " + name);
                    if (val != null)
                        Console.Out.WriteLine(" Value: " + val.ToString());
                    else
                        Console.Out.WriteLine(" Value: <null>");
                }
            }
        }
    }
}
```

Q When I try to set up a subscription, I get the error: `SQL Agent service is not running. This operation requires the SQL Agent service. (rsSchedulerNotResponding)`. What should I do?

A Make sure that the SQL Agent service is running. The agent must be running on the SQL Server that hosts the SSRS catalog.

Q When I click the `Print` icon on the Report Manager's Toolbar, nothing happens. What should I do?

A Because this button invokes an ActiveX control, make sure that the browser you are using supports ActiveX and that the browser's security allows downloading and running of signed ActiveX controls. After you allow your browser to run signed ActiveX, clear temporary Internet files, including offline content. If your browser asks your permission to download a print control, allow your browser to do so.

Q I am getting an error `[rsInvalidReportParameterDependency]: The report parameter 'ParameterA' has a DefaultValue or a ValidValue that depends on the report parameter 'ParameterB'. Forward dependencies are not valid.` What should I do?

A SSRS allows creating dependent parameters. Dependent parameters have to follow in the sequence. In this particular example, `ParameterB` serves as a parameter to a query that retrieves `ParameterA` values. When you open the Report, Report Parameters menu, notice that `ParameterA` is ahead of `ParameterB` in the sequence of parameters. Rearrange the parameters so `ParameterA` follows `ParameterB` by pressing the Up/Down Arrow button in the Report Parameters dialog box.

Q I am getting an error that starts with "`Unable to find Reporting Services WMI`…" while attempting to activate a Report Server. What should I do?

A In a scale-out configuration, when activating a new Report Server, you must activate it from an existing machine in the cluster. From a machine that is already activated, run the following command: `rsactivate -m <machinename>`. The existing machine then gets the symmetric key and encrypts it using the new machine's public key, hence completing the initialization (activation) process.

Index

Symbols

A

B

C

D

E

F

G – H

I

J – K – L

M

N

O

P

Q

How can we make this index more useful? Email us at indexes@samspublishing.com

S

T

U

X – Y – Z

How can we make this index more useful? Email us at indexes@samspublishing.com